Advancements in the New World of Web 3:

A Look Toward the Decentralized Future

Jane Thomason
UCL London Blockchain Centre, UK

Elizabeth Ivwurie
British Blockchain and Frontier Technology Association, UK

A volume in the Advances in Web
Technologies and Engineering
(AWTE) Book Series

Published in the United States of America by
    IGI Global
    Engineering Science Reference (an imprint of IGI Global)
    701 E. Chocolate Avenue
    Hershey PA, USA 17033
    Tel: 717-533-8845
    Fax: 717-533-8661
    E-mail: cust@igi-global.com
    Web site: http://www.igi-global.com

Library of Congress Cataloging-in-Publication Data

Names: Thomason, Jane, 1958- author. | Ivwurie, Elizabeth, 1997- author.
Title: Advancements in the new world of Web 3 : a look toward the
  decentralized future / by Jane Thomason, Elizabeth Ivwurie.
Description: Hershey, PA : Engineering Science Reference, an imprint of IGI
  Global, [2023] | Includes bibliographical references and index. |
  Summary: "As advances in disruptive technologies, the public is
  confronted with changes that move faster than they can comprehend. In
  Advancements in the New World of Web 3: A Look Toward the Decentralized
  Future, the authors explore the possibilities now opening up in Web 3.0
  and the Metaverse. The book provides a description of the critical
  underpinnings of Web 3.0 and Metaverse and an analysis of some of the
  practical, regulatory, and ethical questions that are emerging. The
  purpose of the book is to help leaders, policymakers, regulators,
  researchers, and the public understand the impact that developments in
  Web 3.0 and Metaverse will have on economies, legal and political
  systems, and the way of life and how they can best face the future and
  harness them"-- Provided by publisher.
Identifiers: LCCN 2022059453 (print) | LCCN 2022059454 (ebook) | ISBN
  9781668466582 (h/c) | ISBN 9781668466599 (s/c) | ISBN 9781668466605
  (ebook)
Subjects: LCSH: Metaverse. | Internet--Forecasting. | Internet--Social
  aspects. | Internet commerce.
Classification: LCC TK5105.8864 .T54 2023 (print) | LCC TK5105.8864
  (ebook) | DDC 004.67/80112--dc23/eng/20230113
LC record available at https://lccn.loc.gov/2022059453
LC ebook record available at https://lccn.loc.gov/2022059454

This book is published in the IGI Global book series Advances in Web Technologies and Engineering (AWTE) (ISSN: 2328-2762; eISSN: 2328-2754)

British Cataloguing in Publication Data
A Cataloguing in Publication record for this book is available from the British Library.

All work contributed to this book is new, previously-unpublished material.
The views expressed in this book are those of the authors, but not necessarily of the publisher.

For electronic access to this publication, please contact: eresources@igi-global.com.

Advances in Web Technologies and Engineering (AWTE) Book Series

Ghazi I. Alkhatib
The Hashemite University, Jordan
David C. Rine
George Mason University, USA

ISSN:2328-2762
EISSN:2328-2754

MISSION

The **Advances in Web Technologies and Engineering (AWTE) Book Series** aims to provide a platform for research in the area of Information Technology (IT) concepts, tools, methodologies, and ethnography, in the contexts of global communication systems and Web engineered applications. Organizations are continuously overwhelmed by a variety of new information technologies, many are Web based. These new technologies are capitalizing on the widespread use of network and communication technologies for seamless integration of various issues in information and knowledge sharing within and among organizations. This emphasis on integrated approaches is unique to this book series and dictates cross platform and multidisciplinary strategy to research and practice.

The **Advances in Web Technologies and Engineering (AWTE) Book Series** seeks to create a stage where comprehensive publications are distributed for the objective of bettering and expanding the field of web systems, knowledge capture, and communication technologies. The series will provide researchers and practitioners with solutions for improving how technology is utilized for the purpose of a growing awareness of the importance of web applications and engineering.

COVERAGE

- Data analytics for business and government organizations
- Virtual teams and virtual enterprises: communication, policies, operation, creativity, and innovation
- Integrated user profile, provisioning, and context-based processing
- IT education and training
- Case studies validating Web-based IT solutions
- Information filtering and display adaptation techniques for wireless devices
- Ontology and semantic Web studies
- Quality of service and service level agreement issues among integrated systems
- Radio Frequency Identification (RFID) research and applications in Web engineered systems
- Competitive/intelligent information systems

IGI Global is currently accepting manuscripts for publication within this series. To submit a proposal for a volume in this series, please contact our Acquisition Editors at Acquisitions@igi-global.com or visit: http://www.igi-global.com/publish/.

Titles in this Series

701 East Chocolate Avenue, Hershey, PA 17033, USA
Tel: 717-533-8845 x100 • Fax: 717-533-8661
E-Mail: cust@igi-global.com • www.igi-global.com

Table of Contents

Foreword

It is with great pleasure that I introduce this insightful book, exploring the profound impact of Web 3.0 on society and humanity. In these pages, we embark on a journey that traverses the intricate web of ethics, economics, education, employment, and the environment. In addition, we must consider the implications for a new era as we delve into the transformative power of digital assets, tokenization, DAOs, and the broad impact of distributed ledger technologies (DLTs) on decentralized governance models.

Web 3.0 represents a paradigm shift, a revolution that transcends the boundaries of the digital realm and touches every aspect of our lives. As the world becomes increasingly interconnected, the possibilities and disruptions brought forth by Web 3.0 are staggering. The emergence of digital assets and tokenization has revolutionized the way we perceive and exchange value. It has sparked a new wave of economic opportunities and disrupted traditional financial systems, providing greater access and inclusion for individuals across the globe.

Furthermore, the rise of decentralized autonomous organizations (DAOs) has unlocked innovative models of governance and decision-making. These systems, enabled by DLTs, foster trust, transparency, and accountability, challenging conventional power structures and empowering individuals to actively participate in shaping their destinies. By redistributing power and enabling collective decision-making, Web 3.0 redefines the concept of governance, promising a more equitable and inclusive future.

As we navigate this landscape of immense possibilities, it is crucial to acknowledge the ethical implications that arise. Web 3.0 brings with it unprecedented challenges and responsibilities. Therefore, it is vital to continue optimizing our efforts to enhance data privacy, algorithmic transparency, and the ethical considerations surrounding artificial intelligence. By addressing these issues head-on, we can ensure that the technological advancements of Web 3.0 are harnessed for the greater good and create a society that is not only technologically advanced but also ethically robust.

In the realm of education and employment, Web 3.0 presents both opportunities and challenges. Decentralized educational platforms and personalized learning experiences are reshaping traditional modes of learning. Likewise, the nature of work is undergoing a profound transformation, with remote and decentralized employment models becoming the new norm. However, we must ensure that these shifts are accompanied by comprehensive strategies to bridge the digital divide and equip individuals with the skills needed to thrive in the digital age.

Furthermore, we must recognize the impact of Web 3.0 on the environment. We are morally obligated to build more sustainable and eco-friendly infrastructures as we embrace decentralized systems and reduce reliance on intermediaries. Through using renewable energy sources and optimizing resource consumption, Web 3.0 can play a pivotal role in mitigating climate change and fostering a greener global business ecosystem.

I hope this book serves as a call to action for global collaborative efforts and multilateral web 3.0-centric diplomacy. We must collectively work towards building a trustworthy, responsible, sustainable, inclusive, equitable, and diverse global Metaverse Ecosystem. By harnessing the transformative power of Web 3.0, we can build an urban ecosystem where technological advancements go hand in hand with ethical considerations, where economic opportunities are accessible to all, where education empowers individuals, and where environmental sustainability is at the forefront of our endeavors. Let this book be a catalyst for change, inspiring individuals, organizations, and policymakers to actively participate in the design and implementation of the Web 3.0 revolution. Through global multi-stakeholder collaboration that transcends geographic and socio-cultural boundaries we can forge a new pathway for humanity that leverages technology to build a better world for all.

Before concluding, I would like to express my heartfelt gratitude for the opportunity to contribute to this foreword. It is an honor to be part of a project with such immense significance in Web 3.0. I sincerely appreciate the authors' visionary thinking and tireless dedication to bringing this book to life. Their commitment to exploring the multifaceted impact of Web 3.0 on society and humanity is commendable. Through meticulous research, insightful analysis, and thought-provoking perspectives, they have provided us with a comprehensive understanding of the transformative power of this new era. The authors' unwavering passion for their subject matter shines through on every page, captivating readers and inspiring them to engage in the discourse surrounding Web 3.0.

I am deeply grateful for the diverse range of contributors whose expertise and insights enrich the content of this book. Their collective wisdom and valuable contributions add depth and nuance to the exploration of ethics, economics, education, employment, and the environment in the context of Web 3.0. In addition, their dedication to advancing knowledge and fostering meaningful conversations is genuinely commendable.

Let this book be a guiding resource, highlighting our roadmap toward a trustworthy, responsible, sustainable, inclusive, equitable, and diverse global Metaverse Ecosystem. The challenges and opportunities outlined in this book should be an impetus for collaborative efforts and multilateral web 3.0-centric diplomacy, leading us to a future where technology is a force for positive change and a catalyst for a more equitable world.

Ingrid Vasiliu-Feltes
University of Miami, USA

Preface

OVERVIEW

As advances in disruptive technologies, the public is confronted with changes that move faster than they can comprehend. In *Advancements in the New World of Web 3: A Look Toward the Decentralized Future*, the authors explore the possibilities now opening up in Web 3.0 and the Metaverse. The book provides a description of the critical underpinnings of Web 3.0 and Metaverse and an analysis of some of the practical, regulatory, and ethical questions that are emerging. The purpose of the book is to help leaders, policymakers, regulators, researchers, and the public understand the impact that developments in Web 3.0 and Metaverse will have on economies, legal and political systems, and the way of life and how they can best face the future and harness them.

WHERE THE TOPIC FITS

The many academic areas covered in this publication include, but are not limited to:

- AI Ethics
- Artificial Intelligence (AI)
- Blockchain
- Convergence of Technologies
- Cyber Security
- Decentralized Technologies
- Decentralized Finance
- Digital Ethics
- Emerging Health Technologies
- Ethical Risks

- Extended Reality (XR)
- Gaming
- Geographic Information Systems (GIS)
- Metaverse
- Regulation
- Technology and Investments
- Web 3.0

TARGET AUDIENCE

Covering a broad range of Web 3.0 topics such as Blockchain, artificial intelligence (AI) ethics, Decentralized Finance, Non-Fungible Tokens (NFT), Metaverse, Tokenization, and Sustainability, this book is a dynamic resource for policymakers, civil society, CEOs, ethicists, technologists, security advisors, sociologists, cyber specialists, criminologists, data scientists, global governments, students, researchers, professors, academics, and professionals.

AN INTRODUCTION TO THE BOOK

This book is about possibility. It's not about certainty. The authors believe that when we connect what has already been achieved with Blockchain with future technologies and the affordances of DeFi, NFTs, AR VR, and cloud technology with Web 3.0 or the Internet of Value, these will create possibilities for humankind, that will enable us to review how we live, how we work, how we play, and how we interact with each other. It will allow companies to provide products in different and more convenient ways to consumers. It will enable governments to provide services in a more accessible way and extend their limited human resources to focus on activities that can't be aided or assisted by technology. The motivation for writing this book has been to pull those pieces together so that others can see how the future might unfold.

INTRODUCTION TO WEB 3

This first section of the book aims to set the stage for understanding Web 3.0. In Chapter 1, "Introduction to Web 3.0," the authors discuss how Web 3.0 will be the next iteration of the internet – "The Internet of Value" (IOV).

It outlines the motivation for producing a book on Web 3.0, the change model providing a framework for the book, and a summary of the chapters. The IoV will enable the exchange of any valued asset with another person without the need for an intermediary. Web 3.0 will be open, accessible, and secure, linking technical interconnectivity with the exchange of value, stores of value, proof of authenticity, and smart contracts to create an always-on and borderless internet. Web 3.0 has the potential to take the world forward into a new era of connected digitization. Thus, while the tone of this book is wholly positive, it is also pragmatic. The book represents a snapshot of time. Web 3.0 is emerging fast; in the time it takes you to read this book, there will almost certainly be changes to protocols, terminology, and data management approaches that invite readers to understand the technology with an open mind and a critical eye. The authors hope that you enjoy the journey of learning about this dynamic technology as much as they enjoyed researching it.

BLOCKCHAIN BASICS

This section of the book covers the foundational elements of blockchain. These chapters will introduce and analyze the blockchain ecosystem and components of a fully decentralized ledger that enable complete transparency and shared ownership of resources that will allow the blockchain technology and entire ecosystem to be created, operated, owned, and financed by its users- for other users.

Chapter 2, "Introduction to Blockchain," will outline the history, blockchain technology stack, types of blockchains, and overview of cryptography and consensus algorithms. Token Classification and Platforms will introduce token classification, smart contracts, and some of the current challenges. The ecosystem chapter will look at the major elements, including DeFi, DAOs, NFTs, gamification, and regulation. This chapter explains the primary types of Blockchain: private and public blockchain, and its variants. The chapter will also discuss the positives and negatives of using private and public blockchains. This analysis would help potential blockchain users to discover what system type would best cater to their organizational and business needs. A detailed description of each of the blockchain components: blocks, nodes, miners, cryptography, and consensus, will be provided. It will also give a comparison of the main types of blockchains, public, private, and federated.

It points out that to reap the several benefits that blockchain can provide for businesses, the onus on organizations to carry out an analysis of their business processes to determine the sects where the application of blockchain technology would be most useful and ultimately figure out how to start building their organizational capabilities for blockchain.

Some of the risks involved in experimenting with blockchain are time horizons, barriers to adoption, and sheer complexity that may be involved in the adoption and application of blockchain technology. This notwithstanding, no matter what the context, there is a strong possibility that Blockchain will affect every business owner. The huge question is when, therefore, organizations must equip themselves with the necessary arsenal that would need to employ for successful adoption.

In Chapter 3, "Blockchain Ecosystem," the blockchain trilemma, layers, and limitations of the blockchain ecosystem are outlined. This chapter analyzes these fundamental blockchain issues and proffers suggestions and future research to manage the existing blockchain trilemma. The several limitations of blockchain are described at the end of the chapter, which provides a framework for developmental research. The chapter considers the Scalability Trilema, which involves the prioritization of any two features of the Blockchain (Scalability, security, or decentralization) while compromising on one. There have been several suggestions in the literature for solving the scalability trilemma, and this chapter explains the prominent ones. It also discussed the limitations and criticism of Blockchain systems. It concludes that research is needed to find alternative solutions to the scalability trilemma and other challenges.

DeFi, CeFi, AND TradFi: EVOLUTION OF MONEY

The next section of the book explores money as a much broader concept than what is understood traditionally. It provides an overview of the history of money, explaining the background of Blockchain and digital assets and financial applications, including central bank digital currencies, stablecoins, settlements, and custody. it will also examine the leading blockchain protocols relevant to finances. An overview of DeFi will be provided, as well as an analysis of the DeFi ecosystem and decentralized autonomous organizations (DAOs), and the challenges will be explored.

In Chapter 4, "DeFi and the Future of Money," the emergence of DeFi is explored. This chapter provides an overview of DeFi, an analysis of its ecosystem, and its likely trajectory. Decentralized finance (DeFi) wasn't well understood when it came into the spotlight in 2019. In 2020, it scaled fast and increased from $700 million at the beginning of 2020 to $15 billion by the end of 2020, and as of June 2022, the total value locked (TVL) reached a high of $256 billion. What explains this remarkable increase? The current financial system has left 1.7 billion people unbanked. The barriers to entry are high, the costs are high, transparency is low, and a small group of powerful elites dominates it. DeFi offers an accessible alternative to the current financial system. It explains its exponential growth in borrowing, lending, yield farming, and insurance. Early results suggest that DeFi will redefine the financial system.

DeFi shows great promise, despite some of its growing pains. DeFi solutions are highly interoperable and can potentially be integrated. DeFi offers greater transparency as all the data is stored immutably using blockchain technology, which can be viewed by the participants anytime and anywhere. But it is risky and unregulated. Investors can easily lose money when smart contracts fail or there are problems with open-source computer codes leading to vulnerabilities. It's 24/7, always on the market, and available globally, which means it's hard to undertake meaningful due diligence. Questions remain about definitions, developer liability, the legal status of the code, the application of AML/KYC, and jurisdiction. The history of money is still being written, and the systems that underpin it will continue to evolve. DeFi may very well represent the next step in the evolution of money.

In Chapter 5, "Decentralized Autonomous Organizations: Governing by Code," decentralized autonomous organizations (DAOs), which govern many major DeFi applications, are explained. These oversee the allocation of resources tied to the projects they are associated with and ensure the continuing success of the project they support. The community defines the rules by which a DAO operates and encodes in smart contracts. These are transparent and publicly available so that anyone can understand the protocol operation. DAOs generally receive funding through token issuance, where the protocol sells tokens to raise funds for the DAO treasury. While there are variations in DAO governance and quorum requirements, the only way to change the rules is through member voting. This chapter explores DAOs, their deployment for DeFi, and some of the risks and opportunities of this emerging form of code-led governance.

DAOs govern many major DeFi applications and are an exciting new governance approach. In an optimal situation, the community defines the rules, and these are encoded in smart contracts which are transparent and publicly available. The DAO operates seamlessly and is automated as intended. However, as experience has shown, not all contingencies can be predicted, and sometimes there are vulnerabilities in the code. The concept of DAOs is still relatively young, and significant experimentation with governance is likely to lead to stronger and better models. Regulators will likely be looking closely and determining how they can have visibility into code-governed organizations. Investor education and trusted due diligence sources are critically needed as the industry matures to protect consumers and improve industry standards.

Underpinning Web 3.0 in all its forms is token economics which determines the nature of the resources, their uses, their allocation and distribution, and ways to increase and decrease the resources. Tokenization can democratize access, unlock the value of illiquid assets, enable faster transactions and settlement, improve traceability and transparency, and improve interoperability. This section will comprise one chapter and an overview of investing in digital assets. It will consider market size, investment strategies, portfolio management, custody, trading and technical analysis, investment vehicles, risks, and sustainability. It will describe how and why tokenization will transform industries and examine case studies in banking and financial services, smart cities, real estate, the data economy, healthcare, and social tokens.

Chapter 6, "Digital Assets and the Tokenization of Everything," discusses different types of tokenized assets, including green digital asset solutions, tokenized health data, tokenized real estate, and other potential future tokenized assets. It also discusses the regulatory challenges of a tokenized world. It also provides a brief introduction to digital assets as investments. New business models will emerge, with institutions offering services to manage customer accounts in tokens or providing access to transactions on token exchanges or diverse tokenization platforms. This chapter describes how and why tokenization will transform industries and will examine case studies in banking and financial services; smart cities; real estate; the data economy, health care, and social tokens.

NON-FUNGIBLE TOKENS

This section of the book explores the dynamic concept of NFTs, providing an introduction to non-fungible tokens and how they are being used. The section will explain NFTs, how to make them, why they have become popular, and the sectors that are deploying NFTs. The aim of this section is to transmit knowledge so participants in the ecosystems are aware and involved. This section considers opportunities and risks and the future of NFTs.

Chapter 7, "Introduction to NFTs," outlines the recent history of NFTs. NFTs have been making the news since an NFT for a piece of digital art by the artist Beeple (Mike Winkelmann) sold for $69 million in March 2021. Businesses and their lawyers have been scrambling to understand the legal issues surrounding NFTs, not to mention the meaning and value proposition of this novel class of digital assets for online marketplaces and digital content developers. An NFT is a unique digital asset. This Chapter discusses what NFTs are, their characteristics, marketplaces, and how to mint NFTs. It provides a detailed introduction to the concept of NFTs and common token standards. The characteristics of NFTs are also discussed, including their capabilities to transfer tokens from different accounts, determine token owners and discover the token balance existing in a network. These characteristics also include the qualities of NFTs as being unique, scarce, and indivisible.

It explains NFT marketplaces such as Open Sea, Crypto.com, Rarible, and Binance, where NFTs can be bought and sold. A number of challenges associated with NFTs have been identified by this chapter, particularly the dangers that could arise from the loss of an NFT's private encryption key and the costs associated with distributing a huge quantity of data to the blockchain. Increased exposure and added benefits have been created for aspiring artists, established artists, and several other classes of creatives by NFTs.

Chapter 8, "How Are NFTs Being Used?" discusses different practical applications where NFTs are being used. Some of the areas covered in this chapter include the fashion industry, gaming sector, electoral utilization, ticketing system, regulatory structures, verification of authenticity, medical records, and intellectual property sector. There are two major classifications for the value that NFTs create: novelty and utility. This chapter examines the role of NFTs in various industries and posits that the significance of the NFT ecosystem is amplified as more businesses, artists, producers, and consumers engage with the technology and ecosystem. This chapter emphasizes the multi-utility of NFTs, touching on arguments against the concept of NFTs and other critiques around the threat of NFTs as a medium of over-financialization of every social fabric of society. The importance of NFTs in the blockchain ecosystem cannot be overemphasized in terms of the various intersections it exists in, especially in the metaverse, digital wallets, and traditionally non-bankable assets.

METAVERSE

This section will comprise two chapters, "History of the Metaverse" and "Living in the Metaverse." The section will describe the history of the different elements of a metaverse, including hardware, infrastructure, virtual and augmented reality, digital assets, and gaming. It will examine leading Metaverse platforms and examine the main use cases for Metaverse. It will also look at the likely world of the future and how we will use the Metaverse.

Chapter 9, "History of the Metaverse," describes the metaverse as a futuristic concept combining various technologies, including computer infrastructure, gaming, NFTs, DeFi, AR/VR, and the spatial web. There are more than 160 companies building Metaverses, and it is estimated to be a US$13 trillion market opportunity by 2030. There is yet to be a consensus on what it is. Still, it is thought it will be immersive and persistent, combining virtual and physical worlds with an economy and value that can be earned, lent, borrowed, and extracted from the physical world. Some challenges remain, including interoperability, latency, user interface, and regulation. However, this is arguably one of the most exciting technological developments which will help create new and enhanced ways to live, shop, be entertained, seek services, and be educated. This chapter outlines the immersive and persistent nature of the metaverse, combining virtual and physical worlds with its own economy. It has outlined the many challenges to widespread adoption, including interoperability, latency, user interface, and regulation. It also poses many ethical issues yet to be resolved and ideas on how to do so. The Metaverse is an exciting technological development that will help create new and enhanced ways to live, shop, be entertained, seek services, and be educated. The metaverse could be fulfilling and rewarding and create social purpose. At the same time, there are enormous risks. The Metaverse is an integral part of the future, and its potential is limited only by the framework of our imagination and today's technologies.

This is the beginning of the metaverse journey, and there is much to learn. There are no doubt risks, but the opportunities are immense. This is a new world that is advancing daily, and our knowledge grows with the innovators who are building these new metaverses. Like many innovations, the metaverse is not well-understood and treated with skepticism. Many still see it as a fringe technology fad for gamers and Gen Z. Few understand the potential opportunities to improve services, provision of education, as well as economic opportunities. Increasingly, sectors are exploring how the Metaverse will transform the way to work, shop, socialize, play, and engage with the government. This is the next iteration of the internet, and governments and businesses alike will embrace it, as Gen Z and Gen Alpha do.

Chapter 10, "Living in the Metaverse," describes how as the race for the metaverse continues, many industries are investing by entering existing Metaverses or developing their own. There is substantial innovation and experimentation, from entertainment to commerce to real estate. Metaverse-provided services such as health, education, and government services are all under development. It will be in new "phygital" realms that Metazens (citizens of the metaverse) will explore the new domains. "Phygital" is the use of technology to bridge the digital world with the physical world to provide unique interactive experiences for users. This chapter explores the main developments that underpin the types of activities available in the Metaverse and issues for future growth, including infrastructure, user experience, adoption, and interoperability.

WEB 3.0 AND ESG AND SUSTAINABILITY

The Sustainable Development Goals (SDGs) are aspirational visionary goals for the future state of humankind. However, they are inconceivable to achieve without harnessing the technology. Web 3, Blockchain, and frontier technologies are crucial for social impact.

This section will comprise two chapters. The first will outline how Web 3.0 and blockchain will contribute to improvements in financial inclusion, government, humanitarian settings, cities, gender, and sustainability; and the second will deconstruct the ways that blockchain can contribute to climate action, concluding green digital assets, smart grid management, NFTs and Gamification, measurement and reporting, and how a DAO could support climate action.

Chapter 11, "Web 3.0 and ESG and Sustainability," examines how Web 3.0, blockchain, and frontier technologies are crucial for social impact, especially concerning climate action, financial inclusion, payments, healthcare, humanitarian settings, identity, land registry, philanthropy and fundraising, supply chains, and urbanization. This chapter outlines how Web 3.0, blockchain, and frontier technologies can exponentiate impact on the SDGs, illustrating use cases where possible. It also examines the remaining challenges, such as ethics, privacy, confidentiality, data security, open-source systems, informed consent, data ownership, and the pace of digital transformation. Following this, the chapter examines the role of governments and international organizations in creating an enabling environment for technology transformation.

This chapter contributes to a growing field of knowledge about blockchain and Web 3.0 for sustainability. Innovators and technologists are working globally on implementing blockchain technology to solve many of the SDGs. This chapter provides the readers with an introduction to blockchain and Web 3.0 and its potential applications to improve the lives of the poor and underprivileged. Blockchain and other frontier technologies for sustainability can be tools for social change and improve inequality globally. While these technological tools for groundbreaking innovation exist, many such questions remain unanswered. It is paramount to closely and carefully monitor its evolution and share this information so that maximum impact can be achieved.

Chapter 12, "Blockchain and Climate Action," explains how Web 3.0 and blockchain can promote a climate-resilient, low-carbon, green, inclusive, integrated, and prosperous world, the transition towards a climate-resilient, low-carbon future, and the mobilization of funds to drive green, inclusive, sustainable, and climate-compatible growth. Blockchain has the potential to contribute to adaptation, mitigation, finance, and the enabling environment for climate action. This chapter is structured to educate people on mechanisms for raising capacity for effective climate change-related planning and management using Blockchain. It aims to build the capacity of people involved in climate policy and climate action in blockchain technology's potential to strengthen action on climate change.

This section aims at deploying blockchain technology to scale up climate action and provides practical examples and steps to scale up blockchain and climate action.

SUMMARY AND CONCLUSION

The book is pragmatic, as academics, technologists, industry, and government are coming to understand the demands of the future. The chapters represent a snapshot in time, and the velocity of change is dramatic. In the time it takes you to read this book, there will be new developments. We hope that what we have compiled is a foundation for others to build on.

Throughout the book, the authors explore the challenges and risks, which are many. It's a new technology, and it's still developing. It's had a number of technical failures. It's also been subjected to bad actors who fraudulently hack into projects, steal tokens and give the industry a very bad name. This naturally leads to regulation. However, regulation in most jurisdictions is simply not ready for these new technologies and will need to catch up because it's failing to protect consumers. It's failing to prevent money laundering and generally has the technology being used for social utility rather than harm. Regulation is essential and will come to be able to be interoperable across borders. There will need to be a collaboration between industry and governments.

A final note for the readers of the book, he may be of any demographic. But to remind you, the reader, that the demographic of the future is Gen Z and Gen Alpha. They are already digital. They are already comfortable with immersive experiences. They have grown up knowing the internet and knowing social media. They will not only be the users of Web 3.0 and the metaverse, but they will also be demanding better user experience, and they will be demanding that companies take their sustainability responsibilities seriously. They will be demanding that they have a voice in the development of these products. And they will demand to be remunerated for the contributions that they provide. So with three in the Metaverse is not necessarily for the generation who currently rule the world. It is for their children and for their children's children. And those children will be ready for it.

CONCLUSION

What we need to ensure is that we are handing them something that protects them, doesn't cause harm, takes ethics seriously, and builds a world that can enhance their experience in their lives and not cause catastrophic and painful events and experiences. The future is in our hands. And it's up to us to build it. We hope that people will be able to collect enough knowledge and information from this book, to be able to get a broad understanding of how technology in the Web 3.0 and metaverse spaces is developing and how it may be relevant to their lives and envision them to a new and hopefully better future. The purpose of this book is to provide objective information regarding the emergent field of Web 3.0 and metaverse in a rapidly accelerating digital world. Thus, the authors see that this book is but an introduction to Web 3.0 and metaverse through the perspectives of the authors and invite others to build on it.

Jane Thomason
UCL London Blockchain Centre, UK

Elizabeth Ivwurie
British Blockchain and Frontier Technology Association, UK

Chapter 1
Introduction to Web 3.0

ABSTRACT

Technological tools exist for the first time in human history to connect the bottom billion unbanked to the global economy, provide digital identity to stateless people, provide direct benefits to women and girls, and accelerate climate action. These tools can transform the lives of the world's population. Web 2.0 gave the world access to information. Web 3.0 will be the next iteration of the internet – "The Internet of Value" (IOV). This chapter outlines the motivation for producing a book on Web 3.0, the change model providing a framework for the book, and a summary of the chapters. The internet of value (IoV) will enable the exchange of any valued asset with another person without the need for an intermediary. This will be transformative.

INTRODUCTION

Determining which new exponential technologies will be the most profound is difficult. The authors decided to write a book on Web3 because this is perhaps the most significant Internet transformation ever. The Internet is used by 5.7 billion people worldwide, and Web3 will offer a newer, transformative form of the Internet. Because of the underpinnings of Web3 of Blockchain, Web3 will enable users to share and exchange information and value through Blockchain-based tokenization. In recent months, there has been a rapid explosion in the use of generative AI, notably Chat GPT and many other examples. This has been a powerful demonstration of how technology will sometimes abruptly change the world they live in, how they do their jobs, and

DOI: 10.4018/978-1-6684-6658-2.ch001

possibly cause them to lose their jobs. It will take some time to understand the new technologies, how they work, and how they may fundamentally change what will happen in people's and their children's lives. This is not a highly technical book for technicians. It is designed to introduce the technologies to the government, professionals, industry leaders, and the general public.

The book is designed to provide a basic understanding of Web3, its parts, and how it will be used. There are many risks and regulatory challenges of Web3. The Web3 Metaverse will present significant ethical challenges. These are understood, along with laws and regulations. The key underpinnings of Web3 are those of Blockchain. As a result, the book's first part goes into considerable detail about Blockchains, what it is, their initial use cases, and key developments, including decentralized finance (DeFi) and non-fungible tokens (NFTs). This provides fundamentals of Web3 and its parts. In the book's second part, the authors examine different applications and use in DeFi, NFTs, Metaverse, and applications for society and social impact.

In conclusion, the authors bring all these threads together and propose some recommendations for further research. The research is to be agile and immediate because the developments in technology are happening now. It is almost impossible to examine and produce findings before changes in technological innovation thoughtfully. This book is written in a moment; by the time it is published, many new things will have happened.

WEB 3.0: A FRAMEWORK FOR UNDERSTANDING

The authors believe decentralization is significant and will be part of the future. Web3, in conjunction with AI, will be two of the most profound changes. These will be integrated into Metaverses, where people can interact, learn, exchange, and have experiences that were never possible. A potent possibility enabled by Web3 is the creation of community-owned economies. It is now possible for communities to form and establish a decentralized autonomous organization (DAO) structure to manage the community, encode community rules, and be able to lend, borrow, exchange, and interact within a token economy. The concept of a community-owned economy is profoundly transformational, as will be outlined.

The framework for the book, which is a further extension of the framework for Blockchain outlined in Thomason et al. (2019), tries to capture some of the social, geopolitical, and technological changes that are going to lead to a future with greater decentralization and with the centralization comes greater, individual benefit and ability to be able to participate in the economy in ways that were never previously possible. First, it outlines the key influences and drivers of change. It then considers the enablers: education, government, communities, technology, regulation, and the global economy. Financially it predicts a future world of greater decentralization, a new data economy, and a world where Metaverse will be ubiquitous.

The purpose of this book is not one of persuasion. The intent of producing this book is to provide objective information regarding the technology's capability, its application, and possible evolution. Blockchain is part of a suite of Web 3.0 technologies – its potential is likely to be realized in the following years, coupled with other technologies like artificial intelligence (AI). Thus, the authors see that this book is an introduction to Web3 through the use of case studies, demonstrating which direction this innovation journey leads. The journey is only just beginning.

Figure 1. Web framework for understanding

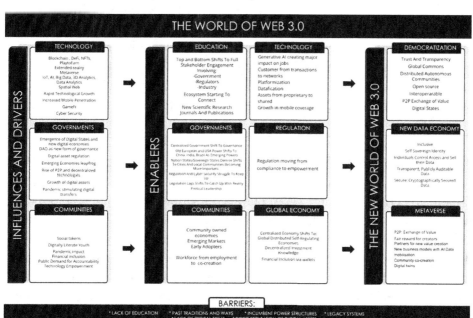

WEB 3.0 FUNDAMENTALS

According to Academy (2022), the Internet has significantly transformed in the last twenty years and has come a long way from Internet Relay Chat (IRC) to current social media platforms. The Internet has become crucial in connecting people and facilitating human relationships. Web2 is the Internet as it exists today (the term "Internet" is sometimes used interchangeably with "Web"), while Web3 is the Internet as it will persist in the future. The initial Internet offered what is now known as Web1. In 1999, author and web designer Darci Di Nucci first used the phrase to distinguish between Web1 and Web2 (Academy, 2022). Websites developed in the early 1990s utilized static HTML pages that could only show data. Users could not upload new data or update the existing data. Simple chat messengers and forums were the only social media outlets available.

A change toward a more participatory internet began in the late 1990s. Web2 allowed users to communicate with websites via social media, forms, databases, and server-side processing. With the help of these tools, the web experience transitioned from static to dynamic (Academy, 2022). User-generated data across various websites and applications have become more viable through Web2. Web 2 was more about participating than it was about watching. Most websites had switched to Web2 by the middle of the 2000s, and big techs had started to develop social networks and cloud-based services, enabling the world to store, access, edit, and share data globally with a few clicks.

Decentralization, transparency, and increased user utility are the fundamental tenets of Web 3.0. Berners-Lee already conceptualized Web 3.0 in the 1990s. He wrote of decentralization with no single point of failure (Team, 2022) because there is no central controlling node, making it possible for anybody to post anything on the Internet, and it offers freedom from arbitrary censorship and supervision. Berners-Lee also saw the bottom-up design; instead of code being created and controlled by a small group, it was developed in full view of everyone, promoting maximum engagement and experimentation (Foundation, 2022). Berners-Lee proposed the idea of the Semantic Web in 2001 (Machine, 2022). Computers cannot reliably process the semantics of the language, and the Semantic Web gave rise to software that would perform complex tasks for users and provide structure to the meaningful content of Web pages. The Semantic Web, as Berners-Lee first imagined it in 2001, has significantly evolved with the advent of Web

3.0. It is partly because translating human language, with all of its nuanced variations, into a format that computers can easily understand is incredibly expensive and highly complex, and Web2 has advanced significantly. Web3 is the Internet as it will exist in the future. Outlier Ventures have described a modular Web3 toolbox (Burke, 2021), combining DeFi, NFTs, Decentralised Governance, Decentralised Cloud Services, and Self Sovereign Identity.

DeFi

The value of DeFi is that it enables anyone to interact directly with peers without intermediaries and no need for costly buildings. This improves efficiency, transparency, and access because a mobile phone is required for access. The proliferation of open, decentralized financial instruments, or Defi, has been made possible by general programmability. These include banking-free borrowing and lending, more complex instruments like options and decentralized exchanges, and new structures like automated market makers (Burke, 2021).

Non-Fungible Tokens (NFTs)

Non-Fungible Tokens (NFTs) are digital assets representing tangible things such as art, music, in-game items, and movies. NFTs have enabled the realization of digital scarcity for particular assets. Ethereum has been the focal point of this innovation. There have been several inventions, initially in the creator economy, which include things like collectibles, tickets, art, virtual land, music, and gaming. It has become clear that they are a powerful tool for content creators and builders of open Metaverse worlds. They function as a doorway through digital consumption and play that will draw in users because every activity in the open Metaverse can be gamified and reimbursed with NFTs, which can subsequently have value on the open market. By extending beyond purely digital sovereign virtual assets, new specialized protocols like the Boson Protocol (Burke, 2021) that represent physical items as NFTs that can be redeemed in the real world without intermediaries, solve the problem of digital to physical redemption. It makes distinguishing between the virtual and physical worlds easier by permitting autonomous decentralized trade throughout the Metaverse.

Decentralized Governance

A Distributed Autonomous Organization (DAO) challenges traditional concepts of governance. The world is accustomed to centralized models of governance, where a central body is in power and control. DAOs enable a community to form and develop its mission, values, and rules, encode these within intelligent contracts, and automate them so the community can grow and be governed according to automated rules. This offers both opportunities and challenges because it means that anyone with a purpose or a community of interest can establish a DAO, can invite members from anywhere in the globe and build an extensive network of people globally and incentivize and activate them, reward them, and monetize their contributions and have a more significant impact possibly than any previous form of social organization. As with all technologies, there are risks and challenges, and DAOs are no exception. Two well-known DAO building blocks are Aragon and DAOStack. They include and extend beyond tools for collaborative asset custody, such as voting systems and multi-signature wallets (Burke, 2021). Decentralized governance provides methods and insights to control the open Web3 platforms and their components, permit economic participation, and aid in organizational structures such as gaming guilds and clans.

Decentralized Cloud

Khan (n.d.) outlines some of the critical features of a decentralized cloud— these contrast with the centralized cloud services in everyday use today. No entity controls the platform in a decentralized cloud network, and multiple providers compete to store user data. Only the customer can access their cloud data, and no one else. Decentralized cloud computing storage means people with excess resources, e.g., hard drive storage or computing capacity, can rent their resources for a fee.

Self-Sovereign Identity

Individuals need to be protected by a digital identity that they can guard and build wealth to create a fully open Web3. The fundamental tenets of Web3 are sovereignty and, thus, self-custody of the user's possessions. Innovations in self-sovereign identity and verifiable claims, in particular, allow them to identify, conduct transactions, and witness facts about themselves without disclosing the underlying or related data (Burke, 2021).

WEB 3.0 SOCIAL STRUCTURAL SHIFTS

The world is undergoing a tremendous structural shift from a society based on material things to an information society based on digital items and digital citizens where value exchanges as freely and easily as information (OpenMarkets, 2015; Tasca, 2020). Paolo Tasca (2020), in his editorial on the Internet of Value, identifies four critical socio-techno trends underpinning this transition: datafication; dematerialization; platformization, and social and resource value.

Datafication

Datafication transforms social action into digitized information (Mayer-Schönberger & Cukier, 2013; Tasca, 2020). It combines with internet connectivity to turn our life into data and enable innovative services to be tailored and delivered to consumers. Data analysis allows for understanding consumers better (Tasca, 2020). It provides an opportunity to build an interconnected network of value exchange.

Dematerialization

Dematerialization is the reduction in the material used in products. Digital technology accelerates dematerialization, creating an emerging service economy. A service is an exchange of value; you get access to it rather than ownership.

Platformization

Platformization, or the use of digital platforms for multiple services, is proliferating, supported by networks, which allow people to be connected and exchange information and value. It includes both marketplaces where buyers and sellers exchange digital or digitized goods and value and idle physical goods, the use of which can be exchanged peer to peer. It has the possibility that consumers will become producers. Platforms scale up by investing in their networks; the more significant their network, the greater their value.

Social and Resource Value

Social and Resource Value reflects a growing awareness of the importance of social and environmental assets, not just economic utility. The tracking and accounting process for different forms of value, such as green bonds, social impact bonds, company loyalty schemes, and carbon accounting, is growing (Tasca, 2020). Web 3.0, or the Internet of Value (IoV), has become the infrastructure that allows us to smoothly exchange this growing number of social and environmental values between companies and people (Tasca, 2020). Web 3.0 is an information network that enables the peer-to-peer value transfer. The Internet of Value, a concept proposed by Ripple, envisions a world where value moves and exchanges like information are exchanged today in the Internet era. Within this concept, value transactions such as foreign currency payments can happen instantly, similar to people sharing messages, images, and videos online for the past few years. Furthermore, it is not just money (Panos, 2021).

The word 'economy' to many is synonymous with money. However, it is a much broader concept. It is understood "traditionally" to be the organization of existing resources and encompassing processes such as creating wealth, production, distribution, trade, and consumption of goods and services. When applied to cryptocurrencies, it becomes the set of standards that govern the laws of digital exchanges through cryptography, encompassing the creation and production of these digital assets, distribution, and exchange. The traditional economy would cover various actors, including but not limited to households, small and medium-sized companies, large corporations, governments, and central banks, and in the cryptocurrency economy, actors would include: Exchanges, cryptocurrency users, developers, investors, regulatory entities, and others to be explored extensively in this Masters. Web3 will do for value what the internet has done for information: decentralize, remove asymmetries, and allow peer-to-peer transactions.

RISKS OF WEB 3.0

Paolo Tasca (2020) identified four crucial risk sources of Web3 - Systemic risk, governance risk, social welfare risk, and privacy risk.

Systemic Risk

This is the risk of a failure of an entire system. Networks have to navigate a trade-off between efficiency and security. They generally have tipping points, where shocks can have a ripple effect, and a small number of failing nodes can cause the entire system to collapse (Gai & Kapadia, 2019; Tasca, 2020). There is also the question of private versus public networks and stable, robust, and efficient system architecture that balances public and private interests.

Governance Risk

This is relevant to accountability, responsibility, and ownership of networks. There exists a divergence of opinions between private centralized governance models (e.g., Hyperledger or the Ethereum Enterprise Alliance) and public decentralized and anonymous governance models (e.g., Tezos). Private governance models centralize by design, but public models tend to become centralized over time. It leads to a dilemma between networks of trust run by centralized but accountable trust providers or keeping direct control of data via a synthetic-trust machine replication run by a small group of anonymous people who could go rogue.

Interoperability

Another governance risk is the need for interoperability between different Web 3.0 networks. As Tasca and Piselli point out (Tasca & Piselli, 2019; Tasca, 2020), "the interoperability between Blockchains is not a mere problem of standards; it is a problem of norms that should be addressed with reciprocal recognition between sovereign powers in their own space.

Social Welfare Risk

Concerns the increase in inequity of the entire society due to inadequate infrastructure supply to meet global needs.

Privacy Risk

Privacy risk is exponentiated with Web 3.0 and the potential that this data explosion will be used to pursue economic or surveillance objectives. What is needed is a privacy-enabling value exchange.

Cybersecurity Risks

Cybersecurity poses several risks in Web 3.0.

1. **Information Quality:** Will there be an agreement in Web 3.0 to accept machine-managed data with accuracy checks? Who makes calls? What are their credentials? Moreover, what drives them to base their choice on the truth rather than pushing an agenda?
2. **Data Manipulation:** A major cybersecurity threat is the deliberate modification of data used to train AI. (Steinberg, 2022).
3. **Availability:** What is the risk that data the systems depend on is unavailable? Links on the Internet today frequently break. Either all of the content on the Internet will need to be made locally by machines, or information will need to be retrieved instantly, as in Web 2.0 (Steinberg, 2022). As a result, there may be a greater reliance on the availability of systems over which IT staff have little control.
4. **Confidentiality of Data:** Constant data breaches put private information at risk. In addition to that risk, content may unintentionally leak or store in an unsafe place. Machines that scan data and store it in their knowledge bases dramatically enhance the possibility that private information will be found and used. Cybersecurity leaders must fortify their defenses to prepare for a system that can spread sensitive details more quickly than ever (Steinberg, 2022).

OVERVIEW OF THE BOOK

Chapter 1 introduces Web 3.0 as a broad overview. It discusses why Web 3.0 will transform many industries and the current trends. It outlines the book's target audience, what readers will learn, and the author's purpose in writing the book.

Chapters 2 and 3 introduce Blockchain and critical concepts. It comprises an introduction to Blockchain, token classification, an introduction to powerful platforms, and an overview of the Blockchain ecosystem. It includes the history, Blockchain technology stack, types of Blockchains, and overview of cryptography and consensus algorithms. Token classification, smart contracts, and current challenges are discussed.

Chapters 4 and 5 are about Decentralised Finance (DeFi), explaining the background of Blockchain and digital assets and financial applications, including central bank digital currencies, stablecoins, settlements, and custody. They also examine the leading Blockchain protocols relevant to finances. An overview of DeFi, an analysis of the DeFi ecosystem, a discussion of Decentralized Autonomous Organizations (DAOs), and several case studies will follow.

Chapter 6 examines trends in tokenization and digital assets. It describes how and why tokenization will transform industries and examines use cases in banking and financial services; smart cities; real estate; the data economy, healthcare, and social tokens.

Chapters 7 and 8 cover NFTs, including an introduction to NFTs and their use cases. It explains NFTs, how to make them, why they have become popular, and the sectors deploying NFTs.

Chapters 9 and 10 describe the history of the different elements of a Metaverse, including hardware, infrastructure, extended reality, digital assets, gaming, leading Metaverse platforms, and the primary use cases for Metaverse. Chapter 9 discusses the likely world of the future and life in the Metaverse.

In Chapters 11 and 12, the book covers technology and sustainability. It outlines how Web 3.0 and Blockchain will improve financial inclusion; government, humanitarian settings; cities; gender, and sustainability. It then deconstructs how Blockchain can contribute to climate action, concluding green digital assets; smart grid management; NFTs and gamification, measurement, and reporting, and how a DAO could support climate action.

The final chapter, 13, synthesizes the book, key challenges and risks, future research needs, and a look forward into the emerging future of Web 3.0.

CONCLUSION

Web3 must be open, accessible, and secure, linking technical interconnectivity with the exchange of value, stores of value, proof of authenticity, and smart contracts to create an always-on and borderless internet. Web3 could take the world forward into a new era of connected digitization. Thus, while the tone of this book is entirely positive, it is also pragmatic. The book represents a snapshot in time. Web3 is emerging fast; when it takes you to read this book, there will likely be changes to protocols, terminology, and data management approaches that invite readers to understand the technology with an open mind and a critical eye. The authors hope that you enjoy the journey of learning about this dynamic technology as much as they enjoyed researching it.

REFERENCES

Academy, B. (2022). *What Is Web 3.0 and Why Does It Matter?* Binance Academy. Retrieved 14 July 2022, from https://academy.binance.com/en/articles/the-evolution-of-the-internet-web-3-0-explained

Burke, J. (2021). *The Web 3 Toolbox.* Retrieved 14 July 2022, from https://outlierventures.io/research/the-web-3-toolbox/

Facts, W. (2022). *Facts About W3C.* Retrieved 14 July 2022, from https://www.w3.org/Consortium/facts

Foundation, W. (2022). *History of the Web.* Retrieved 14 July 2022, from https://webfoundation.org/about/vision/history-of-the-web/

Gai, P., & Kapadia, S. (2019). Networks and systemic risk in the financial system. *Oxford Review of Economic Policy, 35*(4), 586–613. doi:10.1093/oxrep/grz023

Khan, F. (n.d.). *devteam. space.* https://www.devteam.space/blog/what-is-decentralized-cloud-computing

Machine, W. (2022). *Wayback Machine.* Retrieved 14 July 2022, from https://web.archive.org/web/20171010210556/https://pdfs.semanticscholar.org/566c/1c6bd366b4c9e07fc37eb372771690d5ba31.pdf

Mayer-Schönberger, V., & Cukier, K. (2013). *Big data: A revolution that will transform how we live, work, and think.* Houghton Mifflin Harcourt.

OpenMarkets. (2015). *Ripple Labs And The Internet of Value.* CME Group. https://openmarkets.cmegroup.com/10381/what-is-an-internet-of-value

Rene, G. (2019). *An Introduction to The Spatial Web*. Retrieved 15 July 2022, from https://medium.com/swlh/an-introduction-to-the-spatial-web-bb8127f9ac45#:~:text=The%20Spatial%20Web%20integrates%20Convergence,and%20physical%20lives%20become%20one

Research, E. (2022). *Web 3.0 Market Top Companies | Web 3.0 Industry Trends by 2028*. Retrieved 16 July 2022, from https://www.emergenresearch.com/blog/top-10-companies-in-the-world-revolutionizing-the-web-with-web-3-services

Steinberg, L. (2022). *Security Magazine*. Retrieved 14 July 2022, from https://www.securitymagazine.com/articles/96998-4-cybersecurity-risks-of-web-30

Tasca, P. (2020). Internet of Value: A Risky Necessity. *Frontiers in Blockchain, 3*, 39.

Tasca, P., & Piselli, R. (2019). The Blockchain paradox. *Regulating Blockchain: Techno-Social and Legal Challenges*.

Team, I. (2022). *Web 2.0 and Web 3.0 Definitions*. Retrieved 14 July 2022, from https://www.investopedia.com/web-20-web-30-5208698

Thomason, J. (2019). *Blockchain Technology for Global Social Change*. IGI Global. doi:10.4018/978-1-5225-9578-6

Chapter 2
Introduction to Blockchain

ABSTRACT

Blockchain technology underpins Web 3.0. This chapter introduces blockchain technology and details its operation. This chapter explains the primary types of blockchains including public and private and provides their respective benefits and challenges. A detailed description of each of the five blockchain components—blocks, nodes, miners, cryptography, and consensus—is made. This chapter is helpful for readers new to blockchain and Web 3.0 to understand what network configuration might benefit their business needs.

INTRODUCTION

Many complex sets of informal and formal rules organize society. Social norms, policies, regulations, and laws define how we interact with each other, and institutions and individual and social beliefs, values, and expectations define how we respond to behavior. Institutions were established to provide functional efficiencies for society at scale. However, institutional governance is often found not to meet social expectations or to breach governance frameworks.

Against the backdrop of declining trust in institutions across media, not-for-profit organizations, governments, and industry sectors. Blockchain technology provides the promise of enhanced governance, increased trust, and improved performance. With its decentralized and cryptographic structure coupled with multiple validators on the network, Blockchains promise citizens a more trustworthy future. As part of the suite of Web 3.0 technologies, this chapter describes Blockchain's contribution.

DOI: 10.4018/978-1-6684-6658-2.ch002

WHAT IS BLOCKCHAIN?

A Blockchain is a secure distributed ledger that can record transactions between two parties efficiently and in a verifiable and permanent way. The most famous public Blockchains, Bitcoin and Ethereum, are most well-known for providing a secure, decentralized, and transparent record of their respective cryptocurrency transactions – bitcoin (BTC) and Ether (ETH). As a Blockchain is, at its essence, a decentralized database, almost any asset that can be codified can be transacted and stored on the Blockchain efficiently. Its decentralized design means parties can transact directly without using a trusted third party as an intermediary. This means that traditional functions provided by bankers, for example, become unnecessary by using the peer-to-peer network. This chapter explains Blockchain technology in detail, critically examines its types, elaborates on its operation, and provides reasons for its significance.

BLOCKCHAIN FUNDAMENTALS

A Blockchain is simpler to understand than when it first appears. It is a decentralized database that records the entry of every transaction on the network on a shared ledger to affect a secure, transparent transaction. The transaction process involves a party requesting a cryptocurrency, smart contract, storage, record, or other transaction. The transaction is broadcast to the nodes on the specific Blockchain network being used, and the transaction enters the memory pool as 'pending.' A 'gas' fee is registered against the transaction, compensating the miner for the resources used to validate the transaction. As might be expected, the higher the 'gas' offered by the transmitting party, the faster the transaction leaves the memory pool. The collecting miner validates the transaction against network rules, stores it into a 'block,' cryptographically seals it with a hash, and adds it to the 'chain.' The new block is added to the chain, and each node verifies it is correct. If most nodes agree by consensus that the block is correct, then it is added to the Blockchain and cannot be altered.

TYPES OF BLOCKCHAINS

Primarily, there are two types of Blockchains: permissioned and permissionless. Permissionless chains are also called public Blockchains, such as Bitcoin and Ethereum. Permissioned chains are private and consortia Blockchains which are 'by invite only' Blockchains with custom network rules.

Public Blockchains

A public Blockchain is a permissionless, non-restrictive ledger system. Anyone with an internet connection may register on a Blockchain platform to become a certified node and join the Blockchain network. A node or user member of the public Blockchain is granted access to current and historical data, verification of transactions or the proof-of-work for incoming blocks, and mining (Flair, 2022). The most fundamental applications of public Blockchains are cryptocurrency mining and replacement. Bitcoin, Ethereum, and Litecoin are the most prevalent public Blockchains.

Benefits of Public Blockchains

Trustworthy: There are as many nodes on a public network as they are willing to join, providing greater decentralization. The more extensive the network, the more data diffusion, and the more difficult it is for hackers to penetrate the whole network.

Transparent and Accessible: The ledger for a public Blockchain is publicly accessible at each authorized node. This renders the whole Blockchain transparent and accessible.

Disadvantages of Public Blockchains

Lower Transactions per Second (TPS) Than Permissioned Chains: To provide a secure network, public networks are well-decentralized, with thousands of nodes on the network, compromising the volume of transaction throughput. Thus, permissionless Blockchains can be accused of being slow and expensive (higher gas fees attract more attention from miners). Chapter 3 details the Blockchain trilemma – the difficulty of achieving scale when a network is limited by its ability to process transactions efficiently and securely in real time. There are over 17,000 reachable Bitcoin nodes (Bitnodes, 2023).

This makes Bitcoin highly secure but slow – it has a TPS of 7 seconds per transaction. For perspective, it is worth contrasting this transaction volume with Solana – 50,000 TPS (Ledger Academy, 2023).

Difficulties With scalability: The Blockchain trilemma is the tradeoff that projects must make to support decentralization, security, and scalability. The essence of the trilemma is that one cannot have all three elements – one can only have two at the cost of the third. Bitcoin is highly decentralized and secure, making it hard to scale. Chapter 3 provides solutions to the Blockchain trilemma, detailing layer 2 solutions that support efficient transaction processing.

Energy Consumption: Consensus mechanisms (detailed further on) are energy intensive – public Blockchains incur a lot of negative press regarding the energy consumed to mine Bitcoin (Carter, 2021). According to the Cambridge Center for Alternative Finance (CCAF), Bitcoin currently consumes around 110 Terawatt Hours per year—0.55% of global electricity production, or roughly equivalent to the annual energy draw of small countries like Malaysia or Sweden (CCAF, 2023). Calculating energy consumption is a function of looking at a network's hash rate (i.e., the total combined computational power used to mine Bitcoin and process transactions) and making some estimations as to the hardware requirements of miners over a given period. Mining is necessarily energy intensive; however, according to the CCAF, bitcoin mining (138.2 TWh) is compared to gold mining (131) per year (CCAF, 2023).

Private Blockchains

A private Blockchain is a permission based or restricted Blockchain that operates within a closed group by invitation only (Flair, 2022). The governing organization controls the level of protection, authorizations, permissions, and accessibility of each user. Private Blockchain networks are used for voting, chain control, virtual identification, and asset ownership, amongst other applications. Private Blockchains include Multichain and Hyperledger Fabric and Sawtooth, and Corda.

Private Blockchain Benefits

Speed: A private Blockchain is not decentralized; transactions occur faster than on a public Blockchain. A private network has a smaller number of nodes than a public network. This expedites the consensus procedure of a transaction using all of a network's nodes. Private Blockchains can support up to thousands or tens of thousands of transactions per second (Flair, 2022).

Private Blockchains Are Scalable: Thus, one might determine the size of their Blockchain according to their preferences. For instance, if a company wished to build a Blockchain of the top 20 nodes, it could do it relatively quickly. Afterward, they may do so without difficulty if they choose to add larger nodes. This makes personal Blockchains very scalable since it allows an organization to quickly increase or decrease the size of its community.

Disadvantages of a Private Blockchain

Lower Security: A private Blockchain network with fewer nodes or participants is more susceptible to security breaches. If all nodes obtain access to the critical control system (Flair, 2022), it might gain access to all nodes inside the community. This makes it easier for a node to hijack and abuse private Blockchain.

Centralization: Private Blockchains are constrained by the need for an identity and access authorization (IAM) mechanism to function correctly. This computer has all administrative and monitoring privileges. It grants authority to add a new node to the network or sets the access level to the Blockchain-stored data. This entire apparatus opposes decentralization, one of the tenets of Blockchain technology.

Consortium Blockchain

A consortium Blockchain is a blend of private Blockchains, each owned by organizations that have agreed to work together and share information and resources to improve functionality. Each organization's nodes are added to the Blockchain with permissions controlled by the consortium. The nodes remain owned by the organization, but the consortium shares the benefits of the chain. In this way, a consortium Blockchain is a private distributed ledger. Consortium Blockchains best benefit organizations working in similar sectors where knowledge-sharing broadly benefits individual organizations and the sector—for example, banks, airlines, healthcare, supply chain logistics, and government agencies. The governance structure of consortium Blockchains, therefore, is fundamental. Deloitte ran a global Blockchain survey 2019, where 92 percent of its respondents confirmed they already belonged to a consortium or planned to join one within the following year. Given a consortium Blockchain encourages an organization to work and share knowledge directly with its competitors, Deloitte describes this participation as a shift from market competition to market 'coopetition' (Deloitte, 2019).

Among its many benefits, a consortium promotes sensitive data-sharing without breaking data privacy laws by masking unique identifiers of data subjects while enabling the detection of duplication, such as multiple finance applications or insurance claims (Deloitte, 2019). Knowledge-sharing can reduce intermediary and reconciliation costs, introducing processing efficiencies and supply chain transparency. Examples of consortium Blockchains include the Energy web foundation on the Energy Web chain (2019), Bankchain, We: trade (IBM, 2019), and R3.

Hybrid Blockchain

A hybrid Blockchain combines public and private Blockchains (Flair, 2022). With this hybrid network, clients may regulate who has access to which Blockchain-stored information. Only a subset of information or statistics from the Blockchain can be made public, with the remainder kept private within the private network. The Blockchain hybrid flexibility allows users to connect a private Blockchain to many public Blockchains. A transaction in a hybrid Blockchain network is often confirmed within the private network. However, users may also wish to test their tokens on the public Blockchain, increasing the hashing rate and verification nodes. Thus, enhancing security.

Dragonchain (n.d.) is an example of a hybrid commercial-grade Blockchain designed to develop and deploy enterprise Blockchain-based applications rapidly. It aims to optimize speed by introducing a unique context-based consensus mechanism that allows users to choose the level of verification they need for a transaction. Dragonchain's consensus mechanism technology was initially developed at Disney as the Disney Private Blockchain Platform before being released as open-source software.

BLOCKCHAIN ESSENTIALS

The essential components of Blockchain technology include distributed ledgers, consensus, cryptography, blocks, nodes, and miners. This chapter proceeds to consider each of these elements in detail. The technology stack is described with the Blockchain trilemma in Chapter 3.

Distributed Ledgers

Historically a ledger has held records of accounts, whether paper or digital. A Blockchain ledger is a record of accounts on the chain. It is distributed (i.e., replicated) across all nodes on the network, so they all hold the same record of account. Each network node contains a secure copy of the ledger with no way to tamper with the data. As each new transaction is sent to the Blockchain network, the nodes must reach a consensus (detailed later in the chapter) on the blocks of transactions before they are added to the chain. All transactions in the Blockchain network are chronologically grouped to form a linear chain of data blocks, with each new block taking account of all the data from the blocks that came before it. This is how the system became called the "Blockchain."

Blocks

What turns a set of blocks (data) into a secure chain is the inclusion of a cryptographic hash of the previous block into the header of every new block - back to the Genesis block (the first block). Each block must refer to the preceding block's hash. A new block will be created when new transactions need to be added to the network. Once the new block is filled with data, it will be linked to the existing chain of blocks in chronological order. Changing the data once stored on the digital ledger is almost impossible. A Blockchain's security relies on this cryptographic hash. The block's header is one of the metadata fields in the block. The header contains the Blockchain version number, the previous block's hash, the Merkel Root, the timestamp, the difficulty target, and the nonce. The nonce (a portmanteau of number-used-only-once) is a four-byte number added to a hashed - or encrypted - block in a Blockchain that, when rehashed, meets the difficulty level standard set by the Blockchain network.

The nonce validates the information in the block as accurate when solved for. The miner's program then generates a random number to append the hash in the block's header; it then rehashes this value and compares it to the target hash. The miner is awarded the block and the accompanying mining reward if the resulting hash meets the network's difficulty standards. If the resulting hash does not meet the network's difficulty standard, the nonce increases by one, and the process starts again until a miner meets the difficulty target.

As a testament to the network's security, an individual miner is unlikely to have sufficient hashing power alone to generate the number of hashes per second. Keeping up with other miners is necessary to make mining a productive activity. A home computer might have a hashrate of 100 mega hashes per second (6 zeros or million). In contrast, a mining farm full of ASIC miners might hash around 30 exa hashes per second (18 zeros or quintillion). Thus, most blocks are opened by mining pools (Frankenfield, 2022).

Thus, if you are thinking about mining competitively, you will need to invest in powerful computer equipment like a graphics processing unit (GPU) or, more realistically, an application-specific integrated circuit (ASIC) (US$500->US$5000). Consequently, some miners - especially Ethereum - buy individual graphics cards as an affordable way to start mining (Hong, 2022).

Miners

Mining is a metaphor for the computational work undertaken by a node on the Blockchain network in the hopes of being awarded new tokens for validating a block. Mining is also the process by which new coins are released into circulation.

To earn tokens, miners have to be the first node to solve the cryptographic problem the block is secured with. In Bitcoin, this is the Proof-of-Work algorithm. The first miner to solve the 64-digit hexadecimal hash is awarded new tokens.

When bitcoin was first mined in 2009, mining one block would earn 50 BTC. In 2012, this was halved to 25 BTC. By 2016, this was halved again to 12.5 BTC. On May 11, 2020, the reward halved again to 6.25 BTC. As of March 2022, the price of Bitcoin was around US$39,000 per bitcoin (Hong, 2022). Not an insufficient incentive to hash!

Nodes

A node can be any electronic device that stores a copy of the Blockchain ledger and maintains network functionality (yes, that can even be a mobile phone!).

Consensus Mechanisms

Consensus is the procedure by which nodes on a Blockchain network reach an agreement about the state of the network (Crypto.com, 2022). Consensus is said to have been reached if at least 51% of the nodes agree on the next global state of the network (Capital Com SV Investments Ltd, 2022). Different types of consensus mechanisms exist depending on the Blockchain.

Proof-of-Work (PoW)

The Proof-Of-Work (PoW) algorithm is most notably used by the Bitcoin Blockchain – it was, therefore, the very first consensus mechanism created.

In PoW, miners compete to solve complex computational puzzles to create the 64-digit hexadecimal number, earn the right to form the new block, and confirm the transaction (Prestmit, 2022). The successful miner is also rewarded with a predetermined amount of crypto - the 'block reward.'

The operating costs for PoW are notoriously high as it requires large amounts of computational resources and energy to generate new blocks (Daly, 2022). This acts as a barrier of entry for new miners, leading to concerns about centralization and scalability limitations. This has led many potential miners to seek alternative consensus protocols, such as Proof of stake (PoS).

Proof of Stake (PoS)

In a proof of stake (PoS) system, miners are required to pledge a 'stake' of digital currency for a chance to be randomly chosen as a validator (an individual or organization responsible for verifying transactions on a Blockchain) (Kurahashi-Sofue, 2022). Proof of stake works like a lottery. The more coins one stake, the better the odds of becoming a validator. Unlike in PoW, where miners are incentivized by block rewards (newly generated coins), those who contribute to the PoS system earn a transaction fee. PoS is a more environmentally friendly, secure, and sustainable alternative to PoW. However, because this consensus system favors entities with more tokens, PoS has drawn criticism for its potential to lead to centralization. Prominent PoS platforms include Ethereum (ETH), Cardano (ADA), Solana (SOL), and Tezos (XTC).

Delegated Proof of Stake (DPoS)

A modification of the PoS consensus mechanism, delegated Proof of stake (DPoS), relies upon a reputation-based voting system to achieve consensus—users of the network vote to select validators or block producers to secure the network on their behalf. For the DPoS mechanism, a user does not require cryptocurrency to become a validator but must win enough votes to be chosen. A transaction will be formally entered into a ledger after being verified by the validator, and the number of validators that can be included in a single server range between 21 and 101 validators (Bybit Learn, 2021). Only the top tier (those with the most votes) earn the right to validate Blockchain transactions. To vote, users add their tokens to a staking pool, and votes are then weighted according to the size of each voter's stake. Elected validators who successfully verify transactions in a block receive a reward, usually shared with those who voted for them. DPoS is used by Lisk (LSK), EOS. IO (EOS), Steem (STEEM), BitShares (BTS), and Ark (ARK).

Proof of Authority (PoA)

The Proof of authority (PoA) consensus mechanism is a modification of PoS that works by selecting its validators based on reputation. In PoA, validators don't stake coins. Instead, they must put their reputations on the line for the right to validate blocks. This is very different from most Blockchain protocols which usually do not require a revelation of one's identity to participate in them. This mechanism requires almost no computing power, so it is far less resource-intensive than some of its predecessors, particularly PoW (Antolin, 2022). It is also one of the less costly options, making it a heavily favored solution for private networks, such as JP Morgan (JPMCoin). Other PoA-based projects include VeChain (VET) and Ethereum Kovan testnet. Though highly scalable, it is not well-decentralized - only a select few can participate in the network—additionally, the requirement for the validators to be identifiable increases the risk of corruption and third-party manipulation.

Proof of Burn (PoB)

The Proof of Burn (PoB) is a sustainable alternative to Bitcoin's PoW algorithm (Mastropietro, 2021). In PoB, miners gain the power to mine a block by 'burning' (destroying) a predetermined number of tokens, and these tokens are verified by sending them to an eater address (a wallet where they cannot be recovered or spent). The more coins burned, the greater the chances of being randomly selected. Unlike in PoS, where miners can retrieve or sell their locked coins should they ever leave the network, burned coins are irretrievably lost. This method of requiring miners to sacrifice short-term wealth to gain the lifetime privilege of creating new blocks helps to encourage long-term commitment from miners. Burning coins also creates scarcity, limiting inflation and driving up demand. Blockchains that use the Proof of Burn protocol include Slimcoin (SLM), Counterparty (XCP), and Factom (FCT).

Proof of Capacity/Proof of Space (PoC/PoSpace)

This is a unique consensus mechanism because, unlike most of its predecessors, which grant mining rights based on computational power or coins staked, Proof of capacity (PoC), also known as Proof of space (PoSpace), bases its mining algorithm on the amount of space available in a miner's hard drive (Proof of Space, 2022). In PoC, miners generate a list of all the possible hashes beforehand in a process called 'plotting.' These plots are then stored on a hard drive. The more storage capacity a miner has, the more possible solutions, and the more the solutions, the higher the chances of possessing the correct combination of hashes and winning the reward. As it does not require expensive or specialized equipment, PoC opens opportunities for the average person to participate in the network. As such, it is a less energy-intensive, more decentralized, and cost-effective alternative to some of the more prevalent consensus mechanisms (Proof of Space, 2022). However, few developers have chosen to adopt the system, and there are growing concerns about its susceptibility to malware attacks.

This algorithm is currently used by Signum (SIGNA), formerly Burstcoin (BURST), Storj (STORJ), and Chia (XCH).

Proof of History (PoH)

Proof of History (PoH) is a consensus system that provides Proof of historical events. Developed by Solana, PoH allows for 'timestamps' to be built into the Blockchain, verifying the passage of time between transactions without relying on other nodes. This timestamping method is enabled by SHA-256 - a sequential-hashing verifiable delay function (VDF) (Yakovenko, 2019). It works by taking the output of a transaction and using it as input for the next hash, which enables everyone to see which event took place in a particular sequence. As the VFDs can only be solved by a single CPU core, PoH reduces the processing weight of the Blockchain, making it fast and energy efficient. PoH is only employed by Solana; thus, it has yet to be tested at scale.

Proof of Importance (PoI)

First introduced by NEM (XEM), Proof of Importance (PoI) selects its miners based on specific criteria in a process called 'harvesting.' Harvesting involves selecting miners by considering the number and size of transactions in the last 30 days, the amount of vested currency, and network activity to generate a rating or importance score attributed to the nodes (Golden, n.d.). The higher the score, the higher the probability of being chosen to harvest a block and receive the accompanying transaction fee. Though, like PoS, PoI's use of additional metrics does away with the former's tendency to inherently reward the rich by considering participants' overall support of the network (Himanshi, 2022). Simply staking high in POI does not necessarily guarantee a chance of winning the block.

Nakamoto Consensus

The Nakamoto consensus protocol was devised by Satoshi Nakamoto in 2009 as a means of verifying the authenticity of a Blockchain network and preventing double-spending. It is a Byzantine fault-tolerant consensus algorithm that works with Proof of Work (PoW) to govern the Bitcoin Blockchain. Byzantine fault tolerance (BFT) is a condition where a distributed system can remain fault-tolerant due to malicious actors and network imperfection.

Through the combination of BFT and PoW, Nakamoto sought to circumnavigate some of BFT's inherent issues with scalability while deterring bad actors. By creating a standard measurement for the Blockchain's validity – in this case, the number of computational resources (or 'hashing power') spent on it – Nakamoto opened a new direction for solving the Byzantine Generals' Problem in a permissionless setup. One that would lead to the emergence of many new consensus algorithms, including Proof of Stake (PoS), Proof of Authority (PoA), Proof of Reputation (PoR), and Proof of Importance (PoI).

Proof of X

The idea behind this Proof of something (PoX) consensus is to use some scarce resources ('X') where malicious attackers cannot get X quickly. In doing so, the system can remain safe in a decentralized and permissionless manner. Here's how it usually works: To gain the privilege of validating transactions and mining new coins, nodes on a PoX network must provide evidence that they have successfully fulfilled X criteria. Often, this process involves some sacrifice—for example, computational power and effort in PoW and stacked coins in PoS. In different ways, these serve as incentives for miners to stay honest.

Private Blockchains' Consensus Mechanisms (Classical Consensus)

Private Blockchains require permission to participate, and a vetting process allowing participants to come on board is in place to varying degrees. The consensus mechanisms applicable to private Blockchains can be more streamlined and less complicated than those of public Blockchains. Classical consensus reaches consensus through voting. These protocols confirm transactions faster than the types of consensus mechanisms discussed in public Blockchains, as the consensus network size is fixed, and progress can be made as soon as the required votes are seen.

Some examples of classical consensus are:

Practical Byzantine Fault Tolerance (pBFT)

pBFT uses a three-phase state machine and a block election to select the leader. The three phases of pBFT are pre-prepare, prepare, and commit. Usually, the consensus is achieved by exchanging messages among nodes that bring a progressive transition to their local state. Otherwise, in the case of a node failure, a 'view-change' will be triggered, leading to a re-selection of the leader in a round-robin manner. Whereas pBFT can handle less than $\frac{1}{3}$ of Byzantine faults, this can be seen as $3f+1=$ Total nodes where f=amount of Byzantine faults.

Delegated Byzantine Fault Tolerance (dBFT)

In contrast to pBFT, which requires authority services to select the leader, dBFT's voting system allows for large-scale participation similar to delegated Proof of stake (DPoS). The consensus procedure is very similar to pBFT, where it differs in how the votes are counted. In dBFT, the weight of the vote is proportional to the number of tokens that the participants held at the time of voting. Participants can delegate their tokens (votes) to trusted representatives. This extra representation layer enhances the performance and could become more centralized over time. A disadvantage to this method is that elected delegates can no longer be anonymous—for example, delegates on the NEO Blockchain work under their real identities.

Federated Byzantine Agreement (FBA)

The federated Byzantine agreement (FBA) is an algorithm that supports open membership, allowing validators to join the network freely. It is noteworthy for its high throughput, scalability, and low transaction costs. In an FBA system, validators can choose which other validators they trust, and from there, they form what is known as a quorum slice. In a system with many validators, there may be multiple quorum slices; with multiple quorum slices, there becomes overlap with some nodes being trusted in multiple slices. These overlaps come together to form the overarching quorum used to reach a consensus in FBA. Projects that use FBA are Ripple (XRP) and Stellar (XLM).

Leaderless Consensus

As covered earlier, consensus means the agreement of a group of agents on their standard states via local interaction. In a leaderless consensus problem, no virtual leader is needed, while in a leader-following consensus problem, a virtual leader that specifies the objective for the whole group is required. More specifically, consensus with a static virtual leader is called a consensus regulation problem, and consensus with a dynamic virtual leader is called a consensus tracking problem. Examples of leaderless consensus projects include Avalanche, IOTA, and NKN.

Avalanche: Avalanche uses repeated random subsampling for voting to reach a consensus. Each node needs to sample a certain number of neighbors to verify their states to see if it aligns with the majority. If not, they will change their states following the majority. The process will repeat repeatedly, so the whole network will eventually come up with a ubiquitous conclusion in the long run.

IOTA: IOTA uses a directed acyclic graph (DAG) as the underlying data structure for a distributed ledger technology (DLT) instead of Blockchain. The current version of IOTA makes use of a protocol called Tangle:

- Tangle uses a DAG-based data structure to form the transaction graph instead of grouping transactions into chained blocks.
- It removes the role of miners and requires the user to verify two previous (unconfirmed) transactions if they intend to send new transactions to the network.
- Consensus/voting is based on local information and doesn't require interaction with the whole network. Instead, it is achieved via a weighted random walk process called Monte-Carlo Markov Chain (MCMC).

Cryptography

Blockchains are accessed using public key (or asymmetric) cryptography. Cryptography and digital signatures ensure the security of the Blockchain network.

Cryptography seeks to accomplish four goals to ensure the secure transport of data (Miller & Gregory, 2012):

1. Confidentiality ensures that only the intended recipient can decrypt the encrypted communication.
2. **Non-Repudiation:** Accordingly, the sender of the communication cannot refute their motivations for sending or producing the message in the future.
3. **Integrity:** the data inside the message cannot be altered during storage or transmission.
4. **Authentication:** Digital signatures prove that an individual aware of the corresponding private key has created a message.

Any transaction sent over a decentralized network is vulnerable to hacking without cryptographic encryption. In public-key encryption, two sets of keys are used (Saltik & Alemdar, 2022).:

- Public keys, a public 'address', can be distributed and are essential for identification (think of this as an account number that receives transactions). They are used for encryption and to verify a transaction after a transaction has been requested.
- Private keys are secret and are used for authentication and decryption. A private key is necessary to send a transaction. They are also almost impossible to restore – the encrypted transaction cannot be opened if your key is lost. A private key is usually 256 binary digits long, and it is often expressed as a series of 64 numbers and letters like D88C 5E31 8005 A994 C378D 9021 66E9 04E2 69CA 3860 8DBB E274 884F 3010 F004 C08C.

The public key has its origins in the private key, which allows network users to create unforgeable digital signatures, which can only be validated by other participants of the Blockchain network with knowledge of the corresponding public key.

Blockchain network addresses begin with creating a private key, from which the public key is created. When sending virtual assets from a wallet, the sender's identity is authenticated by their private key. Then the transaction is signed with that private key, which communicates the authority to send the funds. The public key can be distributed to receive funds in the receiver's wallet. A private key must never be distributed. The encryption process is as follows:

1. A sender gets the recipient's public key.
2. The sender initiates a transaction, and the public key encrypts information.
3. The sender sends the encrypted information to an addressee.
4. The addressee uses their private key to decrypt the information.

Let's say Bob wants to send Alice 1 BTC. Bob knows her public key and uses it to encrypt his transaction. Alice receives the transaction and decrypts Bob's transfer with her private key. Alice should be the only person who can authorize this transaction as she is the only one that knows her private key.

The goal of public key encryption is, thus, to ensure that the person who authorized the transaction signed for it and the person receiving the transaction is entitled to receive it. This prevents fraudulent transactions and misdirected monies. Various applications and system software use public key cryptography: the SSL protocol, SSH, digitally signed PDF files, OpenPGP, and S/MIME. It is also widely applied to software such as browsers to provide secure connections to insecure networks.

CONCLUSION

This chapter introduced Blockchain technology as part of the suite of Web 3.0 technologies, providing detailed distinctions between the types of Blockchains and how they operate. Chapter 3 introduces the technology stack for Blockchain and details the Blockchain trilemma. Both chapters provide readers an insight into this transformative technology and its contribution to Web development. 3.0 technologies.

REFERENCES

Ahmadu, O. F. (2022, May 30). What Blockchain is and How It Works. *Nicholas Idoko*. https://nicholasidoko.com/blog/2022/05/30/what-Blockchain-is-and-how-it-works/

Alvindayu. (2021). *What Are The Differences Between Rsa Dsa And Ecc Encryption*. https://alvindayu.com/al-what-are-the-differences-between-rsa-dsa-and-ecc-encryption

Antolin, A. (2022). What Is Proof-of-Authority? Cryptocurrency. *CoinDesk*. https://www.coindesk.com/learn/what-is-proof-of-authority/

B-Tech Digital. (2022). *Encryption*. https://btechdigital.com/service/encryption/

Berlove, O. (2019. May 22). What are public and private key pairs and how do they work. *Security Boulevard*. https://securityboulevard.com/2019/05/what-are-public-and-private-key-pairs-and-how-do-they-work/

Binance Academy. (2022). *Proof of Authority Explained*. https://academy.binance.com/en/articles/proof-of-authority-explained

Bitnodes. (2023). *Reachable Bitcoin nodes*. https://bitnodes.io/

Block Runners. (2018). [Audio podcast]. https://podcasts.apple.com/us/podcast/block-runners/id1437172347

BMC. (2020, November 24). What Is the CIA Security Triad? Confidentiality, Integrity, Availability Explained. *Security & Compliance Blog*. https://www.bmc.com/blogs/cia-security-triad/

Bybit Learn. (2021, September 11). *What Is Delegated Proof of Stake (DPoS)?* https://learn.bybit.com/Blockchain/delegated-proof-of-stake-dpos/#2

Cambridge Centre for Alternative Finance. (2023). *Comparisons*. https://ccaf.io/cbnsi/cbeci/comparisons

Capital Com SV Investments Ltd. (n.d.). *What is the consensus mechanism?* https://capital.com/amp/consensus-mechanism-definition

Carter, N. (2021). *How much energy does Bitcoin actually consume?* https://hbr.org/2021/05/how-much-energy-does-bitcoin-actually-consume

Cloudflare. (2022). *What is encryption? Types of encryption*. https://www.cloudflare.com/en-gb/learning/ssl/what-is-encryption/

Crypto.com. (2022, June 9). *How to Agree: Different Types of Consensus for Blockchain*. https://crypto.com/university/different-types-of-consensus-for-Blockchain

Cryptopedia Staff. (2022, March 25). How a Block in the Bitcoin Blockchain Works. Security. Cryptonetworks. *Cryptopedia*. https://www.gemini.com/cryptopedia/what-is-block-in-Blockchain-bitcoin-block-size

Daly, L. (2022, June 28). What Is Proof of Work (PoW) in Crypto? *The Motley Fool*. https://www.fool.com/investing/stock-market/market-sectors/financials/cryptocurrency-stocks/proof-of-work/

Deloitte. (2019). *So, you've decided to join a Blockchain consortium: Defining the benefits of 'coopetition'*. https://www2.deloitte.com/us/en/pages/consulting/articles/the-benefits-of-coopetition-in-Blockchain-consortia.html

Dhyeya, I. A. S. (2022). *Blockchain Technology: Daily Current Affairs*. https://www.dhyeyaias.com/current-affairs/daily-current-affairs/Blockchain-technology

Dobreva, M. (2019, January 18). *Blockchain Glossary from A to Z*. LimeChain. https://limechain.tech/blog/Blockchain-glossary-from-a-to-z

Dragonchain. (n.d.). *Profile.* https://messari.io/asset/dragonchain/profile

Energy Web. (2019). *The Energy Web Chain.* https://www.energyweb.org/wp-content/uploads/2019/05/EWF-Paper-TheEnergyWebChain-v2-201907-FINAL.pdf

Frankenfield, J. (2022). *Nonce: What it means and how it is used in Blockchain.* https://www.investopedia.com/terms/n/nonce.asp

Fruhlinger, J. (2020, February 10. The CIA triad: Definition, components and examples. *CSO.* https://www.csoonline.com/article/3519908/the-cia-triad-definition-components-and-examples.html

GeekForGeeks. (2022, August 3). *Hashing | Set 1 (Introduction).* https://www.geeksforgeeks.org/hashing-set-1-introduction/

Genersis, I. (2021, December 3). Security in the Digital Age: Elements of Cybersecurity That You Should Know. Security. *Tech Trend.* https://the-tech-trend.com/security/security-in-the-digital-age-elements-of-cybersecurity-that-you-should-know/

Golden. (n.d.). *Proof-of-importance (PoI).* https://golden.com/wiki/Proof-of-importance_(PoI)-639YX6M

Guo, H., & Yu, X. (2022). A Survey on Blockchain Technology and its security. *Blockchain: Research and Applications*, *3*(2), 100067.

Himanshi. (2022, March 21). Proof of Importance (PoI) in Blockchain. *Naukri Learning.* https://www.naukri.com/learning/articles/proof-of-importance-poi-in-Blockchain/

Hong, J. (2022). *How does Bitcoin mining work?* https://www.investopedia.com/tech/how-does-bitcoin-mining-work/

Iansiti, M., & Lakhani, K. R. (2017, February). The Truth About Blockchain. Blockchain. *Harvard Business Review.* https://hbr.org/2017/01/the-truth-about-Blockchain

IBM. (2019). *We.Trade.* https://www.ibm.com/case-studies/we-trade-Blockchain

Kurahashi-Sofue, J. (2022). What is a Blockchain validator? *Avalanche.* https://support.avax.network/en/articles/4064704-what-is-a-Blockchain-validator

Leader, S. S. L. (2022, July 10). RSA, ECC, ECDSA: which algorithm is better to choose when ordering a digital certificate in LeaderSSL. *SSL Help.* https://www.leaderssl.com/articles/484-rsa-ecc-ecdsa-which-algorithm-is-better-to-choose-when-ordering-a-digital-certificate-in-leaderssl

Ledger Academy. (2022). *Transactions Per Second (TPS).* https://www.ledger.com/academy/glossary/transactions-per-second-tps

Mastropietro, B. (2021, December 19). What Is Proof-of-Burn (PoB)? *Coinspeaker.* https://www.coinspeaker.com/guides/what-is-proof-of-burn-pob/

Miller, L., & Gregory, P. (2012). *The Role of Cryptography in Information Security. CISSP* (4th ed.). For Dummies., https://learning.oreilly.com/library/view/cissp-for-dummies/9781118417102/a2_13_9781118362396-ch08.html

National Cryptologic Foundation. (2022, September 30). "On This Date in History" Calendar 1983: Three Inventors Receive Patent for Encryption Algorithm RSA. *Cryptologic Bytes.* https://cryptologicfoundation.org/what-we-do/educate/bytes/this_day_in_history_calendar.html/event/2022/09/20/1663650000/1983-three-inventors-receive-patent-for-encryption-algorithm-rsa/78258

PCMag. (2022). Consensus Mechanisms. *Encyclopedia.* https://www.pcmag.com/encyclopedia/term/consensus-mechanism

Preetha, M., & Nithya, M. (2013). A study and performance analysis of RSA algorithm. *International Journal of Computer Science and Mobile Computing*, 2(6), 126–139.

Prestmit. (2022). *What is Hash in Cryptocurrency?* https://prestmit.com/blog/what-is-hash-in-cryptocurrency/?amp=1

Proof of Space. (2022a). In *Wikipedia.* https://en.m.wikipedia.org/wiki/Proof_of_space

Proof of Space. (2022b). In *Wikipedia.* https://en.bitcoinwiki.org/wiki/Proof-of-space

QuantumQuest. (2018, December 23). Intro to Data Structures for Programming. *Physics Forums Insights.* https://www.physicsforums.com/insights/intro-to-data-structures-for-programming/

Rawal, S. (2016). Advanced encryption standard (AES) and it's working. *International Research Journal of Engineering and Technology, 3*(8), 1165–1169.

Saltik, H., & Alemdar, S. (n.d.). *Secure Hash Algorithm–512 In Blockchain.* Academic Press.

Sealpath. (2020, June 23). Protecting the three states of data. *Data Protection.* https://www.sealpath.com/blog/protecting-the-three-states-of-data/

Sectigo. (2021, January 05). What Are the Differences Between RSA, DSA, and ECC Encryption Algorithms? *Blog Post.* https://sectigo.com/resource-library/rsa-vs-dsa-vs-ecc-encryption

SSL247. (n.d.). What is RSA? *Knowledge Base.* https://myssl.ssl247.com/kb/ssl-certificates/generalinformation/what-is-rsa-dsa-ecc

SSL2BUY. (2022). Diffie-Hellman, RSA, DSA, ECC and ECDSA – Asymmetric Key Algorithms. *Information Technology Journal, SSL Information.* https://www.ssl2buy.com/wiki/diffie-hellman-rsa-dsa-ecc-and-ecdsa-asymmetric-key-algorithms

Turner, D. M. (2017, August 7). Applying Cryptographic Security Services - A NIST summary. *Cryptomathic.* https://www.cryptomathic.com/news-events/blog/applying-cryptographic-security-services-a-nist-summary

Tutorials Point. (2022). Cryptography Digital signatures. *Cryptography Tutorial.* https://www.tutorialspoint.com/cryptography/cryptography_digital_signatures.htm

Verghese, R. (2022, July 31). Understanding The Blockchain For Beginners. *Eat My News.* https://www.eatmy.news/2022/07/understanding-Blockchain-for-beginners.html

Yakovenko, A. (2019, April 19). Proof of History: A Clock for Blockchain. *Medium.* https://medium.com/solana-labs/proof-of-history-a-clock-for-Blockchain-cf47a61a9274

Chapter 3
Blockchain Ecosystem

ABSTRACT

This is a relatively technical chapter designed to help readers understand some of the current blockchain technical challenges in more detail. In particular, it explores the blockchain scalability trilemma, protocol layers, and challenges in the blockchain ecosystem. The scalability trilemma prioritizes any two features of the blockchain (scalability, security, or decentralization) while compromising on one. The chapter outlines several solutions under development for solving the scalability trilemma. Developers will continue to solve these issues in years to come.

INTRODUCTION

Blockchain technology has become a significant component of today's global technology ecosystem, with its adoption made possible by the benefits it provides for individuals and businesses alike. This chapter develops the introduction in Chapter 2 to detail the Blockchain scalability trilemma and protocol information essential for understanding the Blockchain ecosystem. This chapter provides some recommendations for addressing scalability and describes ongoing innovation contributing to the development of the Blockchain ecosystem.

DOI: 10.4018/978-1-6684-6658-2.ch003

THE SCALABILITY TRILEMMA

Vitalik Buterin, the founder of the Ethereum project, first summarised the challenge of scaling decentralized networks due to the interplay of contrasting elements in their design. He called this the Blockchain scalability trilemma (Del Monte, Pennino & Pizzonia, 2020; Buterin, 2021). This trilemma can be briefly summarised as the trade-off encountered when seeking to improve any of the three Blockchain components: decentralization, security, and scalability. Buterin posits that any improvement in these aspects will negatively affect the other two (Del Monte, Pennino & Pizzonia, 2020; Buterin, 2021).

The scalability trilemma says that there are three properties that a Blockchain tries to have and that if you stick to "simple" techniques, you can only get two of those three. (Buterin, 2021. Emphasis Buterin's own.)

This chapter will go into further detail about these components. However, in summary, the three properties of the trilemma can be described (Buterin, 2021; CertiK, 2019):

- **Scalability:** The Blockchain can process more transactions than a single–lite - node (such as an individual's regular laptop) can verify and handle increasing numbers of these transactions.
- **Decentralization:** The Blockchain can operate without trust dependencies on any centralized control.
- **Security:** The Blockchain can resist many participating nodes trying to attack it. Buterin's rule of thumb is 'ideally 50%; anything above 25% is fine, 5% is *not* fine' (Buterin, 2021).

This thorny problem is one of the most significant challenges to broader Blockchain adoption – a good argument for continuing centralized networks is speed and security. It is worth noting up front, however, that the 'trilemma' is simply Buterin's snappy way to express a fundamental challenge that Blockchain developers tussle with. Nothing written in stone says these three aspects can never be resolved – but work is ongoing in balancing these design elements.

Public Blockchains (Bitcoin and Ethereum) are Blockchain technology's powerhouse. They offer cryptographically secure means of recording, executing, and auto-executing transactions. The knowledge that these records cannot quickly – or affordably – be altered engenders trust in the decentralized network. Blockchains obviate the traditional reliance on a trusted intermediary (typically a bank, lawyer, accountant, or government agent) to provide a direct, peer-to-peer means of transacting.

As discussed in Chapter 2, for that trust to be insured, transactions are executed across multiple nodes in the network – in the case of Bitcoin and Ethereum, thousands of nodes (Coin Telegraph, 2023) - that all verify the transaction and record copies of the state of the ledger. All nodes on a public network do not have the same technical capacity. Thus, public Blockchains can be limited by the capacity of the nodes' ability to process transactions, especially during periods of high volume. These fundamental processing issues can lead to accusations of Blockchains being slow and expensive in "gas" fees. This chapter will go into these components of the trilemma and possible resolutions further.

Scalability

Scalability is the network's potential to grow in size and scope without compromising effectiveness (Rodda, 2022). The Blockchain can only process as many transactions as its least equipped node. For Blockchain technology to achieve excellent global traction, chains need to handle as much data as the organization or client requires, at faster speeds, so that more people can use the network without it becoming slow or disproportionately expensive. One of the ways to increase Blockchain technology's appeal is to make it more competitive than centralized networks by providing faster speed and settlement times.

Increasing scalability, however, risks weakening decentralization or security. The Blockchain network will take less time to process transactions with fewer nodes, reducing the degree of decentralization and security. Thus. Developers looking to address scalability are innovating with Sharding, side chains, and state channels – discussed more in-depth throughout this chapter.

Decentralization

Decentralization – the essential feature of any Blockchain network – obviates traditional intermediaries, differentiating Blockchains from centralized legacy financial systems. Not all Blockchains are fully decentralized to the same degree, however. Ethereum is well-decentralized, with over 8000 nodes on the network (Ethernodes.org, 2023), EOS less so, with 21 nodes (Koffman, 2020).

Public Blockchains are decentralized to ensure that no one individual or entity can control or censor data moving through the network. Rather than assets passing between counterparties via banks or similar entities, Blockchains allow counterparties to transact directly. In principle, this means that individual authority throughout the network is less concentrated, and individuals have greater control of their assets and information (Rodda, 2022).

Decentralization goes hand in hand with security. As secure as a decentralised system should be (so there is no single point of failure), there are ways to attack decentralised systems. The costs of decentralisation are high, too, however. Consensus algorithms are energy intensive and time-consuming – organizations and clients that require high throughput on their networks may find the performance less than ideal.

Security

Security refers to the defensibility of the network against external malicious actors. It is a measure of a network's internal resistance to change. High-profile attacks on exchanges have demonstrated the need to prioritize security in the trilemma. Due to the transparent nature of the Blockchain's source code, and the lucrative nature of a successful attack, Blockchains can be a prime target for hackers. Scaling at the expense of security creates a more excellent pool of people and funds that can become vulnerable to a security attack.

Centralized networks derive their security from their closed design – whoever controls the system can guarantee security. How can this be insured in a decentralised system? As discussed in Chapter 2, cryptography and consensus algorithms provide the Blockchain's security. Each block in the chain has a digital signature (a hash) connected to the preceding and subsequent blocks. Tampering with a block alters its hash and other blocks in the chain, which nodes quickly pick up on the network. Thus, due to the decentralised nature of the chain and the consensus mechanism, there is no single point of failure vulnerable to attack on the network, and a user cannot change transaction records.

The consensus mechanism employed may depend on whether a chain is permissioned or permissionless. A permissioned network may use a Proof-of-Authority consensus mechanism; others, including the network administrator, must therefore validate users. Permissionless chains allow anyone to participate as a node on the network and validate transactions; however, how much a Blockchain is decentralized relies on the design of the consensus algorithm, network governance, ownership of cryptographic 'private keys,' and the provision of economic incentives. Public Blockchain consensus mechanisms (Bitcoin and Ethereum) are primarily "Proof-of-Work" (PoW) or "Proof-of-Stake" (PoS), respectively. Moving from a PoW consensus mechanism to PoS by Ethereum in 2023 was an attempt to improve scalability and reduce the network's energy consumption, thereby permitting higher transactions per second.

Possible attack vectors on a Blockchain network might include the following (NeonVest, 2018):

- A >50% attack, whereby a user - or group of users - owns>50% of the total tokens outstanding for the network.
- A Collusion attack is where users conspire to perform a malicious action against the network.
- A Penny Spend attack is where a user (or group) floods the network with low-value transactions to halt the network.
- A Distributed Denial of Service attack involves malicious transactions on the network intending to disrupt functioning.
- A Sybil attack involves sets of forged identities created on a system to gain network control.

The scalability trilemma provides a valuable framework to compare and contrast Blockchains – it does not imply a fundamental problem with the ecosystem. It simply identifies which aspects of a project the architects have decided to prioritize. The following section provides insights into how developers balance these critical elements of the trilemma. First, it is essential to understand the Blockchain Stack.

The Main Chain

The main chain is a Blockchain, the most essential and powerful Blockchain and Blockchain network within a specific Blockchain ecosystem. It may also be known as a Layer 1 chain, discussed below. Examples of leading chains are Bitcoin and Ethereum.

Leading chains optimize the foundational layer of a Blockchain protocol to increase transaction throughput and reduce fees. Their capacity is often limited by network congestion, so main chain scaling solutions directly extend the Blockchain protocol to improve scalability, such as the introduction of Ethereum 2.0 (Cointelegraph, 2023).

Side Chains

A sidechain is a Blockchain-adjacent transactional chain used for large batch transactions (Cryptopedia Staff, 2022) to help process some of the data from the mainchain. Sidechains are independent Blockchain ledgers that run parallel to another Blockchain (the main chain) using a two-way peg (Musungate et al., 2019). They may have protocols and implementation strategies dissimilar from the main Blockchain (Singh et al., 2019). A two-way peg, or a Blockchain bridge, is a communication protocol among ledgers (Lerner, 2021). It allows the bidirectional transfer of assets at a fixed or pre-deterministic exchange rate between the mainchain and the sidechain (Singh et al., 2019).

Sidechains use an independent consensus mechanism to the main chain, which can optimize for speed and scalability. Such adjustability allows users access to various other functionalities and features offered on the sidechain using the assets they already possess on the main Blockchain. Furthermore, sidechains are secluded from the main Blockchain so that the harm is confined to the sidechain in case of a cryptographic break (or a maliciously designed sidechain) (Singh et al., 2019). The side chain also allows the execution of business transactions unsuited to the mainchain and helps reduce transaction fees and completion time associated with sole mainchain usage (Gula, 2020).

BLOCKCHAIN LAYERS

Layer 0

Layer 0 is a Blockchain system's foundation comprising hardware, protocols, connections, and other components. Layer 0 is a network architecture underlying the Blockchain (Verma, 2022). This layer allows Blockchains to communicate with one another through interoperability. Interoperability is the propensity for computer systems with dissimilar programs to interpret and exchange information with minute friction. A suitable analogy for comprehending the significance of interoperability in the Blockchain space is to consider Blockchains as massive cities that need a connection via bridges for economic activity to flow in and out (Horizen, 2022). It provides a crucial backbone to address future layer scalability difficulties. Layer 0 enables participation and development via a native token. Examples of Layer 0 Blockchains include Polkadot, Avalanche, Cardano, and Cosmos (Verma, 2022).

Case Study

Cosmos is a proof-of-stake (PoS) Blockchain project empowering the interoperation of multiple independent Blockchains (Kwon & Buchman, 2021; Liu, 2019). The Cosmos development team is behind the most valuable layer 0 on the market, with nearly $150 billion in value created. This Blockchain layer example advocates modularity and interoperability above other factors, such as security. Ignite and the Interchain Foundation are the two most significant contributors to Cosmos, and the three below components created by these contributors help Cosmos pride itself as the "Internet of Blockchains" (Chinedu, 2022).

Tendermint Core is an open-source Blockchain development platform with a consensus algorithm and a peer-to-peer communication solution (Chinedu, 2022). It provides the equivalent of a database, web server, and supporting libraries for Blockchain applications written in some programming language (Tendermint, n.d.). Tendermint facilitated the operation of Cosmos by providing Blockchain software and development kits used by Blockchain projects in the Cosmos ecosystem (Bybit Learn, 2021).

Inter-Blockchain Communication (IBC) is a data exchange solution between several compatible Blockchains for financial and bond transactions. It comes in direct communication channels between each network, allowing the Blockchains to talk to each other (Chinedu, 2022). The Inter Blockchain Communication Protocol brings a robust interchain infrastructure to the Cosmos ecosystem by bridging different Blockchains and facilitating exchanges between a network of interconnected chains (Radmilac, 2022).

Cosmos SDK is a development kit that allows the simple creation of a Blockchain using the Tendermint Core and is compatible with IBC (Chinedu, 2022).

Challenges With Cosmos

Cosmos's governance system is a significant challenge as it easily suspends validator identities. Validators are needed to vote on all proposals. A temporary suspension of the validator identity for a week follows in case of failure to do so promptly (Liu, 2019). Another challenge with using Cosmos is due to its technical nature and the learning curve associated with understanding the project. A crypto novice would first need to understand the individual, siloed Blockchains, why those Blockchains need to be connected, and finally, how Cosmos achieves this. In doing so, Cosmos must introduce complex topics and terminologies like hubs and zones, IBC, interoperability, and Tendermint Core Byzantine Fault Tolerance (Cryptoeq, 2022).

Layer 1 Blockchain

Layer 1 carries out most tasks by maintaining a Blockchain network's fundamental operations, such as dispute resolution, consensus mechanism, programming languages, protocols, and restrictions (Verma, 2022). Layer 1 consists of the base protocols of the Blockchain. Scalability problems at this layer `result from many tasks that this tier must manage frequently. Higher fees and longer processing times occur as more parties enter the Blockchain since the computational power for solving and adding blocks to the chain will grow.

Mitigation techniques for scalability concerns at this layer include improved consensus techniques like moving to a Proof of Stake consensus mechanism by Ethereum and the advent of Sharding (the division of computing operations into smaller parts).

Case Study

Solana is unique because of its Proof of History (PoH) consensus algorithm. PoH cryptographically proves the passage of time and events falling in that timeline (West, 2022), making the Blockchain faster, scalable, and energy-efficient (Tyson, 2022). Solana attracts developers for high-potential and impactful projects in the space (Alchemy, 2022). Solana provides a "stateless" architecture and is scalable due to its reduced memory consumption. The following tools facilitate the functionality of Solana:

The turbine is a protocol used by Solana to break down information into smaller bits, enabling it for easier processing. It facilitates Solana with solving bandwidth problems and increasing the capacity to process transactions. The turbine is similar to Ethereum's plans for Sharding (Alchemy, 2022), splitting a Blockchain into multiple pieces, or shards, and storing them in different places (Nibley, 2020).

The gulf stream is Solana's mempool management solution. A mempool or memory pool is a set of transactions that have not yet been processed in the Blockchain and are waiting to be picked up by the network (Mostafavi, 2021). Solana uses this Gulf Stream protocol to push transaction caching and forwarding to the network's edge. Validators and clients forward transactions to the expected leaders and allow validators to execute transactions in advance. In addition, the Gulf Stream allows for shorter confirmation time, and faster leader switch time, and less memory pressure on validators. This solution is impossible if networks have a non-deterministic leader or cannot know the initial conditions to predict an outcome (Alchemy, 2022).

Sealevel is Solana's smart contract environment that processes multiple contracts in parallel (Samudoka, 2021). Solana uses Sealevel, a hyper-parallelized transaction processing engine that scales across Solid-State Drives (SSDs) and Graphics Processing Units (GPUs), enabling Solana to scale horizontally rather than vertically (Alchemy, 2022).

Pipelining is a technique Solana uses for making sequencing data inputs into hardware components. It enables data verification and duplication across nodes at a fast rate. Overall, it is made to be an effective Central processing unit (CPU) design improvement (Alchemy, 2022).

Cloudbreak is a horizontally-scaled architecture for Solana. Since scaling computing is insufficient, the memory needed to store account information becomes an issue. Cloudbreak allows Solana to scale without using Sharding. Solana made Cloudbreak concurrently utilize all hardware to index data, read the database, and write transaction inputs (Alchemy, 2022).

Solana can store data by using Archives. Archives enable the network to offload data from the validators to the Archives. It allows nodes to duplicate information with fewer hardware requirements. Archives permit using Blockchain data securely and efficiently on a distributed and public ledger. Archives are coherent because they store small parts of the state itself. However, the networks ask Archivers for Proof of storing the data they are supposed to store. This technique is called Proof of Replication (PoRep) (Alchemy, 2022).

Challenges With Solana

A significant challenge associated with Solana is staking centralization. Potential security risks exist if the Standard Custody stakes a substantial portion in Solana. Anything going wrong with the Standard custody could bring down Solana's Blockchain. Finally, liquidity and price data are essential since a great deal of liquidity is on Project Serum, which made a tool on Solana called Serum DEX. Damage to Serum DEX could cause damage to Solana. Recently, Solana suffered a network outage due to bots performing duplicate transactions excessively. This is an increasing problem, as Solana does not guarantee network stability (Alchemy, 2022).

Layer 2 Blockchain

Layer 2 protocols are scaling solutions (separate Blockchains) built atop Layer 1 Blockchains to reduce bottlenecks with data processing (Marcobello, 2022). Solutions at this layer are discussed below: rollups, sidechains, and state channels. Examples of layer 2 solutions are the Bitcoin Lightning Network, Ethereum plasma, Optimism (OP), Arbitrum (ARB), and Polygon.

Case Study: Bitcoin Lightning Network

Lightning Network (LN) is a Layer 2 solution built on top of Bitcoin. LN was made in response to scalability issues with Bitcoin, particularly the speed and cost of Bitcoin transactions (Bitcoin.com, 2022). There are several use cases of the lightning network. A prominent example is that Twitter enables users to send and receive Bitcoin "tips" through the Lightning Network. The Strike is a Lightning Network-compatible payments app that allows Twitter's 360 million monthly active users to send Bitcoin payments to other Twitter accounts instantly and for free (Rodriguez, 2021; Coinbase, 2022).

Challenges With the Lighting Network

There are concerns regarding how easy it is to run an LN node. LN requires a robust network of Bitcoin nodes running the LN protocol. Running an LN node can be perplexing, and there are payment incentive problems for running smaller nodes. Running LN is not much more complex than running a full Bitcoin node. However, since LN mainly targets micro-transactions, the day-to-day experience with LN will be through LN-enabled wallets. However, LN-enabled wallets could be more user-friendly, and most of them caution that since they are still in public testing stages, it is advisable to refrain from investing large sums of money. Unlike some of the more established Bitcoin wallets, the novelty of these LN-enabled wallets means there are ade-offs between custodial and non-custodial versions. The non-custodial LN wallets are harder to use (Bitcoin.com, 2022).

Layer 3

Layer 3 is the last layer of the Blockchain ecosystem and is represented by Blockchain-based applications built upon the Blockchain, such as dApps (decentralized applications).

Historically, web 2.0 architecture consisted of more or less standard components, such as the front end, the back end, and the database. Web 2.0 comprises applications such as Instagram, Yahoo, Meta, Google, and others, which run code created by their respective companies for users to interact with their company. D'apps (Decentralized Applications) service Web 3.0; however, instead of communicating with Google or Meta servers, d'Apps feedback to the Blockchain.

Decentralized Applications are brilliant contract-powered versions of traditional Web 2.0 applications. D'Apps store all their data on a Blockchain and have their back-end code running on a Blockchain instead of with a central authority.

These applications contain cross-chain functionality, which helps users access various Blockchain platforms via a single d'App (Phemex, 2022). Layer 3 protocols take a more front-end role – as opposed to Layers 0-2 – it is the only layer visible to users, as participants can interact with the user interface. Layers 1 and 2 are more back end, as these layers' objectives are to deliver effectiveness and ease to the overall functionality of the Blockchain. Some Layer 3 protocols are seen in Lending Markets, Finance, Market Futures, or Exchanges (dEx).

Types of Layer 3 Protocols

AAVE is a decentralized app that allows users to borrow tokens at different interest rates and helps create specific margin positions. In transaction processing, for instance, as opposed to web 2.0 apps, there will be no need to integrate with a fiat payment provider to accept funds from end-users because users can transact directly using tokens and cryptocurrencies.

Decentralized applications manifesting as an Exchange (DeXes) will allow users and traders to instantly buy and sell their tokens and cryptocurrency with low fees instantly, without background checks, and an example is UniSwap.

Gaming d'Apps utilize Web 3 elements added to a Blockchain as a layer 3 solution for the distribution of games. For example, nine Chronicles, Soccerverse, Tiny World, Alien World and Farmers World are games that run entirely on their own Blockchain. Gamers may remember Crypto Kitties as a Blockchain game. The popularity of the first Blockchain game brought the Ethereum network to a halt on several occasions due to high volumes of NFT trading. Blockchain gaming will evolve fast over the coming years, for the onboarding experience for gaming is not as clunky as during Crypto-kitty times. There is no need to remember private keys and Metamask details anymore. Gamers can create accounts with the host to set up wallets in the back end. Gamers will soon experience a smooth Blockchain onboarding that they will never know the chain powers their game.

Solutions to the Scalability Trilemma

Roll-Ups

Roll-ups are layer 2 protocols that facilitate transaction processing efficiencies by batching up data groups on side chains away from the main chains to save cost and increase transaction speed (Stevens, 2022; Jakub, 2021). Optimistic and Zero-Knowledge (ZK) are the two types of rollups.

Although roll ups are very beneficial, their use also comes with some risks: Both rollups are still new, and their networks are often centralized. At times, the development team of a roll-up keeps some power over the network and can theoretically halt or switch it off wherever they desire. Many roll-ups also rely on centralized "sequencers" to effectively coordinate transactions on the Layer 2 chain. A sequencer cannot spoof or alter transactions, but it can technically censor or re-order them to derive some benefit for itself (Stevens, 2022).

Optimistic Roll-Ups

This roll-up type optimistically assumes that all the transactions accommodating within a rollup are credible. Optimistic roll-ups grant everyone on the network a week to contest fraudulent transactions, after which it assumes that every transaction is ascertained as legitimate. The advantage of the Optimistic roll-up is that it is speedy; by assuming things are legitimate, the network does not waste time confirming things (Stevens, 2022)

ZK-Roll-Ups (Zero Knowledge Roll-Ups)

A ZK-rollup is a Layer-2 Blockchain protocol that processes transactions, performs computations, and stores data off-chain while holding assets in an on-chain smart contract (Panther Team, 2022).

It uses a complex piece of cryptography called a Zero-Knowledge proof for determining a transaction's validity using only minimal details regarding that transaction. It is privacy-preserving, sleek, and, most importantly, fast and cost-effective. Compared with an optimistic rollup, which requires funds to be kept on the network until the end of the dispute resolution period, ZK-rollups allow users to draw out their funds with less delay (Stevens, 2022).

ZK-rollups hold numerous advantages over Optimistic rollups regarding speed and security, but they are reasonably more complex in an obscure manner. Until recently, all of the ZK-rollups known publicly have had specific applications as they can only support specific services or use cases (like swapping a non-fungible token or transferring crypto between addresses) (Stevens, 2022).

ZK-STARK (Zero-Knowledge Scalable Transparent Argument of Knowledge)

ZK-STARK is a highly secure cryptographic testing using Zero Knowledge Testing principles for creating encrypted data for easy verification without revealing sensitive information (Bit2me, 2021). ZK-STARK is transparent in that the prover and verifier did not need to use a third generated parameter to produce the proof and check the claim's validity, respectively (Sasson et al., 2018).

ZK-SNARKs are so-called because they have the following qualities (Alchemy, 2022):

1. **Zero-Knowledge:** The verifier knows nothing about a statement except its validity or falsity.
2. **Succinct:** The proof is small enough for the verifier to verify quickly.
3. **Non-Interactive:** SNARKs are non-interactive because provers and verifiers do not need to exchange information beyond the initial proof submitted. Early zero-knowledge proving systems required provers and verifiers to exchange multiple messages to verify statements.

4. **Argument:** A SNARK is a "computationally sound" statement that satisfies rigorous requirements, making cheating difficult (i.e., generating false proofs).

5. **Knowledge:** SNARK-based proofs cannot be created with access to the underlying information or the witness.

The advantages of ZK-STARK are as follows:

1. **No Need for a Trusted Setup.** ZK-STARKs do not require a trusted setup for functioning. They instead depend on public randomness. This reduces trust assumptions on the users' part and helps improve the security of STARK-based protocols (Alchemy, 2022).

2. **Scalable Properties.** STARKs are computable and verifiable faster at scale compared to SNARKs. Most importantly, ZK-STARKs maintains a low proving and verifying time even as the complexity of the underlying computation grows logarithmically (Alchemy, 2022).

3. **Maximum Throughput.** Like SNARKs, STARKs can scale Blockchains by facilitating off-chain computation in a secure and verifiable manner. A single STARK proof submitted to the Layer 1 chain can legitimize thousands of transactions completed off the main chain. Hence, many high-profile ZK rollup projects utilize ZK-SNARKs to prove the integrity of off-chain computation (Alchemy, 2022).

4. **Higher Security Guarantees.** ZK-STARKs use collision-resistant hashes for encrypting instead of the elliptic curve schemes utilized in ZK-SNARKs. This is considered unsusceptible to quantum computing attacks, deeming it more secure than the elliptic curves used in SNARKs (Alchemy, 2022).

The Disadvantages of ZK-STARKS are outlined below:

1. **Larger proof sizes.** Although STARKs provide proofs faster, the drawback is that these proofs are more significant in comparison to SNARK-based proofs. This makes STARK proofs expensive for verification on Ethereum since computing more considerable proofs incurs costlier gas fees (Alchemy, 2022).

2. **Lack of Trust Resulting From Lower Adoption.** SNARKs were the first practical application of zero-knowledge technology in Blockchains, which is why it has more market share than STARKs. Most ZK rollups use ZK-SNARKs. The developer ecosystem and tooling for SNARK-

based ZK proofs are considerably larger. As a result, most users and developers tend to trust ZK-SNARKS more because of its wide adoption (Alchemy, 2022).

ZK-SNARK (Zero-Knowledge Succinct Non-Interactive Argument of Knowledge)

ZK-SNARK is a protocol that creates a framework in which an entity referred to as the prover can quickly convince another entity referred to as the veriðer of possession or the information without revealing the said information and without any interaction between the two entities (Mayer, 2016).

Other Blockchain Scalability Solutions

Blockchain scalability solutions generally belong to layer-1 or layer-2 levels (Binance Academy, 2022). The main difference between layer-1 vs. layer-2 scalability solutions lies in their role and focus on the Blockchain. Layer-1 here improves the Blockchain architecture, while layer-2 builds third-party networks on top of the leading Blockchain. Layer 1 can provide the most effective solution in large-scale protocol upgrades. However, this method also means the validator must be convinced to accept changes via a hard fork (Zipmex, 2022). Layer 2 provides a faster way to increase scalability. However, users can potentially lose the security of the original Blockchain due to using third parties (Zipmex, 2022).

Layer 1 Scalability Solutions

1. Sharding is the procedure of optimizing database management systems by separating the components of a larger database table into multiple smaller components (Hazelcast, 2022).

Sharding is a unique on-chain scaling solution. It is focused on dividing the Blockchain network into smaller chunks and manageable parts called shards. Then, the network runs the shards in parallel with each other. The processing output will increase substantially across the network, with each shard taking a share of transaction processing in the group. The network can function as the sum of its parts by breaking it into smaller parts. Sharding eliminates the apprehensions of relying on the speed of individual nodes for rapid and improved transaction throughput (Geroni, 2021).

Sharding can be key-based, range-based, or directory based. Key-based Sharding is also known as hash-based Sharding, in which the data is plugged into a hash function to ascertain which shard each data value must go to (Awati & Denman, 2022). Range-based Sharding involves sharding the data according to an attribute's specified range of values. This strategy is simple to understand and implement (Algodaily, 2022). Directory-based shard partitioning involves placing a lookup service before the sharded databases. The lookup service knows the current partitioning scheme and keeps a map of each entity and which database it is stored on (Haldar, 2018).

2. Segregated Witness (SEGWIT) is another notable solution for the scalability of Layer 1 Blockchains (Geroni, 2021). It reduces the size required for storing transactions in a block. This is completed by removing specific signatures by counting serialized witness data as one unit and core block data as four units (Menon, 2018). SEGWIT is a protocol improvement in the Bitcoin Blockchain network which focuses on modifying the manner and structure of storing data. It helps remove signature data associated with each transaction, opening up more capacity and space for storing transactions. Interestingly, the digital signature for verifying ownership and fund availability of the sender consumes around 70% of the entire transaction space. Removing the digital signature can open more space for adding more transactions (Geroni, 2021).

3. A hard fork is a software update implemented by a Blockchain or cryptocurrency's network nodes incompatible with the existing Blockchain protocol, which causes a permanent split into two separate networks that run in parallel (Vermaak, 2021). Hard forking is a process focused on producing structural or fundamental modifications in the property of a Blockchain network. For example, hard forking can involve expanding the block size or diminishing the time required for creating a block. Though hard forking is necessary for Layer 1 Blockchain scalability solutions, a contentious hard fork is the most productive alternative. The contentious hard fork implies a split in the broader Blockchain community, with a specific section defying the core community on specific issues. In such cases, the specific section of a Blockchain community can choose to implement structural changes in the underlying codebase (Geroni, 2021)

Second Layer Scalability Solutions

State channels state is a technique that allows users to make multiple Blockchain transactions, such as state changes or money transfers, without committing all transactions to the Blockchain (Agarwal, 2020). State channels offer a two-way communication channel between off-chain transaction channels and Blockchain networks via distinct mechanisms. As a result, it can ensure productivity improvements concerning the speed and capacity of transactions. State channels do not require the instant involvement of miners for validating transactions. They serve as resources proximal to the network that is integrated with the support of a smart contract or multi-signature mechanism. Once a transaction or group of transactions is completed on a state channel, the concerned Blockchain records the final 'state' of the 'channel' alongside all associated transitions (Geroni, 2021).

Plasma is a layer 2 solution that seeks to drastically increase the efficiency of the Blockchain networks by taking the bulk of the processing duties off of the main chain and redistributing it onto a series of smaller, functional chains referred to as the child chains (Binance Academy, 2021). It focuses on utilizing child chains that begin from the original Blockchain, each acting as an independent Blockchain. The child chains operationalize their transactions while leveraging security advantages in the associated main chain. The independent operation of each child chain parallel to each other provides the perfect opportunity to optimize speed and efficiency. Furthermore, the child chains can have their defined traits and rules. So, one can create plasma for use cases concerning processing a specific category of transactions while ensuring execution in a related ecosystem with more security (Geroni, 2021).

Sidechains are one of the most prominent choices among layer 2 solutions for fixing scalability problems in Blockchains. Sidechains have become necessary for helping pre-existing Blockchains like Bitcoin to scale and become more interoperable (Roth, 2022). Sidechain serves as a transactional chain adjacent to the Blockchain, specifically in the case of large batch transactions. Sidechains leverage independent consensus algorithms as compared to the original chain. Interestingly, the independent consensus mechanisms offer opportunities for optimization to achieve better scalability and speed. Sidechains generally use utility tokens in data transfer between the sidechain and leading chains. In this case, the crucial role of the mainchain will focus on maintaining general security alongside facilitating dispute resolution (Geroni, 2021).

CONCLUSION

This chapter has assessed the Blockchain ecosystem, analyzing a significant issue that exists within the ecosystem: the Scalability Trilemma. This concept was defined as prioritizing any two features of the Blockchain (scalability, security, or decentralization) while compromising on one. The chapter outlines several solutions under development for solving the scalability trilemma. It is also worth remembering that Blockchain technology is a relatively new technology – these developmental problems speak to a balance of priorities for projects. Developers will continue to solve these issues in years to come. The next chapter introduces Decentralized Finance (DeFi), one of the primary uses of Blockchains in Web3 and a significant innovation that will change the future of finance

REFERENCES

Agarwal, G. (2020, January 19). State Channels: An Introduction to Off-chain Transactions. *Talentica*. https://www.talentica.com/blogs/state-channels-an-introduction-to-off-chain-transactions/

Alchemy. (2022, March 10). *Layer 1 Blockchain Ecosystems: Overview*. Learn Web3. https://www.alchemy.com/overviews/layer-1-Blockchain-ecosystems-overview

Alchemy. (2022, May 27). SNARKs vs. STARKS vs. Recursive SNARKs. *ZK Proofs Overview*. https://www.alchemy.com/overviews/snarks-vs-starks

AlgoDaily. (2022). *What is Database Sharding? Scaling DBs*. https://algodaily.com/lessons/what-is-database-sharding/range-based-sharding

Anupam, S. (2019). What Are The Major Limitations, Challenges In Blockchain? *Inc42*. https://www.google.com/amp/s/inc42.com/features/what-are-the-major-limitations-challenges-in-Blockchain/amp/

Atomic, D. E. X. (2022, October 10). What is bitcoin (BTC)? First blockchain and cryptocurrency. *Coin Guides*. https://atomicdex.io/en/blog/what-is-bitcoin-btc/#hold-and-trade-btc-on-atomicdex

Awati, R., & Denman, J. (2022). Sharding. *TechTarget*. https://www.techtarget.com/searchoracle/definition/sharding

Ben-Sasson, E., Bentov, I., Horesh, Y., & Riabzev, M. (2018). Scalable, transparent, and post-quantum secure computational integrity. *Cryptology ePrint Archive*. https://eprint.iacr.org/2018/046

Bit2me Academy. (2021). What are zk-STARKs? *Blockchain*. https://academy.bit2me.com/en/que-son-las-zk-stark/

Binance Academy. (2021). Plasma. *Glossary*. https://academy.binance.com/en/glossary/plasma

Binance Academy. (2022, May 31). *Blockchain Layer 1 vs. Layer 2 Scaling Solutions*. https://academy.binance.com/en/articles/Blockchain-layer-1-vs-layer-2-scaling-solutions

Bitcoin.com. (2022). *What is Lightning Network?* https://www.bitcoin.com/get-started/what-is-lightning-network/

Bogdanov, D. (2021, August 24). Optimistic Rollups vs ZK Rollups: Examining Six of the Most Exciting Layer 2 Scaling Projects for Ethereum. *Limechain*. https://limechain.tech/blog/optimistic-rollups-vs-zk-rollups

Buterin, V. (2021). *The scalability trilemma*. Retrieved from https://vitalik.ca/general/2021/04/07/sharding.html

Bybit Learn. (2021, September 27). What Is Tendermint? *Blockchain*. https://learn.bybit.com/Blockchain/tendermint/

Bybit Learn. (2022, June 27). The Blockchain Trilemma: Can It Ever Be Solved? *Tech Deep Dive*. https://learn.bybit.com/deep-dive/Blockchain-trilemma/#1

Certik. (2019). *The Blockchain trilemma: Decentralised, scalable and secure?* Retrieved from https://medium.com/certik/the-Blockchain-trilemma-decentralized-scalable-and-secure-e9d8c41a87b3

Chauhan, A., Malviya, O. P., Verma, M., & Mor, T. S. (2018). Blockchain and scalability. In *2018 IEEE International Conference on Software Quality, Reliability and Security Companion (QRS-C)* (pp. 122-128). IEEE. https://www.researchgate.net/publication/327000219_Blockchain_and_Scalability

Chinedu. (2022, June 3). *Layer 0, The Foundation of the Blockchain Where Interoperability Reigns*. FXCryptoNews. https://fxcryptonews.com/layer-0-the-foundation-of-the-Blockchain-where-interoperability-reigns/

Coinbase. (2022). What is the Lightning Network? *Crypto Basics*.

Cryptoeq. (2022, September 23). *Cosmos (ATOM): Strengths, Weaknesses, Risks*. Core Report. https://www.cryptoeq.io/corereports/cosmos-abridged

Cryptopedia Staff. (2022, June 28). The Blockchain Trilemma: Fast, Secure, and Scalable Networks. *Cryptopedia.* https://www.gemini.com/cryptopedia/Blockchain-trilemma-decentralization-scalability-definition

Decentralised Dog. (2022). How long does a Bitcoin transaction take? *Coin Market Cap.* https://coinmarketcap.com/alexandria/article/how-long-does-a-bitcoin-transaction-take

Del Monte, G., Pennino, D., & Pizzonia, M. (2020). *Scaling Blockchains without giving up decentralisation and security: A solution to the Blockchain scalability trilemma.* Retrieved from https://arxiv.org/pdf/2005.06665.pdf

Ethernodes.org. (2023). *Ethereum mainnet statistics.* https://ethernodes.org/

Foy, P. (2022). Solana vs Ethereum: Comparing Each Layer 1 Blockchain. *MLQ.ai.* https://www.mlq.ai/solana-vs-ethereum/

Gartner Peer Insights. (2022). Blockchain Platforms Reviews and Ratings. *Blockchain Platforms.* https://www.gartner.com/reviews/market/Blockchain-platforms

Geroni, D. (2021, October 5). Blockchain Scalability Solutions – An Overview. *101 Blockchains.* https://101Blockchains.com/Blockchain-scalability-solutions/

Gonzalez, O. (2022, July 18). Bitcoin Mining: How Much Electricity It Takes and Why People Are Worried. *CNET.* https://www.cnet.com/personal-finance/crypto/bitcoin-mining-how-much-electricity-it-takes-and-why-people-are-worried/

Gula, S. (2020, June 1). Sidechains And Their Applications. Crypto. *Ulam Labs.* https://www.ulam.io/blog/sidechains-and-their-applications-Blockchain

Gupta, P. (2022, July 28). Solving the Blockchain trilemma: A look at some scaling solutions. *Chainstack.* https://chainstack.com/solving-the-Blockchain-trilemma-scaling-solutions-for-ethereum/

Haldar, D. (2018, August 19). System Design Interview Concepts – Database Sharding. *Acoders Journey.* https://www.acodersjourney.com/database-sharding/

Hazelcast. (2022). *What Is Sharding?* https://hazelcast.com/glossary/sharding/

Horizen. (2022). What Is a Layer 0 Blockchain? *Horizon Academy.* https://www.horizen.io/Blockchain-academy/technology/advanced/layer-0/

Investing.com. (2022, July 26). zk-STARKs vs. zk-SNARKs explained. *Cryptocurrency.* https://www.investing.com/news/cryptocurrency-news/zkstarks-vs-zksnarks-explained-2854329

Jakub. (2021, August 2). Rollups – The Ultimate Ethereum Scaling Solution. Crypto. *Finematics.* https://finematics.com/rollups-explained/

Jha, P. (2022, April 20). Brain drain: India's crypto tax forces budding crypto projects to move. *Cointelegraph.* https://cointelegraph.com/news/the-state-of-crypto-in-northern-europe-hostile-scandinavia-and-vibrant-baltics

Knysh, N. (2021, November 22). Introducing Blockchain: Six Limitations For Enterprises To Remember. Innovation. *Forbes.* https://www.forbes.com/sites/forbestechcouncil/2021/11/22/introducing-Blockchain-six-limitations-for-enterprises-to-remember/?sh=4f239c79313f

Koffman, T. (2020). *Google cloud joins forces with EOS.* https://www.forbes.com/sites/tatianakoffman/2020/10/06/google-cloud-joins-forces-with-eos/?sh=675440d7516f

Kruijff, J. D., & Weigand, H. (2017, June). Understanding the Blockchain using enterprise ontology. In *International Conference on Advanced Information Systems Engineering* (pp. 29–43). Springer. doi:10.1007/978-3-319-59536-8_3

Kwon, J., & Buchman, E. (n.d.). *A Network of Distributed Ledgers* [Whitepapers]. Cosmos. https://v1.cosmos.network/resources/whitepaper

Lerner, S. D. (2021, February 25). Bitcoin Sidechains. Innovation Stories. *Medium.* https://medium.com/iovlabs-innovation-stories/bitcoin-sidechains-74a72ceba35d

Liu, Y. (2019, August 14). What are the challenges of the Cosmos and how to tackle them? The Startup. *Medium.* https://cryptoslate.com/cosmos-inter-Blockchain-communication-protocol-ibc-surpassed-11-million-transfers-in-february/ https://medium.com/swlh/what-are-the-flaws-of-the-cosmos-and-how-to-tackle-them-6c114f4f3bd7

Marcobello, M. (2022, June 29). What Are Layer 2s and Why Are They Important? Technology. *CoinDesk.* https://www.coindesk.com/learn/what-are-layer-2s-and-why-are-they-important/

Mayer, H. (2016). *zk-SNARK explained: Basic Principles.* https://blog. coinfabrik. com/wp-content/uploads/2017/03/zkSNARK-explained_basic_ principles. pdf

Menon, S. (2018, February 24). Bitcoin Legacy vs SegWit wallet address. What is the difference? *Medium.* https://medium.com/@buddhasource/bitcoin-legacy-vs-segwit-wallet-address-what-is-the-difference-cb2e71ab8381

Mostafavi, M. (2021). Explaining Solana and its Innovations without technical jargon. *Figment Learn.* https://learn.figment.io/tutorials/explaining-solanas-innovations-without-technical-jargon

Musungate, B. N., Candan, B., Çabuk, U. C., & Dalkılıç, G. (2019, October). Sidechains: Highlights and challenges. In *2019 Innovations in Intelligent Systems and Applications Conference (ASYU)* (pp. 1-5). IEEE.https://www. researchgate.net/publication/335368901_Sidechains_Highlights_and_ Challenges

NeonVest. (2018). *The scalability trilemma in Blockchain.* https://aakash-111. medium.com/the-scalability-trilemma-in-Blockchain-75fb57f646df

Nibley, B. (2022, January 19). A Guide to Sharding in Crypto. *SoFi Learn.* https://www.sofi.com/learn/content/what-is-sharding/

Njoroge, E. (2021, December 15). Understanding a 51% Attack on the Blockchain. *Section.* https://www.section.io/engineering-education/ understanding-the-51-attack-on-Blockchain/

Panther Team. (2022, August 26). ZK-rollup projects: Inner workings, importance & analysis. Panther Academy. *Panther.* https://blog. pantherprotocol.io/zk-rollup-projects-inner-workings-importance-analysis/

Pettinger, T. (2022). Brain Drain Problem. *Economicshelp.* https://www. economicshelp.org/blog/glossary/brain-drain-problem/

Phemex. (2022, April 16). What Are the Blockchain Layers? Layer 3 vs. Layer 2 vs. Layer 1 Crypto. *Crypto Insights.* https://phemex.com/academy/ bitcoin-layer-1-vs-2-vs-3

Radmilac, A. (2022, March 9). Cosmos' Inter-Blockchain Communication Protocol (IBC) surpassed 11 million transfers in February. *Cryptoslate.* https:// cryptoslate.com/cake-defi-launches-100-million-venture-arm-to-fund-web3-gaming-and-fintech-startups/

Rodda, K. (2022, August 18). The three challenges facing the Blockchain Trilemma. *IG Bank*. https://www.ig.com/en-ch/news-and-trade-ideas/the-three-challenges-facing-the-BlockchainBlockchain-trilemma-220818

Rodriguez, S. (2021, September 23). You can now get paid in bitcoin to use Twitter. *CNBC*. https://www.cnbc.com/2021/09/23/you-can-now-get-paid-in-bitcoin-to-use-twitter.html

Romain. (2022, June 29). SNARKs vs STARKs: A Deep Dive Behind Layer-2 Rollups. *Medium*. https://medium.com/coinmonks/snarks-vs-starks-a-deep-dive-behind-layer-2-rollups-d9b3ca6e1386

Rossolillo, N. (2022, September 22). What Is a 51% Attack? *The Motley Fool*. https://www.fool.com/investing/stock-market/market-sectors/financials/cryptocurrency-stocks/51-percent-attack/

Roth, S. (2022, May 7). An Introduction to Sidechains. *CoinDesk*. https://www.coindesk.com/learn/an-introduction-to-sidechains/

Samudoka. (2021, April 15). What is solana. *Remitano*. https://remitano.com/forum/ca/post/10633-what-is-solana

Schweiger, P. (2021). *Improving Usability of Blockchain-Based Decentralized Applications* [Doctoral dissertation]. University of Applied Sciences Technikum.

Singh, A., Click, K., Parizi, R. M., Zhang, Q., Dehghantanha, A., & Choo, K. K. R. (2019). Sidechain technologies in BlockchainBlockchain networks: An examination and state-of-the-art review. *Journal of Network and Computer Applications, 149*. https://sci-hub.se/https://doi.org/10.1016/j.jnca.2019.102471

Stevens, R. (2022, September 7). What Are Rollups? ZK Rollups and Optimistic Rollups Explained. Ethereum. *CoinDesk*. https://www.coindesk.com/learn/what-are-rollups-zk-rollups-and-optimistic-rollups-explained/

Takyar, A. (2022). All About blockchain: Blockchain scalability solutions. *LeewayHertz*. https://www.leewayhertz.com/BlockchainBlockchain-scalability-solutions/

Tendermint. (n.d.). *Tendermint Core*. https://docs.tendermint.com/

Tyson, M. (2022, July 28). Solana BlockchainBlockchain and the Proof of History. *Infor World.* https://www.infoworld.com/article/3666736/solana-BlockchainBlockchain-and-the-proof-of-history.html

Verma, A. (2022). A Beginner's Guide To Understanding The Layers Of Blockchain Technology. *Blockchain-council.* https://www.BlockchainBlockchain-council.org/BlockchainBlockchain/layers-of-BlockchainBlockchain-technology/

Vermaak, W. (2021). What Is a Hard Fork? *Alexandria.* https://coinmarketcap.com/alexandria/article/what-is-a-hard-fork

West, T. (2022, July 29). Solana Blockchain & Proof of History. *CoderOasis.* https://coderoasis.com/solana-and-proof-of-history/

Zipmex. (2022, July 22). *Blockchain Layer 1 VS Layer 2 Scaling Solution: Key Differences.* https://zipmex.com/learn/layer-1-vs-layer-2/

Chapter 4
DeFi and the Future of Money

ABSTRACT

Decentralized finance (DeFi) was not well understood when it came into the spotlight in 2019. In 2020, it scaled fast and increased from $700 million at the beginning of 2020 to $15 billion by the end of 2020, and as of June 2022, the total value locked (TVL) reached a high of $256 billion. What explains this remarkable increase? The current financial system has left 1.7 billion people unbanked. The barriers to entry are high, the costs are high, transparency is low, and a small group of powerful elites dominates it. DeFi offers an accessible alternative to the current financial system. It explains its exponential borrowing, lending, yield farming, and insurance growth. Early results suggest that DeFi will redefine the financial system. This chapter provides an overview of DeFi, an analysis of its ecosystem, and its likely trajectory.

INTRODUCTION

DeFi represents an essential step in the evolution of money. Over history, what is called "money" has had many iterations. Money has three qualities: as a medium of exchange, a unit of measurement, and a storehouse for wealth, which determines its value (Investopedia, 2022). Money has not always been in the exchangeable paper form as it exists today; some of the earliest forms of money were cowrie shells, first used as money in about 1200 BC (Britannica, 2022). Next came metal, reportedly in Babylon before 2000 B.C., and Turkey's first standardized and certified coins emerged in the 7th century

DOI: 10.4018/978-1-6684-6658-2.ch004

(Saggs, 2022). Since then, there have been multiple innovations in money. The next iteration was paper money, invented in China during the reign of Emperor Zhenzong between 997 and 1022. (Britannica, 2022). Paper money spread to other parts of the world by the late 18th and early 19th centuries, and it was in the form of promissory notes to pay specified amounts of gold or silver. In 1821 the Gold Standard was introduced in the United Kingdom. This linked the standard currency unit to the value of a fixed quantity of gold (Britannica, 2022). Countries such as the United States of America, France, and Germany adopted the gold standard, but by the 1970s, it was no longer tied to currency (Britannica, 2022). The next iteration of money was the emergence of the credit card. In 1950, Diners Club introduced the first universal credit card; in 1959, American Express debuted a plastic card (Britannica, 2022).

Bitcoin was the next major innovation in the history of money when the first Bitcoin was mined in 2009, and technology gave the world the potential for digital scarcity. Verification, digital signatures, and cryptography create identity, ownership, and the ability to be traded, which set Bitcoin apart from older mediums of exchange, such as copyable paper currency. The next innovation in virtual assets was the Ethereum public blockchain outlined in the Ethereum Whitepaper (Buterin, V., 2015). Ethereum established the ability to create and issue tokens seamlessly, similar to creating a currency. Initial Coin Offerings (ICO) offer a token. They are conceptually similar to Initial Public Offerings in that ICOs offer ownership stakes as opposed to IPOs as "shares," and these ownership stakes are in the form of tokens. They can be risky and speculative, but the investors hope that the subject blockchain protocol or cryptocurrency will grow in popularity, and such popularity will translate to an increase in the value of the underlying token. The smart contract function of Ethereum laid the groundwork for Decentralized Finance (DeFi), which is envisioned as an open-source alternative to the current financial system which allows people to develop decentralized products which mirror the traditional finance system in a decentralized manner. There are many criticisms of the global financial system, which relies on expensive intermediaries. It takes days and costs money to settle a stock transaction to transfer money from a bank account to anyone. Retailers pay for every customer's credit card transaction.

DeFi does not require the charges that banks, and financial intermediaries apply to the customer. These markets urgently need regulation in DeFi markets to prevent abuses, improve security, reduce volatility, and improve anti-money-laundering (AML) and know-your-customer (KYC) processes. While DeFi and traditional finance have been polarized in the past, it makes sense that there will be a convergence of DeFi and traditional finance. This would allow the cross-fertilization of ideas between DeFi and traditional finance. Traditional finance could benefit from the fast, smooth automation of DeFi. A more robust, cheaper financial system could potentially be attained if DeFi and traditional finance collaborated.

Harvey et al. (2021) argue that the current financial landscape is ripe for disruption, and DeFi will reinvent finance. The advantage of DeFi is that it enables anyone to interact directly with peers without intermediaries and no need for costly buildings. This improves efficiency, transparency, and access because a mobile phone is required for access. This chapter outlines an overview of DeFi. It will also examine the leading blockchain protocols relevant to finances. It covers an overview of DeFi and an analysis of the DeFi ecosystem. DeFi is not without risks, which are elaborated on in this chapter.

DECENTRALIZED FINANCE (DeFi)

DeFi is part of the progression of the remarkable journey of Blockchain. It started with the advent of Bitcoin in 2009 and the Ethereum blockchain (2015), which developed and promulgated smart contracts, a critical underpinning of DeFi. In 2019, DeFi began to become better known and offered an alternative to the current closed financial system, one based on open protocols that are interoperable, programmable, and composable (Nystrom, 2019). Composability has been one of the factors that have enabled rapid growth. Because DeFi code is open source, it has been possible for programmers and innovators to build on existing code rather than develop platforms and products from scratch. It has attracted the term "Lego" as assembling DeFi can occur in multiple combinations based on existing code blocks.

DeFi decentralizes traditional financial services, including:

- **Issuance:** Stablecoins, Borrowing and Lending, Insurances, and NFTs.
- **Trading:** Decentralized Exchanges, Derivatives, SWAPs, Prediction Markets
- **Ownership:** Wallets, Fund Management, and Payment Networks.

DeFi can potentially reduce the cost of financial services and increase financial inclusion, which is a factor in its rapid growth. According to Chainalysis (2021), DeFi represents one of crypto's fastest growing and most innovative sectors. The top 10 countries that use DeFi are the United States,

Vietnam, Thailand, China, the United Kingdom, India, the Netherlands, Canada, Ukraine, and Poland. However, adoption patterns are changing as other geographies learn about DeFi. Chainalysis also reported that initially (from April 2019 to June 2020), most traffic to DeFi protocols came from North America and Western Europe. However, since June 2020, they have seen more traffic from other regions, especially Central and Southern Asia. Chainalysis (2021) reports that large transactions account for more than 60% of DeFi activity, compared to under 50% for all cryptocurrency transactions. This is suggestive of an increase in institutional investment in DeFi.

The two main aspects of DeFi that have accelerated its rapid adoption are inclusive and peer-to-peer. Anyone with a digital wallet and internet connection can access it, and it is composable, meaning anyone can access the open-source code and modify it to launch a new idea. It means that DeFi projects are launchable incredibly quickly. In a new and rapidly developing market, this can also create risks of consumer protection and code vulnerabilities.

DeFi FUNDAMENTALS

The DeFi stack comprises four layers (BTSE, 2022):

1. Layer 0, or the Settlement Layer, comprises a cryptocurrency and a public blockchain. Layer 0 includes the internet, hardware, and connections that enable layer one to run smoothly.
2. Layer 1, or the Protocol Layer, sets the defined norms and regulations that govern operations and provides a list of rules and principles that all participants must follow. Well-known layer-one Blockchains include Bitcoin and Ethereum (Cointelegraph, 2022; Tago, 2022).
3. Layer 2, or the Application Layer, is where core protocols abstract into concise consumer-focused functions in these applications. Protocols use layer two to increase scalability by removing some interactions from the base layer (Head Topics, 2022).
4. Layer 3, or the Aggregation Layer, integrates multiple apps from the preceding layer to give a service to shareholders in the aggregate layer, such as moving funds seamlessly across various financial products to optimize profits. L3 applications provide Blockchains with real-world applicability, as explained in the layered structure of the blockchain architecture.

The elements of DeFi are similar to those of traditional financial systems, but DeFi is decentralized and automated. In the DeFi ecosystem, the elements of DeFi comprise decentralized exchanges, aggregators, wallets, decentralized marketplaces, oracles, prediction markets, smart contracts, and alternative chains Cointelegraph (2022). These are summarized below:

Decentralized Exchanges (DEXs)

In contrast with Centralized Exchanges (CEX), Decentralized exchanges (DEX) do not take custody of user virtual assets (Cointelegraph, 2022). DEXs facilitate the buying and selling of virtual assets without needing to create an account on an exchange. A form of DEX, the Automated Market Maker (AMM), became popular in 2020. These automate the purchase and sale of virtual assets via smart contracts and liquidity pools (Shevchenko, 2020, Tago. Guru, 2022).

Aggregators and Wallets

These are the interfaces that enable users to interact with the DeFi market. Wallets are a place where users can store their assets. Wallets come in two main forms, known as hot and cold wallets. Hot wallets (such as mobile phones) are connected to the internet and are vulnerable to attack. Cold wallets are devices similar to USB sticks, which afford more protection for more significant amounts of virtual assets.

Decentralized Marketplaces

Decentralized marketplaces allow users to transact with one another without the need for an intermediary. These are mainly built on Ethereum at this stage.

Oracles and Prediction Markets

Oracles deliver real-world off-chain data to the Blockchain via a third-party provider (Cointelegraph, 2022). Oracles enable prediction markets for DeFi, where users can place bets on the outcome of an event, and payouts are initiated via a smart contract-governed automated process.

Smart Contracts

Smart contracts are written agreements within computer code that self-execute once criteria meet, eliminating the need for a central authority or third-party enforcement mechanism. Smart contracts are executed upon fulfillment of specific conditions. The transaction is added to the Blockchain when the smart contracts process, making it transparent and irreversible. Smart contracts enable new designs of digital asset trading to be executed on decentralized networks accessible to anyone with an internet connection. Smart contracts provide the essential platform for DeFi applications.

Alternative DeFi Chains

Ethereum has a first-mover advantage in DeFi, and most DeFi applications are built on Ethereum. Other platforms, such as Binance Smart Chain, Solana, and Polkadot, have emerged more recently, competing with Ethereum for DeFi applications and community (Novum Insights, 2021).

Tokens

Understanding DeFi also requires understanding the different types of tokens in the DeFi space. There is a universal lack of clarity on definitions in the digital asset space, and no globally accepted token asset classification system exists. The "sensible token classification system" was developed by the Global Blockchain Convergence (GBC) (GBC, 2021). This classification system is summarized below:

1. **Physical Asset Tokens:** Representations of tangible assets on a blockchain, such as gold and artworks.
2. **Services Tokens:** Representations of services provided, such as music, digital art, cleaning, and concert tokens.
3. **Intangible Asset Tokens:** Representation of intangible assets, including securities, real estate, and intellectual property.
4. Native Tokens exist only to service a particular blockchain. Smart contracts create the native token's functions and features on a specific blockchain.
5. Stablecoins are linked to an asset, reference currency, or basket of assets to maintain a more stable asset value.

DEFI USE CASES

DeFi mirrors the traditional financial system but in a decentralized manner. Its use cases include issuance, trading, and ownership. The open-source nature of DeFi has enabled the rapid deployment of innovations, leveraged existing strings of code and adding additional elements. DeFi is also being deployed by central banks in France, Switzerland, and Singapore to automate foreign exchange markets using decentralized protocols to reduce the cost of cross-border payments (Schickler, 2022).

The following section summarizes the main use cases for DeFi.

ISSUANCE: STABLECOINS, DEBT, SECURITIES, INSURANCES, NFTs

Stablecoins

A stablecoin is a cryptocurrency with a value pegged to a traditional financial or a pool of such assets as fiat currencies and commodities (Synapse, 2022). The market capitalization of stablecoins rose to $29 billion by the end of 2020 (Novum Insights, 2021). In 2021 the market almost quadrupled to $112 billion. Stablecoins are seen as a more stable investment because a real-world asset backs them and is less volatile than some virtual assets. They can be used for savings, lending, passive income, and liquidity pools. Stablecoins leverage the benefits of cryptocurrencies without price volatility. Stablecoins allow digital traders to quickly lock in their gains without cashing out. In times of adverse market events, traders can convert their crypto into stablecoins without potential losses, in this case serving as a store of value, within seconds.

Fiat-backed stablecoins are collateralized by currencies such as USD, JPY, EUR, or GBP. A 1:1 collateral ratio backs the peg, and the collateral is held in the issuing company's cash or cash equivalents reserves. When a holder wants to redeem cash with stablecoins, the corresponding coins are withdrawn. As centralized parties issue fiat-backed stablecoins, they require regular audits to ensure sufficient reserves. Commonly used stablecoins include Tether, USDC, GUSD, BUSD, PAX, and TrueUSD.

Crypto-backed stablecoins are issued on-chain and use over-collateralization to absorb price changes in the digital collateral. However, the volatile nature of digital backing of the crypto-backed stablecoins can destabilize the peg, cause a steep tank in the crypto markets, and trigger an auto-liquidation. The most popular crypto-collateralized stablecoin is Dai. Dai's value is pegged to USD but is backed by crypto locked up in MakerDAO's smart contracts. DAI is created by taking a collateralized debt position. Dai has immensely contributed to the growth of DeFi by helping unlock digital assets' value without compromising their price increase potential.

Synthetic asset protocols provide a valuable mechanism for real-world assets to live on a blockchain in a decentralized manner. On such protocols as Synthetix, users can create synthetic USD along with many other real-life assets, including indices, stocks, commodities, and forex. Synthetic's USD, created by locking in its native token SNX, has grown mainly due to its native use case in the Synthetix ecosystem.

Algorithmic stablecoins maintain the price peg via an algorithm that elastically controls the coin supply based on price changes. This stablecoin type intends to address Capital's inefficient use in digital asset-collateralized stablecoins. Since the first draft of the book, a significant collapse of the stablecoin Terra and related token Luna caused half a trillion USD to be wiped from the digital currency markets (Loo, 2022). Terra used a stablecoin token called Terra (USDT) and a related token called Luna, which formed an algorithmic stablecoin that aimed to maintain a value of 1 USD for each USDT. In May 2022, the value of Luna collapsed, resulting in over $400 billion in losses for digital asset markets (Loo, 2022). This has stimulated the focus of regulators and is likely to lead to more regulation.

Lending and Borrowing

The most popular activities in DeFi are lending and borrowing. Through lending protocols, users can borrow funds using digital currency as collateral (Wiki Tien ao, 2022). Users can also utilize margin and leverage to borrow virtual assets using other assets as collateral (Dfadf, 2022). User returns can increase by programming the smart contracts to include leverage (Wiki Tien ao, 2022). Since the system is based upon algorithms without any human component, this increases the risk of exposure if there is a problem (Wiki Tien ao, 2022). Liquidity pools allow owners to earn passive income from interacting with the pool.

Insurance

With more significant risks of hacks in DeFi, has come a growth in insurance products. Nexus Mutual is the most well-known DeFi insurance platform and provides insurance on smart contract exploits on the Ethereum Blockchain. According to nexustracker.io, the Nexus Mutual Tracker, the active cover amount is over $600 million.

NFTs

NFTs are covered extensively in Chapter Six and will only be summarized here. A non-fungible token (NFT) is a digital file that is not interchangeable. It is a digital file recorded on a blockchain and is often used to represent digital artwork, video, or music file sold on an auction market. Tokens can then be bought with virtual assets and resold. Because of their unique nature, they can serve as rewards with pre-set rules based on loyal behavior. They can also increase in value, be freely traded, and bring yield through a royalties-like feature.

TRADING: DECENTRALIZED EXCHANGES, DERIVATIVES, PREDICTION MARKETS

Decentralized Exchanges (DEX)

DEXs are peer-to-peer marketplaces that allow digital asset owners to transact in a peer-to-peer manner. In other words, there is no intermediary. Smart contracts facilitate transactions. Automated market makers (AMMs) are a type of DEX that use algorithms to provide liquidity for buying and selling virtual assets. AMMs use liquidity pools to enable virtual assets to be traded automatically without intermediaries.

Anyone can become a liquidity provider by posting any ERC20 token and an equivalent value of ETH to a pool. Ethereum and Binance dominate the market. However, AMMs face a significant impermanent loss risk. As an algorithm determines the prices of the tokens held in a pool that adjusts the ratios of the tokens in the pool, there will be high slippage if the ratio between the two tokens changes acutely after depositing them. Some projects provide solutions for impermanent loss (City A.M., 2021).

Staking

Staking is a mechanism by which individuals support their conviction of action with Capital. Ethereum requires a stake of 32 ETH to validate blocks. This deters people from acting in bad faith because their stake can be seized. There is no blocking period for funds in flexible staking, which can be withdrawn anytime. However, the withdrawal is usually effective after hours or a few days, so it is a factor to consider. Due to this "flexibility" in the deposit, the profitability is usually lower. In Blocked Staking, funds are blocked for a specific time before withdrawal. This period is variable. It allows users to obtain simple and passive rewards by delegating coins and generating a return, providing utility to the network without investing in mining hardware. It usually offers stable reward percentages and allows compound interest from the beginning since the rewards are paid daily. However, the rewards are minimal compared to mining the proof of work protocol, and some charge a low percentage of the Capital deposited to monetize the maintenance of the node (energy resources such as electricity and computing).

Borrowing and Lending

As in traditional finance, users can lend or borrow virtual assets and earn or pay interest. Lenders make interest in their digital assets, and borrowers can deploy borrowed virtual assets to trading strategies that yield better than the interest rate they pay (Aki, 2020).

Lending Protocols

Aave, Curve, and Compound are among the best-known lending protocols. The most lent-out coins are stablecoins - USDC, DAI, and USDT, with market sizes of $4.59 billion, $1.66 billion, and $928.7 million, respectively. These top three tokens take up about 60% of the total market size of Aave V2.

Yield Farming

Yield farming, often called liquidity mining, allows users to earn money for "locking" their tokens in a DeFi platform. Various yield products have emerged to simplify this multi-layered farming process. For example, yield aggregators detect the finest lending rates across various lending protocols, and users can create action plans and subscribe to existing yield farming strategies. Vaults pool users' deposited assets and mechanically allocates optimizing returns. Vaults deploy complex and often riskier strategies rather than jumping from one lending protocol to another. It can include investing the returns from one project to fund another (Novum Insights, 2021).

Derivatives

Derivatives are financial instruments deriving value from underlying assets such as stocks, bonds, currencies, interest rates, indices, commodities, and virtual assets. Derivatives allow contract holders to gain exposure to the underlying assets without owning them. Derivatives also will enable the use of leverage to magnify profits. Common types of derivatives include futures, forwards, swaps, and options.

Derivatives are mainly used for speculative and hedging purposes. Derivatives market participants speculate on the future price movements of assets. These speculative activities drive increased market liquidity, enabling participants to hedge their risks to meet their needs. For example, with futures contracts, as the name implies, you predict the price of an asset in the future at the expiry date, e.g., in 3 months. When the expiry date approaches, the investor can either 1) offset the position by realizing the gains or losses of your position or 2) roll over to the next month's contract if the investor wishes to keep the position going. Futures markets serve an essential role in price discovery in virtual asset markets.

Like futures contracts, perpetual contracts enable traders to hold leveraged positions without having to own the underlying asset but without expiry dates. Perpetual contracts incentivize traders to stabilize the perpetual price using funding rates. When the price of a perpetual contract trades below the underlying asset's spot price, the long perpetual holders pay funding fees to short traders. Perpetuals are derivatives with no expiration date or settlement, so they can be held or traded indefinitely. Perpetual futures are gaining momentum in DeFi because they enable traders to take leveraged positions without expiry dates causing inconveniences. The largest derivatives exchange is Binance, followed by Huobi, which supports up to 125 x leverage, and The margin requirements vary.

Options contracts give you an 'option' to buy or sell an underlying asset within a specific time frame at a stated price. Unlike futures contracts, options holders are not obligated to buy or sell upon expiry if they don't want to. Despite being the largest financial market in the world, estimated to be worth over $1 quadrillion, the global derivatives markets have only been accessible to institutional investors or accredited investors. DeFi protocols such as Synthetix and UMA have enabled anyone to access the derivatives markets. Synthetic assets are financial instruments designed to simulate the underlying asset's payoff. They require less initial Capital. Synthetics can mirror the payoff profiles without laying out much Capital. They can be customized - investors can design synthetics based on their desired maturities, risk appetite, and more. Crypto synthetic assets allow users to gain exposure to diverse assets - from virtual assets, stocks, and forex to commodities and more - without owning them.

One critical aspect is that these are open protocols. UMA (n.d.) is creating a derivatives platform that provides standardized contracts for financial products. Synthetix (n.d.) is a protocol that enables the creation and issuing of synthetic assets such as virtual currency, fiat currency, and commodities. Synthetic assets and derivatives provided by open-source protocols will generate value for investors seeking to hedge against risk, diversify capital allocation, and find mechanisms for increasing investment returns. The types of derivatives are endless for traditional and virtual assets (Nystrom, 2019).

OWNERSHIP: WALLETS AND FUND MANAGEMENT

Wallets

A DeFi wallet provides its users with solutions that eliminate the need for a third party for financial transactions. Considerations in wallet selection include the assets that the wallet supports and its reputation for security (Jansen, 2021). Du'Mmett (2022) lists the four common DeFi wallets:

1. MetaMask (2022) is the link that allows you to access DeFi from any web browser. It is mainly used as a web browser plugin. MetaMask may be easily connected with various plugins, allowing multiple tasks across different applications.
2. Coinbase saves private keys on users' smartphones. Users may buy and reserve any ERC20 token, acquire NFTs, and use decentralized Apps without giving up control of their assets (Dribble, 2022).

3.   Argent has developed a digital wallet that requires no paper backups or accessible addresses and provides low-cost (free) transactions (Du'Mmett, 2022).

4.   Trezor (2022) is a cold storage wallet, and users may keep their digital assets online using wallets and benefit from extra security features.

Virtual Asset Fund Management

Emerging digital asset funds are arising to function as the hybrid between the old financial system and the new. They combine the power of DeFi technology to build future financial products with their TradFi background, compliance training, and licensing under the existing regulatory framework. Bernegger (2020) describes the digital asset hedge fund industry as the future of finance. PWC's Crypto Hedge Fund Report (2020) estimated that global digital asset hedge funds assets increased to over USD$2 billion in 2019 from USD$1 billion the previous year. Funds generally saw a 4X increase in 2019. They report that most investors (90%) are family offices (48%) or high-net-worth individuals (42%). The leading traded assets are Bitcoin (97%), followed by Ethereum (67%), XRP (38%), Litecoin (38%), Bitcoin Cash (31%), and EOS (25%). Some digital asset hedge funds are also involved in digital asset currency staking (42%), lending (38%), and borrowing (27%).

Toby Lewis of Novum Insights (personal communication) has been tracking the industry since about 2016 when digital asset funds started with $2 to $4 million under management or even less. He noted a gradual institutionalization of funds with $10 million to $50 million under management, which became a niche alternative space. He observed that "the space provides access to eye-popping returns, sometimes in the 100% to 200% range. For anyone participating in traditional markets, it's quite hard to get those kinds of returns in doing any strategy in the traditional space, making this niche more attractive."

PWC also reported that digital asset hedge funds using an independent custodian increased in 2019 from 52% to 81%. The percentage of crypto hedge funds using third-party research increased from 7% to 38% in 2019. Digital asset custody solutions safeguard virtual assets (Sharma, 2020). Digital asset custody solutions provide storage and security services for virtual assets and are mainly aimed at institutional investors, such as hedge funds. Digital asset custodians securely store digital assets for investors who want to minimize the potential loss of funds due to a lack of technical expertise or are required to use a qualified custodian by law. Custodians are directly tied to commercial and investment banks, as their success hinges on their growth to secure more assets under management. As the bank brings in assets, the custodian secures those assets and charges a small fee. Today, four large custodians (BNY Mellon, State Street, JPMorgan, and Citi) provide the most custody services globally, with nearly $120 trillion in assets. Professional investors need compliant cold storage and insurance from brand-name companies with a strong reputation.

Many banks and financial institutions are also developing digital asset products and services. For example, Basler Kantonalbank, a Switzerland-based bank backed by the country's government, is set to offer crypto trading and custody services via its subsidiary Bank Cler; Custodians such as Copper and Fidelity Digital Assets layered on offerings such as lending, staking, trading, portfolio management, and tax administration; Digital asset management company CoinShares offers custody for institutional investors; Dutch bank ING is working on developing technology to help clients safely store virtual assets; Swiss bank Vontobel also launched a Digital Asset Vault aimed at institutional investors in the crypto space.

Icoinic Capital is registered with the Dutch financial authority, has a Dutch bank account, and is fully audited quarterly. Icoinic operates out of the Amsterdam Stock Exchange, the oldest exchange in the world – the perfect symbol of crypto's evolution. Icoinic Capital fully complies with best practices from traditional finance and reports annually to the Dutch Central Bank. A recently listed regulated fund in London, Kasei Holdings offers investors a diversified portfolio of virtual assets using traditional portfolio management techniques as tradeable listed security. These instruments enable investors to participate in the digital asset market without setting up wallets.

RISKS AND REGULATORY ISSUES

While this is an exciting and swiftly developing sector, it is also risky. Higher yields come with higher risks, including price, interest rate, hacks, and intelligent contract failure risks. About $120 million (Manoylov, 2021) of assets was stolen from DeFi platforms in 2020. With greater liquidity in DeFi, there was $156 million stolen from DeFi hacks between January and April 2021 (Gottsegen, 2021).

DeFi is a new and experimental market and poses a range of risks. There are several risks related to automation. Consumers have no recourse if smart contracts are flawed and no human intermediaries exist. Price risk is the price of the token put as collateral to take out a loan. It can drop below the cost of the loan. Lenders earn interest on digital assets, and borrowers can deploy borrowed digital assets to trading strategies that yield better than the interest rate they pay. Lending protocols that take virtual assets as collateral assets to absorb market volatility require high collateralization ratios.

Regulatory risks tend to be around the volatility of digital asset markets and the nature of their use in connection with illicit or illegal activities. Some governments have addressed achieving this balance using regulatory sandboxes, like the U.K., Bermuda, India, South Korea, Mauritius, Australia, Papua New Guinea, and Singapore. Some have gone straight to legislating (San Marino, Bermuda, Malta, Liechtenstein) (Cryptoboom, 2021). In 2019 the Law Library of Congress recorded 130 countries managing the regulatory issues surrounding virtual assets. Some countries, such as Spain, Belarus, the Cayman Islands, Luxemburg, San Marino, and Bermuda, are developing digital currency-friendly regulatory regimes to attract investment and innovation. Some countries are developing their system of virtual assets, reportedly including the Marshall Islands, Venezuela, the Eastern Caribbean Central Bank (ECCB) member states, and Lithuania.

The absence of standards and a common lexicon hamper regulation. For example, what is the difference between Blockchain, Blockchain, or the Blockchain? Is there a difference between a public blockchain, a permissionless Blockchain, or an open blockchain? Is the technology tamper-proof, tamper-resistant, append-only, or immutable? All these terms are used interchangeably in a working context – yet finding an uncontested definition to establish a legal framework is challenging.

Technology changes exponentially, social, and legal systems change incrementally, and the pace of DeFi development is currently rendering regulation outdated almost immediately. Regulators need to work closely with technologists to continue to understand the evolving landscape of DeFi and its relationship to other disruptive technologies as part of the Web3 ecosystem and stay abreast of the developments international standards organizations are making in this regard.

Legal and Regulatory Challenges include jurisdiction, ownership and IP, data privacy and security, cybercrime, and consumer rights. Key regulatory bodies will need to agree on definitions and harmonize principles and technical standards for virtual assets, including (i) Regulatory Technical Standards, (ii) Supervisory policies and procedures, (iii) Information exchange requirements, and (iv) Regulatory and license criteria and guidelines.

Anti Money Laundering (AML) and Counter-Terrorist Financing (CTF) regulations must be fit for purpose. The Financial Action Task Force 'travel rule' needs to be addressed and amended into current AML/CTF legislation.[1] It is necessary to clarify the regulations governing the taxation of virtual assets. Digital assets in the EU are set to be regulated by the new Markets in Crypto-Assets (MiCA) (European Regulation Parliament (2023). Securities token sales and digital offerings of tangible asset classes have caught the attention of both regular investors and financial institutions, especially decentralized finance, and non-fungible tokens. Cryptocurrencies have already impacted economies in the developing world, so regulators can't afford to take a "wait and see" approach.

An international regulatory framework will allow countries to collaborate more effectively. It's essential to have a common set of standards. Regulatory frameworks must protect consumers and investors and mitigate the risks of money laundering and terrorist financing that nefarious actors propagate. A prime example is the notorious currency mixer Tornado Cash, which has been used to wash over USD 7 billion in virtual currency.

DeFi relies on Decentralized Autonomous Organizations (DAO) governed by code, and it's a 24/7 market. The question arises of how regulators should think about activities that cross borders seamlessly and operate on a 24/7 basis. As long as the smart contract is acting as a single or centrally controlled intermediary between the various parties involved in the transaction, there is no way to protect the interests of the participants, including consumers and investors, who have no way of knowing who is doing what or who is in control of any of these activities.

New definitions, developer liability, the legal status of the code, application of AML/KYC and jurisdiction, governance, and mechanisms for change are required. For example, how do you stop consumers and investors from getting hurt when activities are not controlled, moderated, intermediated, hosted, or validated by a single or centralized party other than the smart contract? The task of the hour is to look at innovative ways to regulate platforms, much as was done with high-frequency trading models in the 1990s. Also, there is the problem of scalability. Decentralized exchange (DEX) scalability is determined by the number of transactions the network can process before it reaches the capacity of its underlying network infrastructure.

Another problem for regulators is the decentralization of the financial sector and the ability to maintain economic stability and defend consumer interests. A relevant statement from Stani Kulechov (Aave founder) on the issues of peer-to-peer auditing "Auditors are not here to guarantee the security of a protocol, and merely they help to spot something that the team itself wasn't aware of. Eventually, it's about peer review, and we need to find a community incentive to empower more security experts into the space." Emeliano Bonassi (Reviews DAO) suggests a Peer review forum for connecting security experts and projects looking for reviews is needed in the space and stated that "This can become a learning opportunity where people with specialized knowledge can branch into other areas and young developers can grow into fully-fledged auditors."

The most apparent targets for regulation in this arena are decentralized exchanges and wallet providers. In a peer-to-peer (P2P) fashion, individuals can trade digital currency straight from their wallets using Decentralized exchanges (DEXes) without intermediaries. Cointelegraph reported that Financial Action Task Force (FATF) rules suggest that DApps (DEXs and other DeFi applications) will be held responsible for complying with country-specific legislation enforcing FATF, AML, and Counter-Terrorism Financing requirements.

Further, only four of the 16 major exchange platforms examined by LSE were found to be subject to significant trade regulation, indicating a glaring oversight deficit. A project must now be audited to be listed on any major exchange; however, absolute security doesn't stop at auditing.

New rules are required urgently for innovation and technological advancements in blockchain technology and virtual and virtual assets. A defined legal and regulatory framework gives the DeFi industry clarity. It will be expected to cover licensing, disclosure requirements, prevention of market abuse, environmental sustainability requirements, and implementation of the FATF's "Travel Rule," which requires identifying information on the sender and receiver in digital asset transactions in most circumstances. DeFi, and its applications which operate in a fully decentralized manner without any intermediary, will likely be subject to regulatory requirements. To approach this, regulators will require mapping DeFi and Web 3.0 projects and new blockchain protocols and whether the regulatory treatment of these new applications is adequate. Regulation should also take account of novel features and specific risks of digital -assets and address potential financial stability risks that could arise from the growing interlinkages between the digital -asset ecosystem and the traditional financial system. An urgent need will be for key regulatory bodies to agree on definitions, principles, and technical standards to ensure the industry has legal certainty and clarity.

For many, crypto investing is new, and many lack the knowledge and experience to make sound investment decisions. Due diligence actions for investors to carry out due diligence include simple steps such as: looking for the website and checking the LinkedIn profiles of the team, and finding teams founded by experienced developers who have done quantitative trading with years of experience. One of the risks in the market is that many of the developers creating the trading algorithms do not have the years of experience that traditional quant fund developers have. When unexpected volatility or other pitfalls occur, they may not know how to deal with them and risk crashing the fund. Look up the company registry in the country where it's domiciled to ensure it's real. Request net asset value (NAV) reports the net value of an entity and is calculated as the total value of the entity's assets minus the total value of its liabilities and only considers funds that have been trading for at least a year. Look for the month-to-month reports for the amount of time the fund has been around and contact people at the fund for an overview. Third-party auditing is essential.

The world of code and protocol architecture in creating virtual assets differs significantly from traditional asset classes. Regulators must be well-versed in computer science and emerging technology trends like never before. Regulators must continue working with digital asset industry players to understand the ecosystem.

RESEARCH AND DEVELOPMENT

As an emergent technology, there is a role for ongoing research and development in DeFi. It will be core to Web3 in all its variants and to the development of the Metaverse. Research is needed to keep up with and document the innovations and to help explore existing challenges, such as governance and regulation of code-governed organizations. Furthermore, DeFi is global in reach, and the protocols do not have defined jurisdiction for their operations, introducing cross-border challenges and regulatory arbitrage. Research is needed to document the challenges, issues, and emerging solutions. Policy-based research can help policymakers understand the DeFi market, its mechanics, benefits, and risks. More analysis of the benefits of DeFi to the traditional financial system and better-quality data is required.

For key sectors, research can document use cases and innovations in each sector. In gaming, for example, how is DeFi used? DeFi offers some benefits to gaming, including liquidity, scarcity, the opportunity to self-custody, audibility, and opportunities to be involved in governance. NFTs are likely key for Web3 games, with unified logins through wallets, allowing a player's history to move across platforms and game environments. DeFi will also facilitate new revenue opportunities for developers. As DeFi is applied in sectors, industries, and policymakers, need to understand opportunities and challenges.

CONCLUSION

DeFi shows excellent promise; DeFi solutions are highly interoperable and can potentially be integrated. DeFi offers greater transparency as all the data is stored immutably using Blockchain technology, which can be viewed by the participants anytime and anywhere. But it is risky and unregulated. Investors can quickly lose money when smart contracts fail or problems with open-source computer codes lead to vulnerabilities. It's an "always on" market and available globally, so it's hard to undertake meaningful due diligence or regulation. Questions remain about definitions, developer liability, the legal status of the code, the application of AML/KYC, and jurisdiction. The history of money is still being written, and the systems that underpin it will continue to evolve. DeFi may very well represent the next step in the evolution of money. It is a fundamental building block of Web 3 and the open Metaverse and will continue to grow, innovate, and attract investment. This Chapter has outlined the fundamentals of DeFi and its risks and challenges. The following Chapter will explore the Decentralized Autonomous Organizations that oversee DeFi transactions.

REFERENCES

A beginner's guide to Decentralized finance (DeFi). (2022, July 15). Wiki Tiên Áo. https://wikitienao.net/en/3684-2

A look at DeFi AMM protocols | SushiSwap Deep Dive. (2021, June 2). Novum Insights. https://novuminsights.com/post/a-look-at-defi-amm-protocols-or-sushiswap-deep-dive/

Aki, J. (2020, December 30). *DeFi Explained: The Guide To Decentralized Finance - Forkast*. Forkast.news. https://forkast.news/explainer-decentralized-finance-defi-guide

Association for Computing Machinery. (2018, June 22). *ACM Code of Ethics and Professional Conduct*. Association for Computing Machinery. https://www.acm.org/code-of-ethics

Bernegger, M. P. (n.d.). *The emergence of cryptocurrency hedge funds*. Cointelegraph. https://cointelegraph.com/news/the-emergence-of-cryptocurrency-hedge-funds

BTSE | Your Favorite Crypto Exchange. (n.d.). BTSE. https://www.btse.com/en/about-us

Buterin, V. (2014). *Ethereum Whitepaper*. Ethereum.org. https://ethereum.org/en/whitepaper/

Clark, M. (2022, June 6). *NFTs, Explained*. The Verge. https://www.theverge.com/22310188/nft-explainer-what-is-blockchain-crypto-art-faq

Cointelegraph. (2022, July 19). *A beginner's guide to understanding the layers of blockchain technology*. Head Topics. https://headtopics.com/us/a-beginner-s-guide-to-understanding-the-layers-of-blockchain-technology-28236152

Cointelegraph Consulting: DeFi projects launch on Polygon, usage skyrockets. (2021, May 24). Cointelegraph. https://cointelegraph.com/news/cointelegraph-consulting-defi-projects-launch-on-polygon-usage-skyrockets

Cosmos (ATOM) Price · Price Index, Charts. (2023, May 24). Cointelegraph. https://cointelegraph.com/cosmos-price-index

Cousaert, S. (2021, September 17). *Insurance: Token-based solutions on blockchain — A summary*. UCL CBT. https://medium.com/uclcbt/insurance-token-based-solutions-on-blockchain-a-summary-e7b5a6805197

Cowrie | marine snail. (2019). In *Encyclopædia Britannica*. https://www.britannica.com/animal/cowrie

Credit card | Britannica Money. (2023, May 5). Www.britannica.com. https://www.britannica.com/money/topic/credit-card

Credit rating agency warns potential risks of stablecoins | How are stablecoins doing so far? (2021, July 7). Novum Insights. https://novuminsights.com/post/credit-rating-agency-warns-potential-risks-of-stablecoins-or-how-are-stablecoins-doing-so-far/

Crypto Research, Data, and Tools. (n.d.). Messari.io. https://messari.io/asset/cover-protocol/profile

Deep dive into Polygon | Ethereum off-chain scaling solutions. (2021, May 26). Novum Insights. https://novuminsights.com/post/deep-dive-into-polygon-or-ethereum-off-chain-scaling-solutions/

DeFi, C. A. D. (2021, February 4). *DeFi Bursts onto the Finance Scene - What is it and why does it matter?* CityAM. https://www.cityam.com/defi-bursts-onto-the-finance-scene-what-is-it-and-why-does-it-matter/

DeFi: A comprehensive guide to decentralized finance. (n.d.). Cointelegraph. https://cointelegraph.com/defi-101/defi-a-comprehensive-guide-to-decentralized-finance

DeFi: the possible future of finance. (2022, March 23). Mntrading.com. https://eightglobal.com/blog/de-fi-the-possible-future-of-finance

Dharma. (n.d.). https://www.dharma.io/

Ethereum Killers. (2021, May 12). Novum Insights. https://novuminsights.com/post/ethereum-killers/

Exploring the Cryptocurrency and Blockchain Ecosystem | United States Committee on Banking, Housing, and Urban Affairs. (n.d.). Retrieved June 3, 2023, from https://www.banking.senate.gov/hearings/exploring-the-cryptocurrency-and-blockchain-ecosystem

Financial Stability Board. (2021). Regulation, Supervision and Oversight of "Global Stablecoin" Arrangements. *Financial Stability Board.* https://www.fsb.org/

Global Blockchain Convergence: A "Sensible" Token Classification System. (2020). https://theblockchaintest.com/uploads/resources/A%20%27Sensible%27%20Token%20Classification%20System%20-%20Global%20Blockchain%20Convergence%20-%202020%20-%20paper.pdf

Godbole, O. (2021, June 10). *Bitcoin Futures "Backwardation" Points to Weak Institutional Demand: JPMorgan.* Yahoo Finance. https://finance.yahoo.com/news/bitcoin-futures-backwardation-points-weak-173527377.html

Gold standard | Definition & History | Britannica Money. (2023, May 5). Www.britannica.com. https://www.britannica.com/money/topic/gold-standard

Hamilton, S. G. K., & Kerry, B. (2021, October 29). *OFAC Publishes Sanctions Compliance Guidance for the Virtual Currency Industry and Updates its Frequently Asked Questions*. Sanctions & Export Controls Update. https://sanctionsnews.bakermckenzie.com/ofac-publishes-sanctions-compliance-guidance-for-the-virtual-currency-industry-and-updates-its-frequently-asked-questions/

Harding, C. (2021, August 22). *DeFi regulation must not kill the values behind decentralization*. Cointelegraph. https://cointelegraph.com/news/defi-regulation-must-not-kill-the-values-behind-decentralization

Harvey, C. R., Ramachandran, A., & Santoro, J. (2020). *DeFi and the Future of Finance*. SSRN Electronic Journal., doi:10.2139srn.3711777

Hok, D. (2021, March 21). *Default auditing for DeFi projects is a must for growing the industry*. Cointelegraph. https://cointelegraph.com/news/default-auditing-for-defi-projects-is-a-must-for-growing-the-industry

Investopedia. (2019). *What Is Money?* Investopedia. https://www.investopedia.com/insights/what-is-money/

Jansen, S. (2021, December 6). *How to choose a secure DeFi wallet, explained*. Cointelegraph. https://cointelegraph.com/explained/how-to-choose-a-secure-defi-wallet-explained

Kuznetsov, N. (2021, January 28). *DeFi liquidity pools, explained*. Cointelegraph. https://cointelegraph.com/explained/defi-liquidity-pools-explained

Macwan, A. (n.d.). *Coinbase Wallet Logo Redesign*. Dribbble. https://dribbble.com/shots/16062179-Coinbase-Wallet-Logo-Redesign

Manoylov, M. (2021, January 1). *Hackers stole $120 million via 15 DeFi hacks in 2020*. The Block. https://www.theblock.co/linked/89830/hackers-stole-120-million-via-15-defi-hacks-in-2020

Mark Cuban shares his yield farming strategies | Yield farming 101. (2021, June 17). Novum Insights. https://novuminsights.com/post/mark-cuban-shares-his-yield-farming-strategies-or-yield-farming-101/

Markets in crypto-assets (MiCA) | Think Tank | European Parliament. (2022, November 9). Www.europarl.europa.eu. https://www.europarl.europa.eu/thinktank/en/document/EPRS_BRI(2022)739221

McMorris, C. (2022, February 18). *Resources | Synapse*. Synapsefi.com. https://synapsefi.com/resources/stablecoins-guide

Mitre shell | marine snail | Britannica. (n.d.). Www.britannica.com. https://www.britannica.com/animal/mitre-shell

Mmett, S. D. (2022, June). *DeFi Wallet Review: Crypto Wallet Choices – Cryptopolitan*. Www.cryptopolitan.com. https://www.cryptopolitan.com/defi-wallet-review/

Nystrom, M. (2019, December 5). *2019 Was The Year of Defi (and Why 2020 Will be Too)*. ConsenSys. https://consensys.net/blog/news/2019-was-the-year-of-defi-and-why-2020-will-be-too/

Pells, R. H., & Romer, C. D. (2019). Great Depression. In *Britannica*. https://www.britannica.com/event/Great-Depression

Public consultation on FATF draft guidance on a risk-based approach to virtual assets and virtual asset service providers. (n.d.). https://www.fatf-gafi.org/en/publications/Fatfrecommendations/Public-consultation-guidance-vasp.html

RiskHarbor. (n.d.). https://www.riskharbor.com

Saggs, H. (2019). Babylon | History, Religion, & Facts. In *Encyclopædia Britannica*. https://www.britannica.com/place/Babylon-ancient-city-Mesopotamia-Asia

Schickler, J. (2022, November 2). *France, Switzerland, Singapore to Test DeFi in Forex Markets*. https://www.coindesk.com/policy/2022/11/02/france-switzerland-singapore-to-test-defi-in-forex-markets/?ref=gomry.co

Sharma, R. (2020, June 21). *What Are Cryptocurrency Custody Solutions?* Investopedia. https://www.investopedia.com/news/what-are-cryptocurrency-custody-solutions/

Shevchenko, A. (2020, August 29). *Uniswap and automated market makers, explained*. Cointelegraph. https://cointelegraph.com/explained/uniswap-and-automated-market-makers-explained

Should all digital assets be subject to financial regulation? - Introducing a "sensible" token classification system. (2021, June 10). Novum Insights. https://novuminsights.com/post/not-all-digital-assets-should-be-subject-to-financial-regulation-introducing-a-sensible-token-classification-system/

Singh, J. (2020, September 26). *What is yield farming in DeFi?* Cointelegraph. https://cointelegraph.com/explained/defi-yield-farming-explained

Solana (SOL) Price · Price Index, Charts. (2023, June 2). Cointelegraph. https://cointelegraph.com/solana-price-index

Synthetix. (n.d.). Synthetix.io. https://synthetix.io

tago-admin. (2022, June 16). *Decentralized finance (DeFi): A beginner's guide.* Tago | Tagoverse | Talk to Earn - TalkFi | Tago Soul | Mental Metaverse. https://tago.guru/decentralized-finance-defi-a-beginners-guide

Team, C. (2022, October 13). *What Happened to Terra?* Corporate Finance Institute. https://corporatefinanceinstitute.com/resources/cryptocurrency/what-happened-to-terra/

Tezos (XTZ) Price · Price Index, Charts. (2023, April 22). Cointelegraph. https://cointelegraph.com/xtz-price-index

The 2021 Geography of Cryptocurrency Report Analysis of Geographic Trends in Cryptocurrency Adoption and Usage. (2021). https://go.chainalysis.com/rs/503-FAP-074/images/Geography-of-Cryptocurrency-2021.pdf

Thomason, C. A. B. (2022, April 4). *Regulating for a decentralised future.* CityAM. https://www.cityam.com/regulating-for-a-decentralised-future/

Thomason, J. (2021, September 25). *DeFi: Who, what and how to regulate in a borderless, code-governed world?* Cointelegraph. https://cointelegraph.com/news/defi-who-what-and-how-to-regulate-in-a-borderless-code-governed-world

Thurman, A. (2021, February 18). *As faith in audits falter, the DeFi community ponders security alternatives.* Cointelegraph. https://cointelegraph.com/news/as-faith-in-audits-falter-the-defi-community-ponders-security-alternatives

UMA - Universal Market Access. (n.d.). Uma.xyz. Retrieved June 3, 2023, from https://umaproject.org

U.S. Treasury Sanctions Notorious Virtual Currency Mixer Tornado Cash. (2022, August 8). U.S. Department of the Treasury. https://home.treasury.gov/news/press-releases/jy0916

Walker, M. C. W., & Mosioma, W. (2021, April 13). *Regulated cryptocurrency exchanges: sign of a maturing market or oxymoron?* LSE Business Review. https://blogs.lse.ac.uk/businessreview/2021/04/13/regulated-cryptocurrency-exchanges-sign-of-a-maturing-market-or-oxymoron/

What are decentralized exchanges, and how do DEXs work? (n.d.). Cointelegraph. https://cointelegraph.com/defi-101/what-are-decentralized-exchanges-and-how-do-dexs-work

What is a decentralized autonomous organization, and how does a DAO work? (n.d.). Cointelegraph. https://cointelegraph.com/learn/what-is-a-dao#:~:text=as%20investment%20advice

What is Polkadot (DOT): A beginner's guide to the decentralized Web 3.0 blockchain. (2022). Cointelegraph. https://cointelegraph.com/blockchain-for-beginners/what-is-polkadot-dot-a-beginners-guide-to-the-decentralized-web-3-0-blockchain

Zhenzong | emperor of Song dynasty | Britannica. (n.d.). Www.britannica.com. https://www.britannica.com/biography/Zhenzong

Chapter 5

Decentralized Autonomous Organizations:
Governing by Code

ABSTRACT

Decentralized autonomous organizations (DAOs) govern many major DeFi applications. These oversee the allocation of resources tied to the projects they are associated with and ensure the continuing success of the project they support. The community defines the rules by which a DAO operates and encodes in smart contracts. These are transparent and publicly available so anyone can understand the protocol operation. DAOs generally receive funding through token issuance, where the protocol sells tokens to raise funds for the DAO treasury. While there are variations in DAO governance and quorum requirements, the only way to change the rules is through member voting. This chapter explores DAOs, their deployment for DeFi, and some of the risks and opportunities of this emerging form of code-led governance.

INTRODUCTION

Decentralized Autonomous Organizations (DAOs) are the predominant DeFi governance mechanism. They oversee over $480 million in DeFi assets (Beck & Ashner, 2020). A single accepted definition of a DAO doesn't exist, but the definition by Shuttleworth (2021) will be used for the purposes of the book. DAO is "A community-led entity with no central authority. It is fully

DOI: 10.4018/978-1-6684-6658-2.ch005

autonomous and transparent: smart contracts lay the foundational rules, execute the agreed upon decisions, and at any point, proposals, voting, and even the code itself can be publicly audited."

Critical features of DAOs outlined by Morrison et al. (2020) are that: (i) Smart contracts operate and govern the organization; (ii) Computer code writes and executes smart contracts; (iii) Monitoring and enforcing smart contracts is by computer algorithms; (iv) Since the "code is law," and all participants agree in advance to abide by the code of the smart contract(s), the mechanisms for dispute resolution are weak or non-existent.

A decentralized DAO structure enables information symmetry in the governance design. DAO group decision-making metrics and DAO governance protocol needs are exchanged and evaluated directly between DAO members in a continuous and iterative stream of information that provides dynamic feedback effects. Thus DAOs involve people corresponding with each other according to a self-enforcing open-source protocol (Gupta & ArchiDAO, 2022). Native network tokens are rewarded for keeping the network safe and performing other network tasks (Voshmgir, 2019). Blockchains and smart contracts reduce management transaction costs, provide higher levels of transparency, and align the interest of all stakeholders through the consensus rules tied to the native token (OIN Finance, 2021; Medium, 2021). Individual behavior is incentivized with a token to contribute to a common goal. A legal entity does not bind together members of a DAO, nor have they entered into any formal legal contracts. Instead, they are steered by incentives tied to the network tokens and fully transparent rules written into the software enforced by machine consensus. The protocol or smart contract regulates the behavior of all network participants. Due to the open-source nature of the code, new projects tend to use existing DAO structures like Aragon (n.d.) and MolochDAO (n.d.).

Each DAO needs a set of rules by which it will abide. Smart contracts encode such rules (Shakirov, 2020). Once established, a DAO can commence raising funding. A DAO has to have tokens that can be spent by the organization or used to reward certain activities. Users get voting rights and can influence how it operates by investing in DAO (Shakirov, 2020). Once a DAO operates, all the decisions and specifications on spending its funds are made when a consensus is reached. Everyone with a stake in a DAO can make proposals regarding its future. A monetary deposit could be required to create one to prevent the network (Bizzer, 2018) from being spammed with proposals.

Subsequently, the stakeholders vote on the proposal. The majority needs to have an agreement to perform any action. The percentage required to reach that majority can be specified in its code and varies depending on a DAO (Shakirov, 2020).

Every investor has an opportunity to shape the organization in a DAO. Innovative ideas can be put forward by anyone and considered by the entire organization since there's no hierarchical structure. There is no room for dispute due to pre-written rules and regulations that investors know before joining the organization and the voting system (Shakirov, 2020). As proposing and voting require an investor to spend some money, it forces them to evaluate their decisions and prevents them from wasting time on ineffective solutions (Bizzer, 2018; Shakirov, 2020; Saive, 2021). The decentralized nature of DAOs should enhance coordination efficiency because DAO members typically know best how to assess other users / DAO members (Okaformbah, 2019). DAOs can feature information asymmetries between participants when they do not know each other or have motivations to invest in the DAO or their values and priorities. When priorities and values do not align, there should be contingencies to define, manage, or control these conflicts.

DAOs have two governance components (Zwitter & Hazenberg, 2020). The first component is internal governance, which tends to get the most attention, with non-hierarchical management and democratic features, where voting rights are based on several parameters. For example, voting weight can depend on the ownership of tokens, or the importance can cap at certain levels (Quiniou, 2019). The second component is external governance, which relies on server clusters and individual nodes for the functioning of the network and decision-making. These actors maintain the infrastructure, so they can exert a more decisive influence on decision-making than others because they control more nodes and server capacity. Developers are also influencing because they can offer code upgrades through open participation and self-selection, and miners can vote on protocol changes based on computing power (Hsieh et al., 2018).

There are also different levels of decentralization, depending on the governance rules. The entire network might be geographically decentralized and have many independent but equal network actors. However, the governance rules written in the smart contracts or blockchain protocols will remain a point of centralization and loss of direct autonomy. DAOs can be architecturally(independent actors run different nodes) and geographically decentralized (subject to various jurisdictions) (Novum Insights, 2021), but they are logically centralized (the protocol) (Novum Insights, 2021).

DAO GOVERNANCE

Web3 DAOs use Blockchain for governance, which has attracted increasing attention in academic circles and the technology community. (Cagigas et al., 2021; Risius & Spohrer, 2017; Rozas et al., 2021). It is well documented in the "Analysis of the Potentials of Blockchain for the Governance of Global Digital Commons" by Rozas, Tenorio-Fornes, and Hassan (2021), where they outline blockchain-based tools for shared governance, summarized below.

Blockchain Tools for Governance

Tokenization

Tokenization refers to transforming the rights to act on an asset into a transferable token. The capacity of Blockchain for tokenization provides new capabilities to experiment with the use of different types of tokens in collaboration platforms. In particular, the distribution of tokens allows participation rights to be more easily and granularly defined, propagated, and revoked. Blockchain tokens can represent the participation in an organization and each actor's voting rights and power. In some blockchain networks, such as Aragon, DAOStack, and Colony, using tokens to represent rights and power in the blockchain systems is crucial (Karjalainen, 2020; Rozas et al., 2021).

Self-Enforcement and Formalization of Rules

This refers to embedding organizational practices in intelligent contracts. Blockchain provides opportunities to make these rules more available and visible for discussion, increasing the degree of reflection, which may lead to higher adaptability. New projects focus on expanding the customization and adaptability of blockchain applications. It raises the question of which participant groups should be involved in creating and modifying which rules (Rozas et al., 2021).

Autonomous Automatization

This refers to defining complex sets of smart contracts as DAOs, enabling multiple parties' interaction with each other, even without human interaction. Self-enforcement of smart contracts and autonomous automatization provide additional means to track and communally fiscal new aspects of the organizational processes. It also facilitates self-enforcement and autonomous automatization for blockchain-based governance. The communities can use smart contracts to automatically self-enforce the rules that regulate the graduated sanctions agreed upon in the community. DAOs react autonomously upon circumstances or user actions, which increases the impersonalization of the application of the sanctions decided by the community (Rozas et al., 2021).

Decentralization of Power Over the Infrastructure

This refers to communalizing the ownership and control of technological tools. The community employs technological tools by decentralizing collaboration platforms (and their servers) for coordination (Rozas et al., 2021). It raises the question of how Blockchain can impact the interaction among social (e.g., users) and technical power (e.g., platform developers and owners)(Rozas et al., 2021). The ability of Blockchain to decentralize the power over the infrastructure (e.g., servers), which sustain the leading collaboration platforms, commonly emerges as a point of organizational tension.

Increased Transparency

This refers to opening the organizational processes and the associated data by relying on blockchain technologies' persistence and immutability properties. Increasing transparency may enable higher accountability and lead to more peer-to-peer monitoring forms. Thus, Blockchain can facilitate the monitoring of community rules. On the one hand, smart contracts represent the rules of online communities. It could include automatic procedures for specific monitoring purposes.

On the other hand, all correspondences are recorded in the Blockchain and observable in real-time by any party (Rozas et al., 2021). It enables users to detect and mitigate the effects of users behaving against the perceived community rules. Using Blockchain to support transparent and open peer-reviewing (Ford, 2013) is another example of the applications of Blockchain for community monitoring (Rozas et al., 2021).

Codification of Trust

Blockchain can self-enforce rules and formalize and codify agreements for facilitating the trust scaling up. Blockchain in Decentraland (Chaudhari et al., 2019) offers an example of its application in promoting the enforcement of rules locally. Users can purchase virtual land in Decentraland. The virtual land is modifiable by incorporating 3D elements and changing its color and texture. Land modification and selling to others are only allowed to the users. Furthermore, they can participate in the decisions that affect the functioning of Decentraland, such as the rules regulating land auctions (Rozas et al., 2021). Another example is the autonomous management of funding in Gitcoin (Qayum & Razzaq, 2020).

Objectives and Mechanisms of Governance

The ecosystem and the ledgers receive maintenance, updates, and upgrades through governance mechanisms. Although the importance of mechanisms for implementation is evident, substantial research is needed to determine mechanisms providing conditions for viable decentralization of ecosystems. It is helpful to explore the objectives of governance of a DAO. Honkanen et al. (2021) outline six potential DAO governance objectives:

1. Governance can provide a guarantee against the centralization of a network.
2. Governance can act as an arbitration process.
3. Governance can be a resource and reward allocator or incentive enabler and creator.
4. Governance as content control.
5. Democracy as a governance target.
6. Decentralization as a governance target.

The data analysis by Honkanen, Nylund, and Westerlund (2021) also found that stakeholders might have different interests and values for introducing governance mechanisms, which may be incompatible or competing.

Governance Mechanisms

There is a wide range of approaches to governance mechanisms, and these are listed below:

1. The proof of Stake (PoS) model is weighted according to the tokens they stake.
2. Progressive PoS system, where voting power is progressive. Each incremental token from more oversized holders has less voting power, giving smaller stakeholders more say in aggregate (Honkanen et al., 2021).
3. One individual equals one vote
4. Voting with expertise, which uses voters' expertise, is considered in addition to token wealth. It helps make decisions that are best for the project in the long run (Honkanen et al., 2021).
5. Voting by participation, here, each token holder is an influencer in the platform in an amount directly proportionate to their participation.
6. Non-Binding voting, where voting results won't be binding, but they will be strongly considered in decision-making.
7. Liquid democracy by Direct or Proxy voting (DPoS), where token holders make decisions, and the weight of decisions hinges on the number of tokens owned. Voters can either vote directly or delegate that power to proxies (Honkanen et al., 2021) and have the right to make proposals considered within the ecosystem.
8. Forking can be seen as a type of governance mechanism. Forking is usually an extreme solution for resolving conflicts.
9. Blockchain-supported courts and other arbitration mechanisms (Metzger, 2019). could lower the conflict-solving cost within global communities and provide transparency in conflict-resolution processes.

Voting Processes and Rights

The right to vote is a crucial governance mechanism. However, voting is one part of decentralized governance, and it need not be synonymous with it. Honkanen, Nylund, and Westerlund (2021) identified the following voting models from their white paper analysis: (i) Reputation-based rule systems which incentivize stakeholders to act desirably, and (ii) Participation and incentives in which users can receive influence about their level of investment.

Stakeholder Sanctions

Poor behavior can lead to the sanctioning of stakeholders. Such sanctioning can be connected to governance, meaning the right to vote can be suspended (Honkanen et al., 2021). A constitution is crucial for formalizing governance and creating trustworthiness for the ecosystem. Ecosystems still have open questions concerning the need for arbitration mechanisms if all the governance rules are assumed to be coded as smart contracts.

Governance Stakeholders

A crucial feature of a decentralized ecosystem is the existence of stakeholders with interests and roles within the ecosystem. A governance design must prevent centralization at conceptual and practical levels (Honkanen et al., 2021). According to Honkanen, Nylund, and Westerlund (2021), the purpose of governance as a guarantee against centralization is considered imperative for decentralized governance.

Changes in external circumstances might force amendments to the ecosystem, even though decentralized ecosystems are independently self-governed. Ecosystems need formal proposing, decision-making, and execution mechanisms to survive in the presence of external challenges. According to Finck (2019), technology needs to react to unexpected circumstances that inevitably arise without governance (Finck, 2019; Honkanen et al., 2021).

Mining Nodes (Miners)

Miners validate blockchain transactions in PoW model-based ecosystems by solving puzzles and receiving rewards for mining. Although the role of miners in governance is indirect, it is still crucial. The governance process decides the potential block rewards for miners. It is paramount that the rewards are adequate to incentivize miners to mine blocks to keep the ecosystem going (Honkanen et al., 2021).

Miners and other types of block validators have a considerable role in governance in proof of work (PoW) ecosystems. Miners have the final decision on adopting new software changes and forking the ecosystem, which gives them an essential position in ecosystems (Honkanen et al., 2021).

Developers

Developers have a crucial role in creating and developing ecosystems. While constructing the initial software, they usually try to improve it continuously (Honkanen et al., 2021).

Users (Content Producers, Viewers, Reviewers)

Decentralized ecosystems are developed and maintained by different types of users. Users can play a role in governance through participation, recommendation, and reputation processes (Honkanen et al., 2021).

Delegates

Delegates selected by vote can make decisions in governance processes in Proof of Stake (PoS) protocols (Honkanen et al., 2021).

Full Nodes

Blockchain ecosystems run on nodes. All computers connected to an ecosystem are a node. A node locally stores the full copy of a ledger (Honkanen et al., 2021).

Masternodes

Masternodes keep a complete copy of theBlockchain in real time. They are responsible for facilitating instant transactions, participation in governance, and voting. Masternodes are granted a portion of block rewards due to their unique contribution to the ecosystem. A certain amount of funds must be locked away as collateral in establishing a masternode (Honkanen et al., 2021).

Foundation

In the initial stages of an ecosystem's development, a foundation is usually the owner, decision-maker, or both. However, the foundation cannot remain a centralized owner or decision-maker and needs to ensure the ecosystem is decentralized (Honkanen et al., 2021).

Stakers (Validators)

The PoS consensus protocol entails the staking process. A staker mostly requires a full node and the ability to maintain and validate transactions on theBlockchain. The target is to determine the next person to validate a transaction/block and potentially get a reward based on a predefined set of rules and a random factor (Honkanen et al., 2021).

When It All Goes Wrong: The DAO Hack

Despite all the planning, codification, and smart contracts, decentralized automated organizations can go wrong In 2016, the DAO was the largest crowdfunded project of its time, raising over $150 million from more than 10,000 supporters (Siegel, 2016; Vigna, 2016; Ducree, 2020). It suffered a hack, and this attack concerned the cunning exploitation of its blockchain-encoded smart contracts.

In "The DAO Controversy: The Case for a New Species of Corporate Governance?" Morrison, Mazey, and Wingreen (2020) deconstruct the infamous DAO Hack. In the case of The DAO, smart contracts granted investors voting rights proportionate to their investment level and led their subsequent votes on investment proposals accordingly. The consensus of the investing company determined entire decisions about distributing and managing its $150 million fund, risks, residual claims, voting rights, and voting (Jentzsch, 2016a; DuPont, 2017; Morrison et al., 2020).

Less than three months after its launch, the DAO suffered a hack, and the hackers stole $60 million. The DAO left the governance operations to an algorithm, which operated according to previously-agreed rules. CoinTelegraph (2022) points out, "The most urgent problem, especially after The DAO hack, is a security problem, and it is connected with the 'unstoppable code' principle. During the attack, observers and investors watched helplessly as the funds were siphoned out of The DAO, but couldn't do anything, as the attacker was technically following the rules" (Shakirav, 2020).

RISKS WITH DAO GOVERNANCE

The DAO hack highlights a significant flaw with DAO voting systems: if there is a security problem in the initial code, its rectification remains on hold until the majority votes. While the voting takes place, hackers can exploit the vulnerability in the code. The DAO did not have implicit work contracts to back up failing or inoperable smart contracts. Therefore, long-term organizational success for DAOs may depend on implicit work contracts as a fail-safe mechanism in case of adverse circumstances or organizational crises (Morrison et al., 2020).

This experience highlights the question of whether someone should be accountable in DAOs. How will DAOs evolve to ensure the details of governance, legalities, ethics, and logic flaws in the code are sound? No single person is morally culpable for group decisions, but this may be different from legal culpability. According to Hinkes (2016) and Morrison, Mazey, and Wingreen (2020), sharing legal accountability and liability in partnership entities and many governance mechanisms is common. Regulators may suggest this for DAOs.

There are risks when corporate and IT governance are the same, and computer algorithms implement investor decisions rather than people. It differs from all other known forms of corporate governance in which governance of the information technology function is subordinate to the overall corporate governance (Morrison et al., 2020).

A DAO is an almost entirely flat organization with no governing board, executive leaders, or executive functions beyond the vote of investors. In principle, an optimally operating DAO shows that using smart contracts may effectively manage organizational decisions and work (Morrison et al., 2020). But this only lasts as long as The DAO's operating conditions remain stable. It is challenging to design rules and logic for all possible contingencies. There has been substantial progress in smart contract security and other mitigation techniques, and since then, larger projects raising several billion dollars have been launched (Rooney, 2018; Block. One, 2020; Ducree, 2020).

DAOs have internal governance and external governance components, which relies on clusters of servers and nodes for the functioning of the network. DAOs exist autonomously but also heavily rely on specialist individuals or smaller organizations to perform tasks that automation can't replace, like keeping the network safe and performing other network tasks rewarded with the native network tokens. As a result, they can exert more influence on decision-making than other actors if they control more nodes and server capacity. Some of the risks are outlined below.

User Attitudes

Users view tokens as yield, not voting rights (SubDAO Protocol, 2021). Protocols started using their governance tokens as "rewards" for users participating in the network. It can encourage competitive and speculative behavior, leading to a centralized governance structure since tokens slowly accumulate in a few hands.

Incentives

The economic incentives of providing liquidity to get rewarded with governance tokens encourage competitive and speculative behavior, leading back to a centralized governance structure as tokens slowly concentrate in a few hands (Cousaert, 2021).

Centralized Tendencies

Projects are prone to attack vulnerability because of excessive centralization, and parties with a conflict of interest can push through proposals (SubDAO, 2021). Computer algorithms enable smart contract enforcement, which participants have agreed to in advance, leaving limited mechanisms for change.

Speed of Response

A problem with DAO voting systems is that even if there is a security hole in an initial code, its rectification can't occur until the majority votes. While voting takes place, hackers can exploit a bug in the code.

Legal Status

Another issue is the legal status of a DAO (Okaformbah, 2019). Who is to sue and sues if a case arises, or in case of liquidating a tangible asset owned by the DAO, what rules are to be followed? In an adverse event, what happens when who can be sued and who sues?

User Understanding

It's not unusual that users don't fully understand the governance of the projects they invest in and the risks they take. If a professional assessment of risks doesn't occur, losing funds via a protocol error or a malicious attack puts the users' funds at risk.

Emerging Governance Solutions

DAOs are experimenting with governance structures mechanisms, including tokens as a governance mechanism, constitution, reputation, participation and incentives, mining, staking, validating, stakeholder sanctions, voting processes and rights, proposals, and forking (Beck & Asher, 2021). Wulf Kaal further outlines improvements to DAO governance that have been suggested, such as: releasing smart contracts in stages; certification and review processes as well as multiple security audits from respected institutions in combination with formal verification programs for smart contracts; and designing the DAO such that it can be stopped (Kaal, 2020).

As reported in Cointelegraph (Thurman, 2021), Stani Kulechov from Aave suggests that peer review will be the future. "Eventually, it's about peer review, and we need to find incentives to empower more security experts into the space as a community." In the same article, Emeliano Bonassi speaks about ReviewsDAO, a peer review forum for connecting security experts and projects looking for reviews. Bonassi envisions this potential to become a learning opportunity in which people with specialized knowledge can contribute to improving the ecosystem's security (Thurman, 2021).

Due diligence is essential for DeFi, which is transparent and open-source. CNBC reported that over $10 billion of user funds were stolen from DeFi products in 2021(Browne, 2021). How can the non-expert user think about due diligence in this fast-moving 24-hour, seven-day-a-week industry? A salutary example of this was the DAO mentioned above hack exploiting a vulnerability in the smart contract (Zwitter & Hazenberg, 2020).

As an alternative, Othmane Zizi has developed a way of ranking DAOs based on a net community score (Zizi, 2021). He hypothesizes that the strength of a DAO's community is essential to its future success. Illuvium.io (2022) and Uniswap (n.d.) had the highest scores based on this approach.

Regulatory Issues

There are many issues that regulators will concern themselves with, including all the questions on virtual assets outlined in Chapter Four. Kozak, K. (2021) outlines the main legal and governance considerations about DAOs. (i) Which jurisdiction(s) need to be considered? (ii) Which regulatory bodies might be concerned? (iii) How do we design smart contracts to be legally compliant? (iv) Does the jurisdiction need to be changed to cater to tokenization? (v) Where will the token be issued? And (vi) Will there be a DAO for the NFT Marketplace?

Hinkes, A. (2016) points out that legal accountability and liability are often shared in partnership entities and many types of governance mechanisms and suggests it seems reasonable that members of DAO communities should be held jointly liable for losses, as they are jointly rewarded for gains The global legal and regulatory community is working actively to solve these questions.

Further research is needed to propose specific and viable requirements for decentralized blockchain governance. A centralized ecosystem may find it easier to address rapid development issues due to shorter decision flows and clear stakeholder benefits. DAO governance must design incentives to align stakeholder views and provide an immediate response to critical incidents.

CONCLUSION

DAOs are a powerful tool for Web3 ecosystem building. They are open source and allow communities to form around a common objective. They are distributed organizations that live on the internet and exist autonomously. They are the essence of community token economies. In an optimal situation, the community defines the rules, and these are encoded in smart contracts, which are transparent and publicly available. The DAO operates seamlessly and is automated as intended. However, as experience has shown, not all contingencies can be predicted, and sometimes there are vulnerabilities in the code The concept of DAOs is still relatively young, and significant experimentation with governance is likely to lead to more robust and better models Regulators will likely be looking closely and determining how they can access code governed organizations Investor education and trusted due diligence sources are critically needed as the industry matures to protect consumers and improve industry standards.

REFERENCES

Aragon. (n.d.). *Homepage.* https://aragon.org

Beck, J., & Asher, M. (2021, February 3). *Why Decentralized Autonomous Organizations (DAOs) Are Essential to DeFi.* ConsenSys. https://consensys. net/blog/codefi/daos/

Bizzer. (2018, September 5). What is DAO? *Medium.* https://medium.com/ bizzer-daico/what-is-dao-5f00b9888273

Blockchain Consulting. (2021). *An overview of Decentralized Autonomous Organizations (DAOs).* https://bcc-munich.com/everything-you-need-to-know-about-decentralized-autonomous-organizations-daos/

Block.one. (2020). *Is a Leader in Providing High-Performance Blockchain Solutions.* https://block.one/

Browne, R. (2021, November 19). Criminals have made off with over $10 billion in 'DeFi' scams and thefts this year. *CNBC.* https://www.cnbc. com/2021/11/19/over-10-billion-lost-to-defi-scams-and-thefts-in-2021.html

Cagigas, D., Clifton, J., Diaz-Fuentes, D., & Fernández-Gutiérrez, M. (2021). Blockchain for public services: A systematic literature review. *IEEE Access : Practical Innovations, Open Solutions, 9,* 13904–13921. doi:10.1109/ ACCESS.2021.3052019

Chaudhari, A. A., Laddha, D., & Potdar, M. (2019). Decentraland – a Blockchain based model for smart property experience. *Int. Eng. J. Res. Dev., 4,* 5.

Cointelegraph. (2022). *What is a decentralized autonomous organization, and how does a DAO work?* https://cointelegraph.com/decentralized-automated-organizations-daos-guide-for-beginners/what-is-decentralized-autonomous-organization-and-how-does-a-dao-work

Cousaert, S. (2021, March 25). Generalizing knowledge on DEXs with AMMs — Part I. *UCL CBT.* Medium. https://medium.com/uclcbt/generalizing-knowledge-on-dexs-with-amms-2963d07ebac7

DeFi Rate. (2022, September 9). *Crypto News.* https://defirate.com/news

Ducrée, J., Etzrodt, M., Gordijn, B., Gravitt, M., Bartling, S., Walshe, R., & Harrington, T. (2020). Blockchain for Organizing Effective Grass-Roots Actions on a Global Commons: Saving the Planet. *Front. Blockchain*, *3*, 33. doi:10.3389/fbloc.2020.00033

DuPont, Q. (2017). Experiments in algorithmic governance: A history and ethnography of "The DAO," a failed decentralized autonomous organization. In Bitcoin and beyond (pp. 157-177). Routledge.

Finance, O. I. N. (2021, February). How OINDAO is different from MakerDAO. *Medium*. https://medium.com/oin-finance/how-oindao-is-different-from-makerdao-5a46feddcc81

Finck, M. (2019). *Blockchain Regulation and Governance in Europe.* Cambridge University Press.

Ford, E. (2013). Defining and characterizing open peer review: A review of the literature. *Journal of Scholarly Publishing*, *44*(4), 311–326. doi:10.3138/jsp.44-4-001

Gupta, R., & Archi, D. A. O. (2022, April 16). Top 10 words to know about DAO (Decentralized Autonomous Organization). *ArchiDao*. https://archidao.substack.com/p/top-10-words-to-know-about-dao-decentralized

Hinkes, A. (2016). *The Law of the DAO.* https://www.coindesk.com/the-law-of-the-dao/

Honkanen, P., Nylund, M., & Westerlund, M. (2021). Organizational Building Blocks for Blockchain Governance: A Survey of 241 Blockchain White Papers. *Front. Blockchain*, *4*, 613115. doi:10.3389/fbloc.2021.613115

Hsieh, Y. Y., Vergne, J. P., Anderson, P., Lakhani, K., & Reitzig, M. (2018). Bitcoin and the rise of decentralized autonomous organizations. *Journal of Organization Design*, *7*(1), 1–16. doi:10.118641469-018-0038-1

Iluvium. (2022). *Home Page.* https://www.illuvium.io

Jentzsch, C. (2016b). *What an Accomplishment!* https://blog.slock.it/what-an-accomplishment-3e7ddea8b91d

Kaal, W. (2020, July 18). DAOs — Governance & Legal Design Experimentation. *Medium.* https://wulfkaal.medium.com/daos-governance-legal-design-experimentation-25b2d0f58a29

Karjalainen, R. (2020). *Governance in decentralized networks.* Available at SSRN 3551099.

Kozak, K. (2021, October 20). *Organizational Building Blocks for Blockchain Governance: A Survey of 241 Blockchain White Papers.* Frontiers. Retrieved May 30, 2023, from https://www.frontiersin.org/articles/10.3389/fbloc.2021.613115/full

Metzger, J. (2019). The current landscape of blockchain-based, crowdsourced arbitration. *Macquarie L. J, 19*, 81–102.

MolochD. A. O. (n.d.). *Homepage.* https://molochdao.com

Morrison, R., Mazey, N. C. H. L., & Wingreen, S. C. (2020). The DAO Controversy: The Case for a New Species of Corporate Governance? *Front. Blockchain, 3*, 25. doi:10.3389/fbloc.2020.00025

Novum Insights. (2021, June 23). *Deep dive into decentralized governance - DAO.* https://novuminsights.com/post/deep-dive-into-decentralized-governance-dao/

Okaformbah, C. (2019, February 19). *Governance in a Decentralized Autonomous Organization.* Medium. https://justcharles.medium.com/governance-in-a-decentralized-autonomous-organization-425f56b3e8bb

Qayum, A., & Razzaq, A. (2020). A self-evolving design of blockchain-based open source community – IEEE conference publication. *2020 3rd International Conference on Computing, Mathematics and Engineering Technologies (iCoMET)*, 1–11.

Quiniou, M. (2019). *Blockchain: The advent of disintermediation.* John Wiley & Sons. doi:10.1002/9781119629573

Risius, M., & Spohrer, K. (2017). A blockchain research framework. *Business & Information Systems Engineering, 59*(6), 385–409. doi:10.100712599-017-0506-0

Rooney, K. (2018). *A Blockchain Start-Up Just Raised $4 Billion Without a Live Product.* https://www.cnbc.com/2018/05/31/a-blockchain-start-up-just-raised-4-billion-without-a-live-product.html

Rozas, D., Tenorio-Fornés, A., & Hassan, S. (2021). Analysis of the Potentials of Blockchain for the Governance of Global Digital Commons. *Front. Blockchain, 4*, 577680. doi:10.3389/fbloc.2021.577680

Saive, G. (2021, January 20). What is dao. *UBC Digital Magazine*. https://ubc.digital/what-is-dao

Shakirov, I. (2020, September 29). *Research on Decentralized Autonomous Organizations (DAO)*. Grom. Medium. https://medium.com/gromorg/dao-research-42709eda6675

Shuttleworth, D. (2021, October 7). *What Is A DAO And How Do They Work?* ConsenSys. https://consensys.net/blog/blockchain-explained/what-is-a-dao-and-how-do-they-work/

Siegel, D. (2016). *Understanding The DAO Attack*. https://www.coindesk.com/understanding-dao-hack-journalists

Stroponiati, K., Abugov, I., Varelas, Y., Stroponiatis, K., Jurgeleviciene, M., & Savannah, Y. (n.d.). Decentralized governance in DeFi: Examples and pitfalls. *Static*. Squarespace. https://static1.squarespace.com/static/5966eb2ff7e0ab3d29b6b55d/t/5f989987fc086a1d8482ae70/1603837124500/defi_governance_paper.pdf

SubDAO Protocol. (2021, October 9). Learn on SubDAO: DAO Governance Matters for DeFi. *Medium*. https://subdao.medium.com/learn-on-subdao-dao-governance-matters-for-defi-35ae40260f5b

Thurman, A. (2021, February 18). As faith in audits falter, the DeFi community ponders security alternatives. *Cointelegraph*. https://cointelegraph.com/news/as-faith-in-audits-falter-the-defi-community-ponders-security-alternatives

Uniswap. (n.d.). *Home Page*. https://uniswap.org

Vigna, P. (2016). Chiefless Company Rakes. In *More Than $100 Million - Group called DAO is running itself via computer code*. Wall Street J.

Voshmgir, S. (2019). Tokenized Networks: What is a DAO? *Blockchainhub Berlin*. https://blockchainhub.net/dao-decentralized-autonomous-organization/

Zizi, O. (2021, December 24). Ranking DAOs: We computed their "net community score" to see how they stack up. *Business of Business*. https://www.businessofbusiness.com/about/

Zwitter, A., & Hazenberg, J. (2020). Decentralized Network Governance: Blockchain Technology and the Future of Regulation. *Front. Blockchain*, *3*, 12. doi:10.3389/fbloc.2020.00012

Chapter 6
Digital Assets and the Tokenization of Everything

ABSTRACT

Underpinning Web 3.0 in all its forms is the token economics that will determine the nature of the resources, their uses, their allocation and distribution, and ways to increase and decrease the resources within a Web 3.0 economy. Tokenization can democratize access, unlock the value of illiquid assets, enable faster transactions and settlement, improve traceability and transparency, and improve interoperability. This chapter will discuss different types of tokenized assets, including green digital asset solutions, tokenized health data, tokenized real estate, and other potential future tokenized assets. It will also discuss the regulatory challenges of a tokenized world. It will also provide a brief introduction to virtual assets as investments. There are many types and uses of tokens, and this chapter aims to provide an overview of this growing trend, which will change how people exchange value in a Web 3.0 future.

INTRODUCTION

Building on Chapters 2-5, which outline the fundamental building blocks of Web 3.0, Blockchain, Decentralized Finance (DeFi), and Decentralized Governance, this Chapter will discuss tokenization, which enables the ownership or rights attached to an asset to be split into small units or tokens and which can be traded, held, bought, sold, and exchanged. The ability to

DOI: 10.4018/978-1-6684-6658-2.ch006

exchange that value is a crucial affordance of Web3 and the building block for many innovations.

As Chapter 1 outlines, Web 3.0 will be the next iteration of the Internet, "The Internet of Value." Tokenization creates Blockchain-based tokens that may be exchanged, stored, and transferred digitally. These tokens reside on a Blockchain, operate as a store of value, and bear the rights of the assets they represent, but the real-world assets they represent remain off-chain.

Tokenization will enable virtual asset movement and utilize fungible and non-fungible tokens (NFTs) to speculate on new projects. Non-fungible tokens are digital certificates of ownership and often represent rights. These are growing in utility, such as documents for real estate and insurance policies. NFTs will be primary enablers of tokenization and will be discussed in Chapters Seven and Eight. There are many distinct types of tokens, as elucidated by Global Blockchain Convergence (2021) and summarized below:

Physical Asset Tokens

Any digital representation of a tangible (real world) asset created and maintained on a Blockchain (Schneider et al., 2021). This category can break down into smaller categories based on the particular type of substantial assets like Gold Coin Physical Asset Tokens, Air Jordan Physical Asset Tokens, and a cup of coffee physical asset tokens versus coffee cup physical tokens (Schneider et al., 2021).

Services Tokens

Any digital representation of services. This category can also include music and purely digital art files. This category includes services susceptible to sub-categorization, like cleaning services tokens, personal performance tokens versus concert tokens, and legal services tokens (including music and digital art) (Schneider et al., 2021).

Intangible Asset Tokens

Any traditional intangible (non-physical) assets. It is another broad category susceptible to sub-categories based on the asset class, such as bond tokens (security tokens), tokens of real estate ownership, government program tokens, and loyalty points program tokens (Schneider et al., 2021).

Native Tokens

A narrow category of truly native tokens (e.g., Bitcoin, Ether, EOS). These tokens are a bundle of rights with no physical items involved, although some may have an element of services (e.g., using a token for resource allocation on the network.) Native tokens have no existence or purpose without the associated Blockchain (Schneider et al., 2021).

Stablecoins

They are designed to maintain a stable value against some underlying, reference, or linked asset or pool/basket of assets (Schneider et al., 2021).

BENEFITS OF TOKENIZATION

Tokenization offers multiple benefits improving access to investment, increasing efficiency, and reducing intermediaries.

Investment

With investment, tokenization can democratize access with fractional ownership, enabling even small retail investors to diversify their portfolios and access formerly exclusive markets only accessible to large-scale investors. Tokenization of equity shares allows companies to interact with shareholders by providing information on a shared and immutable ledger. Investors can invest in small percentages of tokenized assets. It removes the barriers for billions of investors to enter the market. It will also broaden the investor base as asset tokenization makes selling or buying tokens representing fractions of ownership possible. It opens opportunities for new investors and allows them to diversify their investment portfolio into assets they previously could not afford. Investment barriers are high in the conventional financial industry. The minimum investment requirement can be reduced with tokenization, enabling even small-scale retail investors to diversify portfolios. They can access formerly exclusive markets accessible to large-scale investors far beyond their grasp (Thomason, 2022). It will also open other geographies for investment. An investor can invest in a property anywhere in the world without physically visiting. Investment becomes secure, fast, and easy with asset tokenization on the Blockchain. Finally, it allows people with assets to unlock the value of illiquid assets, realizing their liquid potential and becoming tradable on secondary markets via fractional ownership.

Efficiency

In relation to efficiency, tokenization enables faster transactions and settlement, with quicker transactions through automation and smart contracts. It also improves traceability and transparency, as an immutable shared ledger keeps track of all actions on a given asset as all parties have visibility. Tokenized assets enable quicker transactions with less paperwork. Many inefficient manual operations can be automated and streamlined using smart contracts, while clearing and settlement processes may be simplified and built more efficiently.

Removes Need for Intermediaries

Tokenization removes the need for intermediaries with Blockchain's ability to provide immutability and transparency. In the following sections, fungible and non-fungible tokens will be considered.

Investing and Trading

This section will briefly touch on virtual assets used for investing and trading, as this has become a widely adopted use case for virtual assets. The Global Blockchain Convergence defines these as Native DLT tokens like Bitcoin, Ether, and EOS (Schneider et al., 2021). These tokens have become popular globally, and according to Coinmarketcap.com, the global cryptocurrency market cap today is $1.17 Trillion, a -0.75% change in the last 24 hours and a -13.72% change one year ago. The market cap of Bitcoin (BTC) is $521 Billion, representing a Bitcoin dominance of 44.53%.

A challenge for users is the management of their tokens or virtual assets. As outlined in earlier Chapters, Metamask stores users' public and private keys and provides an interface to manage crypto balances. They also support virtual asset transfers through the Blockchain (University, 2022). Some wallets allow users to perform specific actions like buying and selling or interacting with decentralized applications (dApps). There are different types of wallets, hot and cold wallets. Hot wallets are connected to the internet, while cold wallets are kept offline (University, 2022). This means funds stored in hot wallets are more accessible and vulnerable to hackers. In hot wallets, private keys are stored and encrypted on the app, which is kept online. Using a hot wallet can be risky because computer networks have hidden vulnerabilities that can be targeted by hackers or malware programs to break into the system (University, 2022). A hardware wallet is an external device (USB or Bluetooth) that stores user keys. For cryptocurrency assets that do not require instant access, the best practice is to keep them offline in a cold wallet (University, 2022). However, there is a risk that it could be lost or stolen.

An alternative is a hosted wallet, such as Coinbase, where virtual assets are automatically held in a hosted wallet (Learn, 2022). It is hosted because a third party keeps custody of digital assets, similar to how a bank holds money in an account. There is no risk of losing the keys in a hosted wallet.

The main benefit of keeping virtual assets in a hosted wallet is that the crypto can still be accessed if the password is forgotten. (Learn, 2022).

An alternative to holding digital assets personally is investing in a fund. Virtual Asset investment funds have been growing. Grayscale Investments (Scale, 2022), Assets Under Management (AUM) increased from $2.02 billion in 2020 to $20.2 billion. Grayscale Bitcoin Trust has grown the most among its funds, from $1.8 billion AUM to $17.5 billion AUM. 86% of the investment in Grayscale's funds came from institutional investors.

TOKENIZING REAL-WORLD ASSETS

Early tokenized physical assets can be traced to commodities like wine, medications, and jewels. Research and surveys conducted by the World Economic Forum (WEF) and Deloitte suggest that tokenizing digital and physical assets will drive a large portion of the future economy (Utopian Global & Coinmonks, 2022). The projected business value-add of tokenization will grow to more than $176 billion by 2025 and exceed $3.1 trillion by 2030 (Tradestrike, n.d.). The tokenization of physical assets has a variety of use cases and applications and can apply to almost every asset class.

Gold

Gold has always been a stable store of wealth for investors, offering stability during periods of economic uncertainty and financial instability. Tokenizing gold reduces the paperwork involved in keeping, storing, and transferring the item. Investors are buying rights to actual physical gold, which is kept secure in vaults but is immediately available on the ledger. Due to the unchangeable nature of Blockchain, selling the same ownership certificate to multiple people is impossible.

The Universal Protocol Alliance (2018), which includes Bittrex Global, Ledger, CertiK, and Uphold, launched a token backed by the Perth Mint. The Perth Mint, which the Western Australian government controls, is the world's biggest refiner of new gold. The "Universal Gold" or UPXAU tokens were released in October this year. UPXAU tokens may be bought for $1 and are free to retain. They are backed one-to-one by GoldPass certificates issued by the Perth Mint.

JP Morgan also announced plans to tokenize gold bars on Ethereum and represent them on Quorum, their business blockchain. In an interview with Australia's Financial Review, the company's head of blockchain efforts, Umar Farooq, revealed the information. He said that data about gold bars would be reflected on Quorum's distributed ledger, enabling buyers and sellers to verify their gold sources from socially responsible mines (Fries, 2018; Fries, 2021).

Real Estate

Tokenized real estate assets provide an opportunity to expand real estate investment markets. The worldwide real estate market hit an all-time high of $830 billion in 2019 (Prophecy Market Insights, 2022). Despite this, the industry is one of the most illiquid asset classes. To own a piece of real estate, one must purchase the whole property and overcome high entrance hurdles, lengthy transaction procedures, and expensive administrative expenditures.

Blockchain has various applications in the real estate sector, from leveraging smart contracts for property transactions to eliminating intermediaries and lowering expenses. Tokenizing assets is one of the most potential use cases of Blockchain in the real estate market. Real estate tokenization may fractionalize a property's ownership into several tokens representing a portion of the property. The tokens are available to a broader range of investors and may be exchanged on various exchanges, cutting entry barriers and minimizing buyer-seller friction. Tokenization in real estate uses blockchain-based tokens to create fractional ownership of an asset, aiding in liquidating illiquid real estate assets. Serious projects include TrustMe Property Exchange (TPX) (TPX, 2019) and SolidBlock (2022).

There have already been several significant initiatives announced. A $30 million Manhattan apartment became the first real estate tokenized on the Ethereum blockchain in October 2018. The following year, Mata Capital, a French asset management company, tokenized a Paris hotel to reach a bigger audience and lower minimum membership quantities. The €26 million issues that resulted became one of Europe's most prominent real estate tokenization operations (Iredale, 2021).

Commodities

Tokenization will create new market opportunities by converting physical assets into tradable digital assets and lowering barriers to entry in asset classes led by institutional investors. This is currently being experimented on for Nickel Wire (Nikeltech.com) and Jade (https://jadecity.io). Tokenization can also apply to illiquid assets such as artwork, wine, and partnership shares to enable provenance, lending, and price discovery.

Art

According to a report published by Art Basel and UBS's Art Market 2021, the global art market hit $50.1 billion in 2020. The art market share in the US is 42%, while Great China and the UK have 20% global sales (Jenny, 2021). However, the art market has not modified its business model in decades, resulting in a lack of transparency, high investment hurdles, poor liquidity, and many copyright difficulties. Tokenizing artworks might address some of these issues and make the art market more accessible to the general population. It is also cost-effective to construct an immutable register of art copyright data, promote transparency for all ecosystem members, and offer liquidity with lower prices.

Maecenas, a little-known firm, launched a blockchain-based art marketplace that tokenizes works of art and enables anybody to purchase, sell, and swap fractional ownership in masterpieces. Pieces of art are tokenized and split into tokens that may sell for a fraction of their original price. Smart contracts provide a fair and transparent procedure and distribute the tokens, which may enable acquisition by bank transfer, credit card, or cryptocurrency. Maecenas successfully tokenized a multi-million dollar piece of art, Andy Warhol's 14 Small Electric Chairs, for the first time in 2018. (1980). The auction included 100 hand-selected bidders who could buy fractions of 14 Small Electric Chairs using Bitcoin, Ethereum, or the ART token. At US$5.6 million, the beta auction generated US$1.7 million for 31.5 percent of the piece.

Over the years, a slew of new fascinating ventures has developed. For example, Riddle and Code (2018) has partnered with RDI Digital and the famous Tretyakov Gallery in Moscow to examine the application of Blockchain for micro-investment in art pieces while confirming their validity and provenance.

Health and Medical Data

The tokenization of health data is a new and emerging innovation in the medical research industry. The patient identifier is de-identified in this process by generating a patient-specific encrypted token (Weng, 2022; MarksMan Healthcare Communications, 2022). It helps researchers link Real-World Data from the patient's previous medical history from diverse sources. It also facilitates tracking different active engagements across the healthcare system without compromising patients' privacy (Weng, 2022; MarksMan Healthcare Communications, 2022). Tokenization enables replacing a patient's identity with a unique identification symbol in the form of tokens, ensuring the retention of essential information without compromising confidentiality. Tokenization can eliminate the need for decrypting and re-encrypting data (MarksMan Healthcare Communications, 2022).

Using blockchain technology to create tokens ensures that healthcare data remains secure and free of manipulation. Tokenization also helps prevent data duplication while collecting data for the Real-World Evidence (RWE) generation, as it is consistent across different formats of RWE (MarksMan Healthcare Communications, 2022). Examples include *Encrypgen* (2021), which is creating a platform that would increase the amount of genetic data available for research while increasing privacy, security, and ownership of data for individuals and allowing them to profit from their data. *BurstIQ* (2022) provides end-to-end data rights management, an entire chain of custody, granular ownership, revocable consent, and advanced security using on-chain data.

Health data will be the new healthcare currency. This demand for data, and the ability to monetize data, will lead to the development of health data marketplaces that connect health data to medical researchers to accelerate crucial medical research and scientific discovery. Such health data marketplaces will enable and accelerate the development of vital medical research by mobilizing passive datasets to meet medical research and scientific discovery needs. It will allow data owners to create passive income from data sets and provide high-quality anonymous medical data to researchers and tech companies to assist their research or train their AI solutions. Even anonymized, the data command premium prices. For example, Pfizer spends $12 million to buy health data from various sources (Thomason, 2022). Health data marketplaces will be tokenized. This will enable data to be interconnected, interoperable, and accessible in real-time, allowing information to be shared easily between all stakeholders and resulting in improved patient outcomes.

Tokenization of Green Digital Asset Solutions

The recent focus on Voluntary Carbon Markets has stimulated the development of Green Digital Asset Solutions (Green Digital Finance Alliance, 2021), including Green utility tokens - a reward for lowering carbon emissions; Green asset tokens - tokenized carbon credit or biodiversity offset; Green crypto - programmed only to be spent on green products and Green STO (Security Token Offering) issuance platforms - designed to enable green proof of impact reporting (Thomason, 2022). This is discussed in further detail in Chapter 12.

Tokenization can help improve and manage smart grids in decentralized energy markets and allow for the P2P trade of power reliably and transparently. Power Ledger enables (n.d) consumers to buy, sell, or exchange excess renewable electricity directly with each other. Solstroem (n.d) focuses on accelerating the energy transition in developing and emerging countries. It provides off-grid solar and geotagged, timestamped micro-carbon credits that individuals or companies can purchase (Mackreides, 2022). TransActive (n.d.) Grid is a blockchain-based energy marketplace focusing on local peer-to-peer home-produced energy trading.

Tokenization can address the current problems in the energy sector in several ways. Firstly, by ensuring liquidity. Though the projects can have a long-term investment period of 15-20 years, investors do not necessarily have to wait. They can sell their tokens at any time and exit quickly. They can also hold tokens, receive payouts, and watch the tokens rise in value. Secondly, the company's valuation will rise if the tokens grow in price. This increase in the company's valuation will help it raise funds in the subsequent funding rounds (US Energy Media, 2022).

Sports, Entertainment, and Music

Tokenization is also used to allow brands, influencers, and creators to monetize experiences and services. Liquefy, a security token issuance platform, tokenizes sports teams, making it easier for investors to invest in clubs and athletes (News Desk, 2019). Spencer Dinwiddie, a well-known basketball player, was the first athlete to tokenize his basketball contract to maximize his skill and promote fan involvement (Ledger Insights, 2021).

REGULATORY CHALLENGES

Since the emergence of virtual assets, governments have focused on regulation and legal compliance (Werbach, 2016). Different nations have reacted in various ways (Rebecca, 2018). To draw commercial activity as digital assets centers, Switzerland, Singapore, and Malta created specialized regulatory frameworks (Nathaniel, 2016). On the other hand, cryptocurrencies were outlawed entirely in Bangladesh, Kyrgyzstan, and Bolivia and heavily restricted in China, South Korea, and India (Apolline, 2019). Most European nations, including the US, Japan, Canada, Australia, and other countries, have made an effort to integrate digital assets into their current financial regulatory frameworks (Apolline, 2019). The critical issue with the surge of ICO activity was whether tokens qualify as securities. The US Securities and Exchange Commission (SEC) noted that the usual security classification analysis still applied even if Switzerland established a new category of "utility tokens" not marketed primarily for financial purposes (Securities, 2017).

Most countries, except China's notable exception, did not outright forbid exchanges. Several exchanges were successful in obtaining licenses in numerous nations. Significant traditional institutions are now making inroads into digital assets, including the corporate owners of the New York Stock Exchange (Shawn, 2018). Some of the common regulatory challenges are outlined below.

Custody

The cornerstone of the developing virtual asset industry is the custody of virtual assets. Several problems arise when protecting the private key linked to the digital asset, especially for the public. Private keys are readily misplaced or forgotten, making the associated assets unavailable. Serious problems also occur when passing on assets after death because an heir cannot inherit digital assets without access to the private key. Any solution to the custody issue must balance security against spending ability, with the latter requiring that transactions be quickly and easily signed. The ideal answer should strike a balance between the two extremes and, in particular, meet the following criteria (Nicola, 2020): Usability: A legitimate user should have no trouble accessing the funds; Security: Opponents must be unable to seize control of the assets; Safety: In the event of an accident (such as the loss of a regularly used device), the system should maintain or restore access to the funds and Universality: The solution must work with all virtual assets and not just one specific type.

Volatility

Many projects are still in a period of explosive price discovery as a young and developing industry (Center, 2022). As a result, there is an exceptionally high level of price volatility. Virtual assets exchanges operate continuously, in contrast to traditional stock markets. The market is highly automated, another reason causing price volatility. A large number of programs are continuously scanning the network for recognizable patterns. It may have a cascading effect when this happens because numerous algorithms rely on the same factors to forecast future price fluctuations.

Taxation

Government agencies worldwide are looking at ways to change their tax rules and regulations to address digital assets because this is a relatively new technology and market (Center, 2022). This means that the legal environment might change fast, and it may not be clear how new or existing tax rules will affect certain tokenized operations (Center, 2022).

Consumer Risk

Consumer risk remains a challenge. One must enter a receiving address when sending digital assets. These take the shape of a long string that combines letters and numbers. Even experienced users occasionally make mistakes when typing, copying, and pasting a receiving address. The money cannot be recovered once sent to the wrong address since blockchain transactions are irreversible (Center, 2022). Before sending each transfer, double- or even triple-checking the address is essential.

Cybersecurity

Cybersecurity is a growing problem since digital assets have grown to billions, and cyber criminals have targeted tokens. While blockchains offer a high degree of security, there remain points of vulnerability—for example, the protection of private keys. Jurisdiction, regulatory and legislative frameworks can change from jurisdiction to jurisdiction, and tokens must be compliant both in the investor's and issuer's jurisdictions. Anti-money laundering and KYC will be essential, and new operational measures will be required to meet compliance requirements in the digital space. The Financial Action Task Force (FATF), the global money laundering and terrorist financing watchdog., has made a recommendation to all countries known as FATF Travel Rule Recommendation 16 related to Wire Transfers as it relates to the Virtual Asset industry and the sending of the originator and beneficiary PII to a Virtual Asset transaction between two Virtual Asset Service Providers (VASPs). Since June 2019, several FATF Travel Rule TSPs (Travel Rule Service Providers) have built Travel Rule Solutions to facilitate the immediate and secure transmission of originator and beneficiary information, such as wallet addresses and names, between VASPs.

Money Laundering and Terrorist Financing

Using Bitcoin and other virtual assets to launder money or raise money outside the reach of law enforcement has been attempted by terrorist groups, transnational criminal gangs, and sanctioned countries like North Korea (Times, 2022).

Regulatory Uncertainty

Regulatory uncertainty is a critical barrier in tokenization, and the multiplicity of token types also means there is not a single regulator that may be involved. Industry segments make regulations. Central Banks monitor financial stability, securities regulators protect investors and consumers, and FATF (2022) oversees anti-money laundering and terrorist financing. Companies need regulatory certainty for society to access the utility of the use cases outlined here.

Current uncertainties include: The lack of a code of conduct and common standards for developing and managing tokenized assets, The lack of regulations within jurisdictions, and the borderless nature of blockchain technology present a challenge for investors and institutions to hold tokenized assets confidently. Proper KYC and regulatory compliance will enable the adoption of asset tokenization.

As a well-known Blockchain influencer Jonny Fry points out, the UK Government, Bank of England, and Australia have made supportive statements about the potential opportunities that digital assets and crypto offer and intend to regulate. He notes, *"Given the digital nature of digital assets, the location of a crypto-friendly jurisdiction is less relevant; all that is required is clear guidance and legal certainty"* (Fry, 2022). The UAE has also embraced Blockchain, becoming a leading center in February 2022, and passed its Virtual Asset regulation (Akin Gump Strauss Hauer & Feld LLP & Muzz 2022). Dr. Marwan, Head of the Dubai Blockchain Centre, emphasized, *"The idea of regulations is thinking of possibilities, not limitations"* (Alzarouni, 2022).

CONCLUSION

Web 3 will be underpinned by tokenization, which can democratize access, unlock the value of illiquid assets, enable faster transactions and settlement, improve traceability and transparency, and improve interoperability. To date tokenization has focussed on speculative digital assets, green digital asset solutions, tokenized health data, and tokenized real estate. However, this is only the beginning as many other asset classes will be tokenized in the future. New business models will emerge, with institutions offering services to manage customer accounts in tokens or providing access to transactions on token exchanges or diverse tokenization platforms. The following Chapters outline the role of Non-fungible Tokens (NFTs) which will be a key aspect to the Web3 economy and the exchange of value.

REFERENCES

Adams, H., Zinsmeister, N., & Robinson, D. (2020). *Unsiwap v2 Core*. https://uniswap.org/whitepaper.pdf

Agarwal, V., Hanouna, P. E., Moussawi, R., & Stahel, C. W. (2018). *Do ETFs increase the commonality in liquidity of underlying stocks?* Working paper, Villanova University.

Akin Gump Strauss Hauer & Feld LLP. (2022). Dubai Passes Landmark Law Regulating Virtual Assets (Including Cryptocurrencies). *JDSUPRA*. https://www.jdsupra.com/legalnews/dubai-passes-landmark-law-regulating-8666988/#:~:text=Dubai%20Passes%20Landmark%20Law%20Regulating%20Virtual%20Assets%20(Including%20Cryptocurrencies),-Sahar%20Abas%2C%20Mazen&text=On%20February%2028%2C%202022%2C%20Sheikh,"Virtual%20Assets%20Law"

Alzarouni, M. [@drmarwan]. (2022, June). *The idea of regulations is actually thinking of possibilities, not limitations* [Tweet]. Twitter. https://twitter.com/khaleejtimes/status/1543146246000578565

Antoniewicz, R. S., & Heinrichs, J. (2014). Understanding exchange-traded funds: How ETFs work. ICI Research Perspective, 20, 11–13.

Apolline, B. (2019). *Global Cryptoasset Regulatory Landscape Study*. Cambridge Centre for Alternative Finance.

Aydar, M., Cetin, S. C., Ayvaz, S., & Aygun, B. (2019). *Private key encryption and recovery in Blockchain*. doi:10.48550/arxiv.1907.04156

Barbon, A., & Ranaldo, A. (2022). *On The Quality Of Cryptocurrency Markets: Centralized Versus Decentralized Exchanges*. Retrieved 21 July 2022, from https://arxiv.org/pdf/2112.07386.pdf

Baydakova, A. (2019). *IBM Completes Blockchain Trial Tracking a 28-Ton Shipment of Oranges*. CoinDesk. https://www.coindesk.com/markets/2019/02/01/ibm-completes-blockchain-trial-tracking-a-28-ton-shipment-of-oranges/

Ben-David, I., Franzoni, F., & Moussawi, R. (2012). Hedge fund stock trading in the ðnancial crisis of 2007–2009. *Review of Financial Studies*, 25(1), 1–54. doi:10.1093/rfs/hhr114

Blocher, J., & Whaley, R. E. (2016). *Two-sided markets in asset management: exchange-traded funds and securities lending.* Working paper, Vanderbilt University.

Bradley, H. S., & Litan, R. E. (2010). *Choking the recovery: Why new growth companies aren't going public and unrecognized risks of future market disruptions.* Working paper, Ewing Marion Kauffman Foundation.

Bradley, H. S., & Litan, R. E. (2011). *ETFs and the present danger to capital formation.* Working paper, Ewing Marion Kauffman Foundation.

BurstI. Q. (2022). *Home Page.* https://burstiq.com/get-started/

Cap, C. (2022). *Cryptocurrency Prices, Charts, And Market Capitalizations | CoinMarketCap.* Retrieved 3 August 2022, from https://coinmarketcap.com/

Coin, L. (2022). Retrieved 7 August 2022, from https://litecoin.com/en/

Cosper, A. (2019). *Buried Treasures: One startup's story of tokens, sunken ships, robots, and intrigue.* Creative Business Network. https://cbnet.com/2019/04/15/po8/?amp

Deville, L., Gresse, C., & de Séverac, B. (2014). Direct and indirect effects of index ETFs on spot-futures pricing and liquidity: Evidence from the CAC 40 index. *European Financial Management*, 20(2), 352–373. doi:10.1111/j.1468-036X.2011.00638.x

Dewan, N. (2008). *Indian Life and Health Insurance Industry.* Gabler. doi:10.1007/978-38349-9788-3

Dlamini, N. (2017). *Development of an SMS system used to access Bitcoin wallets. In IST-Africa Week Conference.* IEEE.

Dorit, R., & Adi, S. (2013). Quantitative Analysis of the Full Bitcoin Transaction Graph. In *Financial Cryptography and Data Security - 17th International Conference, FC 2013, Okinawa, Japan, April 1-5, Revised Selected Papers. Lecture Notes in Computer Science* (vol. 7859, pp. 6-24). Springer.

EncrypGen. (2021). *Home Page.* https://encrypgen.com

Exchange, T. P. X. (2019). *Real estate: The ultimate asset that you can now own and trade.* https://www.tpx-london.io

FATF. (2022). *Home Page.* https://www.fatf-gafi.org

Foucault, T., Kozhan, R., & Tham, W. (2017). Toxic Arbitrage. *Review of Financial Studies, 30*(4), 1053–1094. doi:10.1093/rfs/hhw103

Frank, T. (2020). *Paul Tudor Jones calls bitcoin a 'great speculation,' says he has almost 2% of his assets in it.* Retrieved 7 August 2022, from https://www.cnbc.com/2020/05/11/paul-tudor-jones-calls-bitcoin-a-great-speculation-says-he-has-almost-2percent-of-his-assets-in-it.html

Fries, T. (2018). *JPMorgan to Tokenize Gold Bars.* The Tokenist. https://tokenist.com/jpmorgan-to-tokenize-gold-bars/

Fries, T. (2021). *JPMorgan to Tokenize Gold Bars.* The Tokenist. https://tokenist.com/jpmorgan-to-tokenize-gold-bars/

Fry, J. (2022). *#digitalbytes In 2021, the Collins Dictionary declared 'NFT' (Non-Fungible Token) its word of the year. NFT joined 'metaverse' and 'crypto', making three of the top ten words in the Collin* [LinkedIn]. https://www.linkedin.com/posts/jonnyfry_2022-predictions-and-thoughts-activity-6884541506393313280-9oR4/

Gecko, C. (2022). *Cryptocurrency Prices, Charts, and Crypto Market Cap | CoinGecko.* Retrieved 7 August 2022, from https://www.coingecko.com/

Gentilal, M. (2017). TrustZone-backed bitcoin wallet. *Proceedings of the Fourth Workshop on Cryptography and Security in Computing Systems,* 25–28. 10.1145/3031836.3031841

Global, U. (2022). *The Economy of Everything Will Be Powered by Tokenized Physical Assets.* Coinmonks. Medium. https://medium.com/coinmonks/the-economy-of-everything-will-be-powered-by-tokenized-physical-assets-f7255bc00398

Global Blockchain Convergence. (2021). *Creating Organic Opportunities for Collaboration Across the Blockchain Tech Stack.* https://globalbc.io

Green Digital Finance Alliance. (2021). *The world's first green fintech taxonomy.* https://greendigitalfinancealliance.org/a-green-fintech-taxonomy-and-data-landscaping/

Hamm, S. J. W. (2014). *The effect of ETFs on stock liquidity.* Working paper, Tulane University.

Horst, L., Choo, K. K. R., & Le-Khac, N. A. (2017). Process memory investigation of the Bitcoin Clients Electrum and Bitcoin Core. *IEEE Access*, 22385–22398. doi:10.1109/ACCESS.2017.275976

Insights, C. B. (2021). *How Blockchain Is Disrupting Insurance.* https://www.cbinsights.com/research/blockchain-insurance-disruption/

Insights, L. (2021). *NBA's Dinwiddie talks about tokenizing personalities on Blockchain.* https://www.ledgerinsights.com/nbas-dinwiddie-talks-about-tokenizing-personalities-on-blockchain/

International, F. (2022). *Fnality International.* Retrieved 7 August 2022, from https://www.fnality.org/home

Iredale, G. (2021). *How Tokenization Of Physical Assets Enables The Economy Of Everything?* Blockchain 101. https://101blockchains.com/tokenization/

Irrera, A. (2020). *S&P Dow Jones Indices to launch cryptocurrency indexes in 2021.* Retrieved 7 August 2022, from https://www.reuters.com/article/cryptocurrencies-sp/sp-dow-jones-indices-to-launch-cryptocurrency-indexes-in-2021-idUSL1N2IJ0TG

Israeli, D., Lee, C., & Sridharan, S. (2017). Is there a dark side to exchange traded funds? An information perspective. *Review of Accounting Studies*, *22*(3), 1048–1083. doi:10.100711142-017-9400-8

James, M. (2022). *How blockchain technology is transforming climate action.* Investments. Bulgarian Financial Investment Agency (BFIA). https://www.bfia.org/2022/04/09/how-blockchain-technology-is-transforming-climate-action/

Jenny. (2021). *What Is An Emerging Art Market?* Nomad Salon. https://www.thenomadsalon.com/post/what-is-an-emerging-art-market

Johnson, B. (2022). *How Actively and Passively Managed Funds Performed: Year-End 2018.* Retrieved 3 August 2022, from https://www.morningstar.com/insights/2019/02/12/active-passive-funds

Kaushal, P. (2017). Evolution of bitcoin and security risk in bitcoin wallets. *Computer, Communications and Electronics (Comptelix), International Conference on*, 172–177. 10.1109/COMPTELIX.2017.8003959

Khaleej Times [@khaleejtimes]. (2022, June). *"The idea of regulations is actually thinking of possibilities, not limitations," said @drmarwan, founder, CEO - #DubaiBlockchainCenter and Managing Partner at #AccellianceBuilder's tribe at the #MetaDecrypt Web 3.0 Summit.* Twitter.

Khedkar, A. (2022). *Exchange Traded Funds (ETF) Global Investment.* https:// ashokakhedkar.com/blog/exchange-traded-funds-etf-global-investment/

Learn, C. (2022). *How to set up a crypto wallet.* Retrieved 3 August 2022, from https://www.coinbase.com/learn/tips-and-tutorials/how-to-set-up-a-crypto-wallet

Lettau, M., & Madhavan, A. (2018). Exchange-traded funds 101 for economists. *The Journal of Economic Perspectives, 32*(1), 135–153. doi:10.1257/jep.32.1.135

Liebi, L. J. (2020). The effect of ETFs on financial markets: A literature review. *Financial Markets and Portfolio Management, 34*(2), 165–178. doi:10.100711408-020-00349-1

Lielacher, A. (2022). *Best Crypto Exchanges.* Retrieved 3 August 2022, from https://www.investopedia.com/best-crypto-exchanges-5071855

Mann, C., & Loebenberger, D. (2017). Two-factor authentication for the Bitcoin protocol. *International Journal of Information Security, 16*(2), 213–226. doi:10.100710207-016-0325-1

MarketplaceE. (n.d.). *Carbon Hub.* https://www.ecosystemmarketplace.com/carbon-markets/

MarksMan Healthcare. (2022). *Tokenization in Real World Evidence Studies: What and Why?* Data Privacy. https://marksmanhealthcare.com/tokenization-in-real-world-evidence-studies-what-and-why/

Marta, T. J., & Joseph, B. (2010). *Forex Analysis and Trading: Effective Top-down Strategies Combining Fundamental, Position, and Technical Analyses.* John Wiley & Sons.

Montanez, A. (2014). *Investigation of cryptocurrency wallets on iOS and Android mobile devices for potential forensic artifacts. Dept. Forensic Sci., Marshall Univ.* Tech. Rep.

Morgan, J. (2022). *Liink | Onyx by J.P. Morgan.* Retrieved 7 August 2022, from https://www.jpmorgan.com/onyx/liink

Nathaniel, P. (2016). *Digital Gold: Bitcoin and the Inside Story of the Misfits and Millionaires Trying to Reinvent Money*. Harper.

News Desk. (2019). *Liquefy security token platform aims to tokenize real-estate in MENA*. Unlock Media. https://www.unlock-bc.com/news/2019-07-22/liquefy-security-token-platform-aims-to-tokenize-real-estate-in-mena

Nicola, V. D., Longo, R., Mazzone, F., & Russo, G. (2020). Resilient Custody of Crypto-Assets, and Threshold Multi signatures. *Mathematics, 8*(10), 1–17. https://EconPapers.repec.org/RePEc:gam:jmathe:v:8:y:2020:i:10:p:1773-:d:427729

Pagnotta, E., & Buraschi, A. (2021). *An Equilibrium Valuation of Bitcoin and Decentralized Network Assets*. Retrieved 21 July 2022, from https://papers.ssrn.com/sol3/papers.cfm?abstract_id=3142022

Peterson, B. (2017). *Thieves stole potentially millions of dollars in bitcoin in a hacking attack on a cryptocurrency company*. Retrieved 21 July 2022, from https://www.businessinsider.com/nicehash-bitcoin-wallet-hacked-contents-stolen-in-security-breach-2017-12

Powerledger. (n.d.). *The Power Behind New Energy*. https://www.powerledger.io

Prophecy Market Insights. (2022). *Global Real Estate Tokenization Market is estimated to grow with a significant CAGR during the forecast period - By PMI*. https://www.globenewswire.com/en/news-release/2022/03/10/2400892/0/en/Global-Real-Estate-Tokenization-Market-is-estimated-to-grow-with-a-significant-CAGR-during-the-forecast-period-By-PMI.html

Protocol, U. (2018). *Every Asset Class will be Digitized and Tokenized*. https://www.universalprotocol.io

Rebecca, M. (2018). *International Approaches to Digital Currencies*. Congressional Research Service. https://crsreports.congress.gov/

Riddle & Code. (2018). *We're Building the Tretyakov Gallery's Blockchain-Powered App to Bring Art Patronage to a New Level*. Medium. https://medium.com/riddle-code/were-building-the-tretyakov-gallery-s-blockchain-powered-app-to-bring-art-patronage-to-a-new-level-d3c2d6602b81

Satoshi, N. (2018). *Bitcoin: A Peer-to-Peer Electronic Cash System*. https://bitcoin.org/bitcoin.pdf

Scale, G. (2022). *Grayscale*. Retrieved 7 August 2022, from https://grayscale.com/

Schneider, L. A., Channing, E., Garcia, J., Ho, J., Patchay, J., Pike, E., Saunders, W., & Thomason, D. J. (2021). *A Sensible Token Classification System*. Novum insights. https://novuminsights.com/post/sensible-token-classification-system/

Securities and Exchange Commission. (2017). *Company Halts ICO After SEC Raises Registration Concerns*. https://www.sec.gov/news/press-release/2017-227

Services Group. (n.d.). *Tokenization*. http://www.bullservices.co.za/#tokenization

Seth, S. (2022). *Technical Analysis Strategies for Beginners*. Retrieved 22 July 2022, from https://www.investopedia.com/articles/active-trading/102914/technical-analysis-strategies-beginners.asp

Shawn, T. (2018). The NYSE's Owner Wants to Bring Bitcoin to Your 401(k). Are Crypto Credit Cards Next? *Fortune*. https://fortune.com/longform/nyse-owner-bitcoin-exchangestartup

Solstroem. (n.d.). *The CO_2 avoidance programme for off-grid solar*. https://www.solstroem.com

Staff, E. (2022). *ETF League Table As Of 24 February, 2021*. Retrieved 3 August 2022, from https://www.etf.com/sections/etf-league-tables/etf-league-table-2021-02-24

Statista. (2020). *Insurance*. https://www.statista.com/markets/414/topic/461/insurance/#statistic2

Sun, C. (2022). *Financial Institutions Move Closer to Realizing a Blockchain Solution for Syndicated Loans*. Retrieved 7 August 2022, from https://www.credit-suisse.com/about-us-news/en/articles/media-releases/financial-institutions-move-closer-to-realizing-a-blockchain-solution-for-syndicated-loans-201703.html

Suresh, A. S. (2013). A study on fundamental and technical analysis. *International Journal of Marketing, Financial Services & Management Research, 2*(5), 44–59.

Technology, R. (2022). *Renaissance*. Retrieved 7 August 2022, from https://www.rentec.com/Home.action?index=true

Thomason, D. J. (2022). *Web 3 and tokenization of everything*. Medium. https://medium.com/coinmonks/web-3-and-tokenisation-of-everything-19b53d4ca535

Times, T. (2022). *Terrorists Turn to Bitcoin for Funding, and They're Learning Fast (Published 2019)*. Retrieved 22 July 2022, from https://www.nytimes.com/2019/08/18/technology/terrorists-bitcoin.html

Tradestrike. (n.d.). *We'll change the way you trade* [PowerPoint Slides]. StrikeX. https://strikex.com/wp-content/uploads/2022/07/TradeStrike-Pitch-Deck.pdf

TransActive Grid. (n.d.). *New Grid on the Block*. http://www.solutionsandco.org/project/transactive-grid/

US Energy Media. (2022). Benefits of Tokenization in Energy Business. *Energies Magazine*. https://energiesmagazine.com/benefits-of-tokenization-in-energy-business/

Vaughan, E. J. (1996). *Risk Management*. https://www.amazon.co.uk/Risk-Management-Emmett-JVaughan/dp/047110759X

Volety, T. (2018). Cracking Bitcoin wallets: I want what you have in the wallets. *Future Generation Computer Systems*. Advance online publication. doi:10.1016/j.future.2018.08.029

Weng, I. (2022). *Linking RWE to Clinical Trials*. Komodo. https://www.komodohealth.com/insights/linking-rwe-to-clinical-trials

Werbach, K. (2016). *Trustless Trust*. SSRN Electronic Journal. doi:10.2139srn.2844409

XRP. (2022). *XRP - Digital Asset for Global Economic Utility | Ripple*. Retrieved 7 August 2022, from https://ripple.com/xrp/

Chapter 7
Introduction to NFTs

ABSTRACT

Non-fungible tokens (NFTs) have been making the news since an NFT for a piece of digital art by the artist Beeple (Mike Winkelmann) sold for $69 million in March 2021. Regulators and lawyers have been scrambling to understand the legal issues surrounding NFTs, not to mention the meaning and value proposition of this novel class of digital assets for online marketplaces and digital content developers. According to GlobeNewsWire, the global NFT market size is expected to grow from USD 3.0 billion in 2022 to USD 13.6 billion by 2027. An NFT is a unique digital asset. This chapter discusses NFTs; their characteristics; how to buy, sell, and mint NFTs; and some key legal and regulatory issues.

INTRODUCTION

A key element of Web 3.0 is NFTs. Non-Fungible Tokens (NFTs) are digital assets representing tangible things such as art, music, in-game items, and movies. They are purchased and sold online, frequently using cryptocurrency. NFTs are generated through a process called "minting." Once an NFT has been minted, it may be bought, sold, or traded. Even if a copy of the underlying file is created, the ownership record cannot be updated without the existing owner's consent. The complex technology allows for records to be protected as digital assets - by prohibiting a token from being duplicated and used in multiple transactions.

DOI: 10.4018/978-1-6684-6658-2.ch007

Before the invention of NFTs, virtual items could easily be duplicated. Thus, the ERC-721 token standard introduces the ability to connect digital or physical items to an ERC-721 token (NFT). NFTs are a way to create a digitally scarce item that cannot be copied or tampered with. CryptoKitties were introduced in late 2017 as a game centered around breedable and collectible virtual pets called CryptoKitties. Each pet was represented by an ERC 721 token: distinct, unable to be replicated, taken away, or destroyed. In late 2017, CryptoKitties transactions accounted for more than 10% of Ethereum traffic in early December 2017 (Jiang & Liu, 2021).

NFTs use blockchain technology to represent ownership, making them more comparable to a car title than the actual vehicle. To understand how NFTs function, understanding what it means for something to be "fungible" is necessary. If an asset is fungible, it can be swapped for another of the same type without depreciation. For instance, if a one-dollar bill is exchanged, it is still worth one dollar. NFTs are one-of-a-kind, or at least one of minimal runs, and have unique identifying codes. This is in stark contrast to the great majority of digital products, which are almost always available in an infinite supply, and theoretically, if an asset is in high demand, reducing its supply should improve its value (Kong & Lin, 2021). Additionally, asset ownership that has been tokenized into an NFT is more quickly and efficiently transferable between people worldwide (Ante, 2021).

In recent times, NFTs are rapidly gaining attraction for a multiplicity of uses, and according to GlobeNewsWire, the global NFT market size is expected to grow from USD 3.0 billion in 2022 to USD 13.6 billion by 2027 (ReportLinker, 2022). Many NFTs have been digital works that already exist in some form elsewhere, such as legendary video clips from NBA games or securitized copies of digital art that are already circulating on Instagram, at least in the early stages of the cryptocurrency's existence. While individual shots or the entire image collage can be seen online for free, an NFT confers ownership of the original object to the purchaser. It also has built-in authentication that serves as proof of ownership.

Token creation allows for the creation of a token on a network. The Ethereum network enables participants to issue assets on a Blockchain using the Ethereum protocol, and this process was introduced in the ERC-20 standard on Ethereum (Vogelsteller & Buterin, 2019). The standard introduced and provided an interface for tokens, establishing the transfer function and allowing tokens to be approved for use by another on-chain third party. Other blockchain platforms for issuing tokens exist. However, the Ethereum blockchain is the most secure and popular way to create an NFT today (Lantz & Cawrey, D. 2020).

In creating tokens, it is crucial to discern whether they are fungible or non-fungible. The concept of fungible tokens was introduced in the ERC 20 standard, and the concept of NFTs was introduced in the ERC 721 token standard. ERC721 is a standard for representing ownership of non-fungible or non-interchangeable tokens. In other words, this type of token is unique and may have a different value than other tokens of the same smart contract due to age, rarity, or appearance. ERC721 is a more complex standard than ERC20, including various optional extensions and contracts. Since the inception of ERC-721 introducing the concept of NFTs, other token standards, which are derivatives of ERC-721, now exist, such as ERC-1155 and ERC 4907.

ERC-1155 Token Standard

In 2019, The ERC-1155 token standard was developed as a combination of the ERC-20 and ERC-721 standards to focus on blockchain-based solutions for video games. The token standard was introduced by Enjin (2022), who considered the ERC 721 NFT standard as limiting and rigid, primarily due to the inability to perform batch transfers. The ERC-1155 standard permits batch transfers of many assets on a single, smart contract, resulting in the transfer of all tokens simultaneously, resulting in a less congested network and lower gas costs. When a user tries to sell a thousand items to another user in a game, for instance, the user can utilize the batch token transfer feature of ERC-1155 to transmit them all at once (Ante, 2021).

This multi-token standard can accommodate both fungible and NFTs. A fungible token may be used with an address to perform in-game payments and transfer NFT assets. ERC-1155 also permits the creation of Semi-Fungible Tokens (SFTs), an important feature. SFTs are fungible tokens that can be traded, but when redeemed, they transform into NFTs. A ticket to a concert is a fungible asset.

In contrast, the ticket loses its resale value after the performance and becomes unique memorabilia. SFTs include this feature directly in the code of the ticket. Finally, token transfers based on this standard can be reversed in error. According to the ERC-721 standard, assets sent to an incorrect address cannot be recovered- in contrast, the ERC-1155 standard provides a function that addresses this. The safe transfer function and a variety of additional controls are in place.

ERC-4907 Token Standard: A Rentable Token

ERC-4907 introduces a rentable NFT standard as an extension of EIP-721, which proposes an additional role for users, which can be granted to addresses, and a time when that role is automatically revoked or reaches expiration. The role granted to users is much like renting; therefore, it is permitted to use the NFT but not the ability to transfer it or set users, which is reserved for the actual owner. This standard effectively captures the need for the possibility that an owner and user can sometimes be different, especially given the many use cases for NFTs. It is logical to have separate roles identifying whether an address represents an "owner" or a "user" and managing permissions to perform actions accordingly.

The ERC-4907 standard is necessary because of how easily it assigns rights. With dual roles in place for bankable assets, for instance, it becomes easier to manage what lenders and borrowers can and cannot do with the NFT or their rights. The ERC-4907 standard also assists in tidying. The chain, as the concept of rentable NFTs, creates on-chain time management, at which point the expiration of the rental period, the user role is reset, and the "user" loses access to the right to use the NFT. Before the introduction of the ERC-4907, a second on-chain transaction would have been carried out, which could be more scalable and gas efficient and, in most cases, leads to complications due to imprecision on-chain. The ERC-4907 standard, by introducing the expiration function, essentially removes the need for a second on-chain transaction, as the "user" is automatically invalidated upon the expiration of the role. Therefore, there is no need for the production of another transaction to carry out a transaction already done.

The ERC-4907 standard additionally facilitates permissionless interoperability and easy third-party integration for other protocols, as other blockchain protocols can manage NFT to adopt a user role and get usage rights without permission from the NFT issuer or the NFT application (Anders et al., 2022).

CHARACTERISTICS OF NFTs

NFTs capabilities include moving tokens from one account to another, obtaining the current token balance of an account, determining the owner of a particular token, and determining the total amount of a token available on the network. NFTs also allow for the authorization of transfers of a specified number of tokens from one account to another, as well as transferability between accounts and exchanges for other digital assets. NFTs also enable the determination of an object's owner throughout the chain. Some of the qualities that make NFTs very dynamic include: (i) Uniqueness: Each NFT has unique characteristics that are frequently included in the token information, as no two NFTs are identical; (ii) Scarcity: NFTs are digitally scarce, which drive their value.; and (iii) Indivisibility: NFTs cannot be divided into smaller amounts, and fractions cannot be purchased or traded.

The long-term value of NFTs is heavily influenced by uniqueness, scarcity, indivisibility, and community. Blockchain technology guarantees an NFT's unique and unreplaceable trait, ensuring scarcity and the demand for NFTs are driven by this blockchain-guaranteed scarcity, which confers value.

Minting NFTs

As discussed earlier, tokens can be issued or "minted" on multiple Blockchains, but Ethereum is singlehandedly the most accessible and most secure medium for token creation. Despite Ethereums attributes, ERC 721 tokens can be issued on other blockchains, as Cardano, Ethereum, and Solana (Vasile, 2022) is the most prevalent (Owie, 2022).

Minting refers to the creation of a new asset. The process is used to increase token supply. Minting an NFT entails changing digital data into cryptographic collections or digital assets on a blockchain. The digital products or files will be stored in a distributed ledger or decentralized database and will be unmodifiable, immutable, and non-erasable. The NFT creators can arrange royalties from each subsequent sale throughout the printing process, which they can collect whenever their work is resold or traded on the secondary market.

When an NFT is minted, it must be confirmed as an asset on the Blockchain (Ethereum, Solana, Cardano, etc.), as the ownership of the token is transferred to the owner's wallet via their public address. The owner or user's account or wallet must reflect the NFT as an asset. This step contributes to one of the upsides of NFTs, which is the ease of proving ownership, as proof of ownership of an Ethereum NFT is similar to the proof of ownership of Ethereum in the user's wallet. A user's NFT token proves that the user's copy of the digital file is the original, and the public key serves as a certificate of authenticity for the digital art and permanent historical data of the token, immortalized on the chain (Use Ethereum, 2022). The owner's public key demonstrates that the NFT was created by the owner, which contributes to the NFT's market value and sets it aside from a counterfeit NFT.

The processes that ensure proof of ownership on-chain are made possible by block producers and validators who add NFT transactions to the block and broadcast it on the chain. Much like other blockchain processes, the validators are incentivized to check that the transaction is valid and then add it to the block, which curbs fraudulent transfer of ownership.

How to Store an NFT

In the same way, physical tokens store value in a wallet. The same is the case for an NFT. For distributed ledger technology, a wallet is like a keychain that holds private keys. Each key is associated with a public key address, which lets the owner prove to the network that they are indeed the owner of the tokens associated with that public key address. In theory, wallets do not hold tokens but keys. The concept of wallets can be thought of as holding the keys (private) to the owner's money or the token's residence. A user may have various addresses owned by one key.

NFTs are stored on the Blockchain's network, not in the user's wallet. In reality, the transaction is stored in the wallet, and what is being traded is not coins or tokens but ownership of the tokens, which can be traced to when it was mined. For instance, if User J transfers tokens to User L on the network, a search is carried out backwards to see if User J received enough coins or tokens in the past even to carry out a transfer to L. There is no account balance like a bank account, just a list of token debits and credit historical data.

Users may explore various wallet options, from Paper and Hardware wallets which are non-custodial (not hosted by an exchange or other third parties), where a user becomes their bank, to custodial wallets like software wallets (hosted by third parties or exchanges). A hardware wallet is a physical wallet, much like a hard drive but comes in various forms. A Ledger is a hardware wallet capable of holding a variety of tokens, including NFTs. If a significant amount of money in NFTs is to be invested, a secure means to protect the funds is using a hardware wallet. A software wallet is an application-based wallet, which can be mobile or desktop. MetaMask is a decentralized application built on Ethereum. It allows a browser to interact with blockchain technology without running a node and for users using a browser to connect with Ethereum dApps through their browsers. It is a digital asset wallet and gateway to Blockchain applications. Users can buy, store, send, and swap tokens as a browser extension. As a mobile application, MetaMask provides users with a key vault, secure login, token wallet, and token exchange, all the tools required to manage the users' digital assets.

Currently, the NFT ecosystem and investors face attacks and hacks due to the widespread use of software wallets. Software wallets lack the same security protections that hardware wallets afford. Authors argue that paper and hardware non-custodial wallets are more suited for storing digital assets (Mackay, 2019). Evaluation of Security in Hardware and Software Cryptocurrency Wallets). These arguments are based on ownership, where non-custodial ownership of private keys belongs to the user, and custodial ownership is technically the property of the third party or exchange. Despite the security of hardware wallets, software wallets are much more accessible at any time, which in terms of convenience, prevails over paper and hardware wallets. Ultimately, the decision on forms of wallets to store an NFT should be based on security.

NFT MARKETPLACES

An NFT marketplace is a digital platform for buying and selling NFTs. Much like an Exchange is for the trade of fungible tokens, an NFT marketplace enables users to store, sell, trade, and display their NFTs for digital assets. An NFT may also be minted on a marketplace, depending on the platform. Similar to dEx's, in exchange for a fee, an NFT marketplace facilitates the transfer of an NFT from one party to the other. A crucial consideration before an NFT minting is deciding on its designated NFT marketplace. There are many NFT platforms, but the prevalent ones include OpenSea, Rarible, Binance, and NiftyGateway.

OpenSea

OpenSea is a marketplace for NFTs built on Ethereum. Users can exchange NFTs for Bitcoin via network interaction. It contains a vast assortment of digital artifacts, including video games and digital works of art. The platform requires a web3 digital wallet, such as MetaMask. Some services, like as OpenSea, use the Ethereum wallet address as the login and password (Valeonti et al., 2021). OpenSea requires an Ethereum wallet for registration.

The user must download MetaMask, generate a wallet, and send purchased ETH to the wallet.

Rarible

The Rarible NFT marketplace permits customers to purchase and hold or sell tokens for profit. Several sorts of tokens are available for purchase on the website. Among the categories are art, photography, gaming, metaverses, music, domains, and DeFi (Kong & Lin, 2022). The Rarible platform enables users to earn royalties on purchasing and selling NFTs, giving the potential for a passive revenue stream. When tokens are purchased on Rarible, users are rewarded with RARI tokens, which grant users platform governance privileges.

RISKS AND CHALLENGES

Fees (Gas Price)

One significant challenge for NFTs has been the fees. The rise of NFTs comes with the increase in the price of mandatory transaction fees (gas fees). This challenge serves as one of the barriers to entry for the mainstream adoption of NFTs. Much like other transactions on the Ethereum blockchain, NFTs require minting, which can be expensive regardless of the NFT platform the NFT is listed. The cost of minting and trading NFTs essentially discourages users from minting their NFTS on Ethereum. However, other alternatives exist as a solution to this problem. For instance, minting on Solana (n.d.) negates the need to pay high transaction prices, as some gas fees are as low as under a cent. These low gas fees have led to increased adoption of the Solana blockchain. Low gas fees and ease of use drive adoption for Solana.

Storage

Art requires storage, and the best way to store NFT data is through a token Uniform Resource Indicator (URI). Pictures are hosted on an Interplanetary File System (IPFS), and the URI is linked to this. Before a purchase occurs, the token attributes may need to be viewed. Therefore, users will have to refer to the metadata for information relating to imagery, such as, e.g., colors, shapes, etc. NFTs were designed to exist in perpetuity on the Blockchain. However, due to frequent cost and storage capacity limits on the Blockchain, only the ownership record, including metadata linked to the original NFT content, is kept. Consumers are directed to a URL (through the HTTP protocol) rather than a particular piece of content via these links. It implies that the information referenced by the link could alter or disappear at any time, resulting in the irreversible loss of original assets (Wang et al., 2021).

Due to the necessity to store and preserve off-chain NFT data, IPFS was created and deployed (Interplanetary File System). IPFS can aid in eliminating these issues and ensuring the long-term accessibility and availability of NFT data on a decentralized network. It employs a peer-to-peer edition filesystem and hypermedia protocol to store and retrieve data. IPFS could uniquely identify each file in a global namespace for NFTs to merge the NFT metadata for the stored digital asset with the content addressing capabilities. In contrast to centralized systems such as Dropbox or Google Drive, IPFS provides more permanent data pinning (Singh, 2021). IPFS enables decentralized data storage and retrieval, enabling the long-term preservation of NFT metadata.

NFTs and Intellectual Property (IP)

Okonkwo (2019) states that digital inventions are usually associated with several intellectual property issues. Assessing the concept of (IP) should be a significant avenue for future research, especially about the risks and obstacles it poses for NFTs. The important subtopics that can be covered are the evaluation of ownership rights to a certain NFT and determining whether a seller genuinely possesses the NFT before purchasing. As Sharma et al. (2016) explained, there have been several instances of someone photographing NFTs or minting reproductions of NFTs. As a result, when an NFT is purchased, the owner gets the rights to utilize it only but not the rights for intellectual property. As celebrities endorse NFTs, a massive market hype bubble surrounds them, and the trading volume of NFTs has surged. However, little or no literature provides intellectual property restrictions for the trade of NFTs. This work is needed.

Environmental Impact

The amount of electricity used for mining Bitcoins is easily comparable to that of countries like Malaysia and Sweden (Goldberg et al., 2021). Before the Ethereum Merge, Ethereum was estimated to use 44.94 terawatt-hours of electricity per year, nearly equivalent to the annual power consumption of countries such as Qatar and Hungary (Popescu, 2021). The Merge reduced Ethereum's annualized electricity consumption by more than 99.988%. Likewise, Ethereum's carbon footprint was decreased by approximately 99.992%. According to a recent study by (Fesenfeld et al., 2018), if blockchain-based technologies become as widely adopted as other new technologies, they could push the Earth's temperature two degrees Celsius above historical levels. The above are the detrimental environmental impacts that have resulted from the creation of transactions involving NFTs and other digital assets. At the same time, NFTs encourage digital art creation. For painters and similar designers, the growth and predominance of NFTs would translate to a reduction in the use of canvas prints, paper, nylon, and other materials that substantially harm the environment. Exploring the possibilities to minimize pollution through NFTs is an option for future research.

Wash Trading

Wash trading, or the practice of the same person buying and selling the same NFTs and artificially inflating the price, has been a problem, according to Chainalys. They reported 262 users who had sold NFTs to a self-financed address more than 25 times.

Money Laundering

Money laundering is a risk with NFTs. A money launderer may create two accounts on an NFT marketplace. One can auction an art NFT, and the other is used to purchase the asset, thus moving illegal funds to another wallet as legitimate purchases.

Legal Issues

As with other digital assets, NFTs have no specific jurisdiction, and it is unclear what jurisdictional legal requirements may apply. The legal recognition of proof of ownership of NFTs is not yet evident in many jurisdictions. Other legal issues relate to copyright protection, which law still needs to establish. The legal fraternity is working on defining the key issues and creating legal certainty for NFT purchasers.

CONCLUSION

This chapter has provided a detailed introduction to NFTs, defining NFTs as digital assets generated through minting, capable of representing arts, video games, and several tangible items. NFTs are Blockchain-based digital assets that can be swapped for others without depreciating. Several token standards exist based on their operation mode and capability to accommodate. Since ERC-721 originally introduced NFTs, other token standard developments, such as ERC-1155, have been developed to provide blockchain solutions for video games; the standard can accommodate fungible and nontangible tokens. ERC-4907 was also developed to modify ERC-721 because it quickly assigns roles and allows users to rent NFTs (Use NFTs without being able to transfer them). The characteristics of NFTs are also discussed, including their capabilities to transfer tokens from different accounts, determine token owners and discover the token balance existing in a network. These characteristics also include the qualities of NFTs as being unique, scarce, and indivisible. Minting NFTs involve a cryptographic conversion of digital data to be stored on an unmodifiable, immutable, and non-erasable distributed ledger, after which it must be confirmed as an asset on the Blockchain.

The chapter also covers NFT marketplaces such as Open Sea, Crypto. com, Rarible, and Binance. This chapter has identified several challenges with NFTs, particularly the dangers of losing an NFT's private encryption key and the costs associated with distributing massive amounts of data to the Blockchain. Recommendations such as uploading NFTs to the IPFS platform were made to counter these challenges.

Increased exposure and added benefits have been created for aspiring artists, established artists, and several other classes of creatives by NFTs. The potential positives that NFTs could provide are endless and would represent a more significant part of the digital economy in the coming years. It is essential to treat NFTs as any other investment: dedicated research should be carried out to understand the dangers while factoring in the possibility that money invested could be lost. The next chapter further elaborates on the NFT use cases.

REFERENCES

Anders, Lance, & Shrug. (2022, March 11). EIP-4907: Rental NFT, an Extension of EIP-721. *Ethereum Improvement Proposals*. https://eips.ethereum.org/EIPS/eip-4907

Ante, L. (2021). The Non-Fungible Token (NFT) Market and Its Relationship with Bitcoin and Ethereum. *SSRN Electronic Journal*. https://papers.ssrn.com/sol3/papers.cfm?abstract_id=3861106

Browne, R. (2022, March 10). *Trading in NFTs spiked 21,000% to more than $17 billion in 2021, report says.* CNBC. https://www.cnbc.com/2022/03/10/trading-in-nfts-spiked-21000percent-to-top-17-billion-in-2021-report.html

Enjin. (2022). *Home Page.* https://enjin.io/

Fesenfeld, L. P., Schmidt, T. S., & Schrode, A. (2018). Climate policy for short-and long-lived pollutants. *Nature Climate Change, 8*(11), 933–936. doi:10.103841558-018-0328-1

Goldberg, M., Kugler, P., & Schär, F. (2021). *The economics of blockchain-based virtual worlds: A hedonic regression model for virtual land.* Available at SSRN 3932189.

Jiang, X.-J., & Liu, X. F. (2021). CryptoKitties Transaction Network Analysis: The Rise and Fall of the First Blockchain Game Mania. *Frontiers in Physics, 9*, 631665. doi:10.3389/fphy.2021.631665

Kong, D. R., & Lin, T. C. (2021). Alternative investments in the Fintech era: The risk and return of Non-Fungible Token (NFT). *Available at SSRN 3914085.*

Lantz, L., & Cawrey, D. (2020). *Mastering Blockchain.* O'Reilly Media.

Mackay, B. (2019). Evaluation of Security in Hardware and Software Cryptocurrency Wallets. School of Computing Edinburgh, Napier University.

Okonkwo, I.E. (2019). *Valuation of Intellectual Property: Prospects for African Countries.* Paper submitted in partial fulfilment of the mini-dissertation in LLM, University of Cape Town.

Owie, B. (2022). NFTs Enter A New Era As Solana Closes The Gap With Ethereum. *Bitcoinist.* https://bitcoinist.com/solana-closes-the-gap-with-ethereum/

Popescu, A. D. (2021). Non-Fungible Tokens (NFT)–Innovation beyond the craze. *5th International Conference on Innovation in Business, Economics and Marketing Research.*

ReportLinker. (2022, May 13). The global NFT market size is expected to grow from USD 3.0 billion in 2022 to USD 13.6 billion by 2027, at a Compound Annual Growth Rate (CAGR) of 35.0% from 2022 to 2027. *GlobeNews.* https://www.globenewswire.com/news-release/2022/05/13/2442960/0/en/ The-global-NFT-market-size-is-expected-to-grow-from-USD-3-0-billion-in-2022-to-USD-13-6-billion-by-2027-at-a-Compound-Annual-Growth-Rate-CAGR-of-35-0-from-2022-to-2027.html

Sharma, T., Zhou, Z., Huang, Y., & Wang, Y. (2022). *"It's A Blessing and A Curse": Unpacking Creators' Practices with Non-Fungible Tokens (NFTs) and Their Communities.* arXiv preprint arXiv:2201.13233.

Singh, A. K. (2021, July). *An Introductory Guide to IPFS (InterPlanetary File System).* https://www.linkedin.com/pulse/introductory-guide-ipfs-interplanetary-file-system-aman-kumar-singh/.LinkedIn

Solana. (n.d.). *Home Page.* https://rejolut.com/blockchain/solana-nft-marketplace-development/

Use Ethereum. (2022). Non-fungible tokens (NFT). *Ethereum Use Cases.* https://ethereum.org/en/nft/#how-nfts-work

Valeonti, F., Bikakis, A., Terras, M., Speed, C., Hudson-Smith, A., & Chalkias, K. (2021). Crypto collectibles, museum funding and OpenGLAM: Challenges, opportunities and the potential of Non-Fungible Tokens (NFTs). *Applied Sciences (Basel, Switzerland), 11*(21), 9931. doi:10.3390/app11219931

Vasile, I. (2022, July 29). Solana vs. Ethereum: An Ultimate Comparison. *BeInCrypto.* https://beincrypto.com/about/

Vogelsteller, F., & Buterin, V. (2019, November 19). EIP-20: Token Standard. *Ethereum Improvement Proposals.* https://eips.ethereum.org/EIPS/eip-20

Chapter 8
How Are NFTs Being Used?

ABSTRACT

NFTs will have a prominent role in Web 3.0 as a primary means of value exchange, and there is already a proliferation of use cases. NFTs will be used as digital receipts for automating royalty payments, proof of ownership, and fractionalizing assets across various industries. This chapter discusses different practical applications of NFTs in the fashion industry, gaming sector, electoral utilization, ticketing system, regulatory structures, verification of authenticity, medical records, intellectual property, and not-for-profit sector. It also highlights some key risks and regulatory issues.

INTRODUCTION

As outlined in Chapter 7, NFTs are coded with smart contracts that govern aspects such as ownership verification and transferability management of the NFTs. NFTs can also include other applications and functionalities, such as linking the NFT to other digital assets. For example, a smart contract can be written to automatically allot a portion of the amounts paid for any subsequent sale of the NFT back to the initial owner, thus allowing the owner to realize the benefits of the secondary marketplace. Therefore, when Someone makes (or "mints") an NFT, they write the underlying smart contract code that governs the NFT's qualities, which adds to the relevant Blockchain where the NFT is managed (DeNuzzo, 2022).

DOI: 10.4018/978-1-6684-6658-2.ch008

NFTs can represent actual objects, digital content, and even immaterial notions such as intellectual property. NFTs are a means to authenticate digital assets. NFTs attach to images on JPEG files, particularly MP3s, GIFs, videos, or other digital assets, and certify their authenticity and ownership (McDonell, 2021). It establishes provenance, creating a digitized chain of titles. NFTs represent ownership of a specific digital asset and act as a permanent record through its Blockchain of the ownership transfer of that asset.

NFTs essentially are the vehicle to mediate the exchange of digital collectibles. Fundamentally, it is a framework that exists as a computer code to create digital objects that possess the attributes of both physical objects and digital, which is to be transmittable, all while providing uniqueness. Critics argue that the defining characteristic of NFTs, "strict uniqueness and scarcity" (Folding Ideas, 2022), is a way of saying that: two different things are different despite being different copies of the same thing. To this point, critics argue that NFT's claimed functionality (uniqueness and scarcity) is exaggerated and will lead to a slippery slope toward the financialization of any benefits of digital uniqueness. (Folding Ideas, 2022).

Upon inception, towards and after the Covid-19 pandemic, the NFT ecosystem was utilized in every medium possible (Overgaauw, 2020), creating an atmosphere susceptible to rug pulling and overappraisal. This led to questions about NFT content in circulation being sold, valuations, fictitious activities, and Intellectual Property Rights concerns (Gerard, 2021). Intensifying the arguments against NFTs are the circumstances in which artists have ended up losing money due to costs of gas fees and art theft due to there being no way to verify that the creator of the NFT owns the copyrights or is the artist (Abdunabi, 2021). This has fuelled kickback against NFTs (Hovhannisyan, 2021) as platforms built to financialize every corner of social existence. Intellectual Property protection, wash trading, money laundering, and rug pulls remain legitimate concerns. This chapter will discuss different practical applications of NFTs and highlight some key risks and regulatory issues.

THE CREATOR ECONOMY

In the creator economy, NFTs offer the most significant value. In art and music, they offer the opportunity for creators to monetize their content and create ongoing automated royalty streams. The section below outlines the main applications of NFTs in the creator economy.

Art

NFTs create the potential to tokenize artwork and introduce newer and higher levels of identity management to help promote authenticity and secure ownership for the artist. Original works by old masters will soon be able to be marked for tracking through NFTs. It also applies to yet-to-be-created physical pieces of art, which can transform into NFTs, and NFTs can be transformed into physical art while maintaining the digital token. NFTs can also aid in tracing the originality of a particular item and decrease the distribution of fake artwork. It also assures NFT owners that their item is legitimate if they purchased them at auction (Rean, 2022).

Music

Since the emergence of the internet, musicians have struggled with the issue of ownership (Wang et al., 2021). With NFTs, artists can independently publish, copyright, distribute, and interact with fans. Artists can claim ownership of their works by minting audio NFTs, concert tickets, merchandising, and other items through decentralized platforms. NFTs can also assist creators in recovering control over the supply chain and associated master and property rights. NFTs create scarcity in the music industry by granting musicians complete control over how their work is distributed and its associated rights. As a result, NFTs enable musicians to engage with their audiences on a more fundamental and granular level, build communities around them, and have much-improved work performance. Even when NFTs are sold on the secondary market, artists retain all rights to their music and receive a royalty for each NFT transfer, creating a global music market (Kong & Lin, 2022).

Artists such as Akon bypassed his record label and released his upcoming album as an NFT to begin monetizing it in advance. Fans who acquired these items have total openness regarding their purchases' authenticity and provenance. Thus, NFTs allow anyone to acquire property rights to art or music while enabling artists to verify their work outside the traditional music industry. In addition, by permitting audience participation in the musical process, NFTs create new funding opportunities. Fans become investors in the endeavor for a variety of reasons. While some may invest in and acquire

NFTs to collect them, others may do so for speculative reasons, to hold, to earn royalties, or to profit from trading them in secondary NFT Marketplaces. This can benefit artists who have battled with exploitation in some form in acquiring up-front funds without losing their master rights or experiencing substantial revenue reductions. It also permits them to receive a fair share of the profit generated by their accomplishments (Trautman, 2021).

Fans can also purchase shares of the royalties generated by the streamed songs, and token holders will get a part of the revenue as long as the music is being streamed. Asset tokenization enables a large number of persons to possess Blockchain-based assets. Thus, even casual fans immediately engage in the value and ethos of the artist or creative they support without needing a streaming service or record label as a middleman. Consequently, fan groups can now participate in the evolution of their favorite creators in unprecedented ways (Pompili, n.d.). Additionally, conversations about transforming paparazzi images into non-fungible tokens (NFTs) to generate royalties have emerged, another way NFT applications can level the playing field in the music business (Sharma et al., 2022).

Fashion

The role of NFTs in the fashion industry lies in identity management, where the ability to verify ownership information of items curbs counterfeits. NFTs provide a powerful tool against piracy in various respects, but in the fashion industry, NFTs can help brand owners to curb counterfeits through traceability throughout the garment lifecycle. Suppose brands incorporate NFT technology in their cycles by creating a system to mint, exchange, and fuse cryptography by linking digital items to the physical product. In that case, the level of counterfeiting in the industry will reduce, as NFTs can uncover fictitious data in future sales if the data entered initially is false or incorrect.

The fashion industry has worked diligently in recent years to alter and adapt fashion to the digital environment digitally. Globally, brands utilize NFTs to attract, register and connect with customers. As gaming and digital fashion have risen, NFTs have become more prevalent in fashion. Gucci and Christie's collaborated on an NFT film titled "Aria" for their autumn 2021 collection, which sold in June for $25,000. This year, the most famous digital inventor purchased his work at Christie's for $69 million. Due to the unexpected surge in NFTs, Christie's is now allowing bids in Ethereum, a popular digital asset. Other brands have put their toes in the digital waters in various ways, hoping to capitalize on the demand that has caused NFT collections to sell out in minutes (Umer & Kishan, 2022).

In April, Hermes launched a lawsuit against artist Mason Rothschild after he auctioned 100 "MetaBirkins" - a digital "tribute" to the label's iconic Birkin bag, some reaching tens of thousands of dollars. Nike is the latest company to sue over this issue, accusing shopping platform StockX of utilizing its name and identity to produce and promote NFTs. Although StockX has not yet asserted that their NFTs are a form of art, the Nike case is more commercially focused. Nike sneakers are popular on StockX, and the Vault tokens are related to the name and picture of the things they represent. Nike asserts that the created digital assets violate trademark law, including trademark infringement, a deceptive indication of origin, and dilution of copyright. The case outcome rests on whether StockX's NFTs are an extension of the company's standard reselling process (such as a digital receipt of ownership) or standalone items, with potentially significant ramifications for NFTs in general (Baytas et al., 2022).

Nike has a financial stake in preventing brand confusion. The company acquired the NFT studio RTFKT (pronounced "artifact") to develop its own NFT collections. Before the acquisition, RTFKT announced a sneaker NFT collection and intended, like StockX, to allow users to exchange their NFTs for authentic sneakers. Conversely, the NFTs featured shoes with a custom design that did not include the product's logo; however, it is anticipated to emphasize Nike-branded tokens more.

The charges of trademark infringement, in this case, create numerous challenges. A legal concept known as the first sale doctrine allows marketplaces to resell items often and display trademarked images of those commodities without the permission of the intellectual property owners. Moish Eli Peltz, an attorney specializing in NFT and Web3 legislation, believes that StockX can offer a consumer market where Nike merchandise is shown. However, it remains to be seen how trademark law will fare in the digital era. In a briefing paper for Lexology, attorney Danielle Garno stated, "The reach of these safeguards in the digital arena and the available remedies have yet to be examined" (Pompili, n.d.).

Sports

The role of NFTs in sports is rooted in the possibility of tokenizing game tickets and merchandise by issuing these items on the Blockchain to prevent counterfeit tickets and merchandise. Deloitte predicts that sales of NFTs in the sports industry will top $2 billion. Regarding NFTs and sports, here is the line-up. The only way to obtain sports-themed non-game tokens is to trade them in licensed collectible card games. Some athletes have gone directly to the market to sell NFTs on websites such as Nifty Gateway and OpenSea (Sharma et al., 2022).

Although there are previously established souvenirs, such as baseball cards, that fans can purchase and keep, NFTs bring them onto the Blockchain. For example, baseball, ice hockey, and American football have substantial fan bases. In addition to evoking a powerful nostalgia, collecting trading cards is an excellent way to show support for one's favorite athletes. When tokenizing trading cards on the network, their value and security increase (Wang et al., 2021).

Non-fungible tokens utilize a variety of Blockchain characteristics to increase the value of sports properties in various ways. When something is scarce, demand increases. Tokenization of sporting items, especially single units, raises their worth. By eliminating the need for intermediaries, NFTs provide an open, transparent market where sports fans can communicate with their heroes and purchase their stuff directly. Many people collect digital collectibles to keep and resell at a later date. Due to the rising number of individuals attracted to the NFT market by sports, collectibles trading has assumed a new (read: liquid) form. Athletic royalties Trading in NFTs provides outstanding value, with the bonus of royalties on subsequent sales (Umer & Kishan, 2022).

Twitter is one of the most effective early-stage platforms for spotting new NFTs. The NFT community is highly active on Twitter, with many prominent buyers and influencers debating various projects. Discord is another fantastic resource for spotting NFT concepts with real possibilities. Most major creators or project has a Discord Server, with interaction levels varying based on the project's popularity. Nansen.ai is a starting point for learning more about popular or hyped initiatives. It is a data aggregator that collects buyer data from OpenSea and delivers it in several ways to the audience.

Checking the NFT collection's route map is one of the best ways to determine its quality. This is a crucial component of every newly launched NFT project, as it indicates all critical dates, such as airdrops, new events, and the creator's collecting goals. The BAYC road map, for instance, featured dates for events like their Annual ApeFest, the release of a new game, the introduction of new models, and critical milestones. Collaborations and partnerships with other NFT producers indicate the project's duration (Ahmad, 2022).

Royalties

NFT artists and content creators can receive and control royalties for digital asset productions. NFT royalties are payments made to the original NFT owner when the original owner's work is resold. During minting, the original owner selects the NFT royalty on the market or Blockchain platform. They are tracking royalties using Blockchain technology. During minting, when adding NFT content to the Blockchain, content providers manually calculate the royalty rate. The innovator does so by encoding the criteria in a smart contract, a sort of Blockchain programming. Royalties can be paid automatically after the Blockchain's smart contract terms are established. NFT royalties are computed as a percentage of the selling price chosen by the artist/creator, even though NFT smart contracts differ across marketplaces and are not standardized. If there is a remainder after computing the royalty fee, the fee may be rounded up or down (Chevet, 2018).

NFT royalties are collected through secondary marketplace transactions, often after the first sale. Using a stock market example, this is comparable to trading on the secondary market after an Initial Public Offering (IPO). Renting out NFTs, particularly those in high demand, is one way to make passive income. Some card trading games, for instance, encourage players to borrow non-fungible trading cards to boost their chances of winning. As intended, smart contracts govern the agreement parameters between the two parties.

Consequently, NFT consumers frequently have the option to select their preferred rental agreement duration and NFT lease rate. reNFT is an exemplary platform that lets users rent or lend NFTs. This enables lenders to determine maximum borrowing durations and daily rates.

As a result of the underlying technology that supports NFTs, developers can stipulate terms that impose royalties whenever their NFTs change hands on the secondary market. In other words, the artists might continue to generate passive revenue even after selling their works to collectors. If they do this, they will be able to receive a portion of the NFTs' sales price forever. If a digital artwork's royalty is set at 10 percent, the original creator will receive 10 percent of its total selling price if it is resold to a new owner. It is important to note that writers typically provide these predetermined percentages when minting NFTs. Smart contracts, which are computer programs that execute themselves and enforce business agreements, also govern the allocation of royalties. As a result, as a creator, the company should not worry about enforcing royalty rules or keeping track of payments, as the process is entirely automated (Kong & Lin, 2022).

Investors and content producers can sell NFTs. The material's creator can earn from both the sale of the NFT and royalties on later sales. NFTs may be purchased and resold by investors for a profit. However, it is essential to recognize that making money with NFTs is never guaranteed. Currently, the market is saturated, and most NFT developers do not sell for a substantial amount. Frequently, NFTs are offered for sale at auction. Like eBay auctions, the owner of an NFT can choose a minimum selling price. If the minimum price is not met or surpassed by the end of the auction, the bidding will end. The NFT remains in the ownership of its original owner (Chevet, 2018).

VERIFICATION AND CERTIFICATION

Verification of Authenticity

NFTs can be used to guarantee the authenticity of the goods individuals are purchasing. Since the Blockchain can permanently retain information about the commodity, it will soon be possible to verify the uniqueness and validity of physical goods. Additionally, NFTs can retain information on the manufacturing process, guaranteeing that all transactions are conducted fairly. NFT applications are not limited to consumer goods. Numerous businesses have already utilized NFTs for industrial design prototyping with success. By tracking and tracing food goods, NFTs can assist in resolving the issue of counterfeit food products, such as dietary supplements and pharmaceuticals. Imagine scanning the QR code of an online-purchased nutritional supplement to view the full path from manufacturing to shipping. Since the track record is transparent, products that falsely claim they were manufactured and produced in a given country will eventually be exposed (Rean, 2022).

Academic Credentials

NFTs are also an effective means of demonstrating academic credentials. NFTs can give proof of attendance, degree achieved, and other crucial information that will be saved on the NFT chain and is hack proof. By distributing tokens for each finished course and certifying degrees through smart contract verification mechanisms, NFTs may generate immutable records for courses taken (Rean, 2022). It will no longer be possible to issue paper certificates in the future. NFTs will be used for recording academic accomplishments. NFT education tokens will be transferrable to other individuals as evidence that the token holder has achieved an NFT (Rean, 2022)

Medical Records

NFT ledgers can store an individual's medical records without compromising confidentiality or risking tampering from external sources. NFT transactions receive validation on multiple nodes before they are permanently added to the Blockchain, ensuring that every record is accurate and secure from malicious attempts to manipulate it.

NFT applications have also been developed to assist healthcare professionals; healthcare providers can issue NFT birth certificates for newborns (Rean, 2022). Issuing one of these NFTs for each child can efficiently generate a permanent identity on the Blockchain that is linked to their birth certificate – which is then confirmed using NFT verification applications. Additionally, NFT ledgers offer safer solutions for storing sensitive medical data while allowing authorized healthcare providers to access the information when necessary. In recent years, narrowly defined NFT use cases have emerged, with hospitals, health insurers, and other organizations exploring how Blockchains could improve hospital operations by authenticating patient IDs and recording medical procedures without compromising patient privacy.

Intellectual Property

NFTs are highly effective at safeguarding intellectual property and patents. NFT tokens also enable users to demonstrate ownership of any content, which is impossible with traditional Intellectual Property rights instruments such as trademarks and copyrights. The ownership of Intellectual Property can be recognized, particularly with the timestamps and the Intellectual Property's whole history. The NFT chain would be immutable, allowing the NFT owner to demonstrate, at any moment, that they were the original creator of a work. Like patents, NFTs can protect and validate ownership of innovation or invention. NFTs could also supply the required data for verification, creating a public ledger that documents all patent-related transactions (Rean, 2022).

Identification

In many nations, voters must present photo identification and proof of domicile to the polls. However, many are disenfranchised because they lack copies of their IDs, or any evidence proving their residency or are not registered to vote. NFTs can assist in resolving this issue because they would provide a digital identity to those lacking physical papers proving their identity and country of residence. NFTs will serve as an official record of people who voted and their votes, which will also help eliminate voter fraud and cheating (Rean, 2022).

Supply Chain Provenance

Provenance is a critical use case. For example, in the food business, using Blockchain technology, however, NFTs may be tied to a product, giving it an immutable NFT identifier. This is a prime example of NFTs collaborating with the supply chain. In addition, NFTs can enable businesses to track their products from when they are manufactured until they are shipped. This gives customers insight into what they spend their money on and maintains supply chain openness (Rean, 2022).

Name and Service Domains

Artists can now distinguish themselves by taking control of their digital environments, for instance, by constructing a decentralized art exhibition. In this arena, artists can immediately display, auction, and offer their skills to their audience utilizing direct payments linked to their Blockchain domain. Virtual or private art exhibitions may be held on the Blockchain in the future, accessible only to those who have received unique NFT invitations (Chalmers et al., 2022).

In other areas of digital life, using Blockchain to trade NFTs to transfer ownership of digital art is gaining support. In the NFT market, domain names are gaining value and will soon be considered commodities. For instance, selling "win. crypto" for $100,000 sets a new record for the highest amount paid for a Blockchain domain. Since domain names are the digital cornerstone of a business, they can fetch a high price, and a clean, professional, and well-known domain immediately enhances its reputation (Bolton & Cora, 2021).

Domains are the gateway to content that billions of online customers can access with a single click; consequently, memorable, and meaningful domain names on the NFT market will undoubtedly contribute to the long-term success of a business. Since domain names are the digital cornerstone of a business, they can fetch a high price, and a clean, professional, and easily recognizable domain immediately boosts reputation. Websites are the gateway to content billions of internet users can access with a single click; hence, memorable, and pertinent domain names on the NFT market will undoubtedly fuel long-term growth (Chohan, 2022).

TOKENIZATION OF ASSETS

Gaming

The role of NFTs in gaming is to enable any form of in-game elements to be tokenized and exchanged with other gamers. This tackles the rigidity in traditional gaming, where in-game elements or collectibles are purchased but is non-transferable to others or yourself when other newer or similar versions are released—the concept of NFTs in gaming proffers authentic ownership and transferable ownership in the gaming experience.

NFTs and the gaming business are a perfect combination. NFTs can be merged into the gaming world if they are playable across several platforms. NFTs provide game producers with another chance to spread their brand and generate additional cash while providing gamers with a greater incentive to continue playing a game if they already own it is characters or objects. NFTs also facilitate game trading, which might boost their value since NFT objects can vary in their rarity (Rean, 2022). Due to the absence of an intermediary, NFT owners will not have to worry about fraud. Transactions are executed quickly over the Blockchain. This brings up unimaginable opportunities, including purchasing firearms or other equipment evaluated by those who have used it. This use case is already extensively utilized by games such as Axie Infinity and other forthcoming Blockchain games.

A smart NFT could provide a complete history of previous ownership, usage, and trades, giving creators essential data. For Keys to Other Games (KOGs), SmartNFTs offer access to other games under development. The Smart NFTs will grant access to skins, tournament entrances, hidden levels, weapons, and content. Alethea AI is the creator of the "intelligent NFTs," or iNFTs. Alethea is building its token economy based on train-to-earn, inspired by the play-to-earn phenomenon established by Blockchain games like Axie

Infinity during the previous season. iNFT owners can use train-to-earn to train their iNFTs once, then put them to work interacting with other iNFTs and users to passively earn ALI token rewards by providing data to Alethea's shared intelligence AI engine. At the core of Alethea's train-to-earn system is the ALI token, a blend of incentive, governance, and utility tokens that will be used in the economy. ALI is granted to iNFT holders who contribute data and participate in various projects to assist in developing Alethea's shared intelligence engine. It possesses a fixed amount of 10 billion coins. This provides an incentive to develop Alethea's AL engines, but the delivered incentives must also be in demand for the economic structure to function (Trautman, 2021).

Silks, a ground-breaking play-to-earn (P2E) game built on the Ethereum Blockchain, contains a vast metaverse where users can purchase avatars and engage in gaming. Silks' gameplay is heavily modeled on real-world thoroughbred horse racing, which provides the framework for how players can profit from their in-game actions. Digital Silks horses manufactured as NFTs are available for ownership within the Silks realm. Silks goes one step further by guaranteeing that each Silks horse is connected to an actual thoroughbred racehorse. Combining vast datasets on the horse's ancestry, training progress, and racing performance enables this one-to-one link (Bolton & Cora, 2021). When the real-world counterpart of a player's Silks horse wins a race, the player is awarded in Silks' native transaction currency, $STT. In addition to racing incentives, Silks horse owners have access to staking, breeding, and pin hooking — a horse racing industry term referring to buying and selling an unraced horse for a profit, using data and speculative skill to anticipate its value.

Real Estate

The role of NFTs in real estate is to proffer security and identity management solutions for ownership. In real estate, using timestamped NFTs makes it possible to transfer land deeds, offer ownership confirmation, and monitor property value changes over time. The real estate sector is among the most NFT-ready industries. It can be utilized in real estate to simplify and accelerate transactions, enable smart contracts for properties (enabling automatic payments), and even build decentralized house rental services - all while securing sensitive data such as credit card information. Users can know everything there is to know about a property with only a few taps on their smartphone (Rean, 2022), such as when the property was constructed, who initially owned it, what improvements were made, and everything leading up to the purchase.

Non-Profits

For Non-Profits looking to explore other fundraising opportunities, NFTs provide potential to be used to raise money and for charity. Beyond the profit maximizing NFTs, an increasing number of NFTs are being auctioned for charity. The value that NFTs create falls into novelty or Utility. For fundraising and charitable activities, both of these values can be leveraged. Non-profit organizations can utilize NFTs by creating value-aligned art to raise awareness and money, in the same way traditionally, T-shirts, ribbons, or physical merchandise are sold to raise a certain amount of money for a charitable walk or race (Weiner, 2022). Charitable organizations may also mint NFT art as a standalone fundraiser. In 2021, UNICEF launched 1,000 NFTs to mark its 75th anniversary and raise funds to help get schools and students worldwide online (Rauf, 2021).

In 2018, Ethereum Co-Founder Vitalik Buterin and others wrote a paper titled 'Liberal Radicalism: A Flexible Design for Philanthropic Matching Funds' (Cryptograph, 2021). This paper posits an innovative model called 'Quadratic Funding,' which forms the basis of a new general-purpose infrastructure for funding and allows the public to contribute funds to convey to the government voluntarily: how much society as a whole values a public good, how much should be spent on it, and where that funding should be directed(Cryptograph, 2021) and upon launching, Cryptograph, in its first round of auctions, raised more than $50,000.

Additionally, The Sandbox launched an NFT auction for charity to raise money for UNICEF (The Sandbox First Virtual LAND NFT-based Charity Auction In Support of UNICEF, 2020). The Sandbox auction for UNICEF was the first time the organization (UNICEF) had utilized Blockchain technology and non-fungible tokens for charity fundraising. The above instances build the case for NFTs as a vehicle for the facilitation and implementation of the transparent Blockchain application for social welfare organizations on a global scale.

There exists mixed dialogue regarding NFTS and climate. However, NFTs are being leveraged for climate change with initiatives ranging from awareness-raising to fundraising and as an immutable record for impact and carbon credits (Thomason, 2022; Foster, 2022). Phantasma is a Blockchain and ecosystem-focused protocol' designed to enable gamers and artists to use an eco-friendly Blockchain (Phantasma, 2022). In 2021, SavePlanetEarth- an environmental-based NGO, and Phantasma collaborated to bring transparent and immutable carbon credit Smart NFTs to the Phantasma Blockchain (Phantasma, 2021). The same year, First Carbon launched a decentralized carbon credit NFT onboarding platform (First Carbon Corp). This NFT Based Carbon Credit provides carbon credit issuers access to the Blockchain and enables users to track, trade, and burn credits to eliminate double counting. Additionally, DigitalArt4Climate utilizes Blockchain to turn art into digital assets or NFTs to be collected and traded and to help unlock potential for mobilizing resources, youth engagement, and climate empowerment (DigitalArt4Climate, 2021; Thomason, 2022). This is further discussed in Chapter 12.

Metaverse

The role of NFTs in the virtual world is the ability to enable users to own, create and monetize assets in the Metaverse. NFTs can demonstrate ownership of certain regions inside a virtual environment. People are purchasing land, a digital piece of real estate in The Sandbox, using NFTs in the Metaverse (Moura, 2022; Sandbox, 2022). The Sandbox Metaverse aims to displace established game developers like Minecraft and Roblox by granting creators full ownership of their works in the form of NFTs. Game developers can use the land to build digital experiences, such as games or dioramas, and fill them with assets (Sandbox, 2022). In the Sandbox Metaverse, there are 166,464 pieces of land. Each land is a non-fungible, one-of-a-kind token on the Ethereum network coding standard (ERC-721). Once land has been acquired, it can be filled with games and assets. Estates are formed by combining multiple lands. A district is a particular type of estate owned by more than one person (Sandbox, 2022). In the Sandbox Metaverse, anyone can create games and assets using the platform's specialized frameworks. Works are subsequently exported as NFT game assets to The Sandbox Marketplace (Kanellopoulos et al.,2021).

A sandbox game, sometimes known as a "free roam" or "open world" game, is a videogame genre in which players can explore and create as they see fit, encouraging invention and spontaneity in the lack of a clearly stated objective or objective. Minecraft is a popular sandbox game with a similar aesthetic to The Sandbox. Other games, not necessarily of the sandbox type, feature a "sandbox mode" that allows players to explore and modify their environment. Using voxels, players create their assets, including entities, equipment, and wearables, which they may convert into NFTs following the ERC-1155 token specification. Then, these assets can be published to The Sandbox marketplace, where $SAND, the game's utility token, is used to purchase and sell assets. The supply of $SAND is capped at three billion, with more than one billion circulating at press time (Pompili, n.d.).

A voxel is the 3D representation of a picture. NFT-based Metaverses have and can be built on the Ethereum Blockchain and, in recent times, Polygon. This virtual world is entrenched in the NFT ecosystem, and parcels can be bought on OpenSea and Rarible, or individuals may build in free space. NFTs are essential in the Metaverse ecosystem, allowing customers to own virtual real estate, automobiles, yachts, accessories, and artworks. It is because NFTs build on Blockchain technology, which grants holders of NFTs exclusive rights. Therefore, if an individual owns land within the metaverse, they will receive an NFT as a license for the digital property. It signifies the individual as the legitimate owner of the metaverse location and has exclusive access to it and the power to grant others access. NFT-controlled access may facilitate VIP entry to metaverse events (Wang, Li, Wang & Chen, 2021). Additionally, NFTs are useful for airdropping branded assets to followers and establishing their distinct metaverse avatars. Using Blockchain technology, users can create a metaverse-agnostic avatar that can be transported across realms. Due to the immutability of NFTs, users are the exclusive proprietor of their customized NFT-based avatar, and no one else can reproduce or alter it.

RISKS OF NFTs

Wash Trading

Wash Trading refers to a form of market manipulation where a series of transactions by the same trader is made to look like authentic trades (purchases/sales) but, at a closer look, are fictitious (Investopedia, 2021). Investors buy and sell the same financial instruments in a sequence known as "round trip trading," where within a short window and to mislead other market participants about the price or liquidity of an asset, a series of fictitious selling and repurchasing is carried out (Bybit Learn, 2022). NFTs are a series of trading activities involving the same trader buying and selling the same NFT (Suberg, 2022). This artificially creates a high trade volume and a manipulated market price for the NFT (Hu, 2022).

In an NFT Market Report by for the year 2021 by Chainalysis Inc, (2021), it was found that only around 28% of NFTs purchased during minting and after that sold on their platform resulted in a profit and roughly $284,000 worth of virtual assets were sent to NFT marketplaces from addresses with sanctions risk in Q4 2021. The report also indicates that the value sent to NFT marketplaces via illegitimate addresses soared to $1.4 million in Q4 2021. Most of this activity originated from scam-associated addresses sending funds to NFT marketplaces for making purchases.

These sales are to unsuspecting buyers who believe the NFT to be purchased has been or is growing in value and sold from one distinct collector to another. For instance, in 2021, a CryptoPunk (24x24 pixel art images, generated algorithmically) was bought for 124,457.07 ETH on Larvalabs Marketplace. However, it was then reported (Hayward, 2021)) that it was bought and sold by the same user with borrowed money, and the loan was repaid in the same transaction. This is an instance where individuals can collude to generate transaction history, influence the price of an NFT, and profit when uninformed new entrants get in on the trade, leaving the new player with a high-priced and worthless jpg. Chainalysis in detecting significant wash trading and NFT money laundering reported 262 users who sold an NFT to a self-financed address more than 25 times (Chainalysis, 2022).

Money Laundering

Money laundering activities are a risk with NFTs and have been described by authors as the "best money laundering method in the cryptocurrency world" (McCall, 2021). The anonymity in the ecosystem can be exploited by individuals who intend to launder money. In a recent United States Department of the Treasury report, the treasury unit indicated the high risk that NFTs could be used to launder funds. In the report (U.S. Department of Treasury, 2022), the method of conducting this crime is self-laundering, where individuals purchase an NFT with illicit funds and proceed to transact with themselves to create a record of sales on the Blockchain. The executive summary also indicates that NFTs could be sold to unwitting individuals who would compensate the criminal with clean funds unrelated to the prior crime.

This is also the method of operation for "wash trading," which, as explained earlier, is an avenue where criminals purchase an NFT with illicit funds and proceed to transact with themselves to create sales records on the Blockchain. In the same way with money laundering, the NFT could then be sold to an unwitting individual who would compensate the criminal with clean funds not tied to a prior crime. The ability to transfer NFTs online instantaneously and without concern for distance or borders makes NFTS accessible to exploitation without incurring financial, regulatory, or investigative costs that would have otherwise been the case traditionally with non-digital financial instruments.

Rug Pulling

A rug pull is a con involving digital assets prevalent in the Blockchain ecosystem. Rug pulls are prevalent in DeFi but are also increasingly common in NFT. A rug pull in the NFT space typically involves an individual posing as an artist or developer, who attracts investors to a new project, subsequently pulling out from the project(s). The term rug pull is derived from this act of pulling out from the project after investments have been made before or after the project is built. Pulling out before or after launch leaves investors with a worthless asset. In the NFT ecosystem, a rug pull is a con attempt to lure consumers into buying an NFT and, upon purchase or investment, quickly abandon the project and the consumers without any prior warning.

REGULATION

Due to the cross-border nature of DLT platforms, NFTs are accessible and exchanged globally. Consequently, NFT issuers, consultants, and buyers must evaluate numerous jurisdictions' legal recognition and regulatory frameworks. Foreign regulatory guidance regarding whether NFTs are covered by existing digital asset legislation is scant. Although several nations have enacted legislation or announced plans to regulate virtual assets, most nations have yet to adopt NFT-specific legislative frameworks. Liechtenstein, the fourth smallest European country, is exceptional because it has enacted laws establishing a regulatory environment for tagging assets/rights, which would be relevant to some NFTs (Liechtenstein. li, 2021). The legislative regime in the EU was assessed by PwC and relying on the annual crypto tax report for 2021 (Liechtenstein. li, 2021, PricewaterhouseCoopers, 2021).

They found that there is room for improvement in the areas of non-fungible tokens (NFTs), DeFi (decentralized finance), and the tax implications for decentralized autonomous organizations (DAOs) in particular (Liechtenstein. li, 2021). The characteristics of any proposed NFT issuance must be assessed against existing regulations, such as those controlling securities, electronic money, and crowdfunding.

Rights

Typically, the rights associated with an NFT are determined by the NFT's seller. Metadata associated with NFTs describes the assets with which they are associated. Every property underlying the vast majority of historical NFTs is produced by the owner of the investment's intellectual property rights, who then determines which rights to grant to the NFT consumer. Suppose the publisher of an NFT is a copywriter. In that case, the issuer will own all rights to the materials. It will be able to generate NFTs that delegate any other rights, including the ability to use, copy, exhibit, and alter the material, to a customer. When an issuer acquires content from a creator, the issuer receives the rights the creator has assigned or approved for the issuance and can only sell these limited rights to the purchaser. The inclusion of adequate transfer, assignment, or license language (including any constraints on the buyer's capacity to use) in a transaction to complete the transference of rights in the manner intended by the parties to the sale is a typical concern that may emerge in NFT transactions (Umer & Kishan, 2022).

LOOKING FORWARD

Current legislative regimes around NFTs are underdeveloped and regulatory developments move slower than the current NFT development cycle. Actors and stakeholders in the NFT ecosystem need to create a space that breeds accountability and promotes utility like other focuses in the ecosystem, such as adoption, privacy, and interoperability. The utility is the factor that makes NFTs a dynamic technology. This is seen in how NFTs introduce newer and higher security and identification levels and market efficiency. The ability to convert a physical product to a digital asset can improve supply chains, reduce intermediaries, and increase security, and, in the way, NFTs can fractionalize ownership.

The ecosystem will significantly benefit from transaction monitoring software to curb wash trading, money laundering, and similar financial crimes. Awareness and research are also crucial for ecosystem participants and entrants to reduce the rug pulls in the NFT ecosystem. A significant awareness and research culture, coupled with sound regulation to guide the space, will help entrants and participants decipher rogue projects and platforms and serve as deterrents for scammers and rogues.

In establishing a profound research culture, some factors present in identifying a rogue NFT project that ought to be communicated involve Projects with a lack of execution or commitment to the NFT development, absence of project goals or roadmaps, no community or real online presence or engagement and non-credible individuals behind the development. Individuals who stage rug pulls can do so by building a false sense of hype around these would-be worthless NFTs. The false sense of hype creates a false sense of demand, perhaps making a rug pull a complex financial crime to detect for everyday individuals.

Much like all the ecosystems in Blockchain, research is essential for navigation to the suitable projects and away from con projects. Research needs to be carried out on the creators behind these projects, as most NFT rug pullers go on to create other similar and seemingly exciting projects only to create another money trap. Therefore, it is essential to research the individual behind the brand, like research is done before giving money to a stranger. Research also includes looking at the project's roadmap and other objectives. Rug pull projects are often promoted by paid influencers who publicize these projects by doing product giveaways to make the rug pull project look legitimate.

To this end, it is imperative as an investor or purchaser of the NFT to follow the project's road map and only invest in projects with utility in the Blockchain ecosystem. It is also essential to pay attention to social media management and engagement of these projects, as many rug pool scammers create accounts on social media platforms that are unengaged and run by bots. The projects have no legitimate activity or community to provide any value, and this usually is a perfect way to flag a project, as it is essential to spend time in project communities. The absence of one is a clear indication of a rug pull.

The concept of NFTs is promising, with newer extensions of the token standard now present, such as the concept of rentable NFTs introduced in standard ERC-4907, which captures the need for temporary transferability of ownership. NFTs have provided a bridge to digital economies that touch everyone and things from the real to the virtual world. NFTS's future role will extend beyond the scope of digital art and collectibles, as a conduit for tokenizing physical and intellectual property due to NFT smart contracts. Much like the concept of tokenization, the future of NFTS should border around more fractional ownership to increase liquidity pools for buyers, and possibly the establishment of liquidity for traditionally non-bankable assets (Fortnow & Terry, 2021).

CONCLUSION

This chapter examines the role of NFTs in various industries. It posits that the significance of the NFT ecosystem is amplified as more businesses, artists, producers, and consumers engage with the technology and ecosystem. This chapter emphasizes the multi-utility of NFTs, touching on arguments against the concept of NFTs and other critiques around the threat of NFTs as a medium of over-financialization of every social fabric of society. As stated in this chapter, the viability of the landscape can be seen in the presence of NFTs in many things, with various use cases, and in how it can be a combination of all of the above. The importance of NFTs in Web3 cannot be over-emphasized, in terms of the various intersections, especially in the Metaverse, Digital Wallets, and Traditionally Non-Bankable assets.

REFERENCES

Abdunabi, A. (2021, May 21). The world of NFT art. *Medium.* https://allaabdunabi.medium.com/the-world-of-nft-art-ccfd3104ede4

Aharon, D. Y., & Demir, E. (2022). NFTs and asset class spillovers: Lessons from the period around the COVID-19 pandemic. *Finance Research Letters, 47,* 102515. doi:10.1016/j.frl.2021.102515 PMID:36406741

Ahmad, K. (2022, February 13). 7 Tips to Spot Promising NFT Projects Early. *Make Use Of.* https://www.makeuseof.com/tips-spot-nft-projects-early/

Ante, L. (2021). Smart contracts on the Blockchain–A bibliometric analysis and review. *Telematics and Informatics, 57,* 101519. doi:10.1016/j.tele.2020.101519

Bad luck Brian. (2021). https://opensea.io/assets/matic/0x2953399124f0cb b46d2cbacd8a89cf0599974963/ 120685920743174856157680314464578280308178366943356511570353131324980505069697

Baytaş, M. A., Cappellaro, A., & Fernaeus, Y. (2022, April). Stakeholders and Value in the NFT Ecosystem: Towards a Multi-disciplinary Understanding of the NFT Phenomenon. In *CHI Conference on Human Factors in Computing Systems Extended Abstracts* (pp. 1-8). https://dl.acm.org/doi/ abs/10.1145/3491101.3519694

Bolton, S. J., & Cora, J. R. (2021). Virtual Equivalents of Real Objects (VEROs): A type of non-fungible token (NFT) that can help fund the 3D digitization of natural history collections. *Megataxa*, 6(2), 93-95. https:// www.researchgate.net/publication/353679784_Virtual_Equivalents_of_ Real_Objects_VEROs_A_type_of_non-fungible_token_NFT_that_can_ help_fund_the_3D_digitization_of_natural_history_collections

Chain analysis. (2022, February 2). *Crime and NFTs: Chainalysis Detects Significant Wash Trading and Some NFT Money Laundering In this Emerging Asset Class.* Chainanalysis. https://blog.chainalysis.com/reports/2022-crypto-crime-report-preview-nft-wash-trading-money-laundering/

Chainalysis Inc. (2021, December 6). Report Preview: The 2021 NFT Market Explained. *Chainalysis.* https://blog.chainalysis.com/reports/nft-market-report-preview-2021/

Chalmers, D., Fisch, C., Matthews, R., Quinn, W., & Recker, J. (2022). Beyond the bubble: Will NFTs and digital proof of ownership empower creative industry entrepreneurs? *Journal of Business Venturing Insights*, 17, e00309. doi:10.1016/j.jbvi.2022.e00309

Chevet, S. (2018). *Blockchain technology and non-fungible tokens: Reshaping value chains in creative industries.* Available at SSRN 3212662. https:// papers.ssrn.com/sol3/papers.cfm?abstract_id=3212662

Chohan, U. W. (2022). *Cryptocurrencies: A brief thematic review*. Available at SSRN 3024330. https://papers.ssrn.com/sol3/papers.cfm?abstract_ id=3024330

Cointelegraph. (n.d.). https://www.google.com/amp/s/cointelegraph.com/ news/how-Blockchain-technology-is-transforming-climate-action/amp

Cryptograph. (2021). *Quadratic Funding.* https://cryptograph.com/ Cryptograph/Vitalik-Buterin-Quadratic-Funding

DeNuzzo, N. (2022, March 18). NFTs the future of college sports NIL deals: Nick DeNuzzo guest blog. *ON3.* https://www.on3.com/news/nfts-the-future-of-college-sports-nil-deals/

Digitalart4climate. (2021). *Digitalart4climate. About.* https://digitalart4climate. space

Folding Ideas. (2022, February). *Line Goes Up - The Problem With NFTs* [Video]. Youtube. https://www.google.com/url?sa=t&source=web&rct=j&url=https:/ /m.youtube.com/watch%3Fv%3DYQ_xWvX1n9g&ved=2ahUKEwi11OO1_ Kj7AhVv_7sIHfhZCYAQwqsBegQIChAB&usg=AOvVaw1spU1VtqNjyC mO-1iWFg-y

Fortnow, M., & Terry, Q. (2021). *The NFT Handbook: How to Create, Sell and Buy Non-fungible Tokens.* John Wiley & Sons, Incorporated. https://www. amazon.com/NFT-Handbook-Create-Non-Fungible-Tokens/dp/111983838X

Gerard, D. (2021, March 11). NFTs: crypto grifters try to scam artists, again. *Attack of the 50 foot Blockchain.* https://davidgerard.co.uk/ Blockchain/2021/03/11/nfts-crypto-grifters-try-to-scam-artists-again/

Hayward, A. (2021, October 29). No, Someone Didn't Really Pay $532 Million for a CryptoPunk NFT. *Decrypt.* https://www.google.com/amp/s/ decrypt.co/84756/no-someone-didnt-really-pay-532-million-cryptopunk-nft%3famp=1

Homer Pepe. (2021). *Owned by Huskan. People NFTs.* OpenSea. https:// opensea.io/assets/ethereum/0x495f947276749ce646f68ac8c248420045cb7 b5e/ 5639922838748308352589180376984732296195856454582788 2145 350131549684159741953

Hovhannisyan, A. (2021, September 28). *NFTs are a problem.* Blog. https:// www.aleksandrhovhannisyan.com/blog/nfts-are-a-problem/

Hu, E. (2022, January 30). *Clever NFT traders exploit crypto's unregulated landscape by wash trading on LooksRare.* Cointelegraph. https://cointelegraph. com/news/clever-nft-traders-exploit-crypto-s-unregulated-landscape-by-wash-trading-on-looksrare

Kanellopoulos, I. F., Gutt, D., & Li, T. (2021). *Do Non-Fungible Tokens (NFTs) Affect Prices of Physical Products? Evidence from Trading Card Collectibles.* https://papers.ssrn.com/sol3/papers.cfm?abstract_id=3918256

Kong, D. R., & Lin, T. C. (2021). *Alternative investments in the Fintech era: The risk and return of Non-Fungible Token (NFT).* Available at SSRN 3914085. https://papers.ssrn.com/sol3/papers.cfm?abstract_id=3914085

Levesque, J. (2022, February 24). How to Utilize NFTs for Fundraising. *TechSoup.* https://blog.techsoup.org/posts/how-to-utilize-nfts-for-fundraising

liechtenstein.li. (2021, December 20). *Liechtenstein has the clearest crypto tax regulations.* https://www.liechtenstein.li/en/liechtenstein_news/liechtenstein-hat-die-verstandlichsten-krypto-steuern

McCall, I. (2021, April 1). How to Launder Money With NFTs. *Medium.* https://medium.com/yardcouch-com/how-to-launder-money-with-nfts-56f1789e5591

McDonnell, H. (2021, April 9). *The Unknown Legal Future of the Art Market's New Favorite Medium: Non-Fungible Tokens ("NFTs").* Hughes Hubbard & Reed LLP. https://www.hhrartlaw.com/2021/04/the-unknown-legal-future-of-the-art-markets-new-favorite-medium-non-fungible-tokens-nfts/

Moura, S. (n.d.). *How to Buy Digital Real Estate.* Crypto Learning and Education. https://www.sarabmoura.com/how-to-buy-digital-real-estate/#page-content

Nyan Cat Owned by 73B28B. (2020). *OpenSea.* https://opensea.io/assets/ethereum/0x3b3ee1931dc30c1957379fac9aba94d1c48a5405/219

OpenSea Fart #0420 Owned by 80168016. (2021). https://opensea.io/assets/ethereum/0x495f947276749ce646f68ac8c248420045cb7b5e/ 9545159878 65636262860428960109911693878747420455204951361402386249786 89327105

Overgaauw, V. (2020). *What are NFT tokens?* Anycoin Direct. https://anycoindirect.eu/en/blog/what-are-nft-tokens

Phantasma. (2022). *The Phantasma Experience.* https://phantasma.io

Rauf, D. (2021). *TFR. UNICEF to launch NFT collection as new way of fundraising to celebrate 75th anniversary.* https://www.google.com/amp/s/tfr.news/news/2021/12/14/unicef-to-launch-nft-collection-as-new-way-of-fundraising-to-celebrate-75th-anniversarynbsp%3fformat=amp

Rean. (2022, March 4). 10 Practical NFT Use Cases Beyond Digital Artworks. *Hongkiat.* https://www.hongkiat.com/blog/nft-use-cases/

Sandbox. (2022). Buying, selling and renting LAND. *The Sandbox.* https://sandboxgame.gitbook.io/the-sandbox/land/buying-selling-and-renting-land

Sharma, T., Zhou, Z., Huang, Y., & Wang, Y. (2022). *"It's A Blessing and A Curse": Unpacking Creators' Practices with Non-Fungible Tokens (NFTs) and Their Communities.* arXiv preprint arXiv:2201.13233.

Suberg, W. (2022, June 27). Google users think BTC is dead- 5 things to know in bitcoin this week. *Cointelegraph.* https://www.google.com/amp/s/cointelegraph.com/news/google-users-think-btc-is-dead-5-things-to-know-in-bitcoin-this-week/amp

Thomason, J. (2022, April 9). How Blockchain technology is transforming climate action. *Cointelegraph.* https://cointelegraph.com/news/how-Blockchain-technology-is-transforming-climate-action

Trautman, L. J. (2021). *Hofstra Law Review. Virtual art and non-fungible tokens.* https://www.google.com/url?sa=t&source=web&rct=j&url=https://www.hofstralawreview.org/wp-content/uploads/2022/04/aa.4.trautman.pdf&ved=2ahUKEwiI5_qSw6j7AhV0gP0HHTGhBtwQFnoECAkQAQ&usg=AOvVaw3w_0_yWSO-0FCUaz0LcNDD

Umer, S. M., & Kishan, V. (2021). *Application of non-fungible tokens (NFTs) and the intersection with fashion luxury industry.* https://www.google.com/url?sa=t&source=web&rct=j&url=https://www.politesi.polimi.it/bitstream/10589/182823/1/2021_12_Umer_Kishan.pdf&ved=2ahUKEwjjg-r1x6j7AhUM-aQKHdItCjwQFnoECBEQAQ&usg=AOvVaw276ippExoM8FoyMYnMIGvS

U.S. Department of Treasury. (2022, May 13). *Treasury Announces 2022 National Illicit Finance Strategy* [Press Release]. https://home.treasury.gov/news/press-releases/jy0779

Wang, Q., Li, R., Wang, Q., & Chen, S. (2021). *Non-fungible token (NFT): Overview, evaluation, opportunities and challenges.* arXiv preprint arXiv:2105.07447. https://www.researchgate.net/publication/351656444_Non-Fungible_Token_NFT_Overview_Evaluation_Opportunities_and_Challenges

Wiener, G. (2022). NFTs for Nonprofits: Non-Fungible Fundraising. Digital Fundraising. *WholeWhale.* https://www.wholewhale.com/tips/non-fungible-fundraising-nfts-for-good/

Chapter 9
History of the Metaverse

ABSTRACT

Metaverse is a futuristic concept combining various technologies, including computer infrastructure, gaming, NFTs, DeFi, AR/VR, AI, and the spatial web. More than 600 companies are building metaverses, estimated to be a US$13 trillion market opportunity by 2030. However, there is yet to be a consensus on what it is. It will be immersive and persistent, combining virtual and physical worlds with an economy and value that can be earned, lent, borrowed, and extracted from the physical world. Some challenges remain, including interoperability, latency, user interface, and regulation. This is arguably one of the most exciting technological developments, which will help create new and enhanced ways to live, shop, be entertained, seek services, and be educated. This chapter introduces the key elements of the Metaverse and outlines challenges and ethical questions as the world becomes more immersive.

INTRODUCTION

"Metaverse" was first coined by Neal Stephenson in "Snow Crash'' to describe a 3D photo-real digital meeting space in which humans, represented by programmable avatars, interacted. Metaverse brings together developments in computer infrastructure, gaming, Augmented and Virtual Reality (AR/VR), and Blockchain to create a virtual experience with a meta-economy with its currencies which can be exchanged peer-to-peer. (Outlier Ventures, 2021). Blockchain technologies, including virtual assets and non-fungible

DOI: 10.4018/978-1-6684-6658-2.ch009

tokens (NFTs), enable the transfer of digital assets across virtual borders. Increasingly generative Artificial Intelligence (AI) will be incorporated into Metaverse experiences.

Many companies were working on the Metaverse long before October 2021, when Mark Zuckerberg brought global attention to the Metaverse by changing the name of Facebook's parent company to Meta and announcing the Meta Metaverse strategy and its plans to hire 10,000 workers in the EU (Matthews et al., 2021). However, Meta will not be the only Metaverse, and there remains a fierce debate about the merits of an open (Web 3.0) or closed (Meta) Metaverse.

Metaverse experiences have been around for some years in gaming and other social venues and experiences. The pandemic, by causing people to move online, has enabled more immersive online experiences. Video games are the closest thing existing to Metaverses, and gaming companies have the advantage of their large user bases, who are young, tech-savvy, and understand the value of digital goods (Chow, 2021).

The Metaverse is expected to impact many sectors, offering immersive experiences, more efficient processes, enhanced education, and opportunities for collaboration. It is the next frontier for online interaction. This chapter will describe the developments in the Metaverse, its leading proponents, some risks, regulatory challenges, ethical issues, and future development opportunities. The following chapter will give a more detailed examination of use cases.

WHAT IS A METAVERSE?

The infrastructure requirements for the Metaverse are still being developed. Matthew Ball, in "The Metaverse Primer," lays out a framework for the Metaverse, which is a helpful anchor to explore the infrastructure: (i) the hardware and devices used to access the Metaverse; (ii) networking connections, bandwidth, and decentralized data transmission; (iii) computing power; (iv) virtual platforms providing immersive experiences; (v) tools, protocols, formats, services, and engines which serve as standards for interoperability; (vi) digital payments; (vii) content, services, and digital assets; and (viii) user behaviors.

Citi (2022) predicts that Metaverse access via AR smartphones could contribute 30 to 40% of expenditure through Metaverse-like mediums. Over the next year or two, the world will see whether access to the Metaverse will be through goggles, mobile phones, the Internet, or a combination.

A Web 3 Metaverse allows developers to create new projects and build communities openly and decentralized, coordinated by tokens and incentive structures. The peer-to-peer incentive model will enable a decentralized global workforce of millions of creators and developers to create multiple collaboration opportunities in gaming, music, digital art, and much more. The government will have an essential role in supporting Web 3.0 Metaverse to enable people to participate, protect their creative and property rights, and build the foundations for a free and fair immersive future. The Metaverse provides a seamless relationship between the natural world and the Internet through Blockchain technology's interconnectivity and seamless interaction between users, platforms, and developers. (Henderson, 2022). Decentralization allows developers and platforms functionality that was impossible prior to its emergence. It will soon be possible for assets from any Metaverse game and real-world assets to be interchanged and exchanged in some form of futuristic meta-marketplace (Henderson, 2021). Thus the Metaverse will amalgamate hundreds of user experiences through VR, AR, mobile, tablet, or home computer (Roberts, 2021). Some describe it as a combination of immersive virtual reality, a massively multiplayer online role-playing game, and the web (Everette, 2021). The Metaverse will need presence, interoperability, and standardization (Ratan & Lei, 2021).

In recent months, the world has seen the emergence of Chat GPT, a generative AI that helps use artificial intelligence to create content autonomously. This can be for text, images, and even music, and AI will be integrated with Metaverse technologies to create a whole new arena of possibilities for immersive and interactive experiences. It can also allow AI-generated content to be used in the Metaverse, and such AI-generated content can respond to users' actions, thus creating increasingly engaging experiences for users. This is the early days for generative AI, but it will be combined with all future versions of the Metaverse.

INVESTMENTS IN METAVERSE

Cathy Wood (2021) of Ark Invest says the Metaverse could be worth trillions and speculates it may be an $800 billion market opportunity. Citi (2022) estimates it will be worth $13 trillion by 2050. Citi (2022) further points out that the growth of 5G will increase Metaverse-related digital spending because 5G will enable much faster access to the Metaverse. Citi (2022) estimates that the 2030 Metaverse market could be up to and above $10 trillion with billions of users. In the same report, Citi (2022) argues that the open Metaverse is likely to be built by a complex collaboration of different contributors in a composable way. A critical technological element will be the digital passport or the self-sovereign identity that will allow people to move in and out of different virtual worlds.

Outlier Ventures (2023) makes the important point that access will require widespread mobile access to the Metaverse and purports that MetaFi will be a form of financial inclusion in the digital economy. Previously, people spoke of financial inclusion as literal access to money, but Web 3.0 three provides access to the value. Outlier Ventures further highlight how Celo was one of the first blockchains to focus on mobile from an accessibility perspective. Mobile technology will be one of the most important means of access for the broader population. When mobile is combined with the opportunities of play-to-earn games, such as Axie Infinity, Metaverse's potential for economic inclusion is extremely powerful. Technology convergence is powerfully exhibited through AI, driving Web 3.0 adoption and success. This will lead to industry transformation and technological gains and benefit creators and the community.

METAVERSE BUILDERS

There is not a single Metaverse, and four quite different proponents are working to create them across more than 600 companies. These are the BigTechs, the gaming industry, the Web 3.0 community, and government and industry.

BigTech Companies

Meta, Microsoft, and others are investing significant resources into developing Metaverses. Cryptomeria Capital reported that Metaverse mergers and acquisitions totaled $77bn in the 18 months from January 2021, the largest being Microsoft's acquisition of Activision Blizzard for $69bn (Perkins, 2022). Meta has invested a total of $10 billion into acquiring and developing both hardware and software that will be used to provide VR capabilities within the Metaverse (Rees, 2022).

Gaming Industry

The global video game market was valued at USD 195.65 billion in 2021 and is expected to expand at a compound annual growth rate (CAGR) of 12.9% from 2022 to 2030 (Grandview Research, 2022). GameFi is the term for integrating digital assets into games for spending, earning, exchanging, player acquisition, and retention (Meilich & Ordano, 2022). Gaming will be the vector for the widespread adoption of digital assets with the availability of high-performance platforms and improved on and off-ramps for digital assets. Now there are better digital asset storage and distribution tools for gamers, incentivized by the ability of gamers to earn credits that can be used in games. Video games are a huge growth industry; the number of global gamers is expected to surpass 3 billion in 2022, making the major gaming companies like Epic (Fortnite), Roblox, and Unity (Pokémon Go and League of Legends) leaders in GameFi and Metaverse (Insider Intelligence (2022). Online video games will increase their world-building as games evolve into persistent online services and virtual worlds for millions of people.

Web 3.0

The next contenders in the quest for the Metaverse are Web 3.0 companies. Web 3.0 companies include Decentraland, Dapper Labs, Space, The Sandbox, Alien Worlds, Yuga Labs, Upland, MetaMetaverse, SuperWorld, Voxels, Decentral Games, and Animoca Brands. They have recently formed The Open Metaverse Alliance to address interoperability challenges within the Metaverse by creating uniform standards for Blockchain gaming so that users can take the digital items they own from one world to other interconnected virtual worlds. The Web 3 community wants a choice so that a single powerful company does not dominate the Metaverse and makes everyone use a closed system (Takahashi, 2022). Web 3.0 Metaverses combine DeFi, NFTs, decentralized governance, decentralized cloud services, and self-sovereign identity. It can enable the exchange of physical, economic, and content assets. These are described in earlier chapters of this book.

Government and Industry

Several governments are investigating the use of Metaverse for government services. One example is Neom, a new city in Saudi Arabia that plans to build a Metaverse platform bridging the real and virtual worlds. It will deliver a gamified experience with distinctive exploration and entertainment features, an instant language translation tool, a social platform that fosters interaction, and a fully-fledged digital marketplace, all adding to ground-breaking innovation. The city of Seoul in South Korea plans to create a Metaverse for its municipal administration. Singapore simulated its traffic management system on the game system Unity instead of a purpose-built simulation system because it is so advanced now. Dubai in the UAE has launched a Metaverse strategy, and the Dubai regulator is set up in the Metaverse. Digital Twins, a virtual model of a physical thing, will be a key element in government and industrial Metaverses.

METAVERSE ASSETS

Outlier Ventures (2021) describe Metaverse assets as 1. Physical Assets - space, objects, avatars, 2. Economic assets - currency, financial instruments, marketplace, and 3. Content assets - media and data assets.

Physical Assets

Avatars are digital identities created by users. These include 3D avatars that may be utilized in different Metaverses and are often generated in enormous numbers as generative Profile Picture Projects (PFP). PFPs, seen as well-known social clubs, employ homogenized tokens to reinforce NFTs, often featuring functionalities such as governance rights or other perks. Common characteristics include (i) They give a new reality in virtual space; (ii) Subscribers' avatars, which they use to enter the virtual world, are saved on the provider's servers, making hacking (and modifying their belongings outside the virtual world) difficult. (iii) The avatars may communicate with one another, allowing players to connect not just with the computer game's artificial intelligence but also with other gamers all around the globe.

Economic assets

MetaFi is the infrastructure layer that unlocks value in the Metaverse. MetaFi refers to agreements, goods, and services that allow non-homogeneous and homogenized tokens (and their derivatives) to establish complex financial transactions. It contains the DeFi stack, multiple universes, and the fundamental components of the Blockchain space (Cognizant, 2022). It is an all-encompassing term for protocols, products, and services that enable the financial interplay between NFTs and fungible tokens within a Metaverse. MetaFi will use Web3 tools, including NFTs, DAOs, and access to previously inaccessible liquidity through crypto. MetaFi, an umbrella word for protocols, products, and services that enable the complicated financial interaction between non-fungible and fungible tokens, is the primary trend in the Open Metaverse (and their derivatives). MetaFi takes on two of DeFi's main characteristics: unstoppability and composability. The mutualization of risk, gamification of finance, increased availability of financial tools, and an efficient DAO services stack are all driving factors. MetaFi is composable and unstoppable (Blockchain Magazine, 2023). Developers from all around the globe are expected to compete for better payouts by actively participating in the new ecosystem.

The Metaverse allows a mix of non-fungible and fungible tokens to be used under unique community governance models. The cornerstone for a well-developed parallel economy is the confluence of fundamental crypto characteristics, NFTs & MetaFi (Umbala Metaverse, 2022).

DeFi is the most crucial part of any MetaFi system. Using common application logic and security, the core frameworks aid in developing applications that run on top of them. DeFi contains the applications that run on protocols. They operate as unstoppable programs that use smart contracts to enable automated financial dynamics. Verses are the last component in the MetaFi ecosystem's framework. The essential layers of verses will stay linked to the many virtual worlds based on compatibility and cost-effective value transmission.

Four significant themes will promote the rise of Metaverse and DeFi convergence. (i) New NFT platforms have empowered artists and communities to negotiate the conditions of creative exchange with users. (ii) At the same time, with individualized social tokens, NFTs can provide recurrent income for producers. (iii) MetaFi technology may also improve the chances of collecting digital asset value and flow in open free marketplaces. Furthermore, it paves the path for real-time price discovery, allowing for finding hidden value. DAO and other mature governance models may also play a key role in adopting MetaFi with better governance. DeFi has effectively educated all users about the benefits of community-based insurance, especially when combined with DAOs. (iv) Finally, the growth of play-to-earn games and new methods to monetize data may eventually bring Gen Z closer to MetaFi DeFi apps. DeFi apps on the Metaverse will complement and boost the Metaverse's characteristics. It is just as crucial to solving the underlying difficulties as it is to find the prospects for adopting DeFi in the Metaverse (Howell, 2022).

Once MetaFi is developed, it can considerably influence the potential of dApps in various ways. Sports clubs and fan clubs provide fan tokens to give holders unique benefits and privileges. MetaFi can ease the process of minting, purchasing, and trading fan tokens. The technique and cost of establishing and selling them vary on every Blockchain and platform.

With the evolution of the Metaverse, the number of vertical domains and their corresponding definitions will continue to vary. The virtual world is a digital place that may be used for social, commercial, or gaming reasons. It may or may not replicate the physical events of the actual world. Rare elements are frequently represented by NFTs, which may be freely acquired, sold, and created when replicated. Sandbox and Decentraland are two famous examples.

Virtual land is linked to the virtual world in-game money and governance tokens as part of the NFT, which implies that tokens may be used to buy virtual world assets and vote on upgrades. Virtual world adoption has made significant progress, with barely a dozen individuals engaging with them per day at the start of 2021. Sixty-five thousand unique addresses have engaged with Somnium Space, Decentraland, Sandbox, and Crypto Voxels smart contracts. Sandbox was the most important among them regarding monthly active users (4100) and land sales 12,000 ETH or USD 450 million). Metaverse games almost always feature a component of playing and earning. Users or players are compensated in tokens for their contributions to the game. This gives rise to the whole in-game economy, where capital and labor are linked to produce value (Amerikayageldim, 2022).

A market is a digital location where supply and demand are matched, enabling us to find additional NFTs and improve price discovery. Users may freely trade and directly issue NFTs on markets like OpenSea, Super rare, and Rarible. These NFTs may then be utilized as financial assets. By separating high-value NFTs into homogenized tokens and then holding them proportionally, the segmentation function helps them achieve liquidity. The rapid growth of NFTs has resulted in a spike in market activity. In January 2021, Open Sea's 30-day transaction volume was barely $1 million, but by November 2021, it had surpassed $2 million (Inf.news 2202).

An increasing number of designer companies are using NFTs to enter the worldwide market of 2.7 billion gamers. Players may now customize their skins with leading fashion labels and display their preferences to millions of others online. Balenciaga, for example, collaborated with Fortnite to create four sets of virtual clothes. In contrast, Burberry collaborated with Mythical Games to release fashion pieces represented by NFTs. Most Metaverse ideas have as their long-term objective the creation of many durable shared interfaces where users may consume diverse experiences together and engage with one another for various reasons, such as socializing, trading, or playing games. However, once these virtual worlds come to life, interoperability will undoubtedly become a significant problem, similar to DeFi in its early days, when fragmented decentralized exchanges (DEXs) collapsed owing to a lack of liquidity and trade volume.

Content Assets: Media and Data Assets

Complementing this is a growing subgroup of the digital economy known as the digital creator economy. There are now over 50 million content developers in the digital world. However, they must contend with the limitations of Web2 digital platforms and suffer financial losses in exchange for losing ownership of their inventions. Self-Sovereign identity will allow for easier access to data while being able to control how it is used. This also offers the possibility of individuals monetizing their data.

As outlined in Chapter 7, there are NFT markets, including Open Sea, Magic Eden, Rarible, and LooksRare. These platforms use Blockchain networks to provide non-fungible goods such as artwork, music, gaming items, avatars, virtual clothing, domain names, etc. It may be possible to construct markets using MetaFi that list every single asset type that can exist in multiple chains, boosting the user experience of collectors by allowing them to access all NFTs in a single interface, making asset exchange more accessible and efficient.

Protocols

For developers, the Metaverse offers an opportunity for the emergence of new projects that would be impossible in the real world. Individuals enter virtual worlds using avatars, which are computer-based simulated settings. The environments may be two-dimensional or three-dimensional, the avatars can be text-based or visual, and the material can be thematic (in the case of games) or unrestricted.

There still needs to be more consensus on how Metaverse commerce will be facilitated at scale. NFTs provide the means for decentralized Metaverse commerce, which is very different from what it would be. Some fear mounting interest from prominent brands such as Adidas risks centralizing Web 3.0 and returning to corporate dominance. Last year Adidas announced a collaboration with BAYC (Bored Ape Yacht Club) and released its own 'Into the Metaverse' series of NFTs, all 30,000 of which sold out within hours of being launched.

EMERGENT RISKS

Metaverse infrastructure is still in its early stages, and the internet infrastructure needs to be improved and made more user-friendly. A range of risks will also interest policymakers, regulators, the government, and the community. These are summarized below: consent, criminal potential, data privacy, governance, human rights, security, and potential social consequences. There are currently no laws or legal jurisdictions in the Metaverse.

Consent

Data collection will be involuntary and continuous, making collecting consent almost impossible. The Metaverse entails the integration of access points with the content and services. It thus considerably reduces users' capacity to avoid collecting personal data. This covers all Metaverses, and the question arises, should the collection of user consent and the obligation to display privacy notices be done separately for all Metaverses or each entity in a Metaverse? (European Parliament, 2022). Informed consent will be a significant challenge. Firstly, a person needs to be informed of the risks, benefits, and probabilities of some dangerous consequences. Second, they need to understand and appreciate that information, and finally, the decision needs to be voluntary. How does this play out for people who are incapacitated, illiterate, mentally ill, or even children?

In the Metaverse, many people will willingly allow the tracking of track body movement, brainwaves, and physiological responses through wearables. The Metaverse will also increase the number of points of attack. Due to its digital nature, uninformed consent in a Metaverse may include personal, biometric, financial, and emotional data. Many people freely consent for their data to be shared across the Internet, to multiple organizations, and across multiple devices, without understanding that their data may be shared or monetized. This is particularly relevant when dealing with susceptible data, like long-term brain wave data. Can people participate without giving up on privacy and ownership of their data? Is it possible to protect people from being monitored or manipulated?

Criminal Risks

Fraud and misconduct are significant risks, and links across Metaverses and NFTs may increase the complexity of applying Anti-Money Laundering (AML) and Combating the Financing of Terrorism (CFT) rules. Jurisdictional questions may hinder the ability to apply sanctions. Many of the worlds within the Metaverse have their virtual assets, and integration across the worlds (and with other cryptocurrencies) will depend on well-developed and integrity markets. Increased growth could present risks to individuals and the broader economy in case of a crash or market manipulation.

NFTs can be misused in various ways. Fraudulent acts include scams, malware, and hacking to gain unlawful access to digital wallets storing NFTs and other crypto assets. With no clear regulatory framework concerning NFT ownership, criminals can create and sell NFTs without the owners' knowledge or permission. NFTs are valuable to the extent that their ownership can be verified on a public ledger, but even if the owner's identity can be verified, there may be issues with where it is hosted. For example, if an NFT disappears from OpenSea, it also disappears from the owner's wallet.

The nature of the Metaverse poses many challenges related to liabilities, combating illegal and harmful practices and misleading advertising practices, and protecting intellectual property rights.

Data

Interoperability means moving assets like avatars and digital assets between virtual spaces. Integration across virtual worlds and between the digital and physical will require interoperability across the "technology stack," including digital platforms and hardware devices. There is yet to be interoperability or portability between the various Metaverse environments. Each platform needs to link NFTs to its proprietary digital assets. Customers' ability to carry their virtual avatars and properties from one virtual world to another is limited. Companies must establish data-sharing agreements that fulfill data protection requirements. This may be challenging in decentralized Metaverse models. International data transfers must be clarified to enable free movement in the Metaverse.

Governance

The Metaverse can be built in Web 2.0 or Web 3.0. Closed Metaverses are being developed by closed BigTech platforms like Facebook and others built on open protocols like Decentraland. Web 3.0 proponents object to the BigTech offerings in the Metaverse because it will not be more decentralized or equitable. There are legitimate fears that a Facebook Metaverse will leverage user data for monetization and track their every move. The alternative is an open Metaverse built on shared open-source protocols, open infrastructure, and an open financial system. A Web 3.0 Metaverse based on Blockchain and open standards controlled by the users in a decentralized autonomous organization (DAO) could address data protection issues prevalent in more centralized business models, whereby the users would control their data and decide how it could be shared. It is yet to be seen who will build and control the Metaverse.

There is a need to determine the jurisdictional boundaries of the Metaverse, as virtual borders could be just as important as physical borders when formulating policies. Policymakers and executives must also understand the boundaries between Metaverses and consequential regulation. At a nation-state level, the question emerges, where are state borders in the Metaverse? What about virtual states?

With the deployment of digital assets in the Metaverse, participants will be subject to the same risks present in the rapidly evolving virtual asset space. Some risks include market manipulation, volatility, impermanent loss, liquidation, technical, and price risk. If the smart contract powering the economy malfunctions, is hacked, or has a problem, there is no recourse. While DAOs are still experimental, there can be information asymmetries and a lack of transparency about participant ambitions, motivations, values, or priorities. If someone has a problem in the Metaverse, who do they call?

Property Rights

Intellectual property (IP) enforcement is challenging in the Metaverse environment. This is because it is more difficult to identify the provider that can remove infringing content since Metaverse content is distributed and replicated across decentralized networks running on Web 3.0 and Blockchain-based platforms. There may be issues around applicable law and jurisdiction and identifying infringers. Popular brands are also facing unauthorized use of registered trademarks in the Metaverse. Several open questions exist about applying existing intellectual property rights to Metaverse intellectual property. At a more fundamental level, questions surrounding the different property types in the Metaverse exist. Like a company's logo, metaverse intellectual property may require a different regulatory regime than virtual property, like an avatar's hat.

Community Owned Economies are thriving. Innovators are building them, developers are building on them, and players are playing in them (Thomason, 2021). Ideally, the governance of these entities is decentralized, and the community gets to vote on all essential issues. However, in an automated code-governed economy, no one owns it. This is a significant challenge for regulators. The legal and regulatory framework surrounding NFTs is under development, and the extent to which NFTs create an ownership right is still very much disputed. For example, in Europe, ownership of Metaverse assets is governed by contract law rather than property law.

Security

Cybersecurity challenges such as phishing, malware, and hacking will persist and extend to devices enabling a Metaverse experience and avatars. Protecting the integrity of avatars will be a particular issue of concern, as will new forms of cybercrime, such as selling fake NFTs, illicit use of virtual assets, and malicious smart contracts. How will virtual crimes be considered in comparison to offline ones?

A further hurdle in fighting hackers, organized criminals, terrorist groups, and sex offenders will be the multi-layered structure of the virtual environment. The Metaverse may allow them to hide behind encryption and untraceable NFTs, making it difficult to identify them and pursue legal recourse. There are also concerns about the possible connections between the dark web and the Metaverse and, consequently, the need to create a Metaverse criminal justice system to prevent and limit illegal activity. Therefore, security considerations and possible solutions need to be built into the development of the Metaverse from its inception. Ensuring that Metaverses can stay online and are not prone to hacks is essential for developing an ecosystem that attracts users and prospers.

Recent research has revealed that the characteristics of connected devices could lead to severe data breaches, as the sensitive data needed for such devices to function, such as voice control or facial movement, could be reproduced.

VR technology enables and warns that private Metaverse platforms may be contractually given a great deal of control over some critical aspects of digital assets in the Metaverse environment. Legal issues may arise regarding proper verification of ownership.

A particular technical challenge will be building protocols able to mitigate the risk of transfer of harmful code between platforms to enable seamless movement of users between virtual spaces. Entities in the Metaverse will therefore need to look beyond their Metaverse security measures, as they will depend on the cybersecurity of other entities. Implementing interoperability will entail the allocation of responsibilities. Supply chain due diligence will be essential to preserve the security of the platforms.

Social Implications

The social, physical, and mental health impacts are as yet unknown. However, the Metaverse will likely present challenges to people's physical and mental health. For example, it is already known that people who use immersive technologies can become disoriented and cause injury, and they may become oblivious to real-world hazards. A study by the GRM Institute (Gosh, 2022) found while there are no long-term studies, immersive games can lead to depression, isolation, lonely behavior, and even suicide and violence. If used to excess, the Metaverse can cause mental health problems (such as loneliness) and reduce physical activity, leading to a rise in obesity and other physical health problems, contributing to a desire to escape the real world. Addictions to social media and online gaming as a form of escapism already exist, but the Metaverse can reinforce them.

The Metaverse holds the promise of offering children a unique experience. It could enable them to return in time or visit places they could never have explored. It also offers a form of hands-on experience that can help children to understand the world around them and how things work, potentially increasing their motivation to learn. Finding ways to use the Metaverse alongside the natural world will be essential to preserve real teacher-child, caregiver-child, and child-child social relationships. If the Metaverse is left unregulated, it may cause children significant harm. The European Commission (2022) has recently proposed several legislative acts to address age-inappropriate and illegal content online. This proposes a regulation to prevent and combat child sexual abuse online that obliges providers to detect, report, block, and remove child sexual abuse material from their services. They will also have to introduce the necessary age verification measures. This is essential to know who a child is. How do we consider the impacts? The protection of vulnerable groups, particularly children's data, requires special protection under the GDPR. Therefore, means will be needed to prevent children from sharing their data. Regulators have examined the effect of video games on children (Bogost, 2019), and this begs the question, what happens when children are virtually immersed in the Metaverse and inhabit the fictional world around them?

Many platforms are voice chat based and fully immersive, which can lead to moderation challenges regarding hate speech and harassment. Content moderation will be critical, and the concentration of moderation power has already been a source of controversy on Web 2.0 platforms and will likely persist in the Metaverse.

Metaverse and network effects in the digital realm could increase wealth inequality. The existing digital divide of unequal internet access will also affect access to the Metaverse. The Metaverse might be challenging to access, particularly for people with low digital literacy, disabilities, or mental health problems. Access to consistent, reliable broadband might be an obstacle for other groups. In practice, many might need help accessing the Metaverse due to a lack of digital skills and needing more reliable broadband or the proper hardware. Online harms may be exacerbated in the Metaverse, including privacy, discrimination, mental health, and misinformation. Additionally, political and societal problems could be exacerbated.

ETHICS AND THE METAVERSE

These challenges demand an ethical perspective on Metaverse development. Ethics are standards of behavior that outline how people ought to act. They commonly consider factors such as concern for the well-being of others, respect for the autonomy of others, trustworthiness, and honesty, willing compliance with the law, fairness, and preventing harm. Digital ethics are not different from traditional ethics; instead, the possibility of unintentional or deliberate automation of unethical behavior on a large scale raises moral dilemmas for technologists, financiers, users, and regulators at the technology, application, and society levels. Powerful new technologies demand new approaches that are jointly created with industry.

Games

Games continue to evolve into persistent online services and virtual worlds for millions of people. The design community must do more to understand the unique implications of designing for these experiences -- and include game designers in the emerging conversation around design ethics. Game designers must be included in the conversation around tech ethics (Games Industry, 2021). Yet technologists and coders are not trained in ethics and may not have the skills to consider ethical issues.

Ethics and Tech Stack

Creators of the Metaverse need to consider proper safeguards. It is people that are building the future and who are responsible for the things they are building. Get the ethics right, and life in the Metaverse could be better, more equitable, and more inclusive than the current world. How can ethics be incorporated into the tech stack? Can developers be connected to the ethical outcomes of their decisions and algorithms? Should a professional association for software developers with a codified ethical standard exist? How can the community and networks be more active in demanding ethical approaches?

Avatars

There will also be an emerging scientific and legal debate arising about Avatars. There are so many ethical questions about Avatars. Spence (2008) argues that people in the real world and virtual worlds have rights to freedom and well-being. He argues that avatars are virtual representations of real people and purposive agents with moral rights and obligations similar to those of their natural counterparts. If they do and have identification, they risk personal data being copied, stolen, or manipulated. How do you distinguish between an avatar and a human in virtual worlds, and does it matter? If a person is in a virtual world killing people, are they a murderer? Should avatars have agency?

Augmented and virtual reality will create new content moderation challenges, including tackling verbal harassment or hate speech in a virtual space. These inappropriate actions from avatars simulate sexual harassment or assault, pornographic content modeled on avatars, or misinformation or defamatory content generated using augmented reality. Avatars may break civil or criminal laws.

There will also be other issues emerging regarding avatars, including identity theft, avatar duplication, and misuse. Identity authentication built on Blockchain will be crucial in this respect, as it is more resistant to cyber-attacks than a centralized system. Nevertheless, this cannot address criminal activity, such as social engineering, which targets human behavior. State surveillance could increase, given governments' access to data shared in the Metaverse. Intrusive profiling could have harmful consequences, such as loss of control over life and decisions or voter manipulation, particularly for vulnerable groups. In the Metaverse workplace, employers could surveil their employees. Perceptual experiences could lead to biased automated decision-making and inequalities in hiring, performance evaluation, and training processes.

A decentralized identification network, enabling an account verification system built on international standards to enhance user confidence in using avatars across platforms, could be one way to overcome this problem.

FUNDAMENTALS OF DIGITAL ETHICS

Since this is a digital age, data is increasingly used to define what "reality" is. Traditional approaches are insufficient for this new world since they were not designed for non-physical spaces like the Internet. Data manipulation, forgery, and theft are three threats to digital systems that might come from anywhere in the world. New tools for a digital, extraterritorial dimension are required as a reaction. Ethical choices can have exponential effects in the digital age. One action can have far-reaching effects on billions of individuals when the speed and scope of its influence are hard coded into a system. Analysis and communication of the ethical implications of these developments are urgently needed, as are viable solutions to the moral problems our digital society is currently experiencing. There will be no black and white. Ethics deals with shades of gray and "right versus right."

One of the most important things to consider is the various levels of technology, starting with the technology stack, with what the technologists are building, how they're building it, and how they're incorporating ethical considerations into their design. Applications with virtual assets, smart contracts, or other types of AI algorithms should also be considered, along with the benefits and drawbacks they may have for people. Finally, how will this technological shift affect institutions and society?

Ensuring that technology is available to everyone is a requirement for ethically leading teams and organizations. We need leaders who simultaneously consider the technology's design, applications, and societal effects. Therefore, it is necessary to discuss crucial ethical issues at all levels of society, such as those involving accountability in government, organizations, and technical design.

Generational gaps in digital product consumption are constantly growing along with emerging technologies as how society consumes information and participates in economic exchanges continue to evolve along with cutting-edge technologies, which were not available a few years ago.

How can ethics be incorporated into the tech stack? Can developers be connected to the ethical outcomes of their decisions and algorithms? Should a professional association for software developers with a codified ethical standard exist? How can the community and networks be more active in demanding ethical approaches?

Ethics and the Technology Stack

The threat to privacy in Web3 and the Metaverse is more significant than in Web 2.0 because 20 minutes of virtual reality (VR) use generates almost two million unique data components. These include, among many other things, how you breathe, walk, think, move, and stare. Massive data sets will enable assembling data about a user's preferences. Not just a user's outer behavior is recorded in VR experiences. Algorithms also capture the underlying emotional responses of individuals to circumstances through traits like pupil dilation or changes in facial expression.

Although digital privacy on websites has become more regulated recently, the Metaverse is still extremely young and lacks any privacy laws. How should data security, privacy, and accessibility be guaranteed ethically? What ethical information management strategy should be used in system creation and use? These are the main ethical questions at the technological stack level. Metaverse raises some critical privacy and security concerns, such as the potential tracking of user biometrics and data usage for marketing that could lead to manipulating and monetizing schemes and other legal issues involving civil and criminal laws.

Data Ethics: Privacy Concerns and General Data Protection

Data ethics studies and evaluates moral problems related to (i) Data (including generation, recording, curation, processing, dissemination, sharing, and use; (ii) Algorithms (including artificial intelligence, artificial agents, machine learning, and robots); (iii) Corresponding practices (including responsible innovation, programming, hacking, and professional codes), to formulate and support morally good solutions (e.g., proper conduct or values).

Automation has significantly increased processing speed but has also led to more ethical risks and the need to examine the unintended consequences of automated technology. The re-identification of individuals through data mining, linking, merging, and re-using large datasets. Risks for group privacy, when the identification of types of individuals, independently of the de-identification, may lead to serious ethical problems, from group discrimination to group-targeted forms of violence (Floridi & Taddeo, 2016).

How will data, algorithms, and practice ethics be considered during design? How will data be governed, informed consent, customer understanding, the requirement for all data to be necessary for the purpose for which it is collected, and the extent of human oversight or intervention required in the decision process? How do people even know what their data is on the Internet?

Security

Current cybersecurity challenges will persist and extend to Metaverse and avatars. Protecting the integrity of avatars will be a problem. New forms of cybercrime will emerge, such as selling fake NFTs, illicit use of crypto-currencies, and malicious smart contracts. The multi-layered structure of the virtual environment may allow bad actors to hide behind encryption and untraceable NFTs, making it difficult to identify them and pursue legal recourse. Possible connections between the dark web and the Metaverse will mean creating a Metaverse criminal justice system to prevent and limit illegal activity.

Data Breaches

Connected devices could lead to severe data breaches, as the sensitive data needed for such devices to function, e.g., voice control or facial movement, could be reproduced. VR technology enables and warns that private Metaverse platforms may be contractually given a great deal of control over some critical aspects of digital assets in the Metaverse environment. Entities in the Metaverse will need to look beyond their security measures, as they will depend on the cybersecurity of other entities. Supply chain due diligence will be essential to preserve the security of the platforms.

Privacy

The European Union's General Data Privacy Regulation (GDPR) (2018) provides a set of regulations to ensure that the EU can guarantee individual data protection. The GDPR, however, was written with a centralized entity in mind that has the power to control access rights, which is not the case when Blockchain technology is used. It is thus unclear how Blockchain technology will compete with the GDPR (Posadas, 2018). Broader frameworks are also required for recognizing Blockchain records, determining the legal status of tokens, and harmonizing the relationship between the General Data Protection Regulation (GDPR) right to be forgotten and the immutable nature of blocks.

Ethical Data Governance

Data governance is "a system of decision rights and accountabilities for information-related processes, executed according to agreed-upon models which describe who can take what actions with what information, and when, under what circumstances, using what methods." Key issues include: (i) Understanding- Technology is growing exponentially, and knowledge is slower to propagate, and many in governments and society are unaware of what's happening; (ii) Interoperability- Many executives and governments may not grasp the need for ethical data governance at this point. Interoperability is vital. There are many different ways of doing data governance and data curation, making governance challenging when the data sets are not interoperable; and (iii) Portability- this can pose a global challenge as data moves across different markets and industries and, there are many differences in continents and state regulatory guidelines.

Digital Informed Consent

Organizations designing digital informed consent methods must assume responsibility for obtaining agreement ethically. As digital technologies evolve, laws, regulations, and guidelines must change accordingly to maintain the individual at the center. Data collection will be involuntary and continuous, making collecting consent almost impossible. The Metaverse entails the integration of access points with the content and services. This reduces users' capacity to avoid collecting personal data. There are currently no laws or legal jurisdictions in the Metaverse. Informed consent will be a significant challenge. A person needs to be informed of the risks, benefits, and probabilities of some dangerous consequences. They need to understand and appreciate that information, and finally, the decision needs to be voluntary.

How does this play out for people who are incapacitated, illiterate, mentally ill, or even children? Should the collection of user consent and the obligation to display privacy notices be done separately for all metaverses or each entity in a metaverse?

Data Tracking

In the Metaverse, many people willingly allow the tracking of track body movement, brainwaves, and physiological responses through wearables. The Metaverse will also increase the number of places that can be attacked. Due to its digital nature, uninformed consent in a Metaverse may include personal, biometric, financial, and emotional data. Many people freely consent for their data to be shared across the Internet, to multiple organizations, and across multiple devices, without understanding that their data may be transferred or monetized. This is particularly relevant when dealing with compassionate data, like long-term brain wave data. Can people participate without giving up on privacy and ownership of their data? Is it possible to protect people from being monitored or manipulated?

Interoperability

Moving assets like avatars and digital assets between virtual spaces will require interoperability across the "technology stack," including digital platforms and hardware devices. There is yet to be interoperability or portability between the various Metaverse environments; each platform must link NFTs to its proprietary digital assets. Companies will need to establish data-sharing agreements which fulfill data protection requirements. This may be challenging in decentralized Metaverse models. International data transfers must be clarified to enable free movement in the Metaverse. Can users carry their avatars and virtual assets from one virtual world to another?

Digital Identity and Representation

Metaverse blurs the lines between real and virtual, raising questions about ethical obligations and moral rights of avatar creation and the natural person behind digital representations. Avatars will be people's entry points into the Metaverse, allowing them to engage in immersive experiences with new social interactions.

Web3 technology lets people own their Avatar (not the platform it was created on) and use it across decentralized virtual worlds like The Sandbox. In an increasingly digital world, people will want to switch between digital identities and not always have to use the same persona across different applications. Issues will emerge regarding avatars, including identity theft, avatar duplication, and misuse. Identity authentication built on Blockchain will be crucial in this respect, as it is more resistant to cyber-attacks than a centralized system. Nevertheless, this cannot address criminal activity, such as social engineering, which targets human behavior. A decentralized identification network, enabling an account verification system built on international standards to enhance user confidence in using avatars across platforms, could be one way to overcome this problem.

Ethics and Metaverse Applications

Decentralized applications, or dApps, are software programs that run on a platform and communicate with the underlying Blockchain ledger. As this quickly expanding sector innovates with crypto, DeFi, Non-Fungible Tokens (NFTs), and smart contracts, ethical issues arise in the applications built on Blockchains. Consumer protection, money laundering, criminal misdeeds, volatility, and tax evasion are just a few of the risks. DeFi has also posed various ethical difficulties, many connected to consumer safety.

Should investors and consumers be safeguarded throughout this Metaverse experimentation phase? How can consumers and investors be safeguarded when activities are not monitored, moderated, intermediated, hosted, or authenticated by a central point, and there are no intermediaries to regulate since it is entirely P2P? Should those responsible for writing smart contracts be held liable for their actions?

In addition to privacy concerns, user safety is another critical ethical consideration that needs to be addressed in the Metaverse. The course covers issues such as cyberbullying, harassment, and virtual crimes. They are identifying how the Metaverse affects one's mental health in the long term. Frequency and duration of use should be regulated through proper R&D. How do immersive environments affect children and their well-being?

Metaverse Intellectual Property

Intellectual property (IP) enforcement is challenging because it is more difficult to identify the provider that can take down infringing content since Metaverse content is distributed and replicated across decentralized networks running on Web 3.0 and Blockchain-based platforms. There may be issues around applicable law and jurisdiction and identifying infringers. Popular brands are also facing unauthorized use of registered trademarks in the Metaverse.

Metaverse Ethics and Society

Metaverse economies demand a rethinking of governance. Web 3.0 enables the creation of leaderless, decentralized organizations that obfuscate the jurisdictional lines of economic activity. Digital communities will connect and form networks or cooperatives. They can be rewarded or paid with tokens. The user is no longer a passive service consumer; they are a stakeholder. In a Community Token Economy, individuals are the agents of innovation. These communities can be global and will be able to exchange network tokens for contributions to the ecosystem. This allows Blockchain-based metaverse ecosystems to crowdsource talent, products, and user inputs worldwide. It is possible to rapidly develop and implement large-scale structures for incentivizing human behavior.

New frontiers of social media and its systematic exploitation of human emotions, reactions, and biases, blending news and content in one feed to keep users 'in-app' and using powerful algorithms to promote more provocative posts, filter content, and trigger the reward centers of human brains.

The lines between the real and digital worlds are becoming blurrier with the convergence between social networks and geo-locations. People who use immersive technologies can become disoriented, cause injury, and become oblivious to real-world hazards. The Metaverse will likely present challenges to people's physical and mental health. While no long-term studies exist, immersive games can lead to depression, isolation, lonely behavior, and even suicide and violence. If used to excess, the Metaverse can cause mental health problems (such as loneliness) and reduce physical activity, leading to a rise in obesity and other physical health problems, contributing to a desire to escape the real world. Addictions to social media and online gaming as a form of escapism already exist, but the Metaverse can reinforce them.

Who should regulate borderless digital economies? Web 3.0 Metaverse decentralization at the social level facilitates the shift from centralized human governance to decentralized algorithm governance. Who should be responsible? Another crucial topic is how it affects the environment, impacts ESG components, and how it could potentially shape critical industries.

Children in the Metaverse

The Metaverse holds the promise of offering children a unique experience. It could enable them to return in time or visit places they could never have explored. It also offers a form of hands-on experience that can help children to understand the world around them and how things work, potentially increasing their motivation to learn. Finding ways to use the Metaverse alongside the natural world will be essential to preserve real teacher-child, caregiver-child, and child-child social relationships. If the Metaverse is left unregulated, it may cause children significant harm.

The European Commission (2022) has recently proposed several legislative acts to address age-inappropriate and illegal content online. This proposes a regulation to prevent and combat child sexual abuse online that obliges providers to detect, report, block, and remove child sexual abuse material from their services. They will also have to introduce the necessary age verification measures. This is essential to know who a child is. The protection of vulnerable groups, particularly children's data, requires special protection under the GDPR. Therefore, means will be needed to prevent children from sharing their data. Regulators have examined the effect of video games on children (Bogost, 2019). What happens when children are virtually immersed in the Metaverse and inhabit the fictional world around them?

Many platforms are voice chat based and fully immersive, which can lead to moderation challenges regarding hate speech and harassment. Content moderation will be critical, and the concentration of moderation power has already been a source of controversy on Web 2.0 platforms, and it will likely be in the Metaverse.

Avatars

There will be an emerging scientific, ethical, and legal debate about Avatars. As avatars are virtual representations of real people and purposive agents, they have moral rights and obligations similar to those of their natural counterparts. If they do and have identification, they risk personal data being copied, stolen, or manipulated. New content moderation challenges include tackling verbal harassment or hate speech in a virtual space, inappropriate actions from avatars that simulate sexual harassment or assault, pornographic content modeled on avatars, or misinformation or defamatory content generated using augmented reality.

Avatars may break civil or criminal laws. The avatars may communicate with one another, allowing players to connect not just with the computer game's artificial intelligence but also with other gamers all around the globe. How do you distinguish between an avatar and a human in virtual worlds, and does it matter?

Mental Health and Well-Being

In addition to privacy concerns, user safety is another critical ethical consideration that needs to be addressed in the Metaverse. They are identifying how the Metaverse affects one's mental health in the long term. Frequency and duration of use should be regulated through proper R&D. Mainstreaming of data science has been accompanied by expanded daily hours in front of screens and the emergence of a brand-new internet minute, which contains within itself a fundamental dependence and emotional investment into digital solutions as a bridge between families, friends, communities, and societies. The addictive nature of the internet world transformed the internet minute into the first generation of internet lifetimes, where significant milestones in the human experience could exist almost entirely online. Large demographics already buy in the notions of reality TV, streaming entertainment, and social media as forms of escapism, and the lines between the natural world and the digital one are becoming blurrier with the convergence between social networks and geo-locations

Ethical Considerations for Government

Web 3.0 enables the creation of leaderless, decentralized organizations that blur the jurisdictional boundaries of economic activities. In particular, enforcing accountability through technical specifications and smart contracts will require a deep understanding of the objectives of the network and decision rights, incentives, and accountabilities. Who should regulate digital, international, and borderless economies? The transition from centralized human governance to decentralized algorithm governance is made possible by Web3 decentralization at the social level. Possible solutions include:

1. Technical solutions such as standards or explicit normative encoding.
2. Transparency, notably by providing information and raising public awareness of existing rights and regulation.
3. Testing, monitoring, and auditing, the preferred solution of notable data protection offices.
4. Developing or strengthening the rule of law and the right to appeal, recourse, redress, or remedy.
5. Systemic changes and processes such as governmental action and oversight, a more interdisciplinary or otherwise diverse workforce, and better inclusion of civil society or other relevant stakeholders in an interactive manner and increased attention to the distribution of benefits.

Digital Rights Management

How can companies commit to ethical practices for their growth, continuously educate ethical decision-making, and reinforce, monitor, and empower employees to question potential unethical issues? Digital Rights Management is one way to create better and ethically safe online spaces. Digital Rights Management (DRM) is a technology that safeguards data over the application layer from illicit usage using some form of encryption. DRM technologies for Cloud content must be explored to protect Cloud data from unauthorized usage and efficient revocation. Unauthorized Cloud content sharing or maneuvering access licenses may infringe copyrights and online content security policies.

Most online social networking platforms store and serve data using the Cloud computing paradigm. After a user transfers the data to any Cloud-based storage provider, the Cloud provider manages the data itself, and the data owner has little control over its data at rest or when the user shares the data with another user or with the online social media platforms. DRM in the Cloud enables content publishers to access control of its contents for content-consuming devices. DRM in the Cloud is necessary to preserve intellectual property to manage data confidentiality, integrity, and security, especially after sharing content with a third party. This third-party verification feature is an emerging research topic, and optimal access technology can help solve the problem in Cloud DRM.

Institutions and Society

The Metaverse can create a new socio-economic ecosystem, legal and regulatory requirements, and a global workforce. Blending boundaries between physical, digital, and biological worlds will likely continue at an exponential pace with technologies such as AI, IoT, 6G, or next-generation computing having the potential to reshape, recalibrate or disrupt our society and the global economy. With the current exponential advancements of a variety of modern technologies, business leaders must have a higher degree of technical acumen in order and emotional intelligence, lead with purpose and embrace ethics to remain competitive and ensure long-term sustainability for their companies.

Corporate Ethics in the Digital Era

Digital ethics address behaviors related to digital mediums, norms for using digital tools, autonomy, ownership of online data, etc. Business ethics include governance, social and fiduciary responsibilities, discrimination, fraud, abuse, or bribery. Leadership ethics describes the attributes of ethical leaders in this digital world. Data Protection and Integrity- confidentiality, Fidelity, Integrity; artificial intelligence algorithms, neural networks, adversarial networks, and decentralized autonomous organizations are producing large datasets of products or solutions that are vulnerable to cybersecurity attacks, and we will have to design robust, proactive cyber-defense mechanisms to protect our privacy, enhance trust and maintain data integrity.

Some experts have even advocated for creating a Universal Code of Digita Ethics to guide legislators, compliance specialists, regulators, and industry leaders in implementing the values outlined by proactive digital ethics programs. Data ethics and consumer protection will be a key focus for ethicists and regulators alike. The educational aspect and the need to teach ethical and moral issues which may be caused by AI-powered technologies to future generations. Digital informed consent methods instead require adaptations of consent processes and appropriate uses of permissioned data to adhere to ethical principles. Generational gaps in digital product consumption are constantly growing in sync with emerging technologies as how society consumes information (streaming, social networks, digital realities, immersive environment) and participates in economic exchanges (freelancer, influencer economics) continue to evolve along with cutting-edge technologies, which were not available even five years ago.

Digital literacy is instrumental to educational, working, personal, and social lives, and algorithmic literacy needs to include algorithms' ethical design to ensure that decisions are fair and transparent.

Digital ethics frameworks include ethical and digital risk analysis. These tools can be deployed at various stages and in different layers of the business processes, establishing and monitoring digital ethics implementations via KPIs and building a culture of digital ethics while embracing an ongoing quality improvement mindset. A best-in-class cyber-ethics program likely represents one of the significant drivers of success when operationalizing a proactive digital ethics framework. The deployment of these frameworks requires digital ethics literacy and harmonization with other key organizational units such as Compliance, Human Resources, and Marketing. Cybersecurity and ethics tend to be managed in silos and therefore offer the opportunity for cyberattacks or privacy breaches. A state-of-the-art comprehensive digital ethics program must always include a robust cyber-ethics component and be fully integrated or harmonized with the organizational cyber-security systems, key hot topics in cyber-ethics. Digital marketing has several critical ethical challenges, such as mindful data usage, targeted advertising, truthful advertising, and refraining from adverse comments about religion, politics, ethnicity, or other emotionally charged content.

A new subfield of ethics, "techno-ethics," which deals with framing principles and methods to guide technology implementation and use, is emerging. The changing consumer habits and preferences about digital access will drive alternative approaches to ethical approaches. Propositions such as Developing a Universal Code of Conduct for Digital Business Ethics and a Global Digital Ethics Framework are moral imperative. Across the range of perspectives presented is a clear call for digital education, not just for laws and regulations but guidelines and interpretations. These must be developed for corporations, communities, governments, and those who design the systems.

FUTURE DEVELOPMENTS

Despite the levels of enthusiasm and investment in the Metaverse, there remain barriers to wide-scale adoption. Only some people genuinely understand the actual utility of a Metaverse. Creating clear benefits for different use cases will be critical to drawing mass audiences. The VR/AR UX hardware must improve dramatically for widespread adoption. The UX/UI of interacting with Blockchain and NFT-based platforms is still clunky, especially for new users. There needs to be improved user experience to create seamless onboarding for non-technical users.

Avatars will be people's entry points into the Metaverse, allowing them to engage in immersive experiences with new social interactions. Web3 technology lets people own their Avatar (not the platform it was created on) and use it across decentralized virtual worlds like The Sandbox. It is reasonably clear that in an increasingly digital world, people will want to switch between digital identities and not always have to use the same persona across different applications. New combinations will be developed for MetaFi categories and the creation of entirely new ones, e.g., user-generated games in virtual worlds with their own economies or yield-bearing non-fungible assets embedded into wearables or avatars.

Most Metaverse platforms currently have different formats and standards for their in-world assets, which makes it challenging to carry assets from one platform to the next. There is a lack of open protocols for sharing and standardizing identities and assets necessary to achieve portability. And interpretability of decentralized information. Current scalability limits of some leading public Blockchains restrict decentralized gamification's applicability to scenarios involving low-frequency on-chain interactions. However, it would be possible to circumvent these limits by relaxing some decentralization constraints. Government policy will be needed around data rights, privacy, antitrust, and financial legislation. Regulation will be one tool governments use to change the course of development. Standards and common taxonomies and frameworks for audit will also be needed.

CONCLUSION

This chapter has outlined the immersive and persistent nature of the Metaverse, combining virtual and physical worlds with its economy. It has outlined the many challenges to widespread adoption, including interoperability, latency, user interface, and regulation. It also poses many ethical issues yet to be resolved and ideas on how to do so. The Metaverse is an exciting technological development that will help create new and enhanced ways to live, shop, be entertained, seek services, and be educated. The Metaverse could be fulfilling and rewarding and create social purpose. At the same time, there are enormous risks. The Metaverse is an integral part of the future, and its potential is limited only by the framework of our imagination and today's technologies.

REFERENCES

A Guide to MetaFi: Infrastructure for the Virtual Economy. (2022, April 6). CYBAVO. Retrieved November 14, 2022, from https://www.cybavo.com/blog/metafi-insfrastructure-for-virtual-economy/

Blockchain Magazine. (2023, January 5). *YouTube.* Retrieved June 2, 2023, from https://blockchainmagazine.net/lets-meet-Metaverse-avatar-metafi/

Bogost, I. (2019, August 5). *The El Paso Shooting and Video Games as a Partisan Issue.* The Atlantic. Retrieved November 15, 2022, from https://www.theatlantic.com/technology/archive/2019/08/video-game-violence-became-partisan-issue/595456/

Chow, A. R. (2021, November 18). *Why You Should Be Paying Attention to the Metaverse.* TIME. Retrieved November 14, 2022, from https://time.com/6118513/into-the-Metaverse-time-newsletter/

Everette, J. (2021, January 27). *Top Massively Multiplayer Online Role-Playing Games.* Lifewire. Retrieved November 14, 2022, from https://www.lifewire.com/the-top-mmorpgs-813063

Ghosh, S. (n.d.). *A study on METAVERSE - GRM Institute.* Global Risk Management Institute. Retrieved November 15, 2022, from https://grm.institute/blog/a-study-on-Metaverse/

Henderson, R. (2021, October 22). *The Blockchain Metaverse. The way the internet works is changing… | by Novum Insights | Medium.* Novum Insights. Retrieved November 14, 2022, from https://novuminsights.medium.com/the-Blockchain-Metaverse-f58c62cc1285

Home. (n.d.a). YouTube. Retrieved November 14, 2022, from https://outlierventures.io/wp-content/uploads/2021/02/OV-Metaverse-OS-V5.pdfBlockchain

Home. (n.d.b). YouTube. Retrieved November 14, 2022, from https://www.insiderintelligence.com/content/gamers-make-up-more-than-one-third-of-world-population

Home. (n.d.c). YouTube. Retrieved November 14, 2022, from https://medium.com/umbalaMetaverse/nfts-metafi-next-big-investment-trend

Home. (n.d.d). YouTube. Retrieved November 14, 2022, from https://www.amerikayageldim.com/assets/uploads/files/1647380348146-1647331508066.pdf

Home. (n.d.e). YouTube. Retrieved November 15, 2022, from https://www.gamesindustry.biz/game-designers-must-be-included-in-the-emerging-conversation-around-tech-ethics

Howell, J. (2022, March 1). *MetaFi - Where DeFi Meets the Metaverse*. 101 Blockchains. Retrieved November 14, 2022, from https://101Blockchains.com/metafi/

Intelligence, I. (n.d.). *Empower yourself with the data, insights, and analysis you need to make strategic business decisions in a digital world*. Insider Intelligence. https://www.insiderintelligence.com/

Logan, K. (2021, December 3). *Cathie Wood says the Metaverse could be worth trillions and will affect the world in ways 'we cannot even imagine right now'*. Fortune. Retrieved November 14, 2022, from https://fortune.com/2021/12/03/cathie-wood-Metaverse-trillions-affect-every-sector/

Mathews, E., Mukherjee, S., Dang, S., & Samuel, M. (2021, October 18). *Facebook plans to hire 10000 in the EU to build a 'Metaverse*. Reuters. Retrieved November 14, 2022, from https://www.reuters.com/technology/facebook-plans-hire-10000-eu-build-Metaverse-2021-10-17/

Meilich, A., Ordano, E., & Guide, S. (2022, August 3). *What is GameFi? 'Play-to-Earn' Gaming Explained*. Crypto.com. Retrieved November 14, 2022, from https://crypto.com/university/what-is-gamefi-play-to-earn-gaming-explained

MetaFi. (n.d.). *Opportunity Encounter between Metaverse and DeFi.* Retrieved November 14, 2022, from https://inf.news/en/economy/6ae1d599ff088ab35 39c3dd7f0748b60.html

MetaFi: Where DeFi Meets the Metaverse | MetaFi Token - Beginner's Guide. (n.d.). Token Development Company. Retrieved November 14, 2022, from https://www.securitytokenizer.io/metafi-defi-meets-Metaverse

Metaverse. (2022, June 1). European Parliament. Retrieved November 15, 2022, from https://www.europarl.europa.eu/RegData/etudes/BRIE/2022/733557/ EPRS_BRI(2022)733557_EN.pdf

Metaverse and Money - CitiGPS. (2022, March 30). Institutional Clients Group. Retrieved November 14, 2022, from https://icg.citi.com/icghome/ what-we-think/citigps/insights/Metaverse-and-money_20220330

Metaverse maybe $800 billion market, next tech platform Insights. (2021, December 1). Bloomberg.com. Retrieved November 14, 2022, from https:// www.bloomberg.com/professional/blog/Metaverse-may-be-800-billion-market-next-tech-platform/

Metaverse: Opportunities, risks and policy implications | Think Tank. (2022, June 24). European Parliament. Retrieved November 15, 2022, from https:// www.europarl.europa.eu/thinktank/en/document/EPRS_BRI(2022)733557

Perkins, K. (n.d.). *September 2022.* Cryptomeria Capital. Retrieved November 14, 2022, from https://research.cryptomeriacapital.com/Cryptomeria_ Capital_Metaverse_Overview_September_2022.pdf

Ratan, R., & Lei, Y. (2021, August 12). *What is the Metaverse? 2 media and information experts explain.* The Conversation. Retrieved November 14, 2022, from https://theconversation.com/what-is-the-Metaverse-2-media-and-information-experts-explain-165731

Rees, K. (2022, February 16). *These 8 Tech Giants Have Invested Big in The Metaverse.* MakeUseOf. Retrieved November 14, 2022, from https://www. makeuseof.com/companies-investing-in-Metaverse/

Spence, E. (2022, February 26). Retrieved November 15, 2022, from https:// www.researchgate.net/publication/234824743_Meta_Ethics_for_the_ Metaverse_The_Ethics_of_Virtual_Worlds

Takahashi, D. (2022, August 5). *The DeanBeat: Why Web3 companies created the Open Metaverse Alliance.* VentureBeat. Retrieved November 14, 2022, from https://venturebeat.com/games/the-deanbeat-why-web3-companies-created-the-open-Metaverse-alliance/

Thomason, J. (2022, February 16). *It's all oh so very Meta.* City A.M. Retrieved November 14, 2022, from https://www.cityam.com/its-all-oh-so-very-meta/

Thomason, J. A. (2021, November 28). *New tribes of the Metaverse — Community-owned economies.* Cointelegraph. Retrieved November 15, 2022, from https://cointelegraph.com/news/new-tribes-of-the-Metaverse-community-owned-economies

Video Game Market Size & Share Growth Report, 2030. (n.d.). Grand View Research. Retrieved November 14, 2022, from https://www.grandviewresearch.com/industry-analysis/video-game-market

What's the Plural for Metaverse? (2021, July 14). Cognizant. Retrieved November 14, 2022, from https://www.cognizant.com/futureofwork/article/whats-the-plural-for-Metaverse

Chapter 10
Living in the Metaverse

ABSTRACT

As the quest to build Metaverses continues, many industries invest by entering existing metaverses or developing their own. There is substantial innovation and experimentation, from entertainment to commerce to real estate. Metaverse-provided services such as health, education, and government services are all under development. It will be in new "phygital" realms that Metazens (citizens of the Metaverse) will explore these new domains. "Phygital" is the use of technology to bridge the digital world with the physical world to provide unique interactive experiences for users. This chapter explores the sectors utilizing the Metaverse and issues for future growth, including infrastructure, user experience, adoption, and interoperability.

INTRODUCTION

Chapter 9 described how Facebook (Meta), Microsoft, Tencent, Snap, Nvidia, and others have started pouring resources into developing the Metaverse (Chow, 2021). At the same time, gaming companies have already created their thriving virtual worlds. They are increasingly adopting blockchain to enable value creators to earn money directly for their online efforts without intermediaries. This has given creatives new income streams and has spawned a new wave of Web 3.0 companies striving to create an open Metaverse where all contributors can be rewarded.

DOI: 10.4018/978-1-6684-6658-2.ch010

In this Web 3.0 world, everyone can own their data and be compensated directly for their online creations without intermediaries. (Chow, 2021) Web 3 supporters are philosophically opposed to the big Tech Metaverses.

Decentralization allows developers and platforms functionality which, before its emergence, was impossible. This will lead to interoperability among Metaverses, and users can exchange and sell assets from any Metaverse and the real word interchangeably. The powerful combination of game theory and blockchain creates tokenized incentivization in virtual worlds. It is now possible to create tokenized incentivization to architecting people's choices. The combination of cryptography, computer networks, and game theory is used to secure systems and realize a set of economic incentives or disincentives. It is an incentivized framework.

METAVERSE USE CASES

What industries will use the Metaverse, and what will life in the Metaverse be like?

Commerce

Commerce in the Metaverse is growing fast. In the Metaverse, brands can create a virtual world that consumers can visit and explore (Moyers, S. 2022). Moyers (2022) sees this as an opportunity to improve customer experience and create a space tailored to their brand. Including promoting and profiting from digital products; Selling digital products that customers can use in their virtual worlds; creating brand experiences, building customer loyalty; and testing new products before they are released to the public. Regardless of what ends up enabling Metaverse commerce, there have been few times in history when entire markets have been presented with what essentially amounts to a fresh slate.

Decentralized protocols have quickly identified a need for value to be easily transferable. Boson Protocol is one of many projects seeking to facilitate 'Metaverse commerce' or 'MetaFi.' They believe that items and goods purchased within virtual experiences, like The Sandbox or Decentraland, should be considered to hold the same value as their equivalent real-world transaction. Boson allows compatible goods purchased in Metaverse games to be represented as NFTs, which can be redeemed for the real-world asset it represents. Likewise, compatible items purchased in real life can be transferred into the Metaverse through an NFT. The non-fungibility that defines NFTs can allow them to function as 'receipts,' which can prove ownership of a particular product with specific attributes stored within the token. Smart contracts are used to operate peer-to-peer transactions that pay both parties.

Highstreet is another relatively new protocol with similar aims. Products from brands such as Hershey's, L'Oréal, and Victoria's Secret can be tokenized and sold across Metaverse experiences. The protocol's liquidity pools make purchasing tokenized products as seamless as purchasing their real-world counterparts. Another Metaverse platform, Space Metaverse, backed by Animoca Brands, Dapper Labs, Digital Currency Group, and many others, is focused on the commerce side of the Metaverse and enables users to design their own virtual spaces like shops, galleries easily and music halls with the point of sale tools integrated.

While there will surely be ads in the Metaverse, brands can be part of creating the Metaverse itself. Digital clothing, world-building, or marketing can have a tangible impact on brands (Danise et al., 2020). The Metaverse provides a new market in digital-first clothing and allows users to create unique digital identities (Danise et al., 2020). Virtual fashion houses and digital designers have a unique opportunity to build a new digital fashion industry. There still needs to be more consensus on how Metaverse commerce will be facilitated at scale. However, NFTs, as digital receipts, are providing the means for decentralized Metaverse commerce.

Gaming

Gaming will likely be the vector for the widespread adoption of digital assets with the availability of high-performance platforms; improved on and off-ramps for digital assets; and better digital asset storage and distribution tools for gamers, incentivized by the ability for gamers to earn credits that can be used in games. Bloomberg (2021) reports that games like Axie Infinity and the Metaverse are upending how we work, earn, spend, live, plan, and run our lives. Metaverse economists are emerging to oversee and plan the macroeconomics of metaverses, just as they do today's physical economy. In Fortnite, real-world celebrities play the game, and players become celebrities (Danise et al., 2020). People will go to brands in the Metaverse because they feel a connection, not necessarily a need for that product or service.

Social Tokens

Marc Whitten (2021) argues that the Metaverse will be the most potent computer-based innovation the world has ever seen. Socializing, meeting friends, and being with them in person are very appealing, especially in these socially distant times. In the Metaverse, people will socialize, attend concerts, travel, shop, and go to the movies - virtually. Fans can create avatars where they can meet their idols and receive virtual autographs. The Metaverse will grow to include multiple cross-chain possibilities as the virtual economy grows in importance. Gen Alpha will see these digital opportunities to believe that the Metaverse is the place to make their fortunes.

The most significant benefits will come from the emergence of community-owned economies and social tokens in the Metaverse (White, 2021). Digital communities will connect and form networks or cooperatives. They can be rewarded or paid with tokens. The user is no longer a passive service consumer; they are a stakeholder. In a Community Token Economy, individuals are the agents of innovation. These communities can be global and will be able to exchange network tokens for contributions to the ecosystem. Blockchain-based Web 3.0 ecosystems can crowdsource talent, products, and user inputs worldwide. It is possible to rapidly develop and implement large-scale structures for incentivizing human behavior. A central issue is creating incentive systems that align the individual's interest with the overall beneficial outcomes for the planet.

Social tokens will be essential to developing two-way relationships between creators and consumers (Shumba, 2021). This will often be in the form of celebrities and fans, where fans can receive discounts, incentives, and upfront experiences with their celebrities. The tokens will allow the community to connect and feel part of the community (Shumba, 2021).

This is also relevant to social prescribing, which can involve a wide range of services for the vulnerable. These include health care, financial and social services, volunteering, group learning, gardening, befriending, cooking, healthy eating advice, sports, and other activities. This has benefited those with mental health problems, complex needs, social isolation, and multiple long-term conditions (Thomason, 2022). Thomason (2022) envisions primary care professionals and service providers for payments, like the provision of services and a financial instrument tracking the perceived value of that community. Benefits for vulnerable people include improved access to care, fewer travel requirements, reduced costs, better schedule flexibility, greater environmental familiarity, and higher patient engagement rates. Socializing, meeting friends, and feeling there with them are very appealing, especially in socially distant times and for vulnerable people.

Health and Wellness

There is substantial potential for Metaverse to extend and improve health care. The healthcare sector is seeing a massive digital transformation from MRI scans and X-rays to robotic surgeries and virtual reality. The Metaverse is a massive technological game-changer for healthcare in mental health, access to health without geographical limitations, virtual wellness and fitness, and connecting with people. Harnessing technology will give consumers the data and information they need to proactively manage their health and wellness and make better, more informed decisions. (Thomason, 2021). Consumer-focused health care driven by data will change the institutional models of the past (Thomason, 2021). Blockchain and token economies in the Metaverse allow secure sharing and monetization of data and intellectual value. Some of the critical use cases for health care are summarized below.

Clinical Care

There are many concrete applications of Metaverse in health care. The Metaverse will further enhance surgical precision and flexibility for complex procedures. Pre-surgery and post-surgery assessments can also benefit from using A.R. to optimize surgical outcomes with more personalized intervention rooted in data analytics. Among providers, the use of A.R. and V.R. is currently focused on several discrete areas, mainly surgical simulations, diagnostic imaging, patient care management, rehabilitation, and health management. (Grand View Research, 2017). For patients, these technologies can expedite education about conditions or treatment plans.

Avatars will be created for more realistic consultations, personalized care, treatment, and diagnosis through data interconnectivity. Metaverse is already used to treat mental health issues, including phobias, PTSD, anxiety disorders, hallucinations, and delusions. Metaverse is interactive, provides an arena for online therapy, improves access to treatment for disabled people, and renders a life-like experience. Concrete examples include using A.R. headsets to project a digital twin over a physical body during surgery. Surgeons have used this procedure to correct spine problems and remove tumors. (Witham,

2021). This provides a practical use case with real utility. Brainlab has created a virtual replica of its radiotherapy system, which allows health workers to access their technology anytime and anywhere (Brainlab, n.d). Empa uses digital twin technology for chronic pain (Six, 2021), and NASA captures digital twins of astronauts before long missions into space (Coombs, 2019).

Gamification is being used to capture practical challenges for doctors. There are increasing examples of collaboration between healthcare organizations and gaming companies. For example, Animonica, a global player in gamification and blockchain, and GOQii, an innovative tech-enabled healthcare platform, are launching a Health Metaverse partnership (GOQii, 2022). Apollo Hospitals Group is collaborating with 8chili Inc to engage the users in virtual reality-mediated activities to empower their abilities to regulate emotion (Apollo Hospitals, 2022). Many more use cases are under development, and the advent of 5G is expected to accelerate the use of Metaverse and immersive technologies in health care.

Wellness

Hoogendoorn (2021) reported on the "play-to-earn" phenomenon, which became prominent in the Philippines, where gamers could earn income from playing a game called Axie Infinity during lockdowns. This concept is being extended into obesity and long-term chronic disease creating an unsustainable burden on the health care system. Gamification will connect healthcare providers and patients, especially in wellness and fitness, where A.R. delivers more innovative workouts with guidance from virtual instructors. A fast-developing application is "move-to-earn," where players are incentivized to be active. Smartphones or fitness wearables track their data, and players can get rewarded for exercising.

Collaboration and Scientific Discovery

The Metaverse offers 24-hour research, scientific discovery, and design collaboration spaces. Avatars of collaborators can work with digital whiteboards and workstations and meet face-to-face without complex conferencing equipment. With the growing popularity of digital twin technology, industries can test systems and machines and detect vulnerabilities before moving into the physical realm. This is widely used in health care, and increasingly other industries will adopt this approach (Thomason, 2021).

Metaverse Education

A long-term and paradigm-shifting trend is taking place. Computer building is faster and cheaper technology. Everything is digitizing, ChatGPT is disrupting industries, and exponential organizations have changed how people think about ownership. Research into the labor market implications of large language models (Eloundu et al., 2023) has found that approximately 80% of the U.S. workforce could have at least 10% of their work tasks affected by the introduction of GPTs, while around 19% of workers may see at least 50% of their tasks impacted. The findings emphasize the importance of science and critical thinking skills.

According to a report published by the International Association of Virtual Reality and Augmented Reality (IAVAR) in 2022, the global market for virtual and augmented reality in education is expected to reach $17.8 billion by 2025, with a compound annual growth rate of 51.5% from 2020 to 2025 (IAVAR, 2022). The metaverse education market is expected to grow significantly, with increased public and private investment. Revenue in the Metaverse Education segment is projected to reach US$56.73m in 2023. Revenue is expected to show an annual growth rate (CAGR 2023-2030) of 44.98%, resulting in a projected market volume of US$763.70m by 2030.

The Metaverse offers the potential for experiential learning, where students can apply and practice their skills in realistic and authentic environments, such as virtual internships or simulations (Sung et al., 2019). Metaverse education offers the potential for Micro-credentialing, which allows learners to earn more minor, specialized certifications that can be completed in a shorter time than a traditional degree program. These credentials can be stacked together to create a personalized learning pathway. It also enables Personalized learning using algorithms to create customized learning experiences for each learner. These platforms adapt to each learner's strengths and weaknesses and provide targeted feedback to help learners improve.

Artificial intelligence will play a significant role in the future of metaverse education, allowing for more personalized learning experiences and improved data analysis. A.I. can improve the educational experience and outcomes in several ways: (i) Personalized learning: A.I. algorithms can analyze student performance data to identify individual strengths and weaknesses and provide personalized learning experiences. (ii) AI-powered assessments can adapt to the student's level of knowledge and provide real-time feedback. (iii) AI-powered tutoring systems can provide students personalized guidance and support. (iv) A.I. algorithms can automatically grade assignments and exams, saving time and providing students with immediate feedback, and (v) A.I. algorithms can analyze data on student performance and feedback to inform the development of curricula tailored to individual student needs.

The rise of metaverse education will challenge universities to adapt and innovate to stay relevant in a rapidly changing educational landscape. Metaverse education can be more flexible than traditional university education, as learners can access courses and materials anywhere and anytime.

Bubeck et al. (2023) highlight the need for multiyear investment in education, training, and development of expertise and the need to adapt, reskill, or reorient career paths in light of the new capabilities of A.I. Creating a global metaverse education program for skills development would require a significant amount of investment. The exact cost would depend on several factors, including the scope and scale of the program, the technology infrastructure needed, and the development and deployment of content and resources. This would require investments in (i) technology infrastructure; (ii) content development; (iii) instructor and staff costs: and (iv) Marketing and outreach.

Blockchain and gamification can transform education into an immersive experience where learning is fun, success is rewarded, and data analytics target precision learning. New platforms are creating ways that people can "learn to earn" and can be integrated into healthcare. This may be for wellness, community collaboration, or medical education. Users can be rewarded with tokens for class attendance, video viewing, and completed assignments. Augmented reality will allow A.I. instructors to show learners in real life: how to stand correctly and how to appear more confident. People can learn from a game-like setting, using celebrity coaches to demonstrate skills. Interoperability is essential to digital healthcare, as it is a growing need for all. Medical schools are beginning to incorporate augmented reality (A.R.) into the curriculum to provide students with valuable hands-on learning opportunities. With AR, programs can simulate patient and surgical encounters, allowing medical students to visualize and practice techniques during training (Thomason, 2022).

One of the main benefits of education in the Metaverse is that it is not limited by time or location. This allows people on a 24-hour time cycle to enter and participate in learning activities and select the learning activities they want to participate in. So, people from both ends of the globe interact together without the need for walls in a more diverse learning environment. This gives teachers and learners in different places great opportunities to connect with educational settings (Zhang et al., 2022).

The Metaverse will enable people to have customized avatars. Teachers and peers in avatars can interact with the learner's avatar. This way, learners can participate in learning activities and collaborate virtually. For example, field visits for geography could take learners to Croatia or Slovenia to learn about Eastern Europe. It also enables learners to develop higher-order cognitive functions and achieve more comprehensive learning objectives.

It is also possible within the Metaverse environment to construct customized learning scenes that maximize learners' attention. It enables resources to be provided visually rather than in a book. For example, in astronomy, it is possible to represent the planets and demonstrate by zooming in and rotating out which planets are and in what order they go from the sun. It provides more opportunities for interactive learning, much more so than a platform like Zoom. This can include virtual learning experiences where participants engage in activities, such as group field trips, panels, quizzes, and creating spaces. Metaverse also offers opportunities for language training, allowing people to interact with intelligent peers for language practice.

Competency-based education is a way to enable interactive discussions about issues. It allows teachers and learners to share professional knowledge by observing processes in a virtual environment.

Suppose people living in developing countries have access to a mobile phone, and the Metaverse is augmented reality enabled. In that case, it will enable people to connect from places where bricks and mortar schools may not even be available.

Sports

The Qatar World Cup has provided an opportunity to see how the Metaverse can broaden access to exclusive events. Many people worldwide cannot visit Qatar, but they can go through a virtual space and visit one of these stadiums FIFA (2022). Upland Metaverse allows people to travel to the stadium, shop for merchandise, trade these, and win prizes. This will make global events more accessible to people who would otherwise be unable to travel to attend.

Government and Industry

Rob Whitton (2021) predicts that businesses will offer virtual versions of their services, allowing users to try out 3D products before purchase. Every government and major company will have a Metaverse strategy. He predicts employers will use the Metaverse 3D environment to allow distributed workers to collaborate using technology. Governments can visit job sites virtually to monitor progress in highly realistic 3D.

Park (2022) reports that South Korea's government announced a US$170 million fund to invest in the virtual reality idea and its digital technologies to be in the top five nations in metaverse developments by 2026. The capital Seoul is building a Metaverse to provide digital civil services, and other cities have announced their metaverse initiatives. Asia's largest metaverse platform has 20 million monthly active users, one of the largest in Asia (Davies & Jung, 2022).

In Dubai, the Dubai Future Foundation recently convened the Dubai Metaverse assembly and produced an extensive outcomes report (PWC, 2022). The potential possibilities for the Metaverse include the legislative frameworks, bilateral treaties in the Metaverse, and services in a borderless physical environment. The Assembly concluded that governments and businesses must now act to prepare themselves for the Metaverse transformation. Action points included establishing regulators to formulate regulations for Metaverse, the importance of collaboration with all stakeholders in the Metaverse ecosystem, forming partnerships, and developing tangible relatable use cases to gain credibility with users and the public. It concluded that the Metaverse is expected to empower users in new ways. Other governments are expected to follow these pioneers.

Metaverse-as-a-Service

The software industry has been quick to respond to Metaverse with the creation of Metaverse as a service. These subscription services enable people to access various components and technologies of the Metaverse. For example, a retailer could access Metaverse-as-a-Service and develop their virtual retail store. In a study of Metaverse-as-a-Service, Liu, Y. (2022) identified two typical types of Metaverse services. The first is for digital twins, which offer components and technology as a service, allowing them access to hardware and on-demand software. A second kind is the augmented and virtual reality services which offer Metaverse using immersive experiences using A.R. and V.R. So, as an example, a virtual travel scenario on a beach includes augmented reality service with navigation services maps and extended reality experiences, like panoramics of the beach, so people can have a beach experience by exploring the world as avatars. There is a proliferation of platforms that enable people to access digital twin technology, with digital twins-as-a-service making it possible to co-create solutions with digital twins, creating a virtual model of a physical thing.

FUTURE RESEARCH DIRECTIONS

The European Digital University, based in U.S. and Iceland, will be the first to offer an integrated doctorate in Metaverse in collaboration with major Indian universities (Khaleej Times, 2022). This is expected to cover research areas of metaverse economics, technologies and infrastructure, Metaverse and the future of work, MetaFi, Metaverse and industry, Metaverse and government, metaverse education, metaverse ethics, and metaverse standards and regulatory approaches.

Samia Rizk (2022) recommends that the convergence of digital solutions will require an additional set of standards and approaches as new applications arise. In particular, market players developing X.R. solutions must address the risk of bias amplification in A.I. She concludes, "The challenges for ethics will expand as the areas of digital convergence grow, and the scenarios diverge to reflect individual use scenarios."

This leads to the growth of community-led organizations to promote knowledge and standards for the Metaverse. For example, The World Metaverse Council, launched in October 2022 (World Metaverse Council, 2022), states it intends to be a platform leading the dialogue for equity and inclusion. Its Declaration promotes open collaboration sharing of technological advancements and standards. Other industry leaders have stated that the potential of the Metaverse will be best realized if it is built on a foundation of open standards. The Metaverse Standards Forum provides a venue for cooperation between standards organizations and companies to foster the development of interoperability standards for an open and inclusive metaverse and accelerate their development and deployment through practical, action-based projects. Another initiative, Metaverse Safety Week (2022), is an international community effort to explore the challenges of the Metaverse in critical areas of this emerging ecosystem.

CONCLUSION

There needs to be a genuine utility for the Metaverse to be widely adopted, and people must associate it with utility. Specific demographics are more likely to engage. Teenagers are the ones who are embracing the digital-first lifestyle. They have grown up with smartphones and touchscreens and are much more comfortable with these digital-first experiences than people. It has become part of their lives as they have gotten older. They will be comfortable attending a virtual concert. They will want to dress their avatars in branded merchandise, which will be available digitally. They can attend the concert and have a virtual outfit and a physical outfit as well. People can be accountants during the day and play different roles in the Metaverse. Many will want to do just that.

Empowering professionals who understand the space to engage in education and create concrete use cases that help them enhance their practice is a way of giving back power in a creative economy and educating big brands. There are challenges in educating people who may be resistant to the Metaverse. What are some of the things that bring that experience to them? This is just the beginning of the Metaverse journey, and more than 160 companies are creating Metaverses. There is much to learn. There are no doubt risks, but the opportunities are immense. This is a new world that is advancing daily, and our knowledge grows with the innovators who are building these new Metaverses. This is the next iteration of the internet, and governments and businesses will embrace it, as Gen Z and Gen Alpha do.

REFERENCES

Boson Protocol - Web3's Commerce Layer. (n.d.). Retrieved June 8, 2023, from https://www.bosonprotocol.io/

Chow, A. R. (2021, November 18). *Why TIME Is Launching a New Newsletter on the Metaverse*. Time. https://time.com/6118513/into-the-metaverse-time-newsletter/

Coombs, B. (2019, August 30). *From Jedis to astronauts: How NASA tapped a video game maker for training*. CNBC. https://www.cnbc.com/2019/08/30/jedis-to-astronauts-how-nasa-tapped-video-game-maker-for-training.html

Davies, C. D., & Jung-a, S. (2022, September 27). Asia's largest metaverse platform Zepeto ramps up global expansion. *Financial Times*. https://www.ft.com/content/14c88e84-f3c8-485e-a9df-31ead34e48f0

ExacTrac Dynamic® - A New Dimension in Patient Positioning and Monitoring. (n.d.). Brainlab. https://www.brainlab.com/radiosurgery-products/exactrac/

FIFA. (2022, November 8). *FIFA unveils range of new web 3.0 games ahead of FIFA World Cup Qatar 2022*. FIFA. https://www.fifa.com/fifaplus/en/articles/fifa-unveils-range-of-new-web-3-0-games-ahead-of-fifa-world-cup-qatar-2022

GOQii. (2022, March 29). *GOQii To Launch Health Metaverse In Partnership With Animoca Brands*. GOQii. https://goqii.com/blog/goqii-to-launch-health-metaverse-in-partnership-with-animoca-brands/

Hackl, C. (2020, July 5). *The Metaverse Is Coming And It's A Very Big Deal*. Forbes. https://www.forbes.com/sites/cathyhackl/2020/07/05/the-metaverse-is-coming--its-a-very-big-deal/

Highstreet Market. (n.d.). Retrieved June 8, 2023, from https://www.highstreet.market/

Home | Forefront. (n.d.). https://www.forefront.market

In a first-of-its-kind initiative in the healthcare industry, Apollo Hospitals collaborates with 8chili Inc to enter the Metaverse. (n.d.). Apollo Hospitals. Retrieved June 8, 2023, from https://www.apollohospitals.com/apollo-in-the-news/in-a-first-of-its-kind-initiative-in-the-healthcare-industry-apollo-hospitals-collaborates-with-8chili-inc-to-enter-the-metaverse/

Khaleej Times - Dubai News, UAE News, Gulf, News, Latest news, Arab news, Gulf News, Dubai Labour News. (n.d.). Khaleej Times. https://www.khaleejtimes.com

Losing Paradise. (2012, October 29). *YouTube*. Retrieved November 19, 2022, from http://english.seoul.go.kr/seoul-to-provide-public-services-through-its-own-metaverse-platform/?keyword=metaverse&cat=46

Metaverse safety Week 2022 - 10-15 December. (n.d.). Metaverse Safety Week. Retrieved June 8, 2023, from https://metaversesafetyweek.org/

Moyers, S. (2022, August 8). *Why Brands Are Entering the Metaverse! Future of Marketing.* SPINX Digital. Retrieved November 22, 2022, from https://www.spinxdigital.com/blog/why-brands-entering-metaverse/

Parisi, T. (2021, October 22). The Seven Rules of the Metaverse. A framework for the coming immersive.... *Medium.* Retrieved November 19, 2022, from https://medium.com/meta-verses/the-seven-rules-of-the-metaverse-7d4e06fa864c

Park, D. (2022, August 31). *South Korea's capital city launches first stage of "Metaverse Seoul".* Forkast News. Retrieved November 24, 2022, from https://forkast.news/headlines/south-koreas-capital-city-launches-first-stage-of-metaverse-seoul

PWC. (2022, September 28-29). *Metaverse Assembly Outcomes Report.* Retrieved December 31, 2022, from https://www.dubaifuture.ae/wp-content/uploads/2022/12/TheMetaverseAssembly-OutcomesReport-WP-English.pdf

Samia, R. (2022, January 17). *Ethical and Regulatory Challenges of Emerging Health Technologies.* IGI Global. Retrieved November 24, 2022, from https://www.igi-global.com/chapter/ethical-and-regulatory-challenges-of-emerging-health-technologies/291434

Shumba, C. (2021, July 25). *RealVision's Raoul Pal Says Social Tokens Are "Next Big Crypto Thing".* Markets Insider. Retrieved November 22, 2022, from https://markets.businessinsider.com/news/currencies/realvisions-raoul-pal-says-social-tokens-are-next-big-crypto-thing-2021-7

SIX. (2021, June 1). *Communication - EQ71 Digital Twin.* Empa. Retrieved January 1, 2023, from https://www.empa.ch/web/s604/eq71-digital-twin

SPACE Metaverse – The Virtual Commerce Platform. (n.d.). Retrieved June 8, 2023, from https://www.tryspace.com/

Thomason, J. (2022a). *MetaHealth - How will the Metaverse Change Health Care?* DergiPark. Retrieved November 24, 2022, from https://dergipark.org.tr/en/download/article-file/2167692

Thomason, J. (2022b). *The Metaverse could be just the tonic for social prescribing.* City A.M. Retrieved November 24, 2022, from https://www.cityam.com/the-metaverse-could-be-just-the-tonic-for-social-prescribing-2/

Thomason, J. (n.d.). *5 things we will do in the metaverse – Studyum Academy*. Studyum Academy. Retrieved November 22, 2022, from https://academy. studyum.org/5-things-we-will-do-in-the-metaverse/

Wells, C. (2021, October 30). *What Is the Metaverse? Where Crypto, NFT, Capitalism Collide in Games Like Axie*. Bloomberg.com. Retrieved November 19, 2022, from https://www.bloomberg.com/news/features/2021-10-30/what-is-the-metaverse-where-crypto-nft-capitalism-collide-in-games-like-axie

White, W. (2021, April 29). *Social Tokens: Get Ready for the Next Massive Crypto Trend*. Nasdaq. Retrieved November 22, 2022, from https://www. nasdaq.com/articles/social-tokens%3A-get-ready-for-the-next-massive-crypto-trend-2021-04-29

Whitten, M. (2021, October 16). The Amazing Things You'll Do in the 'Metaverse' and What It Will Take to Get There. *Wall Street Journal*. Retrieved November 22, 2022, from https://www.wsj.com/articles/the-amazing-things-youll-do-in-the-metaverse-and-what-it-will-take-to-get-there-11634396401

WithamJ. (2021). https://www.hopkinsmedicine.org/news/publications/neurologic_issues/neurologic-winter-2021

World Metaverse Council. (2022). https://wmetac.com/

Zhang, X., Chen, Y., Hu, L., & Wang, Y. (2022). The Metaverse in education: Definition, framework, features, potential applications, challenges, and future research topics. *Frontiers in Psychology*, *13*, 1016300. Advance online publication. doi:10.3389/fpsyg.2022.1016300 PMID:36304866

Zhu, Y. (2022, October 11). The Metaverse in education: Definition, framework, features, potential applications, challenges, and future research topics. *Frontiers*. Advance online publication. doi:10.3389/fpsyg.2022.1016300

Chapter 11
Web 3.0 and ESG and Sustainability

ABSTRACT

The Sustainable Development Goals (SDGs) are aspirational visionary goals for the future state of humankind. However, they will only be attained by harnessing the potential of technology. Web 3.0, blockchain, and other emerging technologies are crucial tools for social impact. Web 3.0 and blockchain open the possibility for creating transparent collaboration at scale for solving problems of the global commons. Distributed autonomous communities (DAOs) can enable value exchange through token economics to collaborate and invest in global issues like climate change. This chapter will outline how Web 3.0, blockchain, and emerging technologies (artificial intelligence [AI], machine learning, big data, internet of things [IoT], and satellite) can accelerate the achievement of SDG goals.

INTRODUCTION

The Sustainable Development Goals (SDGs), established in 2015, were aspirational goals for the planet. Technology will be crucial in achieving the SDGs by 2030, and it is estimated that 70 percent of 169 targets base-lining the world's sustainability goals can be positively influenced through digital technologies. Web3 and Blockchain have much to contribute to the SDGs. Over 70% of the world's population have mobile phones, which opens accessibility.

DOI: 10.4018/978-1-6684-6658-2.ch011

The underpinning technology of Web 3, or the "Internet of Value," enables the peer-to-peer exchange of value for anyone with a mobile phone.

As outlined in earlier chapters, some of the key features of Blockchain include (1) Tokenization; (ii) Self-enforcement and formalization of rules by embedding organizational practices in smart contracts; (iii) Autonomous automatization using smart contracts to allow multiple parties' interaction with each other, without human interaction.; (iv) Decentralization of power over the infrastructure communalizing the ownership and control of the technological tools; (v) Increasing transparency which may enable higher accountability and lead to more peer-to-peer monitoring forms; and (vi) Codification of trust: Blockchain can self-enforce rules and formalize and codify agreements for facilitating the trust factor. (Rozas et al., 2021). This chapter will outline how Web 3.0, Blockchain, and emerging technologies of (AI), machine learning, big data, IoT, and Satellite) can accelerate the achievement of SDG goals.

KEY SUSTAINABILITY USE CASES

Digitalization can enhance the achievement of the SDGs. Web 3.0 and Blockchain can accelerate economic growth through financial inclusion, social accountability, and algorithmic decision-making. Governments across the globe are exploring Blockchain applications for economic growth and better services for citizens. Blockchain offers the benefits of efficiency, immutability, savings in time and cost, reduced operating costs, and real-time data reporting and transparency.

While much of the development and implementation of Blockchains has taken place in Western countries, its most significant potential resides in emerging markets. Front movers like small states can pivot more nimbly and emerging market innovators. Their trailblazing is setting a high bar for the traditional states to follow. Thomason et al. (2019) explain that emerging markets are fast movers because of the sheer size and scale of the market. There are more people overall and smartphone users under 30 years of age comprising the digitally literate demographic. Mobile penetration is growing rapidly and currently stands at more than two-thirds of the global population. According to Theodorou et al. (2019), 5.1 billion individuals had a mobile subscription by the end of 2018. It amounts to 67% of the total population with a mobile subscription. Developing countries will drive growth, particularly India, China, Pakistan, Indonesia, and Bangladesh, as well as Sub-Saharan

Africa and Latin America. Another driver is that emerging markets have big problems to solve, stimulating innovation. Small states are disadvantaged by isolated geography, Technology can help access knowledge, and scarce human resources can overcome some of these barriers. Finally, emerging market governments are increasingly agile (Thomason et al., 2019), and Mauritius, Kenya, UAE, and Bermuda, for example, are driving the technology innovation agenda. Blockchain applications will likely be embraced, and innovation is expected from these markets.

While promising development exists, other issues need addressing for technologies to scale. Some challenges include the capacity of existing infrastructure, costs, and regulations restricting the use of such technologies. Privacy and security have heightened focus as people caught in humanitarian crises fear having their personal information leaked or their location identified. There are fears of being tracked and the need for further rigorous evaluation of the uses of Blockchain technology in humanitarian contexts.

Climate Action

Blockchain technology has the potential to contribute to climate change efforts. Its traceability and transparency feature makes it critical in measuring and monitoring climate impact (Sandor, 2022). Other climate action deployments of Blockchain for climate action include (i) Green digital asset solutions; (ii) Smart grid management; NFTs and gamification; Tokenization of carbon credits; Verification, measurement, and reporting and use of DAOs for climate action. These are covered in detail in Chapter 12.

Environment

Blockchain and Web 3, in conjunction with AI, machine learning, and big data, can improve transparent data analytics reporting on emissions, air quality, and pollution levels. As discussed in Chapter 12, Blockchain can also support intelligent grids with the speed of exchange, reduction in transacting backlog and overall costs, and improved data availability and reliability.

Combining digital twins with AI and multiple data sets can enable the evaluation of environmental impact on a larger scale, considering more than one variable at a time. For example, Web3 Digital Twins will allow examining climate projections and rainfall with hydrological models and allow forecasting of where a flood would occur. Digital Twins combined with

Augmented Reality can simulate the impact of natural disasters through real-time interaction and accurate 3D registration of virtual and natural objects. Data from IoTs and Satellites can be secured on a Blockchain in combination with measurement reporting and verification to increase the trust and utility of the data to support solutions for sustainability.

Payments and Financial Inclusion

Chainalysis (2022) reported the top 20 countries with holders of virtual assets to be - Vietnam, Philippines, Ukraine, India, United States, Pakistan, Brazil, Thailand, Russia, China, Nigeria, Turkey, Argentina, Morocco, Colombia, Nepal, United Kingdom, Ecuador, Kenya, and Indonesia. The majority are emerging economies, suggesting that where services are poor and financial systems weak, citizens are moving towards virtual assets as a store of value and means of exchange.

Digital assets and the large-scale rollout of mobile money systems could fuel widespread access to financial services for the unbanked. Digital payments provide benefits of traceability and efficiency in disbursement. Blockchain can enable the international development community to increase the impact of the dollars it spends on aid with improved speed, transparency, and efficiency.

Governments and donors allocate significant amounts of money for social welfare but have limited means of ensuring it reaches the intended beneficiary. Cong and He (2018) define smart contracts as digital contracts allowing terms contingent on a decentralized consensus that is tamper-proof and typically self-enforcing through automated execution. Blockchain smart contracts can execute digital agreements through the computer program code entrusted by the parties involved and stored in a Blockchain database. These self-executable codes can facilitate the exchange of money, shares, and property and eliminate the need for an intermediary. All agreements part of the smart contract is recorded on a Blockchain network, and each transaction is transparent (Fauziah et al., 2020). The smart contract can self-execute and make payment upon service delivery to a beneficiary.

Applications are under testing to improve the flow and targeting of donor funds. Rangone and Busolli (2021) demonstrated the impact of Blockchain technology on the development of Charity 4.0 through Charity Wall, an emerging Italian social marketplace. This use case was especially prominent during the COVID-19 pandemic in Italy. It helped regain trust in philanthropy initiatives by avoiding misappropriation of funds, thereby preventing economic, financial, and social repercussions. Charity Wall demonstrated how Blockchain technology helps prevent the fraudulent detriment of beneficiaries, receivers, and donors. It also set an example for establishing a closer network between philanthropic players to support charitable initiatives against COVID-19 and other future pandemics.

The Bahamas launched the Sand Dollar (International Monetary Fund, 2021) to issue a digital representation of the Bahamas Dollar. It is the world's first government-backed, Blockchain-based digital currency (Project Management Institute, 2021). It is a retail Central Bank Digital Currency (CBDC) through which the Central Bank expects to reduce service delivery costs and increase efficiency for financial services, especially to promote inclusive finance options for the banked and unbanked. It is a centralized, regulated, stable, private, and secure unit of account and means of exchange. It is a direct liability of the central bank of the Bahamas and is backed by foreign reserves (Sand Dollar BS, 2022).

Blockchain technology can also have a developmental impact on Small and Medium Enterprises (SMEs). According to the World Bank's Policy Brief on Small and Medium Enterprises (2020), post the COVID-19 pandemic, access to finance constrains SME growth; without it, many SMEs languish and stagnate. Based on Survey results from 13 countries, SMEs were as likely to be shut down as large firms. In countries such as Albania and Togo, they were 30% more likely to have shut down completely. Shock pandemics and unknown disasters have led to reliance on Blockchain-based systems among local SMEs.

An example is AgriLedger, an SME in Haiti, an agriculture-based Blockchain systems provider which has handled the aggregation and distribution of payments to the farmers in the mango sector. Within its first five weeks of commercial shipments to the United States, it ended with a full container, despite logistics providers claiming COVID-19 disrupted the service. It has resulted in a net revenue increase for farmers between 150-400 percent (Adian et al., 2020; OAG, 2019). Policy dialogue with Governments on improving SME financing should be an essential part of the global strategy for financial inclusion.

Philanthropy and Fundraising

Web3 offers new tools for creating financial instruments. New funding mechanisms, including token sales and crowdfunding backed by crypto, are creating new forms of finance. There is potential for even further innovation with token economics using cryptography, computer networks, and game theory to create new incentivized models which benefit people experiencing poverty.

The world is suffering from implications of reversals of poverty reduction performance in the pre-pandemic decade. Owing to the COVID-19 pandemic, climate change, and conflicts, nearly a quarter century of efforts toward a steady global decline in extreme poverty have decelerated. Deepening income inequality will lead to sluggish economic recovery and future growth. Nations need to work together for a resilient recovery. Therefore, policy actions must design safety nets, rebuild jobs, and strengthen human capital for recovery. These relief efforts must reach people in the informal sectors of both rural and urban areas. Some countries, such as the Philippines, Ecuador, and Uganda, have expanded investments in digital technology by facilitating access to finance, enabling logistical support to small and medium enterprises, and encouraging workers' awareness of employment opportunities (Rodríguez et al., 2020).

According to the Kiel Institute for World Economy, more than a quarter of development aid never leaves donor countries. Additionally, there is disproportionately higher spending on refugees from donor countries (Kiel Institute for World Economy, 2019). In 2010, following the earthquake in Haiti, USD 3.5 Billion was pledged by the international community, but it got distributed inefficiently. Such inefficiencies in fund distribution are due to corruption resulting from difficulties in tracking. It calls for developing efficient humanitarian aid for people who need it (Harvard International Review, 2020). Blockchain technology with smart contracts can help ensure that donor funds reach intended recipients transparently without intermediaries and leakage.

Philanthropists, impact investors, donors, and international organizations can be crucial in advancing responsible adoption and scaling technology. The landscape of donor engagement with Blockchain technology discusses the donors' role in supporting and enabling responsible adoption and scaling it. Policymakers must be able to make an informed assessment of the technology, its impacts on public outcomes, and its future direction (Thomason et al., 2019).

Some who have become rich from the early adoption of Bitcoin and other cryptocurrencies have chosen to turn to philanthropy, and several prominent figures in crypto have made sizable personal philanthropic donations. Red Cross, Save the Children, United Way, the Wikimedia Foundation, the Electronic Frontier Foundation, UNICEF, and Save the Children have started to accept crypto donations. These are welcome additions to the philanthropy sector but utilize standard models. Web3 offers new tools for creating financial instruments. Token sales and crowdfunding are creating new forms of finance. There is potential for even further innovation with token economics using cryptography, computer networks, and game theory to create new incentivized models.

Steemit (Wikipedia, 2016), which launched in 2016, enables users to earn tokens for publishing and curating content on a blogging and social media website. Top Steemit user countries are India, Indonesia, Venezuela, and Nigeria, suggesting that Steemit has provided a valuable income-earning opportunity for some of the fastest-growing emerging markets. Good Dollar offers a digital currency that any cell phone owner can claim and convert to local currency. GoodDollar has onboarded thousands of users from over 40 countries, including South Africa, Nigeria, Ghana, Kenya, Senegal, Argentina, and Venezuela.

Electroneum aspires to unlock the global digital economy for millions of people in the developing world. The wallet is entirely mobile based, makes instant transfers, maximizes usability, and empowers users by reducing the lag between earning and receiving. As of May 2020, 4 million wallets, 1,510 merchants, and service providers were on ETN in 174 countries across 25 business categories. Electroneum has partnered with several mobile network operators and has 140 countries worldwide where users can receive airtime. Most vendors currently accepting ETNs are in Uganda, South Africa, Brazil, and Argentina. While it is early days, it is now possible to see how Web3 creates sustainable ways to distribute wealth to people experiencing poverty.

Health Care

Web3 and Blockchain can also contribute to universal health coverage, redesigning business models, removing friction, and improving data sharing in a highly secure environment. This includes managing patient records and data, financing, supply chain management, health workforce management, and surveillance processes. (Thomason et al., 2019). Health facility supply chains are crucial for ensuring the authenticity and quality of life-saving medicines. Poor-quality medicines are a public health threat, particularly in weak regulatory environments. Advances in logistic supply chain management leveraging digital and data analytics will help improve the tracking and authenticity of medicines and ensure consistency of availability and quality.

The health industry can use smart contracts to record data on patient health history.

Blockchain technology has the potential to make ground-breaking innovations in the health sector. It can be leveraged for ethical health financing, streamlining supply chain management, organizing health records, ensuring accurate identification and verification of health apparatus, establishing seamless telehealth procedures, and curbing misinformation. It will help build secure, efficient, cost-effective data storage, analysis, and transfers (Vervoort et al., 2021). However, adopting Blockchain technology for healthcare depends on inter-connected and advanced technologies in the ecosystem. It includes system tracking, healthcare insurance, medicines tracing, and clinical trials (Haleem et al., 2021) and thus needs holistic collaboration between the health, finance, and technology sectors on a global scale.

Emerging health systems face constant challenges in national reporting and sharing information on patient treatment at different health service sites. Distributed databases are, by design, intended to address these issues. Blockchain also allows each transaction to be visible to anyone with access to the system, but where users can remain anonymous or provide proof of their identity to others. Once a transaction enters the database, recording on the database is permanent, chronologically ordered, and available to all others on the network (Thomason et al., 2019).

Finally, Blockchain technology utilizes hashing that gives every block a unique identifier that changes based on its contents. A change in a block of data will also change its hash. Since blocks get stored in chronological order, they directly reference the preceding block's hash. A change in the data of one block will cause a succeeding block to identify a hash change. Therefore, connected blocks form an immutable, reliable, decentralized, and secure chain (Morey, 2021).

Blockchain offers the potential to address interoperability challenges for health data by maintaining interoperable electronic health records with a single transaction layer, enabling uniform authorization protocols and smart contracts (GAVS, 2021). It also assures patient identity and verification of services covered by insurance and rendered by providers. Blockchains offer a solution that enables secure data exchange and places a person's health records within their reach and control rather than being fragmented and inaccessible to the patient in a remote central database. (Thomason, 2019). There is also the potential for patient-owned longitudinal health records based on patient ID. (Thomason et al., 2019). Identifying and tracking the most marginalized and impoverished populations with the highest mortality is important as maternal and child deaths decline (The Republic of Uganda, 2016). Blockchain solutions will enable accurate databases of the population with identity, population level vaccine, and medical intervention studies without any potential breach of privacy and improved health outcomes through better data exchange.

Health Care Supply Chains

Advances in logistic chain management leverage digital and data analytics to improve tracking and authenticity. Blockchain enables participants to see every part of a product's journey from production to end user. It also enables supply chain companies to identify attempted fraud because once a block is on the Blockchain, it remains unaltered (Thomason et al., 2019). To illustrate, the United States Food and Drug Administration (FDA) pilot program uses Blockchain technology for the pharmaceutical supply chain associated with Klynveld Peat Marwick, Goerdeler, Merck, and Walmart. The aim was to address the need to track, identify and trace prescription medicines and vaccines within the vicinity of the United States. Blockchain technology helped connect disparate systems and organizations to record product traceability. The organizations involved in the pilot program also explored the potential of Blockchain technology to minimize the recall period of supply chain products from a few days to a few seconds. It helped increase patient safety by improving supply chain visibility and alerting the supply chain for product recall within seconds (Treshock, 2020). Scaling such applications of Blockchain technology to ensure a seamless supply chain of essential services such as vaccines and medical supplies to developing countries through specialized organizational collaboration will help achieve efficient supply chains at the global level.

IBM offered a Digital Health Pass service built on Blockchain technology to help organizations bring people back to physical locations during COVID-19. It allows organizations to verify the vaccination and test results credentials of their employees, customers, or anyone trying to enter the vicinity of their physical space. It lets organizations maintain the COVID-19 protocol. At the same time, employees and customers can control their health information securely, verifiable, and trusted (IBM, 2020). Blockchain offers a supply chain solution that allows end-to-end track and trace to ensure that medicine and drugs are appropriately sourced. The Specialized Agency of Tuv Province and the Government of Mongolia Feasibility Study piloted a project to counterfeit drugs. The aim was to increase the safety and transparency of the drug industry in Mongolia and globally by tracing the pharmaceutical supply chain (Observatory of Public Sector Innovation, 2018). These solutions need testing in emerging markets and applied to women's and children's health supply chains.

Humanitarian Settings

Mass migration is becoming one of the most significant challenges of the 21st century. According to the United Nations High Commissioner for Refugees (UNHCR, 2022), 100 million people faced forcible displacement from their homes in 2022. When forced to abandon their homes, many leave necessary identity documents such as birth certificates, marriage licenses, and passports (Thomas & Brien, 2018). Blockchain in humanitarian settings can address digital identity, supply chains, cash transfers, and remittances. It can also establish the integrity of donor funds flows, property registry, employment rights, human trafficking, education, and asylum processing (Thomason et al., 2019). This section presents some use cases of Blockchain in humanitarian settings.

According to the World Bank (2018), over a billion people exist without a recognized identification. This population includes refugees, trafficked children, people experiencing homelessness, and others. This problem feeds on itself as the longer a person goes without associations and affiliations, the harder it is to provide enough of a record to create them (Thomason et al., 2019). Refugees commonly have no or little documentation. The 1951 UN Refugee Convention quite sensibly recognizes that individuals subject to the travails of war do not have time or opportunity to go home and find their birth certificates. Economic migrants are also likely to lack a driving license or a passport. It makes the bureaucracy involved in fleeing countries troublesome. As per the Vulnerability Assessment of Syrian Refugees in Lebanon (VASyR, 2021), only 16% of people 15 years of age and above hold legal residency (UNHRC, 2021; United Nations Children's Funds [UNICEF], 2021; United Nations World Food Programme [WFP], 2021).

The window to global inclusion and economic participation is identity. Once a person has an identity, they can access essential services like financial credit, health care, and education. Digital currencies could fuel rapid and widespread access to financial services previously unavailable. This could have a positive benefit on the economic livelihoods of the large segments of rural populations that are unbanked. Government and donor payments often fail to reach their intended recipients. The widespread application of digital and automated payments conditional on specific variables can reduce the amount of leakage in social disbursements. Smart contracts through digital transactions ensure funds transparently reach intended recipients, eliminating the need for a middleman and avoiding leakages. Digital payments provide benefits of traceability and efficiency in disbursement (Thomason et al., 2019).

Identity is necessary for financial inclusion, access to services, and the movement of people. Without identity, low-income people may be excluded from government services, finance, and fundamental human rights. The identity data is held immutably on a Blockchain, and with Self Sovereign Identity, identity data remains in the ownership of the individual, and individuals permit who can see what data is for what purpose and for how long (Thomason, 2017). Blockchain technology records can establish an identity where no state identity exists or is used. There is a difference between identity and government-issued credentials (Shrier, 2017). Blockchain technology provides self-sovereign identity (SSI) that helps counter patient information privacy and security threats in healthcare. SSI gives users more control and a secure identity (Shuaib et al., 2021). Blockchain in humanitarian settings can rapidly speed the transfer of funds to beneficiaries and reduce the costs of transfers. (Thomason, 2017). A smartphone-based prototype identity system in Kenya has enabled families and healthcare providers to register births and mother-baby pairs using verifiable credentials and decentralized identifiers (Freytsis et al., 2021). The New Delhi Municipal Council (NDMC) has implemented birth and death certificate registration using Blockchain technology (Sur, 2021; NDMC, 2022).

When refugees forcibly abandon their homes, many leave necessary documents such as birth certificates, marriage licenses, passports, and ID cards. It forces them to face the challenges of accessing survival services. VASyR (2021) mentioned in their report that the Syrian refugees in Lebanon compromise with availing services, such as accessing food (94%), reducing healthcare (54%), and education expenditure (29%). They take new debts (92%) and purchase food on credit (74%) (UNHRC, 2021; United Nations Children's Funds [UNICEF], 2021; United Nations World Food Programme [WFP], 2021).

Blockchain can digitize the identities of refugees and persons in need. It can also help preserve other essential documents they need to receive aid from governments of refugee-hosting countries. This can be done by creating federated layers of identity and digitizing the records while at the same time imposing federated control structures and technical partnerships between those who look after the data.

Blockchain technology is a suitable way to establish refugee digital identities since these are decentralized systems that keep balance and check power dynamics. Refugees will have more control over their data as their information will be accessible and exportable, and immigration authorities in refugee host countries can vet information quickly, resulting in a smooth process for providing services (Huang, 2019). Blockchain technology can arguably have a significant impact on matters of humanitarian concern.

People need identity proof to avoid exclusion from typical financial systems. In fact, without legal existence proof, everything from getting a job to gaining access to a bank account to finding somewhere to live to access education, healthcare, and voting is difficult. As a result, refugees and displaced people suffer deprivation of protection, access to services, and human rights. Approximately 2 billion people do not use formal financial services, and over 50% of adults in the world's poorest households are unbanked (Thomason et al., 2019). In 2013, the World Bank Group president Jim Yong Kim announced that the Universal Financial Access Goal is for all adults who are currently not part of the traditional financial system to have access to a transaction account that will allow them to store, send and receive money by 2020 (The World Bank, 2018).

Innovations in mobile technology have brought about a shift in the way humanitarian organizations deliver aid to refugees. Cash transfers are a modality for cash-based interventions dispensed via mobile money platforms. It provides benefits to beneficiaries, the humanitarian sector, and the ecosystem. However, in most refugee-hosting countries, Mobile Service Provider Companies are now subject to mandatory SIM registration obligations across 150 countries. Customers must present an approved identity document to activate a SIM card or a mobile money service. Without the identity documents necessary for Know Your Customers (KYC), asylum seekers and refugees face denials or delays in applying for government services, government financial support, financial services, and SIM card/mobile phone service. It disproportionately impacts vulnerable groups across Asia and Sub-Saharan Africa (GSMA 2019).

Blockchain technology can provide access to financial instruments for refugees. As mentioned earlier, when refugees face displacement due to persecution, natural disaster, or war, they often do not have time to carry their life savings. Firms such as Leaf Global Fintech, a Blockchain-based platform providing mobile banking services to refugees, give them opportunities to store their funds in the form of cryptocurrencies. It is based on Unstructured

Supplementary Service Data technology and is available to anyone with a mobile phone, regardless of whether they have an internet connection (Crypto Altruism, 2022). Based on similar technology, Kotani Pay is a startup based out of Kenya, which hosts 500,000 refugees and asylum seekers (United Nations Office for the Coordination of Humanitarian Affairs [OCHA] reliefweb, 2022) to send and receive money via Blockchain technology with the help of a mobile phone (Crypto Altruism, 2022).

Urbanization and Smart Cities

Blockchains can increase the efficiency and effectiveness of city services and enable interoperability between devices and platforms to connect homes, offices, and systems. Urbanization is a global phenomenon, with 70% of the world's population expected to live in cities by 2050. These will be the home of most of the world's most vulnerable. Blockchain can facilitate decentralized neighborhood-scale co-creation, collaboration, and citizen engagement activities and, if embedded in cities' design, can provide a digital layer of trust. (Thomason et al., 2019). Transparency and decentralization are intrinsic to Blockchain technology and often challenge the fundamental structures of centralized governments. For cities, these are opportunities to develop an urban, physical, and political organization that can improve the speed, transparency, and security of cities everywhere.

The World Health Organization (WHO) declared COVID-19 a pandemic in March 2020 (Ghebreyesus, 2020). As the world dealt with the crisis, major urban cities suffered inefficient public health systems, inadequate services, and lockdown-imposed economic harms. Therefore, the United Nations(UN) reports an increase in slum dwellers to over 1 million in 2020. As 85% of the world's population resides in slum areas, 359 million in southern Asia, 306 million in eastern and south-eastern Asia, and 230 million in sub-Saharan Africa. This increase in the slum dwellers population will need adequate health policies, affordable housing, sustainable mobility, and connectivity (UN Economic & Social Council, 2022).

The livability crisis is not restricted to people with low incomes, however. The UN Department of Economic and Social Affairs (DESA) estimates that by 2030, the population in high-income countries will grow from 77 percent in 2000 to 84 percent in 2030. The urban population in middle-income countries will grow from 42 percent in 2000 to 59 percent in 2030. Finally, low-income countries will grow their urban population from 26 percent in 2000 to 38 percent in 2030. The fastest urbanization is experienced in Africa and Asia (UN DESA, 2020). Mass migration to cities implies a need for development measures, as data from 1,072 cities worldwide in 2020 indicates a poor distribution of open public spaces in most regions (UN Economic & Social Council,2022). While the global average municipal solid waste in 2022 is 82% in cities, the global average rate of municipal solid waste management is 55% in controlled facilities in cities. It is alarming as uncollected waste contributes to climate change since it is a source of plastic pollution and greenhouse gas emissions (UN Economic & Social Council, 2022).

Governing globally connected cities requires balancing the demands of soaring poverty, food shortage, corruption, crime, pollution, and ill-health, including the growing mental stress among citizens. In progressive countries like Dubai and China, automated systems and infrastructure sensors use big data and the Internet of Things(IoT). It optimizes urban processes and services and connects with residents. Smart cities need emerging technologies such as Blockchain technology to encourage sustainability solutions from all citizens. Digital technologies like IoT can help incentivize urban individuals and organizations to comply with low-carbon transportation, energy efficiency, and waste diversion. Enterprises such as The Plastic Bank, ECO-Coin, and SolarCoin have already started implementing these solutions to bring impactful behavior change among citizens (Kahya et al., 2021).

Many countries have integrated Blockchains into city services for increased efficiency and effectiveness (Thomason et al., 2019). It encourages beneficial behavioral change for socio-environmental benefits. Currently, most governments are in Blockchain's research and testing stage for city use. However, since 60 percent of the world's population is expectedly to live in cities by 2030 (UN DESA, 2020), many countries have yet to embark on the path of a digital economy. Soon, we may see qualitative changes in social, economic, and environmental aspects of life by eliminating the need for piles of papers, giant traffic jams, documentation errors, and double transactions as interoperability between devices and platforms improve to connect homes, offices, and systems (Thomason et al., 2019). This will include (i) smart grids for household energy efficiency, monitoring energy consumption, and maintaining efficient use of energy: reducing energy loss; (ii) Smart Transportation for autonomous driving and optimizing fuel consumption; and (iii) Smart buildings and cities: mitigating building inefficiencies through sensors and analytics.

CHALLENGES

Challenges include ethics, privacy, confidentiality, data security, open-source systems, informed consent, data ownership, and the pace of digital transformation. The World Economic Forum (2018) highlights five digital transformation inhibitors relevant to international agencies' adoption of Blockchain technology. These are:

1. Incentives need to be put in place to generate social benefits.
2. Regulation and protection of consumer interests as innovation is outpacing regulation.
3. There is a preference by incumbents for evolutionary change rather than revolutionary change; therefore, new business models are needed.
4. Gaps in digital skills are increasing.
5. Technology adoption rates, with many skeptical of technological advances and do not adopt technologies when they become available.

Other challenges in adopting Blockchain technology include security issues due to cybersecurity, scaling, the immature nature of the technology, interoperability, compatibility, and lack of regulation support. Specifically, the health sector faced challenges such as distrust in using Blockchain technology due to the nature and privacy of medical records and data and fear of hacking and assurance of confidentiality. Scalability challenges include a high internet bandwidth connection and computing power requirement to validate each transaction, risks related to demand volatility, and currency fluctuations (Ali et al., 2021).

Digital money allows governments and organizations to track people's choices. Such control might lead authorities and corporations to increase surveillance. Authoritarian states can use sensitive data collected from refugees against them. It can also be used by nations of the global North that lack sympathy for refugees and immigrants' movement toward their home countries. The information can be used to keep refugees and immigrants forcefully in neighboring countries. The refugees and immigrants are not safe in institutionally democratic countries either, as there are debates about manipulating them through fake news, interference in democratic elections, and using search engine algorithms to offer people tailored search results or exposing them to targeted advertisements based on their preferences and choices. Thus, millions of unclassified people can be manipulated and mobilized based on corporations' power and technological superiority.

Therefore, it is also possible that the influence could mobilize refugees in a particular direction or discourage them from making certain decisions. Thus, they could end up in harsh conditions such as modern slavery and cheap labor (Korkmaz, 2018).

Deployment of Blockchain in resource-poor communities requires a strong understanding of local social, cultural, and political contexts to be effective. Users also need to have sufficient digital and health literacy.

Blockchain economies require a new approach to governance, especially when automated. Enforcing accountability through technical specifications and digital contracts requires thorough thinking of the network's objectives, decision rights, incentives, and accountability. This may depart radically from established notions of governance (Beck et al., 2018).

Achieving the SDGs will require global collaboration among governments, regulators, industry, academics, funders, and innovators. Thomason et al. (2019) propose that governments and international organizations can facilitate digital adoption by

- Establishing benchmarks for basic digital infrastructure.
- Supporting emerging economies to build digital as a sector of the economy, develop country-led digital strategies, data use partnerships, and build the digital ecosystem.
- Convening policy discussions on regulatory frameworks, promising public technologies, and economic policies to stimulate digital growth and showcase leadership in digital adoption.
- Disseminating evidence and sharing experiences, education, and common frameworks for regulation, facilitating innovation and entrepreneurship models, and enabling cross-border digital markets.
- Building a connected ecosystem.

This collaboration needs to be based on a frame of mind that, until proven otherwise, someone somewhere already knows what works best. (Ecosystem Innovation, Prism First Semester 2017; Thomas et al., 2021). A connected innovation ecosystem will bring together diverse and complementary capabilities from across the globe. This will require collaboration between hundreds of partners, universities, research institutes, customers, and suppliers. The collaboration is enabled by digital and other rapidly evolving technologies, such as cloud computing. Digital technologies may encourage convergence across industries to create novel solutions around market needs. The availability of (open-source) data and a culture of sharing information and intelligence within a fit-for-purpose IP framework will be essential (Thomason et al., 2019).

Collaboration can help shape technology, as technologists work in a vacuum, and technology needs scaling to suit the context. Governments and international institutions can help shape the application of technology for social benefit and to protect the interests of the poor and vulnerable. Collaboration to understand the political economy for implementation is crucial as intermediaries will be eradicated, and the implications of this change will be necessary for integrating this change into public sector work.

Research collaboration is needed to develop new methods of prospectively reviewing technology impact using rapid cycle analytics to monitor the impacts of technology adoption. This research can inform governments' policy and regulatory environments (Thomason, 2022). NGOs and communities can report on their user experience, and the industry can partner to see how to scale technologies commercially (Thomason et al., 2019).

Regulators are interested in the safety and soundness of the financial system, adherence to consumer protection, Know your Customer (KYC), and Anti Money Laundering (AML). They are cautious about the risks of technologies, consumer protection from speculative cryptocurrencies, privacy risks, and informed consent (Thomason, 2022). Never has a combined approach to regulation among jurisdictions been more critical.

There is a global talent shortage for the new digital economy that understands and can build with Blockchain, AI, and associated technologies. In developing countries, many young people learn digital skills through innovative training approaches, Youtube, TikTok, gamification, Metaverse and fast-track learning that can be global and virtual will be essential for building capacity for a digital future (Thomason et al., 2019).

Governments are critical in implementing policy and regulatory settings to catalyze digital transformation. There are four elements of a government role: (i) political leadership, (ii) talent access, (iii) finance, and (iv) infrastructure. The government needs bold political ambition to build digital transformation and develop policies to attract talent and investors to the country and to be at the forefront of innovation. Governments need to grow their talent for digitization; this requires proactive government policy. Governments can attract investment instruments like government-backed bonds to invest in promising tech companies, fund startups, and incentivize the industry to provide accelerator programs and partnerships for startups. Connectivity is necessary, affordable, and secure access to the internet is a fundamental priority.

CONCLUSION

This chapter contributes to growing knowledge about Blockchain and Web 3.0 for sustainability. Innovators and technologists are working globally on implementing Blockchain technology to solve many of the SDGs. This chapter introduces the readers to Blockchain and Web 3 and its potential applications to improve the lives of the vulnerable and underprivileged. Blockchain and other frontier technologies for sustainability can be tools for social change and improve inequality globally. While these technological tools for groundbreaking innovation exist, many such questions still need to be answered. It is paramount to closely and carefully monitor its evolution and share this information to achieve maximum impact.

REFERENCES

A Basic Income Coin & Wallet. (n.d.). GoodDollar. https://www.gooddollar.org/

Adian, I., Doumbia, D., Gregory, N., Ragoussis, A., Reddy, A., & Timmis, J. (2020). *Small and medium enterprises in the pandemic*. Academic Press.

Ali, O., Jaradat, A., Kulakli, A., & Abuhalimeh, A. (2021). A comparative study: Blockchain technology utilization benefits, challenges and functionalities. *IEEE Access : Practical Innovations, Open Solutions*, 9, 12730–12749. doi:10.1109/ACCESS.2021.3050241

Chainalysis. (2022). https://blog.chainalysis.com/reports/2022-global-crypto-adoption-index/

Cong, L. W., & He, Z. (2019). Blockchain disruption and smart contracts. *Review of Financial Studies*, 32(5), 1754–1797. doi:10.1093/rfs/hhz007

Crypto Altruism. (2021, October 15). *Using Blockchain and cryptocurrency to support and empower refugees*. https://www.cryptoaltruism.org/blog/using-Blockchain-and-cryptocurrency-to-support-and-empower-refugees

Electroneum offers a new way to earn, send and pay. (n.d.). Electroneum. Retrieved June 11, 2023, from https://electroneum.com/

Fauziah, Z., Latifah, H., Omar, X., Khoirunisa, A., & Millah, S. (2020). Application of Blockchain Technology in Smart Contracts: A Systematic Literature Review. *Aptisi Transactions on Technopreneurship, 2*(2), 160–166. doi:10.34306/att.v2i2.97

Freytsis, M., Barclay, I., Radha, S. K., Czajka, A., Siwo, G. H., Taylor, I., & Bucher, S. (2021). Development of a Mobile, Self-Sovereign Identity Approach for Facility Birth Registration in Kenya. *Frontiers in Blockchain, 4*, 631341. doi:10.3389/fbloc.2021.631341

GAVS. (2021, August 31). *Healthcare Interoperability and Blockchain.* https://www.gavstech.com/healthcare-interoperability-and-Blockchain/

Ghebreyesus, T. A. (2020, March 11). *WHO Director-General's opening remarks at the media briefing on COVID-19 - 11 March 2020* [Speech Audio Recording]. World Health Organization. https://www.who.int/director-general/speeches/detail/who-director-general-s-opening-remarks-at-the-media-briefing-on-covid-19---11-march-2020

Haleem, A., Javaid, M., Singh, R. P., Suman, R., & Rab, S. (2021). Blockchain technology applications in healthcare: An overview. *International Journal of Intelligent Networks, 2*, 130–139. doi:10.1016/j.ijin.2021.09.005

Harvard International Review. (2019, December 30). *Where that Used Teddy Bear Really Goes: Corruption and Inefficiency in Humanitarian Aid.* https://hir.harvard.edu/where-that-used-teddy-bear-really-goes-corruption-and-inefficiency-in-humanitarian-aid/

Hassan, Hammad, Iqbal, Hussain, Ullah, AlSalman, Mosleh, & Arif. (2022). A Liquid Democracy Enabled Blockchain-Based Electronic Voting System. *Scientific Programming.* doi:10.1155/2022/13830

Holloway, K., Al Masri, R., & Abu Yahi, A. (2021). *Digital identity, biometrics and inclusion in humanitarian responses to refugee crises.* ODI-HPG. https://cdn.odi.org/media/documents/Digital_IP_Biometrics_case_study_web.pdf

Huang, R. (2019, January 7). *How Blockchain Can Help With The Refugee Crisis.* Forbes. https://www.forbes.com/sites/rogerhuang/2019/01/27/how-Blockchain-can-help-with-the-refugee-crisis/?sh=6c6721366562

Human Rights Watch. (2021, March 30). *IMF: Scant Transparency for Covid-19 Emergency Loans.* https://www.hrw.org/news/2021/03/30/imf-scant-transparency-covid-19-emergency-loans

IBM. (2020). *Digital Health Pass*. https://www.ibm.com/products/digital-health-pass/businesses

International Monetary Fund. (2021, April 14). *Leveraging Digital Money to Facilitate Remittances*. https://www.imf.org/en/News/Articles/2021/04/14/sp041421-leveraging-digital-money-to-facilitate-remittances

Kahya, A., Avyukt, A., Ramachandran, G. S., & Krishnamachari, B. (2021, July). Blockchain-enabled Personalized Incentives for Sustainable Behavior in Smart Cities. In *2021 International Conference on Computer Communications and Networks (ICCCN)* (pp. 1-6). IEEE. 10.1109/ICCCN52240.2021.9522340

Kiel Institute for World Economy. (2019, August 26). *More than a quarter of development aid never leaves donor countries*. https://www.ifw-kiel.de/publications/media-information/2019/more-than-a-quarter-of-development-aid-never-leaves-donor-countries/

Korkmaz, E. (2018). *Blockchain for refugees: great hopes, deep concerns*. University of Oxford https://www.qeh.ox.ac.uk/blog/Blockchain-refugees-great-hopes-deep-concerns

Morey, J. (2021, October 25). The Future Of Blockchain In Healthcare. *Forbes*. https://www.forbes.com/sites/forbestechcouncil/2021/10/25/the-future-of-Blockchain-in-healthcare/?sh=b2f9811541f5

New Delhi Municipal Council. (2022). *Information Technology: On Going Projects*. https://www.ndmc.gov.in/departments/information_technology.aspx

OAG (Open Access Government). (2019). *World Bank Blockchain pilot sows fresh narrative for Haiti's farmers*. https://www.openaccessgovernment.org/world-bank-Blockchain-haitis-farmers/61205/

Observatory of Public Sector Innovation. (2018). *Counterfeit Medicine Detection Using Blockchain and AI*. https://oecd-opsi.org/innovations/counterfeit-medicine-detection-using-Blockchain-and-ai/

OCHA reliefweb. (2022, February 22). *ECHO Factsheet – Kenya – (Last updated 03/02/2022)* [Press Release]. https://reliefweb.int/report/kenya/echo-factsheet-kenya-last-updated-03022022

Project Management Institute. (2021). *Most Influential Projects 2021*. https://www.pmi.org/most-influential-projects-2021/50-most-influential-projects-2021/sand-dollar

Rangone, A., & Busolli, L. (2021). Managing charity 4.0 with Blockchain: A case study at the time of Covid-19. *International Review on Public and Nonprofit Marketing*, *18*(4), 491–521. doi:10.100712208-021-00281-8

Rodríguez, S. F., Woolcock, M., Castañeda, R. A., Cojocaru, A., Howton, E., Lakner, C., Nguyen, M. C., Schoch, M., Yang, J., & Yonzan, N. (2020). *Reversals of fortune*. World Bank Publications. https://openknowledge.worldbank.org/bitstream/handle/10986/34496/211602ov.pdf

Rozas, D., & Hassan, S. (2021). *Analysis of the Potentials of Blockchain for the Governance of Global Digital Commons*. Frontiers in Blockchain. doi:10.3389/fbloc.2021.577680

Sanddollar. (2022). *About Us*. https://www.sanddollar.bs/about

Sandor, D. (2022, January 28). *How Blockchain technology will reshape green finance in 2022*. Eco-Business. https://www.eco-business.com/opinion/how-Blockchain-technology-will-reshape-green-finance-in-2022/

Schletz, M., Nassiry, D., & Lee, M. K. (2020). *Blockchain and tokenized securities: The potential for green finance*. Academic Press.

Shuaib, M., Alam, S., Alam, M. S., & Nasir, M. S. (2021). Self-sovereign identity for healthcare using Blockchain. *Materials Today: Proceedings*.

Sur, A. (2021, June 2). *New Delhi Municipal Corporation To Introduce Blockchain For Birth-Death Certificate and Property Tax*. Medianama. https://www.medianama.com/2021/06/223-ndmc-Blockchain-birth-death-property/

Teshock, M. (2020, May 4). *How the FDA is piloting Blockchain for the pharmaceutical supply chain*. IBM. https://www.ibm.com/blogs/Blockchain/2020/05/how-the-fda-is-piloting-Blockchain-for-the-pharmaceutical-supply-chain/

The Goalkeepers. (2021). *Global Progress and Projections for Maternal Mortality*. Gates Foundation. https://www.gatesfoundation.org/goalkeepers/the-goalkeepers/

The World Bank. (2018, April 25). *ID4D data: Global Identification Challenge by the numbers*. Data | Identification for Development. Retrieved July 21, 2022, from https://id4d.worldbank.org/global-dataset

The World Bank. (2018, October 1). UFA2020 Overview: Universal Financial. https://www.worldbank.org/en/topic/financialinclusion/brief/achieving-universal-financial-access-by-2020

Theodorou, Y., Okong'o, K., & Yongo, E. (2019). Access to mobile services and proof of identity 2019: Assessing the impact on digital and financial inclusion. GSMA.

Thomas, F., Schaaf, B. d., & Sehlstedt, U. (2021, December). *Hyper-collaboration in the healthcare and life science industry – The new imperative.* Arthur Little. https://www.adlittle.com/en/insights/prism/hyper-collaboration-healthcare-and-life-science-industry---new-imperative

Thomason, J. (2017, May 4). Blockchain – Leapfrogging for the Poor? *LinkedIn.* https://www.linkedin.com/pulse/Blockchain-leapfrogging-poori-dr-jane-thomason/

Thomason, J. (2019, April 8). Money, Management, Medicines and Me - Blockchain and Emerging Health Systems. *LinkedIn.* https://www.linkedin.com/pulse/money-management-medicines-me-Blockchain-emerging-health-thomason/

Thomason, J., Bernhardt, S., Kansara, T., & Cooper, N. (2020). *Blockchain technology for global social change.* Engineering Science Reference.

United Nations. Economic and Social Council. (2022). *Progress towards the Sustainable Development Goals Report of the Secretary-General.* United Nations. https://unstats.un.org/sdgs/files/report/2022/secretary-general-sdg-report-2022--EN.pdf

United Nations Department of Economic and Social Affairs. (2020, December). *Population Facts. No. 2020/2.* https://www.un.org/development/desa/pd/sites/www.un.org.development.desa.pd/files/undes_pd_2020_popfacts_urbanization_policies.pdf

United Nations Human Rights Counselling. (2022, May 23). *UNHCR: A record 100 million people forcibly displaced worldwide.* United Nations. https://news.un.org/en/story/2022/05/1118772

Vervoort, D., Guetter, C. R., & Peters, A. W. (2021). Blockchain, health disparities and global health. *BMJ Innovations*, 7(2), 506–514. doi:10.1136/bmjinnov-2021-000667

WFP & UNICEF. (2021). *Vulnerability assessment of Syrian refugees in Lebanon*. Author.

Wikipedia. (2016). https://en.wikipedia.org/wiki/Steemit

World Economic Forum (WEF). (2018). *Digital Transformation Initiative*. Collaboration with Accenture.

World Health Organization. (2022, January 28). *Child mortality (under 5 years)* [Press Release]. https://www.who.int/news-room/fact-sheets/detail/levels-and-trends-in-child-under-5-mortality-in-2020

Chapter 12
Blockchain and Climate Action

ABSTRACT

To promote a climate-resilient, low-carbon, green, inclusive, integrated, and prosperous world, mobilizing funds to drive a green, inclusive, sustainable, and climate-compatible growth is essential. Blockchain and Web 3.0 have the potential to contribute to adaptation, mitigation, finance, and the enabling environment for climate action. This chapter is structured to educate people on mechanisms for raising capacity for effective climate change-related planning and management using blockchain, including focusing on women, youth, and local and marginalized communities. It aims to build the capacity of people involved in climate policy and climate action in blockchain technology's potential to strengthen action on climate change.

INTRODUCTION

SDG Goal 13 (United Nations, 2021) calls for urgent action to combat climate change and its impacts. It summarizes the Paris Agreement (United Nations, 2021) to limit global temperature rise to below 2 degrees Celsius and the Goal 13 objectives:

13.1   Strengthen resilience and adaptive capacity to all countries' climate-related hazards and natural disasters.
13.2   Integrate climate change measures into national policies, strategies, and planning Indicators.

DOI: 10.4018/978-1-6684-6658-2.ch012

13.3   Improve education, awareness-raising, and human and institutional capacity on climate change mitigation, adaptation, impact reduction, and early warning.

13.4   A Implement the commitment undertaken by developed-country parties to the United Nations Framework Convention on Climate Change to a goal of mobilizing jointly $100 billion annually by 2020 from all sources to address the needs of developing countries in the context of meaningful mitigation actions and transparency on implementation and fully operationalize the Green Climate Fund through its capitalization as soon as possible.

13.5   B Promote mechanisms for raising capacity for effective climate change-related planning and management in the least developed countries and small island developing States, focusing on women, youth, and local and marginalized communities.

The COP26 (National Grid, 2022) stimulated the world to commit to curbing contributions to carbon emissions. Achieving a net-zero world (Bouckaert, 2021) in less than 30 years is causing many to turn to the Blockchain, buy carbon offsets, and spark renewed interest in carbon capture. Voluntary Carbon Markets (Ecosystem Marketplace, 2021) hit a record $1 Billion in 2021. The United Nations Environment Programme (UNEP) identified transparency, clean energy, carbon markets, and climate finance areas where Blockchain technology can accelerate climate action (Alstair et al., 2021). At the 2017 Paris Summit, the UN Climate Change Secretariat joined a multi-stakeholder group of organizations to establish an open global initiative, the Climate Chain Coalition (UN Climate Change, 2018), signaling its early support for Blockchain for the climate. Blockchain offers several tools to support climate action, as outlined below.

Several authors have been exploring how Blockchain technology will help verify and trace multistep transactions. Future Thinkers (n.d) have identified ways Blockchain technology can combat climate change:

Supply Chain Management

Blockchain technology can track the supply chain of products. It will help consumers and sellers prevent waste, inefficiency, and fraud and establish transparency. Consumers can purchase products from sellers nearby, resulting in lower carbon emissions, which will cut transportation costs. A Blockchain-powered dApp, known as Foodtrax, created by Blockchain Development Company, enables food tracking from origin to store shelves.

Recycling

In several places in Northern Europe, people receive rewards with cryptographic tokens in exchange for depositing recyclable products such as those made of plastics. Facilitating this incentive distribution will enable transparent tracking of data like volume, cost, and profit to conduct impact evaluations. Social Plastic aims to eliminate poverty through such initiatives.

Environmental Treaties

Blockchain technology can help establish accountability among countries that promise a sustainable future.

Transparent Funds Flow

Blockchain technology can help pass the administrative procedures to ensure faster, transparent, and optimized funds transfers meant for conserving the environment. Developing countries mostly do the least harm yet suffer the most. Appropriate funding can help alleviate climate action.

Carbon Tax

Blockchain technology can help track the carbon footprint of each product. It will help determine the amount of tax to charge. Increasing pricing for products with higher carbon emissions will encourage consumers and producers to buy and sell products with lower carbon emissions to get them at cheaper rates.

GREEN DIGITAL ASSET SOLUTIONS

Green Digital Asset Solutions are crucial to achieving sustainability goals. These are subsidiaries of clean energy projects that find difficulties with financing. Blockchain can help with green investment because it is secure, transparent, auditable, and traceable (Naderi & Tian, 2022). United Nations

13th Sustainable Development Goal (SDGs) calls for urgent action to combat climate change and its impacts (UN, n.d.). Therefore, all crucial sectors of the economy, especially finance, will need sustainable financing solutions that Blockchain technology offers. It can integrate Blockchain-enabled tokenization, new sources of finance, and enthusiastic investors. Though the COVID-19 pandemic has halted investments in green projects, markets and finance experts need to evolve to draw policymakers' attention toward saving the planet from the ramifications of climate change. The United Nations Office For Project Services (2019) states that the Group of Twenty or G20 countries will provide $97 trillion for green infrastructure improvements and sustainable developments by 2040.

Blockchain technology can combat the challenges the energy sector faces in powering the globe post the ramifications of the COVID-19 pandemic. These challenges include high greenhouse gas emissions due to dependence on fossil fuels, financing for green projects, and a lower rate of return in green energy projects. With an emphasis on tokenizing green bonds, Blockchain technology can revolutionize green finance leading to greater efficiency and transparency in the market. Retail investors and donors will participate in climate adaptation and sustainable finance when green assets tokenize and crowdfunding starts (Naderi & Tian, 2022).

Green Blockchains

Blockchain technology has applications for carbon emissions trading and green certificates. Emissions Trading Systems (ETS), green certificates, or carbon offsets represent emissions saved through green technologies or CO_2 removed from the environment. Extending emissions allowance and offset trading schemes with Blockchain technology-based systems could grant improvements. Blockchain technology can enable interactions between standalone markets from various ETSs (European Commission, n.d.; Burke, 2016, Climate Change Authority, n.d.; Thalhammer et al., 2022). It allows transparency and traceability, leading to a higher reputation for the ETSs and their underlying market mechanisms. French Energy Provider Engie and The Energy Origin (TEO) created a platform in a dApp running on the Energy Web Foundation Blockchain. It allows users to monitor the energy origin and sustainability. The TEO platform records energy produced and consumed in real-time using sensors in homes and energy generators. Based on this, it calculates the energy flow of sustainable energy producers to the consumers

(Fleuret & Lyons, 2020; Thalhammer et al., 2022). Another use case example of Blockchain technology is green financing. Green Assets Wallet allows project sponsors to certify the eco-friendliness of undertakings publicly with credibility. The platform is also a space for investors to discover new opportunities and monitor the environmental impact of existing investments (Thalhammer et al., 2022).

Green Tokens

Using Blockchain technology, carbon credits can be easily tracked, traded, and stored as digital tokens (Strack, 2022). According to a report by Tacnalia and Chainlink labs, "Blockchain technology can initiate tokenized cash flows from Clean Energy Projects. Investing in clean energy projects is difficult due to a lack of availability in immediate jurisdictions. Asset tokenization can help ease this difficulty by helping participants buy Blockchain tokens representing equity and cash flows in renewable energy projects. The renewable energy projects can include but are not limited to wind farms and solar fields". They further explain how oracles can be helpful in the same, "Oracles are middleware that delivers off-chain data such as energy data on the Blockchain, perform secure off-chain computation, and facilitate communication between different Blockchain. Oracles can be applied to the dividend distribution processes to gather revenue data and performance output from smart meters to calculate cash flow payouts to token holders. These metrics can be stored on-chain as immutable records to verify the productivity of the investment and inform future initiatives." (Tecnalia & Chainlink labs, 2022).

Green Digital Asset solutions are witnessing a rise in adoption due to the renewed interest in carbon reporting, sequestration, and capture- leveraging Voluntary Carbon Markets (Ecosystems, n.d; Green Fintech Taxonomy and Data Landscaping, 2021). Green Digital Asset solutions can be tokenized and used as commodities in a market system, including Green utility tokens - a reward for lowering carbon emissions; Green asset tokens - tokenized carbon credit or biodiversity offset; Green crypto - programmed only to be spent on green products and Green STO (Security Token Offering) issuance platforms - designed to enable green proof of impact reporting (Mackreides, 2022).

There is an increase in the maturation and proliferation of such projects as people innovate for climate action. E.g., Treecoin (2020) sells asset tokens tied to eucalyptus trees and reinvests them in Paraguay's eucalyptus trees. Carbon and Trust (UpLink, n.d) also create a tokenized carbon credit for forest conservation, and Cambridge Centre for Carbon Credits (Cambridge Centre for Carbon Credits (4C), n.d.) looks forward to purchasing carbon credits to fund nature-based solutions preserving biodiversity. ClimateCoin (CoinNewsExtra.Com, n.d.; DennisBPeterson, 2021) is incentivizing offsetting carbon emissions by awarding tokens to people who reduce CO2 emissions or plant trees. Carbon Offsets To Alleviate Poverty (COTAP) supports projects which reward farmers for planting and maintaining trees on under-utilized portions of their land (Fight Climate Change and Alleviate Poverty with COTAP Carbon Offsets., n.d.). Evercity.io (Evercity Platform, n.d.) works with GloCha on a green chain solution for COP28 (Mackreides, 2022).

One of the most critical ways smart contracts can bring everyday people into the fight against climate change is by enabling regenerative agriculture programs. These include efforts to incentivize communities worldwide to cut their carbon footprints by adopting more sustainable land-use practices, such as planting trees and conservation (Entrepreneursface.com, n.d.; Zhou, 2021). Smart contracts interacting with real-world data make it possible to automatically issue rewards to people who steward these critical tracts of land. For example, in association with Cornell University, the Green World Campaign (Chainlink, 2021) has started the Initiative for Cryptocurrencies and Contracts (IC3). It focuses on building smart contracts that use satellite data to allocate rewards automatically to people. People receive rewards for successfully regenerating bodies of land by increasing tree cover, improving soil, and more. Payouts occur when oracles extract data from satellite images to trigger smart contracts built on a Blockchain. The process guarantees that people on the ground earn rewards fairly and transparently (Zhou, 2021).

Green Crypto

Cryptocurrency can help decarbonize unreliable power grids, optimize economic incentives for people to participate in clean energy, and help countries achieve climate goals. Crypto miners are unique energy buyers that offer flexible interruptible load capacity and are location agnostic. It makes crypto a strategic utility and an energy buyer of last resort that can be turned on or off at any point. This feature helps address the deficiencies of solar and wind energy supply as it is mostly either overabundant or nonexistent. Crypto mining can put the overabundance of such energy supply to good use. It will incentivize more solar & wind power and help retire fossil fuels for the same purpose. As per the US Energy Information Administration, 66%

of the primary energy used to create electricity goes wasted by the time it reaches consumers. HIVE Blockchain draws cheap energy from hydropower producers. The Swedish grid can depend on it whenever there is a disturbance to the local power supply (World Economic Forum, 2022).

Green STO Issuance Platforms

Blockchain technology can be used for tokenized securities to decentralize and democratize the interaction of private (retail) investors with issuers of SME projects. Security Token Offering (STO) is issuing a tokenized security (Scheltz et al., 2020.) It is the digital representation of a security asset in a digital token on a Blockchain platform. Tokenized securities can be divided into three categories: asset-based tokens representing ownership of an asset like real estate or work of art, debt token representing a debt instrument like green bonds or real estate mortgages, and equity tokens representing the value of shares issued by companies. Such tokenized securities must comply with legal regulations and Blockchain technology for greater transparency and issuer-investor protection. STOs have the potential to increase the demand and supply of green assets. The transparency feature of STO increases investor and donor confidence in overseas investments on the demand side. STOs also increase financial inclusion by offering investor ticket sizes of a few hundred US dollars investor ticket sizes. It encourages retail investors and communities to participate and create a diversified portfolio. Further, STOs enable SMEs (Merrill et al., 2019; Scheltz et al., 2020) to invest in green bonds as it offers smaller investment sizes of 3-5 million dollars (STOScope, 2019; Scheltz et al., 2020). The financial inclusion feature of STOs creates the supply side (Scheltz et al., 2020).

CARBON MARKETS

Carbon Markets

Carbon markets are crucial in achieving climate change goals and Nationally Determined Contributions (NDCS) to the Paris Agreement. During the COP26, delegates approved Article 6- the Paris Agreement rulebook governing global carbon markets. This approval helps establish a market where countries can trade carbon credits generated by reducing or removing greenhouse gas

(GHG) emissions from the atmosphere. They can use carbon markets to smoothen the transition to low-carbon transitions due to their potential to mobilize resources and reduce costs. As per estimates, carbon markets can reduce the cost of NDCs by $250 million by 2030. Securing verified data through digital infrastructure and ensuring accurate accounting and tracking of reductions can help reduce global GHG emissions. Some countries have started engaging with carbon markets. Blockchain technology can help ensure transparency. For example, Jordan is the first developing country to build end-to-end digital infrastructure to track and reduce global greenhouse gas emissions (The World Bank, 2022).

A carbon credit reduces, avoids, or removes carbon emissions in one place to compensate for unavoidable emissions somewhere else through certified green-energy projects. Carbon credits represent one ton in carbon emission reduction. They include 1. Avoidance or reduction projects, e.g., renewable energy – wind, solar, hydro, biogas and 2. Removal or sequestration e.g.reforestation, direct carbon capture, and aim at the voluntary carbon market (VCM). Carbon credits can be resold multiple times until it has been retired by the end-user who wants to claim the offset's impact. Carbon credits can also have co-benefits, such as job creation, water conservation, flood prevention, and preservation of biodiversity.

Carbon Registries

Carbon registries store the carbon credits issued by third-party independent, internationally certified auditors or verifiers following independent standards. The verifiers issue serial numbered credits, and the offset reduction claim gets converted to carbon credits that can be traded or retired. Carbon markets turn CO_2 emissions into a commodity or tradable environmental asset by giving it a price.

Carbon Compliance Markets

In the carbon compliance market, carbon allowances are traded. There are currently 64 compliance markets in the world, and pricing is determined by the emitters/polluters. The EU, or ETS, is the largest carbon market, with a 90% share in global trade. Entry into the EU ETS has been restricted to large polluters and the brokers the program's operators regulate. The supply of credits is also controlled to manage the pricing. Only the carbon prices traded in the EU ETS reflect the actual cost of polluting carbon, but access to the market is not equitable.

Voluntary Carbon Markets

Small companies and individuals can only access the Voluntary Carbon Market (VCM), where they buy credits at their discretion to offset emissions from a specific activity. Voluntary credits usually cannot be traded under the compliance market regime. VCM is expected to grow 15-fold by 2030 to respond to increased private sector demand for climate solutions, according to the Taskforce for Scaling the Voluntary Carbon Market and Final Report 2021(Miltenberger et al., 2021). A significant problem with VCM is that carbon credit prices have been low. The low costs of voluntary credits at $2-3 per credit do not motivate or incentivize project developers and do little to capture the actual cost of climate pollution compared to the compliance market. An excellent article for understanding VCM is "The Good Is Never Perfect: Why the Current Flaws of Voluntary Carbon Markets Are Services, Not Barriers to Successful Climate Change Action" (Miltenberger et al., 2021). In this article, Miltenberger et al. highlight critical issues around the design, function, and scale-up of VCMs, listed below.

Greenwashing

Greenwashing with false energy efficiencies being claimed and high rates of ineffective credits being used to offset corporate emissions.

Carbon Accounting

Carbon Accounting for the number of claims for offsetting emissions is unrealistic given ecosystem constraints; net-zero ambitions should have disclosure requirements and be audited.

Double Counting

Double counting can happen intentionally but also due to a lack of complete accounting protocols and alignment between market jurisdictions or operators.

Market Failures

Market Failures and Inefficiencies unfairly burden product and service markets with compliance costs, and there are few incentives for businesses that voluntarily take action to mitigate an environmental impact.

Monitoring Reporting and Verifying

Monitoring, Reporting and Verifying the costs of these activities can constitute a majority of the market value of carbon credit, reducing the incentive for implementation.

Additionality and Baselines

Additionality and Baselines Carbon removal projects utilize inherently subjective baselines.

Permanence

Permanence is the assurance that carbon will remain in stock for an extended time, usually 30–100 years. However, there is an opportunity to protect and expand carbon sinks, incentivize low carbon production, and increase the flow of carbon from the atmosphere to short-term and durable stock, even in cases with shorter-term permanence.

Stakeholder Inclusion and Inequity

Stakeholder Inclusion and Inequity projects can disenfranchise local livelihoods; in some early REDD+ projects, the financialized carbon benefits resulted in local communities' restricted access to their traditional land and livelihoods.

Southpole points out that "Blockchain technology has enormous potential for climate action. However, this is only the case when the right safeguards are in place to ensure environmental integrity. Web3 applications can be part of the climate solution, but they have to be designed and applied correctly" (Puhl, 2022). While the potential exists, there is a need to rectify the problems in Voluntary Carbon Markets, including

1. Strengthening the incentives for decarbonization.
2. Pricing carbon is urgently needed with improved price transparency.
3. Reducing the cost of carbon credit creation.
4. Reducing transaction costs and providing additional liquidity.
5. Make the prices in the spot and futures market higher and more reliable.
6. Building carbon credits as a viable asset class by providing predictable returns on investment and including value protection for buyers and sellers.
7. Create safeguards to protect the reputation and legal processes for dispute settlement.
8. Clarity on taxation exemption of carbon credits, moving from "polluter pays" to "polluter invests," and complete price discovery goes to the green owners on the ground taking direct climate action on their behalf.

Voluntary Carbon Markets are an essential means to catalyze action, but as can be seen from Puhl (2022), they need significant improvements to fulfill that role.

DECENTRALIZED ENERGY MANAGEMENT

Due to the rising cost of Smart Grid (SG) systems, their future in the energy industry is uncertain and complicated. Blockchain helps improve and manage smart grids in decentralized energy markets, allowing for the Peer-to-Peer(P2P) trade of power reliably and transparently. The P2P approach can also support renewable energies and provide economic benefits for both consumers and prosumers. The SG system has distinguished features integrating renewable energy systems, Internet of Things (IoT) devices, Electric vehicles (EV), and smart meters, requiring novel structural support that Blockchain technology can provide. Blockchain technology is helpful in SGs in nine areas: security, energy trading, decentralized energy management, Blockchain testbed, EV, IoT, smart contracts, and environmentalism. The Blockchain application in smart grids is well summarised below by Hasankhani et al. (2021).

Smart Contracts for Demand Response

This helps facilitate financial transactions between the decentralized nodes, increases security in financial transactions, and provides digital incentives to consumers. Smart contracts help empower environmentally conscious individuals and sell to charitable organizations, crowdfunding campaigns, or companies that seek proof of having made a practical green impact. Since the tokenized carbon credits can form only if satellites or Internet of Things (IoT) devices verify meaningful reforestation to a smart contract, these organizations can demonstrate that their funds have made a substantial impact (Entrepreneurs Face, n.d.).

Smart contracts also can enable environmentally conscious consumers to have more options concerning the energy they consume (Zhou, 2021). Several decentralized energy grids, like the Brooklyn Microgrid Project (Zhou, 2021), use smart contracts to enable consumers to produce and trade solar electricity with their neighbors through an exchange using Blockchain as a coordinating medium. The facility and the ability to buy and sell solar energy credits between neighbors using smart contracts can reduce energy transportation costs and greenhouse gas emissions (Entrepreneurs Face, n.d.). Since the smart contracts connect with real-world data, consumers can digitally receive accurate information on billing and penalties based on the impact of their consumption habits, creating behavioral changes that would not have occurred through education alone (Zhou; Hinchliffe,2022). A project called NetObjex (n.d.) is installing IoT devices in select hotels to keep track of guests' water and energy consumption throughout their visit. Smart contracts can interact with the resulting data about a hotel visit through oracles and automatically calculate and reward guests based on their consumption metrics.

Electric Vehicles

This improves security issues in the energy trading between EVs and charging stations, increases security between data transactions between EVs, helps define a digital wallet for each EV, and stores its digital coins to ease financial transactions.

Internet of Things

This helps develop the decentralized control of IoT devices, provides authentication and secure transactions between IoT devices, and facilitates data collection from smart home devices.

Decentralized Energy Management

This helps develop decentralized energy management through distributed ledger technology, facilitates energy management of distributed renewable energy resources, and compensates for their intermittencies.

Energy Trading

This develops the new structure for energy trading according to Ethereum contracts, facilitates energy trading between all nodes in SG, and facilitates financial transactions by utilizing a token-based network.

Financial Transactions

This facilitates the financial transactions between different nodes in SG using the digital currency, decreases the electricity cost compared to the real-time electricity market, addresses the intermittencies in energy trading with renewable resources through smart contracts, and guarantees financial transactions in the Blockchain.

Cyber-Physical Security

This helps avoid cyber attacks on SGs, solves false data injection problems, and decreases the possibility of forgery according to the decentralized structure of Blockchain technology.

Environmentalism

This helps track pollution caused by all units in SG and identify polluting units, encourages people to recycle by defining token-based incentives, and develops renewable energy resources resulting in decreased fossil fuel-based plants.

SMART GRID MANAGEMENT

This section will examine the implementation of Blockchain technology in smart grids in decentralized energy markets and allow for the P2P trade of power reliably and transparently.

P2P Energy Trading

The existing hierarchical grid networks lack security regarding the transactions due to the involvement of mediators and other third parties. It leads to low efficiency of operations (Gartner, 2017; Abdella & Shuaib, 2018; Alladi et al., 2019). Therefore, it is advantageous to use a decentralized, Blockchain-based trading infrastructure enabling the Peer-to-Peer (P2P) energy trade between consumers and prosumers in a secure manner (Alladi et al., 2019). It gives identity privacy and transaction security. The P2P energy trade has practical applications in various areas like the Industrial Internet of Things (IIoT) and micro-grid development for sustainable energy utilization (Li et al., 2019, Mengelkamp et al., 2017; Alladi et al., 2019). P2P energy trading is gaining momentum as UK based Energy Networks Association plans a 17 billion Euros investment in the local energy markets using the smart grid (Ambrose, 2017; Alladi et al., 2019). P2P energy trading utilizes technologies such as virtual currency using Blockchain to represent each unit of electricity. It will facilitate selling surplus energy available with the prosumer to other Blockchain network peers and transferring this electrical energy into the grid. Another technology used is credit-based transactions which facilitate purchasing power without actual possession of virtual currencies. Finally, smart contracts associated with smart meters in grids accommodate the Blockchain. It helps ensure authentic data transfers between the smart meters and supervisory nodes and reports any unauthorized and malicious data tampering.

One example is Power Ledger which enables consumers to buy, sell, or exchange excess renewable electricity directly with each other (Powerledger, n.d.). Solstroem focuses on accelerating the energy transition in developing and emerging countries (Thomason, 2022). It provides off-grid solar and geotagged, timestamped micro-carbon credits that individuals or companies can purchase (Solostroem, n.d.). New technologies significantly reduce fabrication costs and facilitate the massive adoption of mobile phones in developing countries. Therefore, new technologies allow consumers to benefit from distributed generation by connecting solar panels to the Blockchain

(Azuri Technologies, n.d.; Mackreides, 2022); off-grid Electric and Mobisol produce low-cost solar panel solutions for off-grid areas in rural Africa. This smart PayGo system makes solar technology affordable at a fraction of the price of kerosene. When households pay off the solar panels, they move from renting to owning an asset. It helps transform the lives of off-grid rural citizens by giving them ownership of cutting-edge technology, building a safer home environment, and supporting additional sustainability initiatives.

Smart Grids

Smart grids are advancing by leveraging the benefits of Wireless Sensor Networks (WSNs) and the Internet of Things (IoT). Adopting intelligent systems that monitor and communicate with each other offers energy production and consumption optimization. Smart grids also utilize Advanced Metering Devices (AMI) for automating sensor-based metering systems leading to less reliance on human resources. Further, it promises more efficient tapping of renewable energy sources by offering technological support for transferring energy between local energy producers and consumers. Using Blockchain technology helps grid networks decentralize their operations. It eliminates the need for decision-making and transaction flows through centralized systems such as mediators and banks (Alladi et al., 2019).

Energy Marketplaces

Energy marketplaces encourage renewable energy generation through a flexible marketplace connecting buyers and sellers. Since 2021, Energy Web Token (EWT), Power Ledger (POWR), and WePower(WPR) have seen triple-digit gains. EWT is the operational token for the Energy Web Chain, an open-source enterprise Blockchain that supports and develops the energy sector. It utilizes open-source, decentralized digital technologies to accelerate a low-carbon, customer-centric electricity system. The project has a network of partners from global companies such as Volkswagen, Siemens, and Hitachi (Finneseth, 2021).

Solar Energy and Prosumers in Rural Areas

Prosumers result from decentralized energy systems. They use and generate their energy and help increase electrification in remote areas. People can sell access to power throughout the community. Developing countries such as Sri Lanka and India are prime examples of adapting solar-power grids. According to Filippo Carzaniga, Executive Chairman of FIMER, we are witnessing growth in the use of storage systems across all market segments such as utility-scale, commercial & industrial, and residential – particularly in markets such as Taiwan, Vietnam, and the Philippines (Open Access Government, 2021; Koons, 2022). It helps stabilize the grid and provides a continual energy source during intermittency. The residential market supports the rise of prosumers (Carzaniga, 2021; Koons, 2022).

NFTS, GAMIFICATION AND CLIMATE ACTION

This section will examine how NFTs and gamification are used and leveraged for climate change initiatives (Foster, 2022), ranging from awareness-raising to fundraising and an immutable impact and carbon credits record.

For example, the Open Banking World Congress planned to have its entire carbon emissions fully offset (Financial IT, 2021). In association with Carbon Free Brasil, over 1,000 trees will be planted and maintained, restoring over 8,000 square meters of native forests. A special access card is given to each delegate. Once activated, the card provides the delegate with an NFT representing one exceptionally commissioned artwork by Brazilian artist Lincoln Lima. As all pieces are activated, the entire image will be displayed on monitors at the event (Financial IT, 2021). Another example is Moss. Earth is utilizing NFTs and crypto carbon credits to fight climate change in the Amazon (Martson, 2022). For example, the company's customers can purchase non-fungible tokens (NFTs) to own a piece of the Amazon rainforest. Moss acquired the land for these NFTs (N FT Documentation and Property Deeds - Moss Amazon Forest NFT - White Paper and FAQ, 2022) through its subsidiary Terra Vista Gestora de Recursos LTDA. In January 2022, it purchased 50 hectares of the Fazenda Rio Azul (Blue River Farm) in Para state and subsequently made its shares available as NFTs. Moss stresses on its website that when a person purchases an NFT, they buy the actual land and finance its conservation. An NFT that was bought from Moss. Earth is equivalent to one hectare of forest, roughly the size of a football field (Martson, 2022).

Descartes Labs provides remote sensing tools to enable buyers to digitally monitor the owned piece of land (Geospatial Analytics Platform | Satellite Imagery | Remote Sensing, n.d.; Martson, 2022). There are certain legal restrictions and rules that the buyers have to follow. For instance, according to Moss, they cannot "burn, squander, or deforest the land in any way." Aside from this, people can do whatever they want with the land, including reselling it by selling their NFT. However, this should be done without impairing the ecological balance. The company mentioned that it would arrange trips for curious owners to visit their land at some point (Martson, 2022).

As described in Chapter 7, NFTs originate through a process known as "minting" (Filebase, 2022), creating a Blockchain network representation of their material, which forms immutable records of every asset purchase and sale, and who owns it now. Once minted, NFTs can be purchased, sold, or exchanged. NFTs raise concerns regarding climate change, as most NFTs mint on the Ethereum Blockchain; thus, there is the paradox of the balance between harm and good (Calma, 2021). One solution is to build out another "layer" on top of the existing Blockchain, and this can reduce energy consumption because transactions happen "off-chain." For example, two people interested in trading NFTs could open up their own "channel" on the second layer to make virtually unlimited transactions (Calma, 2021).

Scrutiny over the crypto world's environmental impact has grown as the NFT marketplace has exploded over the past few years (Sherrif, 2021). NFT creators that want to make their products carbon neutral choose Blockchain with a proof-of-stake mechanism on Ethereum, where most valuable NFTs are hosted. It uses a layer two solution and offsets the footprint using carbon (Sherrif, 2021).

Truby et al. (2022) examine how the rapidly increasing uptake of NFT transactions has increased social attention toward the level of emissions from proof-of-work Blockchain networks that support NFT transactions. Newer platforms supporting NFTs have also advertised their environmental credentials, avoiding proof-of-work in favor of energy-efficient consensus protocols. Palm uses the Ethereum Blockchain to trade NFTs, claiming to consume 99% less energy than the proof-of-work Blockchain, while Cardano and Flow8 offer alternative models for NFT trading. NFT traders could significantly reduce their carbon impact by avoiding proof-of-work platforms. Regulations could require traders to avoid proof-of-work platforms, or traders could be taxed at the point of transaction based on the energy consumption or emission levels of the type of platform utilized for the transaction. It would align with the polluter pays principle, as accepted in environmental law and policy-making.

Several projects are using NFTs for trading carbon credits. Universal Protocol allows certified projects to convert greenhouse gas reductions into tradable carbon credits (CoinNewsExtra.Com, n.d.; Universal Protocol Alliance, n.d.). First, Carbon NFT Based Carbon Credits provides carbon credit issuers access to the Blockchain, enabling users to track, trade, and burn credits (First Carbon Corp., 2021). Moreover, organizations such as Evercity. io (n.d) and Blockchain Triangle are robust integrated platforms providing guidance, aggregating initiatives, and carbon credits and linking them to investors and financial mechanisms such as digital green bonds through Blockchain-driven platforms (Blockchain Triangle, n.d.). The capacity to include the voluntary market credits in National reporting under the Paris Agreement is also being addressed through initiatives like Blockchain for Climate (Blockchain for Climate Foundation, n.d.) and its BITMO platform and Open Earth Foundation and its Nested Climate Accounting for the Paris Global Stocktake (CoinNewsExtra.Com, n.d.; OpenEarth Foundation, n.d.).

Digital Art for Climate

Another NFT use case, DigitalArt4Climate, is a multi-stakeholder partnership initiative that uses Blockchain technology to turn art into digital assets or NFTs, which can be collected and traded, which helps unlock potential for resource mobilization, youth engagement, and climate empowerment (Thomason, 2022). NFTs are increasingly being leveraged for climate change with initiatives ranging from awareness-raising to fundraising and as an immutable record for impact and carbon credits (Thomason, 2022). Artists like Beeple, Andres Resigner, Refik Anadol, Sara Ludy, and Kyle Gordon have an NFT project called Social Alpha Foundation (SAF) to auction off work donated by NFT artists using Blockchain-focused technology. Open Earth Foundation will receive the proceeds from this auction. It is a registered non-profit focused on cutting-edge research and deployment of open digital infrastructure, including Blockchains, for climate accounting under the Paris Agreement. They have received support from Render Token Price (RNDR); 500 tons of carbon offset is represented as NFTs and auctioned off. The act of registration of carbon offers is a result of this initiative and is set aside for preserving the Amazon rainforest and preventing deforestation (Wintermeyer, 2021).

Gamification and Climate

Play to Earn consists of a dynamic of playing to win, thus creating a monetization of time. It is the unique set that is changing the way of seeing gaming, and with the new generation of games, many people have professionalized being able to live from it. The use of NFTs is essential in the gameplay dynamics of this new gaming world, being the ideal connector between cryptocurrencies and games.

NFTs are being leveraged for climate change initiatives (Foster, n.d.), ranging from awareness-raising to fundraising and an immutable record for impact and carbon credits. It is also possible to use the gameplay to incentivize widespread positive climate action and for people to understand their carbon footprint, and we can expect to see more games where people can play to earn for climate action.

Some use cases of NFTs include Certified Credit Smart NFTs by SavePlanetEarth. Another is NFT-based carbon credits by First Carbon Corp., which give insurers access to the Blockchain, enabling users to track, trade, and burn credits to eliminate double counting. NFTs are used for multi-stakeholder partnership initiatives by DigitalArts4Climate uses Blockchain technology to turn art into digital assets or NFTs that can be collected and traded for multi-stakeholder partnership initiatives. This use case shows NFT's potential for resource mobilization, youth engagement, and climate empowerment. Gameplay is also usable for incentivizing widespread positive climate action. For instance, GreenApes is using gamification to help covey people's carbon footprint to them (Bobby, 2022).

MEASUREMENT AND REPORTING AND VERIFICATION

This section examines how Blockchain and Web 3.0 will be critical tools for measurement and reporting combined with AI and IoT with large-scale interconnected databases (e.g., climate, water, land) to develop action for desertification and deforestation and predict weather events and trends. Climate action accounting is also called Measurement, Reporting, and Verification (MRV) (Hyperledger Foundation, 2021). Blockchain will be a critical tool for measurement and reporting in combination with AI and IoT with large-scale interconnected databases (for climate, water, and land) to develop action for desertification and deforestation and predict weather events and trends. Blockchain smart contracts offer a tamper-proof zero-cost mechanism for connecting positive (or negative) environmental changes or outcomes to financial incentives/disincentives (Bobby, 2022).

Every party to the Paris Agreement needs a Nationally Determined Contribution (NDC). An NDC is a plan for climate action to reduce emissions and adapt to climate impacts. The parties involved must update the NDC every five years (United Nations, n.d.). In 2015 Mexico set an NDC to reduce its greenhouse gas reduction target to 22% by 2030. Further, conditional upon international support, it promised to increase its mitigation targets to 36%. To achieve these, Mexico explored climate transparency systems and enabled trading for emission allowances. In a briefing paper published by Medio Ambiente and GIZ on behalf of the Federal Ministry for the Environment, Nature Conservation, and Nuclear Safety (2019), the study Blockchain for Mexican Climate Instruments: Emissions Tradings and MRV systems, elaborated by Sven Braden, was analyzed. They examined the suitability of Blockchain technology for MRV, and the results show that it offers core principles of results-based finance and therefore facilitates access to international climate finance. The verification of climate action claims enables transparent MRV of a variety of climate policies. MRV gathers and verifies data and processes. It can be valuable for future policy planning (Medio Ambiente, GIZ, Federal Ministry for the Environment, Nature Conservation, and Nuclear Safety, 2019).

Blockchain and Web3 can help with standardized accounting protocols for interoperability across accounting scales and systems; greater transparency from VCM operators and credit purchasers; standalone certifications on rights and ownership of credits; improved traceability, traceability, and liquidity, and smart contracts allow carbon credits to be used in innovative ways, creating additional demand in the overall VCM. Combined with remotely sensed data via satellite imagery, drones, laser-detecting devices, and IoT devices, machine learning, and artificial intelligence analytics can decrease development costs and increase rigor in measurement (Thomason, 2022).

DECENTRALIZED AUTONOMOUS ORGANIZATION (DAO) FOR CLIMATE ACTION

As described in Chapter 5, Blockchain and Web 3.0 can create new digital economies which unite and economically align people around a common purpose. This means there is potential to develop community token economies that value climate action (Thomason, 2022). This section will elaborate on the plan to utilize a DAO to develop economies that value climate action. A DAO can create new digital economies where tokens can unite and economically align people around a common purpose. It is possible to develop economies that value climate action.

Blockchain can enable (Thomason, 2022): (i) Direct financing for community-scale climate actions, (ii) Simplification of results-based climate finance, (iii) Decentralized carbon trading benefits people with low incomes at the household level, (iv) Crowdfunding for climate projects for people experiencing poverty, and Gamification to incentivize climate-friendly action. Social impact and global commons issues require greater cooperation and collaboration among ecosystems that don't typically collaborate or converge (Thomason, 2022).

Dr. Miroslav Plozer of the GloCha United Citizens Organisation (Glocha, 2022)makes the point that technology alone will be insufficient, "Even if Blockchain can offer the solutions to scale up climate actions, they won't be developed and operated on the ground if there are barriers such as policies, regulations and local capacity for using them. Young people from emerging economies will be vital partners in addressing the challenge" (Thomason, 2022).

CONCLUSION

This chapter has covered practical examples and steps to scale up Blockchain and climate action. A key element to scaling will be mobilizing capital through sustainable finance initiatives for climate action through green bonds, fintech solutions, and alternative finance mechanisms. Investment programs are needed to support Blockchain and other technological innovations contributing to climate change mitigation and adaptation. Strengthening the clean technology innovation ecosystem and improving access to finance facilitates clean technology startups and small and medium-sized enterprises is also needed.

Climate change poses an extreme threat to the livelihood, food security, and health of people experiencing poverty, especially women and children. Estimates suggest that a billion people will face forcible displacement out of their homes by 2050 due to climate change. Impoverished communities tend to depend on climate-sensitive sectors and natural resources for survival. The carbon footprint of the poorest billion people in the world is only about 3 percent of the total footprint of the world, yet death rates are about 500 times more (Wikipedia, 2019). The climate response needs to consider the world as a whole, not just a way to allow emissions creators to atone for their harms by buying carbon credits (Thomason, 2022). Blockchain and Web 3.0 are important in carbon markets, as described above.

Green digital asset solutions, carbon markets, decentralized energy trading, smart grid management, NFTs. DAOs, incentivization and transparent measurement and reporting are all ways Blockchain and Web3 can be deployed for climate action. Metaverse and immersive reality will enable the use of Digital Twins across energy, water, and telecoms networks to enable the examination of climate projections and impacts. For example, examining drought and flooding more precisely will be possible with rainfall with hydrological models. Digital twins and AI can use data from different sources and connect and leverage different models to evaluate their impact on a larger scale with multiple variables. Digital twins and augmented reality can simulate natural disasters through real-time interaction and accurate 3D registration of virtual and real objects. It is early days for Metaverse, but the value of digital twins and virtual experiences are also expected to be deployed for climate action. The collaboration will continue to be crucial in developing and adapting web3, Blockchain, Metaverse and other technology-based solutions that support climate actions, bringing together the global community to scale climate action.

REFERENCES

Abdella, J., & Shuaib, K. (2018). Peer to Peer Distributed Energy Trading in Smart Grids: A Survey. *Energies*, *11*(6), 1560. doi:10.3390/en11061560

Alladi, T., Chamola, V., Rodrigues, J. J., & Kozlov, S. A. (2019). Blockchain in smart grids: A review on different use cases. *Sensors (Basel)*, *19*(22), 4862. doi:10.339019224862 PMID:31717262

Ambrose, J. (2017, December 4). Energy networks to unveil plan for £17bn smart-grid boom. T*he Telegraph.* https://www.telegraph.co.uk/business/2017/12/04/energy-networks-unveil-plan-17bn-smart-grid-boom/

Art Meets Climate Change at Open Banking World Congress. (n.d.). *Financial IT.* Retrieved July 29 2022 from https://financialit.net/news/open-banking/art-meets-climate-change-open-banking-world-congress

Azuri. (n.d.). *Solar Innovators.* https://www.azuri-group.com/about

Blockchain for Climate Foundation. (n.d.). *Blockchain for Climate Foundation*. Retrieved July 29 2022 from https://www.Blockchainforclimate.org

Bobby. (2022, April). *How Blockchain Technology Is Transforming Climate Action*. NSBB News. https://nsbb.in/2022/04/09/how-Blockchain-technology-is-transforming-climate-action/

Bouckaert, S., Pales, A. F., McGlade, C., Remme, U., Wanner, B., Varro, L., & Spencer, T. (2021). *Net Zero by 2050: A Roadmap for the Global Energy Sector*. https://iea.blob.core.windows.net/assets/deebef5d-0c34-4539-9d0c-10b13d840027/NetZeroby2050-ARoadmapfortheGlobalEnergySector_CORR.pdf

Bruner, R. (2021, November 18). Environmental Concerns Have Cast Doubt on NFTs—But That's Changing. *Time*. https://time.com/6120237/nfts-environmental-impact/

Burke PJ. (2016). Undermined by adverse selection: Australia's direct action abatement subsidies. *Economic Papers: A Journal of Applied Economics and Policy, 35*(3), 216-229. 10.1111/1759-3441.12138

Calma, J. (2021, March 15). The Climate Controversy Swirling around NFTs. *The Verge; Vox Media*. https://www.theverge.com/2021/3/15/22328203/nft-cryptoart-ethereum-Blockchain-climate-change

Cambridge Centre for Carbon Credits. (n.d.). Retrieved July 29 2022 from https://4c.cst.cam.ac.uk

Carzaniga, F. (2021, December 2). Solar:Vital to Asia's renewable energy success. *Open Access Government*. https://www.openaccessgovernment.org/asias-renewable-energy/125209/

Chainlink. (2021, May 20). *How Hybrid Smart Contracts Incentivize Regenerative Agriculture*. https://blog.chain.link/reversing-climate-change-how-hybrid-smart-contracts-incentivize-regenerative-agriculture

Cheikosman, E. (2022, June 9). Can crypto become a leader in sustainability? *World Economic Forum*. https://www.weforum.org/agenda/2022/06/crypto-sustainability/

Climate Change Authority. (n.d.). *Review of the emissions reduction fund*. https://www.climatechangeauthority.gov.au/review-emissions-reduction-fund

CoinNewsExtra. (n.d.). *How Blockchain technology is transforming climate action.* https://coinnewsextra.com/how-Blockchain-technology-is-transforming-climate-action/

Contributors, W. (2019, October 22). *Carbon footprint.* Wikipedia; Wikimedia Foundation. https://en.wikipedia.org/wiki/Carbon_footprint

DennisBPeterson. (2021 May 27). Climatecoin. *GitHub.* https://github.com/DennisBPeterson/Climatecoin

European Commission. (n.d.). *EU emissions trading system (eu ets).* European Commission. https://ec.europa.eu/clima/eu-action/eu-emissions-trading-system-eu-ets_en

Face, E. (n.d.). *How will Blockchain technology help fight climate change?* https://entrepreneursface.com/how-will-Blockchain-technology-help-fight-climate-change/

Fight climate change and alleviate poverty with COTAP carbon offsets. (n.d.). https://cotap.org

Filebase. (2022, June). *Deep Dive: NFTs.* https://docs.filebase.com/knowledge-base/deep-dives/deep-dive-nfts

Financial, I. T. (2022, May 17). *Art meets Climate Change at Open Banking World Congress.* https://financialit.net/news/open-banking/art-meets-climate-change-open-banking-world-congress

Finneseth, J. (2021, April 3). Blockchain-based renewable energy marketplaces gain traction in 2021. *Cointelegraph.* https://cointelegraph.com/news/Blockchain-based-renewable-energy-marketplaces-gain-traction-in-2021

First Carbon Corp. (2021, October 19). First Carbon Develops Proprietary NFT Based Carbon Credits Trading Platform and Launches Company Website. *GlobeNewswire News Room.* https://www.globenewswire.com/news-release/2021/10/19/2316705/0/en/First-Carbon-Develops-Proprietary-NFT-Based-Carbon-Credits-Trading-Platform-and-Launches-Company-Website.html

Fleuret, F., & Lyons, T. (2020). *Blockchain and the future of digital assets. ConsenSys AG and European Union Blockchain Observatory & Forum.* https://2020.standict.eu/publications/Blockchain-and-future-digital-assets

Foster, K. (2022, March 25). NFTs for Social Impact: Addressing Three Key Challenges. *St. Gallen Symposium.* https://symposium.org/nfts-for-social-impact-addressing-three-key-challenges/

Future thinkers. (n.d.). *7 Ways Blockchain Can Save The Environment and Stop Climate Change.* https://futurethinkers.org/Blockchain-environment-climate-change/

Gartner. (2017, August 15). *Gartner Identifies Three Megatrends That Will Drive Digital Business Into the Next Decade* [Press Release]. https://www.gartner.com/en/newsroom/press-releases/2017-08-15-gartner-identifies-three-megatrends-that-will-drive-digital-business-into-the-next-decade

Geospatial Analytics Platform | Satellite Imagery | Remote Sensing. (n.d.). Retrieved July 29 2022 from https://descarteslabs.com

GloCha. (2022, February 2). *Media Advisory - Announcement of United Citizen Organization Formation at COP26.* https://www.glocha.org

Green Digital Finance Alliance. (2021, November 29). *The World's First Green Finetech Taxonomy.* https://greendigitalfinancealliance.org/a-green-fintech-taxonomy-and-data-landscaping/

Hasankhani, A., Hakimi, S. M., Bisheh-Niasar, M., Shafie-khah, M., & Asadolahi, H. (2021). Blockchain technology in the future smart grids: A comprehensive review and frameworks. *International Journal of Electrical Power & Energy Systems*, *129*, 106811. doi:10.1016/j.ijepes.2021.106811

Li, J., Zhou, Z., Wu, J., Li, J., Mumtaz, S., Lin, X., Gacanin, H., & Alotaibi, S. (2019). Decentralized On-Demand Energy Supply for Blockchain in Internet of Things: A Microgrids Approach. *IEEE Transactions on Computational Social Systems*, *6*(6), 1395–1406. doi:10.1109/TCSS.2019.2917335

Mackreides, J. (2022, April 9). How Blockchain technology is transforming climate action. *BFIA.* https://www.bfia.org/2022/04/09/how-Blockchain-technology-is-transforming-climate-action/

Marke, A., Nellore, S.K., Mihaylov, M., Khvatsky, J., Floyd, H.P., Symes, T., Schlumberger, J.A.F., Baumann, T., Yarger, M., Doebler, F., Mathley, N., Lin, N., Ruslanova, M., Miller, D., Thorne, S.R., Arslan, C., Kilic, S., Chávez, C., Angarita, R., ...Wainstein, M. (2022). *Blockchain for sustainable energy and climate in the Global South. Social Alpha Foundation and United Nations Environment program.* http://www.socialalphafoundation.org/wp-content/uploads/2022/01/saf-Blockchain-report-final-2022.pdf

Marketplace, E. (2021, September 15). *Voluntary Carbon Markets Rocket in 2021 On Track to Break $1B for First Time.* https://www.ecosystemmarketplace.com/articles/press-release-voluntary-carbon-markets-rocket-in-2021-on-track-to-break-1b-for-first-time/

Marston, J. (2022, February 18). Moss.Earth is using NFTs & crypto carbon credits to fight climate change in the Amazon. *AgFunderNews.* https://agfundernews.com/nfts-crypto-carbon-credits-moss-earth-is-using-to-fight-climate-change

Medio Ambiente GIZ Federal Ministry for the Environment Nature Conservation and Nuclear Safety. (2019). *Blockchain for Mexican Climate Instruments: Emissions Trading and MRV System*s. https://www.giz.de/en/downloads/giz2019-en-Blockchain-emissions.pdf

Mengelkamp, E., Notheisen, B., Beer, C., Dauer, D., & Weinhardt, C. (2017). A Blockchain-based smart grid: Towards sustainable local energy markets. *Computer Science - Research for Development, 33*(1-2), 207–214. doi:10.100700450-017-0360-9

Merrill, Schillebeeckx, & Blakstad. (2019). *Sustainable Digital Finance in Asia: Creating Environmental Impact through Bank Transformation.* DBS and UN Environment. https://www.dbs.com/iwov-resources/images/sustainability/reports/Sustainable Digital Finance in Asia_FINAL_22.pdf

Microgrid, B. (n.d.). *About.* https://www.brooklyn.energy/about

Miltenberger, O., Jospe, C., & Pittman, J. (2021). The Good Is Never Perfect: Why the Current Flaws of Voluntary Carbon Markets Are Services Not Barriers to Successful Climate Change Action. *Front. Clim., 3*, 686516. doi:10.3389/fclim.2021.686516

Naderi, N., & Tian, Y. (2022). Leveraging Blockchain Technology and Tokenizing Green Assets to Fill the Green Finance Gap. *Energy Research Letters, 3*(3). Advance online publication. doi:10.46557/001c.33907

Nazarov, S., Preukschat, A., Lage, O., & Fernández, M. (2022, April). *Managing Climate Change in the Energy Industry With Blockchains and Oracles.* Tecnalia and Chainlink Labs. https://pages.chain.link/hubfs/e/managing-climate-change-energy-industry.pdf?_ga=2.253807112.1649722747.1658841288-1828728476.1658841288

netObjex. (n.d.). *NetObjex India - The platform for NFT MarketPlace and Web3 Wallet.* https://www.netobjex.com

NFT documentation and property deeds - Moss Amazon Forest NFT - White Paper and FAQ. (2022). https://moss-earth.gitbook.io/moss-amazon-forest-nft-faq/nft-documentation-and-property-deeds

OpenEarth Foundation. (n.d.). Retrieved July 29 2022 from https://www.openearth.org

Ossinger, J. (2022, February 25). *Polkadot Has Least Carbon Footprint Crypto Researcher Says.* Bloomberg Asia Edition. https://www.bloomberg.com/news/articles/2022-02-02/polkadot-has-smallest-carbon-footprint-crypto-researcher-says#xj4y7vzkg

Platform, E. (n.d.). *Evercity.io.* Retrieved July 29 2022 from https://www.evercity.io

Powerledger. (n.d.). *The Power Behind New Energy.* https://www.powerledger.io

Puhl, I. (2022). *Blockchain and carbon: How to scale climate action while protecting investors and ensuring environmental integrity.* South Pole. https://www.southpole.com/blog/Blockchain-and-carbon

Rozas, D., Tenorio-Fornés, A., & Hassan, S. (2021). Analysis of the Potentials of Blockchain for the Governance of Global Digital Commons. *Front. Blockchain, 4*, 577680. doi:10.3389/fbloc.2021.577680

Scheltz, M., Nassiry, D., & Lee, M. K. (2020). *Blockchain and Tokenized Securities: The Potential For Green Finance* [Working Paper Series]. ADBI Institute.

Sheriff, L. (2022, April 25). How a new generation of NFTs plans to cut its carbon footprint. *Fortune.* https://fortune.com/2022/04/25/how-a-new-generation-of-nfts-plans-to-cut-its-carbon-footprint/amp/

Solstrom. (n.d.). *The CO_2 avoidance programme for off-grid solar.* https://www.solstroem.com

STOScope. (2019). *Security Token Offering (STO) List.* https://stoscope.com/

Strack, B. (2022 April 19). *Blockchain Tech Is Key to Combating Climate Change Report Says.* Blockworks. https://blockworks.co/Blockchain-tech-is-key-to-combating-climate-change-report-says/

Thalhammer, F., Schöttle, P., Janetschek, M., & Ploder, C. (2022). Blockchain Use Cases Against Climate Destruction. *Cloud Computing and Data Science*, 22-38. https://www.wiserpub.com/uploads/1/20220225/cb1859265cfa6a25dfa0bc362237128c.pdf

The Future of Crowdfunding Creative Projects. (n.d.). *Kickstarter.* https://www.kickstarter.com/articles/the-future-of-crowdfunding-creative-projects

The World Bank. (2022, May 24). *Countries on the Cusp of Carbon Markets.* https://www.worldbank.org/en/news/feature/2022/05/24/countries-on-the-cusp-of-carbon-markets

Thomason, J. (2022, January 26). Could a green DAO allow Blockchain to be used for climate action? *CITY.AM.* https://www.cityam.com/could-a-green-dao-allow-Blockchain-to-be-used-for-climate-action/

Thomason, J. (2022, April 9). How Blockchain technology is transforming climate action. *Crypto News.* https://cryptonews.net/news/analytics/4818663/

Thomason, J. (2022, April 23). Green Finance need voluntary carbon markets that work. *Cointelegraph.* https://cointelegraph.com/news/green-finance-needs-voluntary-carbon-markets-that-work

Towards Ontology and Blockchain Based Measurement Reporting and Verification for Climate Action – Hyperledger Foundation. (n.d.). Retrieved July 29 2022 from https://ja.hyperledger.org/learn/webinars/towards-ontology-and-Blockchain-based-measurement-reporting-and-verification-for-climate-action

TreeCoin. (2020, January 31). *2020: A big year for natural forests?* TreeCoin. https://medium.com/treecoin/2020-a-big-year-for-natural-forests-cb3437a2ef75

Triangle, B. (n.d.). Retrieved July 29 2022 from https://www.bctriangle.com

Truby, J., Brown, R. D., Dahdal, A., & Ibrahim, I. (2022). Blockchain climate damage and death: Policy interventions to reduce the carbon emissions mortality and net-zero implications of non-fungible tokens and Bitcoin. *Energy Research & Social Science*, 88, 102499. doi:10.1016/j.erss.2022.102499

United Nations. Climate Change. (2018, January 22). *UN Supports Blockchain Technology for Climate Action.* https://unfccc.int/news/un-supports-Blockchain-technology-for-climate-action

United Nations. (2021). *Climate Change - United Nations Sustainable Development.* Sustainable Development Goals. https://www.un.org/sustainabledevelopment/climate-change/

United Nations. (n.d.). *Take Action for the Sustainable Development Goals.* https://www.un.org/sustainabledevelopment/sustainable-development-goals/

Universal Protocol Alliance. (n.d.). *Universal Protocol Alliance.* Retrieved July 29 2022 from https://www.universalprotocol.io

UNOPS. (2019). Building for a sustainable future. *The Economist.* https://content.unops.org/publications/UNOPS-Building-for-a-sustainable-future.pdf

UpLink. (n.d.). Retrieved July 29 2022 from https://uplink.weforum.org/uplink/s/uplink-contribution/a012o00001pTeuBAAS/carbonland-trust-esg-nfts

What, I. B. T. (2018 March 13). *GOBankingRates.* https://www.gobankingrates.com/investing/crypto/what-is-Blockchain-technology/?utm_campaign=1144566&utm_source=yahoo.com&utm_content=8&utm_medium=rss

Wintermeyer, L. (2021, March 19). Climate-Positive Crypto Art: The Next Big Thing Or NFT Overreach? *Forbes.* Retrieved July 29 2022 from https://www.forbes.com/sites/lawrencewintermeyer/2021/03/19/climate-positive-crypto-art-the-next-big-thing-or-nft-overreach/?sh=19d0c402b0e6

Zhou, A. (2021, July 7). Blockchain can help us beat climate change. Here's How. *CITI I/O.* https://citi.io/2021/07/07/Blockchain-can-help-us-beat-climate-change-heres-how/

Chapter 13
Summary and Conclusion

ABSTRACT

Web 3.0 is a vision for the next generation of the internet or the internet of value. Those building it envision a fairer, more equitable internet. An internet that facilitates the peer-to-peer exchange of value without intermediaries. It will be an internet where creators and content providers can be rewarded for their contributions, and community members can influence the direction of travel. Our children and children's children will use the internet to shape their world. This is not a pre-defined future; it is being built by innovators worldwide. This book has been written to provide a framework for policy research and public engagement and to help leaders, policymakers, and the public understand these technologies' impact on our economies, legal and political systems, and way of life. It elucidates a moment in time in a story that is not yet written. The book is neither correct nor incorrect. It provides a perspective to assist in educating people on the technology and its progress and impacts.

INTRODUCTION

Blockchain, DeFi, NFTs, AI/VR/XR, Big Data, Satellite, Cloud, and Artificial Intelligence (AI) are already converging and creating new possibilities for the Future. Web 3.0 and Metaverse are the recent manifestations of what the convergence of technological innovations can create. But what are Web 3.0 and Metaverse? How will we use them? How will this impact people and their lives in the Future? What are the risks? These are the questions and

DOI: 10.4018/978-1-6684-6658-2.ch013

developments which are explored in this book. It is a compilation of emergent thinking and the author's perspective on the questions above.

As Ray Kurzweil (2001) points out:

An analysis of the history of technology shows that technological change is exponential, contrary to the common-sense "intuitive linear" view. So we won't experience 100 years of progress in the 21st century — it will be more like 20,000 years of progress (at today's rate). The "returns," such as chip speed and cost-effectiveness, also increase exponentially. There's even exponential growth in the rate of exponential growth. (para. 1)

This exponential growth of technology is changing as consumer habits and expectations change. Generational gaps in technology consumption patterns are widening between GenZ and Gen Alpha and the older generations. Children access technology early, allowing them to connect and learn from each other. TikTok recognized this and launched "LearnOnTikTok" in 2020, a long-term effort to grow educational content on the platform. GenZ and Gen Alpha are already utilizing the internet to learn in new ways in their free time, at their convenience.

This book is about possibility. It's not about certainty. The authors believe that linking what has already been achieved with Blockchain and the affordances of DeFi, NFTs, AR/VR, and cloud technology, together with Web 3.0 or the Internet of Value, will create possibilities for humankind. These new possibilities will enable us to review how we live, how we work, how we play, and how we interact with each other. An immersive Web 3.0, or the Metaverse, will enable companies to provide consumers with products in different and more convenient ways. It will allow governments to provide services in a more accessible way and extend their limited human resources to focus on activities that can't be aided or assisted by technology. The motivation for writing this book has been to pull those pieces together so that others can see how the Future might unfold.

In Chapter 1, "Introduction to Web 3.0," the authors discuss how Web3 will be the next Internet iteration, "The Internet of Value" (IOV). It starts with explaining Web3 and how these pieces might come together, providing an overview so the reader can understand where the journey is going. Web3 must be open, accessible, and secure, linking technical interconnectivity with the exchange of value, stores of value, proof of authenticity, and smart contracts to create an always-on and borderless internet. Web3 can potentially advance the world into a new era of connected digitization. Thus, while the tone of this book is fully favourable, it is also pragmatic.

Chapter 2, "Introduction to Blockchain," takes the reader back to the beginnings of Blockchain, what it is, how it works, and how it can be applied to solve problems of safety, efficiency, speed, and security problems. Essential technical detail is provided on Blockchain, the platforms, and the consensus mechanisms. This is more so that the reader can get an overview and understand the different elements of Blockchain, the different types of Blockchain, and the uses of those blockchains for various industries, communities, and governments. In Chapter 3, "Blockchain Ecosystem," the blockchain trilemma, layers, and limitations of the blockchain ecosystem are outlined. This Chapter analyses these fundamental blockchain issues and proffers suggestions and future research to manage the existing blockchain trilemma. The several limitations of Blockchain described at the end of the Chapter provide a framework for developmental research.

Chapter 4, "DeFi and the Future of Money," provides an overview of DeFi, an analysis of its ecosystem, and its likely trajectory is provided. DeFi offers an accessible alternative to the current financial system. Decentralized finance (DeFi) grew exponentially during the pandemic. Before the pandemic, the word had been coined, but few knew much about it. During the pandemic, with everyone staying at home and application developers and software engineers building, there was a dramatic rise in DeFi projects. The Chapter explains its exponential growth in borrowing, lending, yield farming, and insurance. DeFi has the potential to redefine the financial system.

DeFi shows great promise, despite some of its growing pains. DeFi solutions are highly interoperable and can be integrated. DeFi offers greater transparency as all the data is stored immutably using Blockchain technology, which can be viewed by the participants anytime and anywhere. But it is risky and unregulated. Investors can quickly lose money when smart contracts fail or problems with open-source computer codes lead to vulnerabilities. It's 24/7, always on the market, and available globally, so it's hard to undertake meaningful due diligence. Questions remain about definitions, developer liability, the legal status of the code, the application of AML/KYC, and jurisdiction. The history of money is still being written, and the systems that underpin it will continue to evolve. DeFi represents the next step in the evolution of money.

Chapter 5, "Distributed Autonomous Organizations (DAO): Governing by Code," explains new automated forms of organization used to underpin most DeFi projects. The chapter unpicks: How do DAOs work? What are their points of vulnerability? What are the points of centralization? What genuine problems have been seen with DAOs, including the infamous DAO hack? The chapter concludes with a discussion of some of the regulatory issues in dealing with these automated organizations that operate on a 24-hour, seven-day-a-week basis across multiple jurisdictions. DAOs govern many major DeFi applications and are an exciting new governance approach. In an optimal situation, the community defines the rules, and these are encoded in smart contracts which are transparent and publicly available. The DAO operates seamlessly and is automated as intended. However, as experience has shown, not all contingencies can be predicted, and sometimes there are vulnerabilities in the code. The concept of DAOs is still relatively young, and significant experimentation with governance will likely lead to more robust and better models. Regulators will be looking closely and determining how they can have visibility into code-governed organizations. Investor education and trusted due diligence sources are critically needed to protect consumers and improve industry standards as the industry matures.

The book's next chapter briefly covers tokenization it is likely to be critical to any future Web 3.0 Internet or Web 3.0 Metaverse. Underpinning Web 3.0 in all its forms is token economics which determines the nature of the resources, their uses, their allocation and distribution, and ways to increase and decrease the resources. Tokenization can democratize access, unlock the value of illiquid assets, enable faster transactions and settlement, improve traceability and transparency, and improve interoperability. Chapter 5, "The Tokenization of Everything," discusses different tokenized asset types, including green digital asset solutions, tokenized health data, real estate, and other potential future tokenized assets. It also discusses the regulatory challenges of a tokenized world. It will also provide a brief introduction to digital assets as investments. New business models will emerge, with institutions offering services to manage customer accounts in tokens or giving access to transactions on token exchanges or diverse tokenization platforms. This Chapter describes how and why tokenization will transform industries and examines case studies in banking and financial services; smart cities; real estate; the data economy, health care, and social tokens.

Chapters 7 and 8 examine non-fungible tokens (NFTs). COVID spawned the rapid proliferation of NFTs. Many have proposed that it was a bubble, conceivably, it has burst. Inevitably in unregulated financial services, frauds are perpetuated. Wash trading became an issue, and the industry was accused of being used for money laundering. These are the things that can happen in unregulated markets and need to be dealt with by regulation. This does not take away from the essential utility of NFTs as proof of digital ownership or digital ownership certificates and their potential value to many industries, ranging from identity to university certification to certification of land titles and many more. As always in the new sectors, issues of legal certainty remain and a need to clarify what the ownership of a digital asset provides to the owner concerning intellectual property rights and physical assets. A wide range of use cases for NFTs are also discussed.

Chapter 7, "Introduction to NFTs," provides a detailed introduction to the concept of NFTs, capable of representing arts, video games, and other tangible items. NFTs are Blockchain-based digital assets that can be swapped for others without depreciating. NFT marketplaces are platforms such as Open Sea, Crypto.com, Rarible, and Binance, where NFTs can be bought and sold. Several challenges associated with NFTs have been identified in this chapter, including money laundering, wash trading, and the dangers of losing an NFT's private encryption key.

In Chapter 8, "How Are NFTs Being Used?" different practical applications, including the fashion industry, gaming sector, electoral utilization, ticketing systems, verification of authenticity, medical records, and intellectual property sector, are discussed. There are two central values that NFTs create: novelty and utility. The importance of NFTs in the Blockchain ecosystem for the Future cannot be over-emphasized. They will play a vital role in the intersections between the Metaverse, Digital Wallets, and Traditionally Non-Bankable assets.

Following that, the book changes gear to look at the current hot topic of the Metaverse. Chapter 9, "History of the Metaverse," describes Metaverse as a futuristic concept combining various technologies, including computer infrastructure, gaming, NFTs, DeFi, AR/VR, AI, and the spatial web. There is yet to be a consensus on what it is. There is a level of agreement that it will be immersive and persistent, combining virtual and physical worlds with an economy and value that can be earned, lent, borrowed, and extracted from the physical world. This Chapter outlines the immersive and persistent nature of the Metaverse, combining virtual and physical worlds with its economy. It outlines the many challenges to widespread adoption, including interoperability, latency, user interface, and regulation. It also poses many ethical issues yet to be resolved and some ideas on how to do so. The Metaverse is an exciting technological development that will help create new and enhanced ways to live, shop, be entertained, seek services, and be educated. The Metaverse could be fulfilling and rewarding and create social purpose. At the same time, there are enormous risks. The Metaverse is an integral part of the Future, and its potential is limited only by the framework of our imagination and today's technologies.

This is the beginning of the Metaverse journey, and there is much to learn. There are no doubt risks, but the opportunities are immense. This is a new world that is advancing daily, and our knowledge grows with the innovators who are building these new Metaverses. Like many innovations, the Metaverse is not well-understood and treated with scepticism. Many still see it as a fringe technology fad for gamers and Gen Z. Few understand the potential opportunities to improve services, provision of education, as well as economic opportunities. Increasingly, sectors are exploring how the Metaverse will transform how to work, shop, socialize, play, and engage with the government. This is the next iteration of the internet, and governments and businesses alike will embrace it, as Gen Z and Gen Alpha do.

The Web 3.0 Metaverse is an immersive version of the Internet of Value. It is peer-to-peer, open, trusted, and decentralized. However, as explained in the chapter, this is a view and an aspiration held by the Web 3.0 community. It is not necessarily how the Metaverse will play out because there are four leading proponents currently working on Metaverses. The first are Facebook, Meta, Apple, Amazon, Google, and the BigTechs. Their Metaverses will not be open and decentralized and reward contributors fairly. The BigTechs will likely perpetuate their existing models, which are extractive and profitable for the company, but less for the users. The second Metaverse proponents are the gaming industry, a vast and growing industry of almost 3 billion players worldwide. They already use many aspects of the Metaverse experience in their games with an immersive environment, the equivalent of avatars, and the ability to require in-game assets. It's not a giant leap for them to integrate a token economy so players can extract value from the games and bring it into the real world. Some gaming companies are moving in that direction. Others are not. The Future will tell us whether the power of the community will drive the Future of gaming.

The next group building Metaverses is the Web 3.0 community, which is working to build open, decentralized peer-to-peer versions of the internet, where everyone can benefit from their contribution and be rewarded within that ecosystem. At present, while there are many of these being developed; however, the user base could be more significant. For it to be increased, the utility of these Metaverses will need to align with the needs and interests of users. User experience must also improve to make it easy and accessible. The author contends that the most successful Metaverses will be an immersive experience enabled by mobile phones. Over 70% of the world's population has access to mobile phones. If Metaverse experiences are to be made available widely, they must be made available with enough inexpensive technology available to most people. So the Metaverse using the Oculus headset will be for the wealthy few. For many, an AI-enabled mobile phone could provide immense value in health, education, and government services. Some challenges remain, including interoperability, latency, user interface, and regulation. However, this is arguably one of the most exciting technological developments which will help create new and enhanced ways to live, shop, be entertained, seek services, and be educated.

The final group who are building Metaverses is in increasing numbers of governments. Examples include Neom in Saudi Arabia, The Dubai Metaverse strategy, Seoul in South Korea, and others moving forward with similar strategies. Government exploration of the Metaverse will continue, particularly in health and education and government service delivery.

Chapter 10, "Living in the Metaverse," describes the quest to create Metaverses. Many industries are investing by entering existing Metaverses or developing their own. There is substantial innovation and experimentation, from entertainment to commerce to real estate to health care. Metaverse-provided services such as health, education, and government services are all under development. It will be in new "phygital" realms that Metazens (citizens of the Metaverse) will explore the new domains. "Phygital" is the use of technology to bridge the digital world with the physical world to provide unique interactive experiences for users. This Chapter explores the main developments that underpin the types of activities available in the Metaverse and issues for future growth, including infrastructure, user experience, adoption, and interoperability.

The book's final two chapters, on Web 3.0 and ESG and sustainability, are essential because they explore where and how Web 3.0 can contribute and be used to promote, promote, enable and accelerate sustainability. The Sustainable Development Goals (SDGs) are aspirational visionary goals for the future state of humankind. However, they are only possible to achieve by harnessing the technology. Web 3.0, Blockchain, and frontier technologies are crucial for social impact. Chapter 11, "Web 3.0 and ESG and Sustainability," examines the technologies essential for social impact, especially climate action, financial inclusion, payments, health care, humanitarian settings, identity, land registry, philanthropy and fundraising, supply chains, and urbanization. This chapter outlines how Web 3.0, Blockchain, and Frontier Technologies can exponentiate impact on the SDGs, illustrating use cases where possible. It also examines the remaining challenges, such as ethics, privacy, confidentiality, data security, open-source systems, informed consent, data ownership, and the pace of digital transformation. Following this, the chapter examines the role of governments and international organizations in creating an enabling environment for technology transformation. The Chapter contributes to the growing knowledge about Blockchain and Web 3.0 for sustainability. Innovators and technologists are working globally on implementing blockchain technology to solve many SDGs. This Chapter introduces the readers to Blockchain and Web 3 and its potential applications to improve the lives of the underprivileged. Blockchain and other frontier technologies for sustainability can be tools for social change and strengthen inequality globally. While these technological tools for groundbreaking innovation exist, many such questions still need to be answered. It is paramount to closely and carefully monitor its evolution and share this information to achieve maximum impact.

Chapter 12, "Blockchain and Climate Action," is devoted to Web 3.0, Blockchain, and climate action as a predominant global issue. The authors wanted the readers to explain how Web 3.0 and Blockchain are relevant to promote a climate-resilient, low-carbon, green, inclusive, integrated, and prosperous world and the transition towards a climate-resilient, low-carbon Future, and the mobilization of funds to drive green, inclusive, sustainable, and climate-compatible growth. Blockchain can contribute to adaptation, mitigation, finance, and the enabling environment for climate action. This Chapter is structured to educate people on mechanisms for raising capacity for effective climate change-related planning and management using Blockchain, focusing on women, youth, and local and marginalized communities. It aims to build the capacity of people involved in climate policy and climate action in Blockchain technology's potential to strengthen action on climate change.

FUTURE DIRECTIONS

The world is undergoing a profound transformation stemming from several influencing factors, starting with technology, including changes in governments, how governments think about citizens, and changes in the community and social expectations. First, the pandemic forced people to live their lives digitally. As a result, they started to learn how to interact digitally in many sectors, including health and education. At the same time, technologists and innovators were forced to stay home. During this period, they worked vigorously on creating new technologies and new ways of doing things. During the last five years, rapid technological growth and increased mobile penetration have changed how people can interconnect and interact with the economy. Blockchain, DeFi, NFTs, play-to-earn games, extended reality, and the Metaverse have created the possibility of exchanging value in virtual worlds and combined with IoT AI, big data, data analytics, and the spatial web.

This has meant that people can participate using technology in ways that were not possible before. In terms of governance, digital states and new digital economies have emerged, challenging the traditional views of sovereign states, nation-states, and global governance. Distributed Autonomous Organizations (DAOs) have emerged as a new form of automated governance, allowing multi-jurisdictional economies to develop. This has been challenging regulators who are scrambling to keep up with digital asset regulation. It has also stimulated the ability of emerging economies to leapfrog using technology, so the balance of power in the world is changing.

From the point of view of communities, the ability to create community-owned economies with internal social tokens or other kinds of tokens run by digitally literate youth has opened up the world for the peer-to-peer exchange of value using W3. In addition, there's an increasing public demand for accountability, with a loss of trust in government, and concurrently technology is empowering people.

There are several enablers which are enabling profound changes to take place. First of all, in technology, the focus is moving from the customer to the network or the platform. The approach to data is moving from accumulation to mobilization of data. Data will be the fundamental underpinning of the new digital economy. Concerning digital assets, the focus is shifting from proprietary to shared assets. The world is moving to a sharing. Regulation is pressured to move from a compliance-based regulation to an empowerment-based regulation. Regulators must collaborate with industry because they need help to keep up. This will create shifts in the global economy to a more distributed economy.

Investment knowledge will be decentralized; science will be decentralized. Financial inclusion will be possible using wallets and digital assets. The way that the global economy interacts is also changing. Communities have discovered that they're able to create their economies. The Future of work is moving from an employment and jobs-based economy to a skills-based economy. Economies are forming where people within communities co-create products instead of companies providing products to customers.

In terms of education, the old education methods need to change because of the pace with which technology is changing things. For example, consider generative AI and ChatGPT, which has meant that jobs and workforce needs will change significantly. As a result, the traditional school system, which has been preparing people for the past 50 years, needs to transform itself into the ability to teach skills for the new economy very agilely. This is an opportunity for Web 3.0 Metaverse education.

Where is the world going with all of these changes? In the first place, it's likely to be more democratized. With more trust and transparency in peer-to-peer connections. Using Blockchain affordances, the ability to connect on global commons issues is becoming a reality. Distributed autonomous communities are forming around issues like climate change already, and there will likely be many more of these communities forming around common issues.

While interoperability remains a challenge, in the future, the world will see interoperable Web3 and interoperable Metaverses allowing people to interact and exchange value across them. Data will be the foundation of the new world, and people will have the ability, through self-sovereign identity, to control access and monetize their data. The opportunity for transparent and publicly auditable transactions is made possible through Blockchain, and secure cryptographically secured data exchange is now possible. This will make scientific discoveries and medical records, for example, far more accessible.

It is finally moving from Web 3.0 to immersive worlds. The Metaverse is emerging as a powerful concept for the future. Not that everyone will spend their entire time in virtual worlds in the Future. This is unlikely; however, where the Metaverse provides utility for people, it will likely be a commonly used method in entertainment and commerce, healthcare, research, education, government, and industry. Digital twins will allow precision planning for all sorts of things, from buildings and cities to complicated surgical operations.

This is the world of the future. It's exciting to contemplate. There are, of course, barriers, such as lack of education, traditions and ways of doing things, lack of digital skills, and incumbent power structures that will not seek these new economies to develop. The poor reputation of crypto has been unhelpful. And legacy systems provide barriers to new technologies. In many ways, this favours the nations that don't have legacy or inferior systems. Because in the absence of a system, the adoption of a new system, structure, or way of doing things will be much faster. The world is moving at an exponential pace. New technologies are appearing daily. It's an exciting time. This is when it's essential for people to lean in, understand and shape the new digital world in a way that will make it more accessible, more inclusive, and provide more value to more people globally.

Throughout the book, the authors explore the challenges and risks, which are many. It's a new technology, and it's still developing. It's had several technical failures. It's also subject to bad actors who fraudulently hack into projects, steal tokens and give the industry a bad name. This naturally leads to regulation, yet the fact is that regulation in most jurisdictions is not ready for these new technologies and will need to catch up. It needs to protect consumers. It's failing to prevent money laundering and be used for social utility rather than nefarious purposes. Regulation is essential, will come, and has to be interoperable across borders. This will require collaboration between industry and governments.

A final note for the readers of the book, who may be of any demographic. But to remind the reader that the future demographic is Gen Z and Gen Alpha. They are already digital. They are already comfortable with immersive experiences. They have grown up knowing the internet and understanding social media. They will not only be the users of Web 3.0 and the Metaverse, but they will also be demanding better user experience, and they will be demanding that companies take their sustainability responsibilities seriously. They will be demanding that they have a voice in developing these products and demanding to be reimbursed for their contributions. So Web 3.0 in the Metaverse is not necessarily for the generation who currently rule the world. It is for their children and their children's children. And those children will be ready for it. We need to ensure that we are handing them something that protects them, doesn't cause harm, takes ethics seriously, and builds a world that can enhance their life experience and not cause catastrophic and painful events and experiences. The Future is in our hands. And it's up to us to build it. We hope that people will be able to collect enough knowledge and information from this book, to be able to get a broad understanding of how technology in the Web 3.0 and Metaverse spaces is developing and how it may be relevant to their lives and envision them to a new and hopefully better future.

FUTURE RESEARCH

There is so much need and potential for research into Web 3.0 and questions that need to be explored. Some of these are suggested below.

Social Utility

How can Metaverse improve global access to education and improve the educational experience? Impacts on the industry, for example, having the immersive retail space inside where customers can engage with NFTs, with gamification? Case studies on Web 3.0 and government services? How Metaverse will create jobs of the Future? New economic opportunities with token economies?

Web 3.0 and sustainability?

Technical Advancements

Approaches to Self-Sovereign Identity? Use of NFTs as digital verification for KYC and credentials? Interoperability? Improving accessibility, e.g., goggles; XR?

Regulation

Approaches to regulation and governance of DeFi and DAOs? What body would be appropriate to regulate the Metaverse? Cross-border jurisdictional issues?

User Experience and Engagement

How to improve the user experience and user interface? Community engagement models and incentives? Physical and mental health impacts of digital life? Digital Anthropology examines the changing life patterns of young people living digitally? Impact of multiple identities on psychological health?

CONCLUSION

The Internet of Value (IoV) will enable the exchange of any valued asset with another person without the need for an intermediary. Web 3.0 must be open, accessible, and secure, linking technical interconnectivity with the exchange of value, stores of value, proof of authenticity, and smart contracts to create an always-on and borderless internet. Web 3.0 could take the world forward into a new era of connected digitization. Thus, while the tone of this book is entirely positive, it is also pragmatic. The book represents a snapshot of time. Web 3.0 is emerging fast; when it takes you to read this book, there will almost certainly be changes to protocols, terminology, and data management approaches that invite readers to understand the technology with an open mind and a critical eye. The authors hope that you enjoy the journey of learning about this dynamic technology as much as they enjoyed researching it.

Glossary

Blockchain Trilemma: A widely accepted principle that public blockchains or decentralized networks can only provide two of the three benefits simultaneously concerning decentralization, security, and scalability.

Brain Drain: When a country loses talent to other opportunities outside their native country.

Byzantine Fault Tolerance: The property of a system able to resist the class of failures derived from the Byzantine Generals' Problem. A BFT system can continue operating even if nodes fail or act maliciously.

Byzantine General's Problem: A logical dilemma that illustrates how a group of Byzantine generals may have communication problems when trying to agree on their next move.

Consensus: A set of rules which guide the blockchain network that enable the blockchain network to make decisions.

Consortium Blockchain: A blend of private Blockchains, each owned by organisations which have agreed to work together and share information and resources to improve functionality.

Fifty-One Percent Attack: A malevolent miner or group of miners controlling more than fifty percent of a network's mining electricity or hash rate.

Hard Fork: A software update implemented by a blockchain or cryptocurrency's network nodes incompatible with the existing blockchain protocol, which causes a permanent split into two separate networks that run in parallel.

Hybrid Blockchain: A hybrid Blockchain combines public and private Blockchains.

Layer 0: The foundation of a blockchain system that comprises hardware, protocols, connections, and other components.

Layer 1: Maintains a blockchain network's fundamental operations, such as dispute resolution, consensus mechanism, programming languages, protocols, and restrictions.

Layer 2: Off-chain solutions (separate blockchains) built atop Layer 1 to reduce bottlenecks with scaling and data.

Layer 3: The final blockchain layer, hosting decentralised applications (D'Apps).

Miner: A metaphor for the computational work undertaken by a node on the Blockchain network in the hopes of being awarded new tokens for validating a block.

Node: A device equipped to access the Blockchain network and process transactions.

Nonce: A portmanteau of 'number-used-only-once' - a four-byte number added to an encrypted block in a Blockchain that, when it is rehashed, it meets the difficulty level standard set by the Blockchain network.

Plasma: A layer 2 solution that seeks to drastically increase the efficiency of the blockchain networks by taking the bulk of the processing duties off of the main chain and redistributing it onto a series of smaller, functional chains referred to as the child chains.

Private Blockchain: A permissioned blockchain that operates within a closed group by invitation only.

Public Blockchain: A permissionless Blockchain that any user can access and join.

Roll-Ups: Protocols that facilitate transaction processing of a batched-up group of data on side chains away from the main chains in order to save cost and increase transaction speed.

Scalability: The network's potential to grow without compromising its effectiveness.

Security: The need for the blockchain to safely and reliably protect assets and execute transactions.

SEGWIT: Segregated witness reduces the size required for storing transactions in a block by removing certain signatures to create more space for storing transactions.

Sidechain: A blockchain-adjacent transactional chain used for large batch transactions.

Sharding: The division of computing into smaller parts for faster processing.

State Channels: A technique designed to allow users to make multiple blockchain transactions, such as state changes or money transfers, without committing all of the transactions to the blockchain.

Two-Way Peg: A communication protocol among ledgers that allows the bidirectional transfer of assets at a fixed or pre-deterministic exchange rate between the mainchain and the sidechain.

ZK SNARK: A Zero-Knowledge Roll-up – a Layer-2 blockchain protocol that processes transactions, performs computations, and stores data off-chain while holding assets in an on-chain smart contract. It stands for Zero-Knowledge Scalable Transparent Argument of Knowledge.

ZK STARK: A Zero-Knowledge Roll-up – a Layer-2 blockchain protocol that processes transactions, performs computations, and stores data off-chain while holding assets in an on-chain smart contract. It stands for Zero-Knowledge Succinct Non-Interactive Argument of Knowledge.

Compilation of References

A Basic Income Coin & Wallet. (n.d.). GoodDollar. https://www.gooddollar.org/

A beginner's guide to Decentralized finance (DeFi). (2022, July 15). Wiki Tiên Áo. https://wikitienao.net/en/3684-2

A Guide to MetaFi: Infrastructure for the Virtual Economy. (2022, April 6). CYBAVO. Retrieved November 14, 2022, from https://www.cybavo.com/blog/metafi-insfrastructure-for-virtual-economy/

A look at DeFi AMM protocols | SushiSwap Deep Dive. (2021, June 2). Novum Insights. https://novuminsights.com/post/a-look-at-defi-amm-protocols-or-sushiswap-deep-dive/

Abdella, J., & Shuaib, K. (2018). Peer to Peer Distributed Energy Trading in Smart Grids: A Survey. *Energies*, *11*(6), 1560. doi:10.3390/en11061560

Abdunabi, A. (2021, May 21). The world of NFT art. *Medium*. https://allaabdunabi.medium.com/the-world-of-nft-art-ccfd3104ede4

Academy, B. (2022). *What Is Web 3.0 and Why Does It Matter?* Binance Academy. Retrieved 14 July 2022, from https://academy.binance.com/en/articles/the-evolution-of-the-internet-web-3-0-explained

Adams, H., Zinsmeister, N., & Robinson, D. (2020). *Unsiwap v2 Core.* https://uniswap.org/whitepaper.pdf

Adian, I., Doumbia, D., Gregory, N., Ragoussis, A., Reddy, A., & Timmis, J. (2020). *Small and medium enterprises in the pandemic.* Academic Press.

Agarwal, G. (2020, January 19). State Channels: An Introduction to Off-chain Transactions. *Talentica.* https://www.talentica.com/blogs/state-channels-an-introduction-to-off-chain-transactions/

Agarwal, V., Hanouna, P. E., Moussawi, R., & Stahel, C. W. (2018). *Do ETFs increase the commonality in liquidity of underlying stocks?* Working paper, Villanova University.

Aharon, D. Y., & Demir, E. (2022). NFTs and asset class spillovers: Lessons from the period around the COVID-19 pandemic. *Finance Research Letters*, *47*, 102515. doi:10.1016/j.frl.2021.102515 PMID:36406741

Ahmad, K. (2022, February 13). 7 Tips to Spot Promising NFT Projects Early. *Make Use Of*. https://www.makeuseof.com/tips-spot-nft-projects-early/

Ahmadu, O. F. (2022, May 30). What Blockchain is and How It Works. *Nicholas Idoko*. https://nicholasidoko.com/blog/2022/05/30/what-Blockchain-is-and-how-it-works/

Aki, J. (2020, December 30). *DeFi Explained: The Guide To Decentralized Finance - Forkast*. Forkast.news. https://forkast.news/explainer-decentralized-finance-defi-guide

Akin Gump Strauss Hauer & Feld LLP. (2022). Dubai Passes Landmark Law Regulating Virtual Assets (Including Cryptocurrencies). *JDSUPRA*. https://www.jdsupra.com/legalnews/dubai-passes-landmark-law-regulating-8666988/#:~:text=Dubai%20Passes%20Landmark%20Law%20Regulating%20Virtual%20Assets%20(Including%20Cryptocurrencies),-Sahar%20Abas%2C%20Mazen&text=On%20February%2028%2C%202022%2C%20Sheikh,"Virtual%20Assets%20Law"

Alchemy. (2022, March 10). *Layer 1 Blockchain Ecosystems: Overview*. Learn Web3. https://www.alchemy.com/overviews/layer-1-Blockchain-ecosystems-overview

Alchemy. (2022, May 27). SNARKs vs. STARKS vs. Recursive SNARKs. *ZK Proofs Overview*. https://www.alchemy.com/overviews/snarks-vs-starks

AlgoDaily. (2022). *What is Database Sharding? Scaling DBs*. https://algodaily.com/lessons/what-is-database-sharding/range-based-sharding

Ali, O., Jaradat, A., Kulakli, A., & Abuhalimeh, A. (2021). A comparative study: Blockchain technology utilization benefits, challenges and functionalities. *IEEE Access: Practical Innovations, Open Solutions*, *9*, 12730–12749. doi:10.1109/ACCESS.2021.3050241

Alladi, T., Chamola, V., Rodrigues, J. J., & Kozlov, S. A. (2019). Blockchain in smart grids: A review on different use cases. *Sensors (Basel)*, *19*(22), 4862. doi:10.339019224862 PMID:31717262

Alvindayu. (2021). *What Are The Differences Between Rsa Dsa And Ecc Encryption*. https://alvindayu.com/al-what-are-the-differences-between-rsa-dsa-and-ecc-encryption

Alzarouni, M. [@drmarwan]. (2022, June). *The idea of regulations is actually thinking of possibilities, not limitations* [Tweet]. Twitter. https://twitter.com/khaleejtimes/status/1543146246000578565

Ambrose, J. (2017, December 4). Energy networks to unveil plan for £17bn smart-grid boom. *The Telegraph*. https://www.telegraph.co.uk/business/2017/12/04/energy-networks-unveil-plan-17bn-smart-grid-boom/

Anders, Lance, & Shrug. (2022, March 11). EIP-4907: Rental NFT, an Extension of EIP-721. *Ethereum Improvement Proposals*. https://eips.ethereum.org/EIPS/eip-4907

Ante, L. (2021). The Non-Fungible Token (NFT) Market and Its Relationship with Bitcoin and Ethereum. *SSRN Electronic Journal.* https://papers.ssrn.com/sol3/papers.cfm?abstract_id=3861106

Ante, L. (2021). Smart contracts on the Blockchain–A bibliometric analysis and review. *Telematics and Informatics, 57,* 101519. doi:10.1016/j.tele.2020.101519

Antolin, A. (2022). What Is Proof-of-Authority? Cryptocurrency. *CoinDesk.* https://www.coindesk.com/learn/what-is-proof-of-authority/

Antoniewicz, R. S., & Heinrichs, J. (2014). Understanding exchange-traded funds: How ETFs work. ICI Research Perspective, 20, 11–13.

Anupam, S. (2019). What Are The Major Limitations, Challenges In Blockchain? *Inc42.* https://www.google.com/amp/s/inc42.com/features/what-are-the-major-limitations-challenges-in-Blockchain/amp/

Apolline, B. (2019). *Global Cryptoasset Regulatory Landscape Study.* Cambridge Centre for Alternative Finance.

Aragon. (n.d.). *Homepage.* https://aragon.org

Art Meets Climate Change at Open Banking World Congress. (n.d.). *Financial IT.* Retrieved July 29 2022 from https://financialit.net/news/open-banking/art-meets-climate-change-open-banking-world-congress

Association for Computing Machinery. (2018, June 22). *ACM Code of Ethics and Professional Conduct.* Association for Computing Machinery. https://www.acm.org/code-of-ethics

Atomic, D. E. X. (2022, October 10). What is bitcoin (BTC)? First blockchain and cryptocurrency. *Coin Guides.* https://atomicdex.io/en/blog/what-is-bitcoin-btc/#hold-and-trade-btc-on-atomicdex

Awati, R., & Denman, J. (2022). Sharding. *TechTarget.* https://www.techtarget.com/searchoracle/definition/sharding

Aydar, M., Cetin, S. C., Ayvaz, S., & Aygun, B. (2019). *Private key encryption and recovery in Blockchain.* doi:10.48550/arxiv.1907.04156

Azuri. (n.d.). *Solar Innovators.* https://www.azuri-group.com/about

Bad luck Brian. (2021). https://opensea.io/assets/matic/0x2953399124f0cbb46d2cbacd8a89cf0599974963/120685920743174856157680314464578280308178366943356511570353113132498055069697

Barbon, A., & Ranaldo, A. (2022). *On The Quality Of Cryptocurrency Markets: Centralized Versus Decentralized Exchanges.* Retrieved 21 July 2022, from https://arxiv.org/pdf/2112.07386.pdf

Baydakova, A. (2019). *IBM Completes Blockchain Trial Tracking a 28-Ton Shipment of Oranges.* CoinDesk. https://www.coindesk.com/markets/2019/02/01/ibm-completes-blockchain-trial-tracking-a-28-ton-shipment-of-oranges/

Baytaş, M. A., Cappellaro, A., & Fernaeus, Y. (2022, April). Stakeholders and Value in the NFT Ecosystem: Towards a Multi-disciplinary Understanding of the NFT Phenomenon. In *CHI Conference on Human Factors in Computing Systems Extended Abstracts* (pp. 1-8). https://dl.acm.org/doi/abs/10.1145/3491101.3519694

Beck, J., & Asher, M. (2021, February 3). *Why Decentralized Autonomous Organizations (DAOs) Are Essential to DeFi.* ConsenSys. https://consensys.net/blog/codefi/daos/

Ben-David, I., Franzoni, F., & Moussawi, R. (2012). Hedge fund stock trading in the ∂nancial crisis of 2007–2009. *Review of Financial Studies, 25*(1), 1–54. doi:10.1093/rfs/hhr114

Ben-Sasson, E., Bentov, I., Horesh, Y., & Riabzev, M. (2018). Scalable, transparent, and post-quantum secure computational integrity. *Cryptology ePrint Archive.* https://eprint.iacr.org/2018/046

Berlove, O. (2019. May 22). What are public and private key pairs and how do they work. *Security Boulevard.* https://securityboulevard.com/2019/05/what-are-public-and-private-key-pairs-and-how-do-they-work/

Bernegger, M. P. (n.d.). *The emergence of cryptocurrency hedge funds.* Cointelegraph. https://cointelegraph.com/news/the-emergence-of-cryptocurrency-hedge-funds

Binance Academy. (2021). Plasma. *Glossary.* https://academy.binance.com/en/glossary/plasma

Binance Academy. (2022). *Proof of Authority Explained.* https://academy.binance.com/en/articles/proof-of-authority-explained

Binance Academy. (2022, May 31). *Blockchain Layer 1 vs. Layer 2 Scaling Solutions.* https://academy.binance.com/en/articles/Blockchain-layer-1-vs-layer-2-scaling-solutions

Bit2me Academy. (2021). What are zk-STARKs? *Blockchain.* https://academy.bit2me.com/en/que-son-las-zk-stark/

Bitcoin.com. (2022). *What is Lightning Network?* https://www.bitcoin.com/get-started/what-is-lightning-network/

Bitnodes. (2023). *Reachable Bitcoin nodes.* https://bitnodes.io/

Bizzer. (2018, September 5). What is DAO? *Medium.* https://medium.com/bizzer-daico/what-is-dao-5f00b9888273

Blocher, J., & Whaley, R. E. (2016). *Two-sided markets in asset management: exchange-traded funds and securities lending.* Working paper, Vanderbilt University.

Block Runners. (2018). [Audio podcast]. https://podcasts.apple.com/us/podcast/block-runners/id1437172347

Block.one. (2020). *Is a Leader in Providing High-Performance Blockchain Solutions.* https://block.one/

Blockchain Consulting. (2021). *An overview of Decentralized Autonomous Organizations (DAOs).* https://bcc-munich.com/everything-you-need-to-know-about-decentralized-autonomous-organizations-daos/

Blockchain for Climate Foundation. (n.d.). *Blockchain for Climate Foundation.* Retrieved July 29 2022 from https://www.Blockchainforclimate.org

Blockchain Magazine. (2023, January 5). *YouTube.* Retrieved June 2, 2023, from https://blockchainmagazine.net/lets-meet-Metaverse-avatar-metafi/

BMC. (2020, November 24). What Is the CIA Security Triad? Confidentiality, Integrity, Availability Explained. *Security & Compliance Blog.* https://www.bmc.com/blogs/cia-security-triad/

Bobby. (2022, April). *How Blockchain Technology Is Transforming Climate Action.* NSBB News. https://nsbb.in/2022/04/09/how-Blockchain-technology-is-transforming-climate-action/

Bogdanov, D. (2021, August 24). Optimistic Rollups vs ZK Rollups: Examining Six of the Most Exciting Layer 2 Scaling Projects for Ethereum. *Limechain.* https://limechain.tech/blog/optimistic-rollups-vs-zk-rollups

Bogost, I. (2019, August 5). *The El Paso Shooting and Video Games as a Partisan Issue.* The Atlantic. Retrieved November 15, 2022, from https://www.theatlantic.com/technology/archive/2019/08/video-game-violence-became-partisan-issue/595456/

Bolton, S. J., & Cora, J. R. (2021). Virtual Equivalents of Real Objects (VEROs): A type of non-fungible token (NFT) that can help fund the 3D digitization of natural history collections. *Megataxa,* 6(2), 93-95. https://www.researchgate.net/publication/353679784_Virtual_Equivalents_of_Real_Objects_VEROs_A_type_of_non-fungible_token_NFT_that_can_help_fund_the_3D_digitization_of_natural_history_collections

Boson Protocol - Web3's Commerce Layer. (n.d.). Retrieved June 8, 2023, from https://www.bosonprotocol.io/

Bouckaert, S., Pales, A. F., McGlade, C., Remme, U., Wanner, B., Varro, L., & Spencer, T. (2021). *Net Zero by 2050: A Roadmap for the Global Energy Sector.* https://iea.blob.core.windows.net/assets/deebef5d-0c34-4539-9d0c-10b13d840027/NetZeroby2050-ARoadmapfortheGlobalEnergySector_CORR.pdf

Bradley, H. S., & Litan, R. E. (2010). *Choking the recovery: Why new growth companies aren't going public and unrecognized risks of future market disruptions.* Working paper, Ewing Marion Kauffman Foundation.

Bradley, H. S., & Litan, R. E. (2011). *ETFs and the present danger to capital formation.* Working paper, Ewing Marion Kauffman Foundation.

Browne, R. (2021, November 19). Criminals have made off with over $10 billion in 'DeFi' scams and thefts this year. *CNBC.* https://www.cnbc.com/2021/11/19/over-10-billion-lost-to-defi-scams-and-thefts-in-2021.html

Browne, R. (2022, March 10). *Trading in NFTs spiked 21,000% to more than $17 billion in 2021, report says.* CNBC. https://www.cnbc.com/2022/03/10/trading-in-nfts-spiked-21000percent-to-top-17-billion-in-2021-report.html

Bruner, R. (2021, November 18). Environmental Concerns Have Cast Doubt on NFTs—But That's Changing. *Time.* https://time.com/6120237/nfts-environmental-impact/

B-Tech Digital. (2022). *Encryption.* https://btechdigital.com/service/encryption/

BTSE | Your Favorite Crypto Exchange. (n.d.). BTSE. https://www.btse.com/en/about-us

Burke PJ. (2016). Undermined by adverse selection: Australia's direct action abatement subsidies. *Economic Papers: A Journal of Applied Economics and Policy, 35*(3), 216-229. 10.1111/1759-3441.12138

Burke, J. (2021). *The Web 3 Toolbox.* Retrieved 14 July 2022, from https://outlierventures.io/research/the-web-3-toolbox/

BurstI. Q. (2022). *Home Page.* https://burstiq.com/get-started/

Buterin, V. (2014). *Ethereum Whitepaper.* Ethereum.org. https://ethereum.org/en/whitepaper/

Buterin, V. (2021). *The scalability trilemma.* Retrieved from https://vitalik.ca/general/2021/04/07/sharding.html

Bybit Learn. (2021, September 11). *What Is Delegated Proof of Stake (DPoS)?* https://learn.bybit.com/Blockchain/delegated-proof-of-stake-dpos/#2

Bybit Learn. (2021, September 27). What Is Tendermint? *Blockchain.* https://learn.bybit.com/Blockchain/tendermint/

Bybit Learn. (2022, June 27). The Blockchain Trilemma: Can It Ever Be Solved? *Tech Deep Dive.* https://learn.bybit.com/deep-dive/Blockchain-trilemma/#1

Cagigas, D., Clifton, J., Diaz-Fuentes, D., & Fernández-Gutiérrez, M. (2021). Blockchain for public services: A systematic literature review. *IEEE Access : Practical Innovations, Open Solutions, 9,* 13904–13921. doi:10.1109/ACCESS.2021.3052019

Calma, J. (2021, March 15). The Climate Controversy Swirling around NFTs. *The Verge; Vox Media.* https://www.theverge.com/2021/3/15/22328203/nft-cryptoart-ethereum-Blockchain-climate-change

Cambridge Centre for Alternative Finance. (2023). *Comparisons.* https://ccaf.io/cbnsi/cbeci/comparisons

Cambridge Centre for Carbon Credits. (n.d.). Retrieved July 29 2022 from https://4c.cst.cam.ac.uk

Cap, C. (2022). *Cryptocurrency Prices, Charts, And Market Capitalizations | CoinMarketCap.* Retrieved 3 August 2022, from https://coinmarketcap.com/

Capital Com SV Investments Ltd. (n.d.). *What is the consensus mechanism?* https://capital.com/amp/consensus-mechanism-definition

Carter, N. (2021). *How much energy does Bitcoin actually consume?* https://hbr.org/2021/05/how-much-energy-does-bitcoin-actually-consume

Carzaniga, F. (2021, December 2). Solar:Vital to Asia's renewable energy success. *Open Access Government.* https://www.openaccessgovernment.org/asias-renewable-energy/125209/

Certik. (2019). *The Blockchain trilemma: Decentralised, scalable and secure?* Retrieved from https://medium.com/certik/the-Blockchain-trilemma-decentralized-scalable-and-secure-e9d8c41a87b3

Chain analysis. (2022, February 2). *Crime and NFTs: Chainalysis Detects Significant Wash Trading and Some NFT Money Laundering In this Emerging Asset Class.* Chainanalysis. https://blog.chainalysis.com/reports/2022-crypto-crime-report-preview-nft-wash-trading-money-laundering/

Chainalysis Inc. (2021, December 6). Report Preview: The 2021 NFT Market Explained. *Chainalysis.* https://blog.chainalysis.com/reports/nft-market-report-preview-2021/

Chainalysis. (2022). https://blog.chainalysis.com/reports/2022-global-crypto-adoption-index/

Chainlink. (2021, May 20). *How Hybrid Smart Contracts Incentivize Regenerative Agriculture.* https://blog.chain.link/reversing-climate-change-how-hybrid-smart-contracts-incentivize-regenerative-agriculture

Chalmers, D., Fisch, C., Matthews, R., Quinn, W., & Recker, J. (2022). Beyond the bubble: Will NFTs and digital proof of ownership empower creative industry entrepreneurs? *Journal of Business Venturing Insights*, *17*, e00309. doi:10.1016/j.jbvi.2022.e00309

Chaudhari, A. A., Laddha, D., & Potdar, M. (2019). Decentraland – aBlockchain based model for smart property experience. *Int. Eng. J. Res. Dev.*, *4*, 5.

Chauhan, A., Malviya, O. P., Verma, M., & Mor, T. S. (2018). Blockchain and scalability. In *2018 IEEE International Conference on Software Quality, Reliability and Security Companion (QRS-C)* (pp. 122-128). IEEE.https://www.researchgate.net/publication/327000219_Blockchain_and_Scalability

Cheikosman, E. (2022, June 9). Can crypto become a leader in sustainability? *World Economic Forum.* https://www.weforum.org/agenda/2022/06/crypto-sustainability/

Chevet, S. (2018). *Blockchain technology and non-fungible tokens: Reshaping value chains in creative industries.* Available at SSRN 3212662. https://papers.ssrn.com/sol3/papers.cfm?abstract_id=3212662

Chinedu. (2022, June 3). *Layer 0, The Foundation of the Blockchain Where Interoperability Reigns.* FXCryptoNews. https://fxcryptonews.com/layer-0-the-foundation-of-the-Blockchain-where-interoperability-reigns/

Chohan, U. W. (2022). *Cryptocurrencies: A brief thematic review.* Available at SSRN 3024330. https://papers.ssrn.com/sol3/papers.cfm?abstract_id=3024330

Chow, A. R. (2021, November 18). *Why TIME Is Launching a New Newsletter on the Metaverse.* Time. https://time.com/6118513/into-the-metaverse-time-newsletter/

Chow, A. R. (2021, November 18). *Why You Should Be Paying Attention to the Metaverse.* TIME. Retrieved November 14, 2022, from https://time.com/6118513/into-the-Metaverse-time-newsletter/

Clark, M. (2022, June 6). *NFTs, Explained.* The Verge. https://www.theverge.com/22310188/nft-explainer-what-is-blockchain-crypto-art-faq

Climate Change Authority. (n.d.). *Review of the emissions reduction fund.* https://www.climatechangeauthority.gov.au/review-emissions-reduction-fund

Cloudflare. (2022). *What is encryption? Types of encryption.* https://www.cloudflare.com/en-gb/learning/ssl/what-is-encryption/

Coin, L. (2022). Retrieved 7 August 2022, from https://litecoin.com/en/

Coinbase. (2022). What is the Lightning Network? *Crypto Basics.*

CoinNewsExtra. (n.d.). *How Blockchain technology is transforming climate action.* https://coinnewsextra.com/how-Blockchain-technology-is-transforming-climate-action/

Cointelegraph Consulting: DeFi projects launch on Polygon, usage skyrockets. (2021, May 24). Cointelegraph. https://cointelegraph.com/news/cointelegraph-consulting-defi-projects-launch-on-polygon-usage-skyrockets

Cointelegraph. (2022). *What is a decentralized autonomous organization, and how does a DAO work?* https://cointelegraph.com/decentralized-automated-organizations-daos-guide-for-beginners/what-is-decentralized-autonomous-organization-and-how-does-a-dao-work

Cointelegraph. (2022, July 19). *A beginner's guide to understanding the layers of blockchain technology.* Head Topics. https://headtopics.com/us/a-beginner-s-guide-to-understanding-the-layers-of-blockchain-technology-28236152

Cointelegraph. (n.d.). https://www.google.com/amp/s/cointelegraph.com/news/how-Blockchain-technology-is-transforming-climate-action/amp

Cong, L. W., & He, Z. (2019). Blockchain disruption and smart contracts. *Review of Financial Studies, 32*(5), 1754–1797. doi:10.1093/rfs/hhz007

Contributors, W. (2019, October 22). *Carbon footprint.* Wikipedia; Wikimedia Foundation. https://en.wikipedia.org/wiki/Carbon_footprint

Coombs, B. (2019, August 30). *From Jedis to astronauts: How NASA tapped a video game maker for training.* CNBC. https://www.cnbc.com/2019/08/30/jedis-to-astronauts-how-nasa-tapped-video-game-maker-for-training.html

Cosmos (ATOM) Price · Price Index, Charts. (2023, May 24). Cointelegraph. https://cointelegraph.com/cosmos-price-index

Cosper, A. (2019). *Buried Treasures: One startup's story of tokens, sunken ships, robots, and intrigue.* Creative Business Network. https://cbnet.com/2019/04/15/po8/?amp

Cousaert, S. (2021, March 25). Generalizing knowledge on DEXs with AMMs — Part I. *UCL CBT.* Medium. https://medium.com/uclcbt/generalizing-knowledge-on-dexs-with-amms-2963d07ebac7

Cousaert, S. (2021, September 17). *Insurance: Token-based solutions on blockchain — A summary.* UCL CBT. https://medium.com/uclcbt/insurance-token-based-solutions-on-blockchain-a-summary-e7b5a6805197

Cowrie | marine snail. (2019). In *Encyclopædia Britannica.* https://www.britannica.com/animal/cowrie

Credit card | Britannica Money. (2023, May 5). Www.britannica.com. https://www.britannica.com/money/topic/credit-card

Credit rating agency warns potential risks of stablecoins | How are stablecoins doing so far ? (2021, July 7). Novum Insights. https://novuminsights.com/post/credit-rating-agency-warns-potential-risks-of-stablecoins-or-how-are-stablecoins-doing-so-far/

Crypto Altruism. (2021, October 15). *Using Blockchain and cryptocurrency to support and empower refugees.* https://www.cryptoaltruism.org/blog/using-Blockchain-and-cryptocurrency-to-support-and-empower-refugees

Crypto Research, Data, and Tools. (n.d.). Messari.io. https://messari.io/asset/cover-protocol/profile

Crypto.com. (2022, June 9). *How to Agree: Different Types of Consensus for Blockchain.* https://crypto.com/university/different-types-of-consensus-for-Blockchain

Cryptoeq. (2022, September 23). *Cosmos (ATOM): Strengths, Weaknesses, Risks.* Core Report. https://www.cryptoeq.io/corereports/cosmos-abridged

Cryptograph. (2021). *Quadratic Funding.* https://cryptograph.com/Cryptograph/Vitalik-Buterin-Quadratic-Funding

Cryptopedia Staff. (2022, June 28). The Blockchain Trilemma: Fast, Secure, and Scalable Networks. *Cryptopedia.* https://www.gemini.com/cryptopedia/Blockchain-trilemma-decentralization-scalability-definition

Cryptopedia Staff. (2022, March 25). How a Block in the Bitcoin Blockchain Works. Security. Cryptonetworks. *Cryptopedia.* https://www.gemini.com/cryptopedia/what-is-block-in-Blockchain-bitcoin-block-size

Daly, L. (2022, June 28). What Is Proof of Work (PoW) in Crypto? *The Motley Fool.* https://www.fool.com/investing/stock-market/market-sectors/financials/cryptocurrency-stocks/proof-of-work/

Davies, C. D., & Jung-a, S. (2022, September 27). Asia's largest metaverse platform Zepeto ramps up global expansion. *Financial Times*. https://www.ft.com/content/14c88e84-f3c8-485e-a9df-31ead34e48f0

Decentralised Dog. (2022). How long does a Bitcoin transaction take? *Coin Market Cap*. https://coinmarketcap.com/alexandria/article/how-long-does-a-bitcoin-transaction-take

Deep dive into Polygon | Ethereum off-chain scaling solutions. (2021, May 26). Novum Insights. https://novuminsights.com/post/deep-dive-into-polygon-or-ethereum-off-chain-scaling-solutions/

DeFi Rate. (2022, September 9). *Crypto News*. https://defirate.com/news

DeFi, C. A. D. (2021, February 4). *DeFi Bursts onto the Finance Scene - What is it and why does it matter?* CityAM. https://www.cityam.com/defi-bursts-onto-the-finance-scene-what-is-it-and-why-does-it-matter/

DeFi: A comprehensive guide to decentralized finance. (n.d.). Cointelegraph. https://cointelegraph.com/defi-101/defi-a-comprehensive-guide-to-decentralized-finance

DeFi: the possible future of finance. (2022, March 23). Mntrading.com. https://eightglobal.com/blog/de-fi-the-possible-future-of-finance

Del Monte, G., Pennino, D., & Pizzonia, M. (2020). *Scaling Blockchains without giving up decentralisation and security: A solution to the Blockchain scalability trilemma*. Retrieved from https://arxiv.org/pdf/2005.06665.pdf

Deloitte. (2019). *So, you've decided to join a Blockchain consortium: Defining the benefits of 'coopetition'*. https://www2.deloitte.com/us/en/pages/consulting/articles/the-benefits-of-coopetition-in-Blockchain-consortia.html

DennisBPeterson. (2021 May 27). Climatecoin. *GitHub*. https://github.com/DennisBPeterson/Climatecoin

DeNuzzo, N. (2022, March 18). NFTs the future of college sports NIL deals: Nick DeNuzzo guest blog. *ON3*. https://www.on3.com/news/nfts-the-future-of-college-sports-nil-deals/

Deville, L., Gresse, C., & de Séverac, B. (2014). Direct and indirect effects of index ETFs on spot-futures pricing and liquidity: Evidence from the CAC 40 index. *European Financial Management*, *20*(2), 352–373. doi:10.1111/j.1468-036X.2011.00638.x

Dewan, N. (2008). *Indian Life and Health Insurance Industry*. Gabler. doi:10.1007/978-38349-9788-3

Dharma. (n.d.). https://www.dharma.io/

Dhyeya, I. A. S. (2022). *Blockchain Technology: Daily Current Affairs*. https://www.dhyeyaias.com/current-affairs/daily-current-affairs/Blockchain-technology

Digitalart4climate. (2021). *Digitalart4climate. About*. https://digitalart4climate.space

Dlamini, N. (2017). *Development of an SMS system used to access Bitcoin wallets. In IST-Africa Week Conference*. IEEE.

Dobreva, M. (2019, January 18). *Blockchain Glossary from A to Z*. LimeChain. https://limechain.tech/blog/Blockchain-glossary-from-a-to-z

Dorit, R., & Adi, S. (2013). Quantitative Analysis of the Full Bitcoin Transaction Graph. In *Financial Cryptography and Data Security - 17th International Conference, FC 2013, Okinawa, Japan, April 1-5, Revised Selected Papers. Lecture Notes in Computer Science* (vol. 7859, pp. 6-24). Springer.

Dragonchain. (n.d.). *Profile*. https://messari.io/asset/dragonchain/profile

Ducrée, J., Etzrodt, M., Gordijn, B., Gravitt, M., Bartling, S., Walshe, R., & Harrington, T. (2020). Blockchain for Organizing Effective Grass-Roots Actions on a Global Commons: Saving the Planet. *Front. Blockchain*, *3*, 33. doi:10.3389/fbloc.2020.00033

DuPont, Q. (2017). Experiments in algorithmic governance: A history and ethnography of "The DAO," a failed decentralized autonomous organization. In Bitcoin and beyond (pp. 157-177). Routledge.

Electroneum offers a new way to earn, send and pay. (n.d.). Electroneum. Retrieved June 11, 2023, from https://electroneum.com/

EncrypGen. (2021). *Home Page*. https://encrypgen.com

Energy Web. (2019). *The Energy Web Chain*. https://www.energyweb.org/wp-content/uploads/2019/05/EWF-Paper-TheEnergyWebChain-v2-201907-FINAL.pdf

Enjin. (2022). *Home Page*. https://enjin.io/

Ethereum Killers. (2021, May 12). Novum Insights. https://novuminsights.com/post/ethereum-killers/

Ethernodes.org. (2023). *Ethereum mainnet statistics*. https://ethernodes.org/

European Commission. (n.d.). *EU emissions trading system (eu ets)*. European Commission. https://ec.europa.eu/clima/eu-action/eu-emissions-trading-system-eu-ets_en

Everette, J. (2021, January 27). *Top Massively Multiplayer Online Role-Playing Games*. Lifewire. Retrieved November 14, 2022, from https://www.lifewire.com/the-top-mmorpgs-813063

ExacTrac Dynamic® - A New Dimension in Patient Positioning and Monitoring. (n.d.). Brainlab. https://www.brainlab.com/radiosurgery-products/exactrac/

Exchange, T. P. X. (2019). *Real estate: The ultimate asset that you can now own and trade*. https://www.tpx-london.io

Exploring the Cryptocurrency and Blockchain Ecosystem | United States Committee on Banking, Housing, and Urban Affairs. (n.d.). Retrieved June 3, 2023, from https://www.banking.senate.gov/hearings/exploring-the-cryptocurrency-and-blockchain-ecosystem

Face, E. (n.d.). *How will Blockchain technology help fight climate change?* https://entrepreneursface.com/how-will-Blockchain-technology-help-fight-climate-change/

Facts, W. (2022). *Facts About W3C*. Retrieved 14 July 2022, from https://www.w3.org/Consortium/facts

FATF. (2022). *Home Page*. https://www.fatf-gafi.org

Fauziah, Z., Latifah, H., Omar, X., Khoirunisa, A., & Millah, S. (2020). Application of Blockchain Technology in Smart Contracts: A Systematic Literature Review. *Aptisi Transactions on Technopreneurship*, 2(2), 160–166. doi:10.34306/att.v2i2.97

Fesenfeld, L. P., Schmidt, T. S., & Schrode, A. (2018). Climate policy for short-and long-lived pollutants. *Nature Climate Change*, 8(11), 933–936. doi:10.103841558-018-0328-1

FIFA. (2022, November 8). *FIFA unveils range of new web 3.0 games ahead of FIFA World Cup Qatar 2022*. FIFA. https://www.fifa.com/fifaplus/en/articles/fifa-unveils-range-of-new-web-3-0-games-ahead-of-fifa-world-cup-qatar-2022

Fight climate change and alleviate poverty with COTAP carbon offsets. (n.d.). https://cotap.org

Filebase. (2022, June). *Deep Dive: NFTs*. https://docs.filebase.com/knowledge-base/deep-dives/deep-dive-nfts

Finance, O. I. N. (2021, February). How OINDAO is different from MakerDAO. *Medium*. https://medium.com/oin-finance/how-oindao-is-different-from-makerdao-5a46feddcc81

Financial Stability Board. (2021). Regulation, Supervision and Oversight of "Global Stablecoin" Arrangements. *Financial Stability Board*. https://www.fsb.org/

Financial, I. T. (2022, May 17). *Art meets Climate Change at Open Banking World Congress*. https://financialit.net/news/open-banking/art-meets-climate-change-open-banking-world-congress

Finck, M. (2019). *Blockchain Regulation and Governance in Europe*. Cambridge University Press.

Finneseth, J. (2021, April 3). Blockchain-based renewable energy marketplaces gain traction in 2021. *Cointelegraph*. https://cointelegraph.com/news/Blockchain-based-renewable-energy-marketplaces-gain-traction-in-2021

First Carbon Corp. (2021, October 19). First Carbon Develops Proprietary NFT Based Carbon Credits Trading Platform and Launches Company Website. *GlobeNewswire News Room*. https://www.globenewswire.com/news-release/2021/10/19/2316705/0/en/First-Carbon-Develops-Proprietary-NFT-Based-Carbon-Credits-Trading-Platform-and-Launches-Company-Website.html

Fleuret, F., & Lyons, T. (2020). *Blockchain and the future of digital assets. ConsenSys AG and European Union Blockchain Observatory & Forum.* https://2020.standict.eu/publications/Blockchain-and-future-digital-assets

Folding Ideas. (2022, February). *Line Goes Up- The Problem With NFTs* [Video]. Youtube. https://www.google.com/url?sa=t&source=web&rct=j&url=https://m.youtube.com/watch%3Fv%3DYQ_xWvX1n9g&ved=2ahUKEwi11OO1_Kj7AhVv_7sIHfhZCYAQwqsBeg QIChAB&usg=AOvVaw1spU1VtqNjyCmO-1iWFg-y

Ford, E. (2013). Defining and characterizing open peer review: A review of the literature. *Journal of Scholarly Publishing, 44*(4), 311–326. doi:10.3138/jsp.44-4-001

Fortnow, M., & Terry, Q. (2021). *The NFT Handbook: How to Create, Sell and Buy Non-fungible Tokens.* John Wiley & Sons, Incorporated. https://www.amazon.com/NFT-Handbook-Create-Non-Fungible-Tokens/dp/111983838X

Foster, K. (2022, March 25). NFTs for Social Impact: Addressing Three Key Challenges. *St. Gallen Symposium.* https://symposium.org/nfts-for-social-impact-addressing-three-key-challenges/

Foucault, T., Kozhan, R., & Tham, W. (2017). Toxic Arbitrage. *Review of Financial Studies, 30*(4), 1053–1094. doi:10.1093/rfs/hhw103

Foundation, W. (2022). *History of the Web.* Retrieved 14 July 2022, from https://webfoundation.org/about/vision/history-of-the-web/

Foy, P. (2022). Solana vs Ethereum: Comparing Each Layer 1 Blockchain. *MLQ.ai.* https://www.mlq.ai/solana-vs-ethereum/

Frank, T. (2020). *Paul Tudor Jones calls bitcoin a 'great speculation,' says he has almost 2% of his assets in it.* Retrieved 7 August 2022, from https://www.cnbc.com/2020/05/11/paul-tudor-jones-calls-bitcoin-a-great-speculation-says-he-has-almost-2percent-of-his-assets-in-it.html

Frankenfield, J. (2022). *Nonce: What it means and how it is used in Blockchain.* https://www.investopedia.com/terms/n/nonce.asp

Freytsis, M., Barclay, I., Radha, S. K., Czajka, A., Siwo, G. H., Taylor, I., & Bucher, S. (2021). Development of a Mobile, Self-Sovereign Identity Approach for Facility Birth Registration in Kenya. *Frontiers in Blockchain, 4*, 631341. doi:10.3389/fbloc.2021.631341

Fries, T. (2018). *JPMorgan to Tokenize Gold Bars.* The Tokenist. https://tokenist.com/jpmorgan-to-tokenize-gold-bars/

Fries, T. (2021). *JPMorgan to Tokenize Gold Bars.* The Tokenist. https://tokenist.com/jpmorgan-to-tokenize-gold-bars/

Fruhlinger, J. (2020, February 10. The CIA triad: Definition, components and examples. *CSO.* https://www.csoonline.com/article/3519908/the-cia-triad-definition-components-and-examples.html

Fry, J. (2022). *#digitalbytes In 2021, the Collins Dictionary declared 'NFT' (Non-Fungible Token) its word of the year. NFT joined 'metaverse' and 'crypto', making three of the top ten words in the Collin* [LinkedIn]. https://www.linkedin.com/posts/jonnyfry_2022-predictions-and-thoughts-activity-6884541506393313280-9oR4/

Future thinkers. (n.d.). *7 Ways Blockchain Can Save The Environment and Stop Climate Change.* https://futurethinkers.org/Blockchain-environment-climate-change/

Gai, P., & Kapadia, S. (2019). Networks and systemic risk in the financial system. *Oxford Review of Economic Policy*, *35*(4), 586–613. doi:10.1093/oxrep/grz023

Gartner Peer Insights. (2022). Blockchain Platforms Reviews and Ratings. *Blockchain Platforms.* https://www.gartner.com/reviews/market/Blockchain-platforms

Gartner. (2017, August 15). *Gartner Identifies Three Megatrends That Will Drive Digital Business Into the Next Decade* [Press Release]. https://www.gartner.com/en/newsroom/press-releases/2017-08-15-gartner-identifies-three-megatrends-that-will-drive-digital-business-into-the-next-decade

GAVS. (2021, August 31). *Healthcare Interoperability and Blockchain.* https://www.gavstech.com/healthcare-interoperability-and-Blockchain/

Gecko, C. (2022). *Cryptocurrency Prices, Charts, and Crypto Market Cap | CoinGecko.* Retrieved 7 August 2022, from https://www.coingecko.com/

GeekForGeeks. (2022, August 3). *Hashing | Set 1 (Introduction).* https://www.geeksforgeeks.org/hashing-set-1-introduction/

Genersis, I. (2021, December 3). Security in the Digital Age: Elements of Cybersecurity That You Should Know. Security. *Tech Trend.* https://the-tech-trend.com/security/security-in-the-digital-age-elements-of-cybersecurity-that-you-should-know/

Gentilal, M. (2017). TrustZone-backed bitcoin wallet. *Proceedings of the Fourth Workshop on Cryptography and Security in Computing Systems*, 25–28. 10.1145/3031836.3031841

Geospatial Analytics Platform | Satellite Imagery | Remote Sensing. (n.d.). Retrieved July 29 2022 from https://descarteslabs.com

Gerard, D. (2021, March 11). NFTs: crypto grifters try to scam artists, again. *Attack of the 50 foot Blockchain.* https://davidgerard.co.uk/Blockchain/2021/03/11/nfts-crypto-grifters-try-to-scam-artists-again/

Geroni, D. (2021, October 5). Blockchain Scalability Solutions – An Overview. *101 Blockchains.* https://101Blockchains.com/Blockchain-scalability-solutions/

Ghebreyesus, T. A. (2020, March 11). *WHO Director-General's opening remarks at the media briefing on COVID-19 - 11 March 2020* [Speech Audio Recording]. World Health Organization. https://www.who.int/director-general/speeches/detail/who-director-general-s-opening-remarks-at-the-media-briefing-on-covid-19---11-march-2020

Ghosh, S. (n.d.). *A study on METAVERSE - GRM Institute.* Global Risk Management Institute. Retrieved November 15, 2022, from https://grm.institute/blog/a-study-on-Metaverse/

Global Blockchain Convergence. (2021). *Creating Organic Opportunities for Collaboration Across the Blockchain Tech Stack.* https://globalbc.io

Global Blockchain Convergence: A "Sensible" Token Classification System. (2020). https://theblockchaintest.com/uploads/resources/A%20%27Sensible%27%20Token%20 Classification%20System%20-%20Global%20Blockchain%20Convergence%20-%202020%20 -%20paper.pdf

Global, U. (2022). *The Economy of Everything Will Be Powered by Tokenized Physical Assets.* Coinmonks. Medium. https://medium.com/coinmonks/the-economy-of-everything-will-be-powered-by-tokenized-physical-assets-f7255bc00398

GloCha. (2022, February 2). *Media Advisory - Announcement of United Citizen Organization Formation at COP26.* https://www.glocha.org

Godbole, O. (2021, June 10). *Bitcoin Futures "Backwardation" Points to Weak Institutional Demand: JPMorgan.* Yahoo Finance. https://finance.yahoo.com/news/bitcoin-futures-backwardation-points-weak-173527377.html

Gold standard | Definition & History | Britannica Money. (2023, May 5). Www.britannica.com. https://www.britannica.com/money/topic/gold-standard

Goldberg, M., Kugler, P., & Schär, F. (2021). *The economics of blockchain-based virtual worlds: A hedonic regression model for virtual land.* Available at SSRN 3932189.

Golden. (n.d.). *Proof-of-importance (PoI).* https://golden.com/wiki/Proof-of-importance_(PoI)-639YX6M

Gonzalez, O. (2022, July 18). Bitcoin Mining: How Much Electricity It Takes and Why People Are Worried. *CNET.* https://www.cnet.com/personal-finance/crypto/bitcoin-mining-how-much-electricity-it-takes-and-why-people-are-worried/

GOQii. (2022, March 29). *GOQii To Launch Health Metaverse In Partnership With Animoca Brands.* GOQii. https://goqii.com/blog/goqii-to-launch-health-metaverse-in-partnership-with-animoca-brands/

Green Digital Finance Alliance. (2021). *The world's first green fintech taxonomy.* https://greendigitalfinancealliance.org/a-green-fintech-taxonomy-and-data-landscaping/

Green Digital Finance Alliance. (2021, November 29). *The World's First Green Finetech Taxonomy.* https://greendigitalfinancealliance.org/a-green-fintech-taxonomy-and-data-landscaping/

Gula, S. (2020, June 1). Sidechains And Their Applications. Crypto. *Ulam Labs.* https://www.ulam.io/blog/sidechains-and-their-applications-Blockchain

Guo, H., & Yu, X. (2022). A Survey on Blockchain Technology and its security. *Blockchain: Research and Applications*, *3*(2), 100067.

Gupta, P. (2022, July 28). Solving the Blockchain trilemma: A look at some scaling solutions. *Chainstack*. https://chainstack.com/solving-the-Blockchain-trilemma-scaling-solutions-for-ethereum/

Gupta, R., & Archi, D. A. O. (2022, April 16). Top 10 words to know about DAO (Decentralized Autonomous Organization). *ArchiDao*. https://archidao.substack.com/p/top-10-words-to-know-about-dao-decentralized

Hackl, C. (2020, July 5). *The Metaverse Is Coming And It's A Very Big Deal*. Forbes. https://www.forbes.com/sites/cathyhackl/2020/07/05/the-metaverse-is-coming--its-a-very-big-deal/

Haldar, D. (2018, August 19). System Design Interview Concepts – Database Sharding. *Acoders Journey*. https://www.acodersjourney.com/database-sharding/

Haleem, A., Javaid, M., Singh, R. P., Suman, R., & Rab, S. (2021). Blockchain technology applications in healthcare: An overview. *International Journal of Intelligent Networks*, *2*, 130–139. doi:10.1016/j.ijin.2021.09.005

Hamilton, S. G. K., & Kerry, B. (2021, October 29). *OFAC Publishes Sanctions Compliance Guidance for the Virtual Currency Industry and Updates its Frequently Asked Questions*. Sanctions & Export Controls Update. https://sanctionsnews.bakermckenzie.com/ofac-publishes-sanctions-compliance-guidance-for-the-virtual-currency-industry-and-updates-its-frequently-asked-questions/

Hamm, S. J. W. (2014). *The effect of ETFs on stock liquidity*. Working paper, Tulane University.

Harding, C. (2021, August 22). *DeFi regulation must not kill the values behind decentralization*. Cointelegraph. https://cointelegraph.com/news/defi-regulation-must-not-kill-the-values-behind-decentralization

Harvard International Review. (2019, December 30). *Where that Used Teddy Bear Really Goes: Corruption and Inefficiency in Humanitarian Aid*. https://hir.harvard.edu/where-that-used-teddy-bear-really-goes-corruption-and-inefficiency-in-humanitarian-aid/

Harvey, C. R., Ramachandran, A., & Santoro, J. (2020). *DeFi and the Future of Finance*. SSRN Electronic Journal., doi:10.2139srn.3711777

Hasankhani, A., Hakimi, S. M., Bisheh-Niasar, M., Shafie-khah, M., & Asadolahi, H. (2021). Blockchain technology in the future smart grids: A comprehensive review and frameworks. *International Journal of Electrical Power & Energy Systems*, *129*, 106811. doi:10.1016/j.ijepes.2021.106811

Hassan, Hammad, Iqbal, Hussain, Ullah, AlSalman, Mosleh, & Arif. (2022). A Liquid Democracy Enabled Blockchain-Based Electronic Voting System. *Scientific Programming*. doi:10.1155/2022/13830

Hayward, A. (2021, October 29). No, Someone Didn't Really Pay $532 Million for a CryptoPunk NFT. *Decrypt*. https://www.google.com/amp/s/decrypt.co/84756/no-someone-didnt-really-pay-532-million-cryptopunk-nft%3famp=1

Hazelcast. (2022). *What Is Sharding?* https://hazelcast.com/glossary/sharding/

Henderson, R. (2021, October 22). *The Blockchain Metaverse. The way the internet works is changing… | by Novum Insights | Medium*. Novum Insights. Retrieved November 14, 2022, from https://novuminsights.medium.com/the-Blockchain-Metaverse-f58c62cc1285

Highstreet Market. (n.d.). Retrieved June 8, 2023, from https://www.highstreet.market/

Himanshi. (2022, March 21). Proof of Importance (PoI) in Blockchain. *Naukri Learning*. https://www.naukri.com/learning/articles/proof-of-importance-poi-in-Blockchain/

Hinkes, A. (2016). *The Law of the DAO*. https://www.coindesk.com/the-law-of-the-dao/

Hok, D. (2021, March 21). *Default auditing for DeFi projects is a must for growing the industry*. Cointelegraph. https://cointelegraph.com/news/default-auditing-for-defi-projects-is-a-must-for-growing-the-industry

Holloway, K., Al Masri, R., & Abu Yahi, A. (2021). *Digital identity, biometrics and inclusion in humanitarian responses to refugee crises*. ODI-HPG. https://cdn. odi.org/media/documents/Digital_IP_Biometrics_case_study_web. pdf

Home | Forefront. (n.d.). https://www.forefront.market

Home. (n.d.a). YouTube. Retrieved November 14, 2022, from https://outlierventures.io/wp-content/uploads/2021/02/OV-Metaverse-OS-V5.pdfBlockchain

Home. (n.d.b). YouTube. Retrieved November 14, 2022, from https://www.insiderintelligence.com/content/gamers-make-up-more-than-one-third-of-world-population

Home. (n.d.c). YouTube. Retrieved November 14, 2022, from https://medium.com/umbalaMetaverse/nfts-metafi-next-big-investment-trend

Home. (n.d.d). YouTube. Retrieved November 14, 2022, from https://www.amerikayageldim.com/assets/uploads/files/1647380348146-1647331508066.pdf

Home. (n.d.e). YouTube. Retrieved November 15, 2022, from https://www.gamesindustry.biz/game-designers-must-be-included-in-the-emerging-conversation-around-tech-ethics

Homer Pepe. (2021). *Owned by Huskan. People NFTs*. OpenSea. https://opensea.io/assets/ethereum/0x495f947276749ce646f68ac8c248420045cb7b5e/ 56399228387483083525891803769847322961958564545827882145350131549684159741953

Hong, J. (2022). *How does Bitcoin mining work?* https://www.investopedia.com/tech/how-does-bitcoin-mining-work/

Honkanen, P., Nylund, M., & Westerlund, M. (2021). Organizational Building Blocks for Blockchain Governance: A Survey of 241 Blockchain White Papers. *Front. Blockchain, 4*, 613115. doi:10.3389/fbloc.2021.613115

Horizen. (2022). What Is a Layer 0 Blockchain? *Horizon Academy.* https://www.horizen.io/Blockchain-academy/technology/advanced/layer-0/

Horst, L., Choo, K. K. R., & Le-Khac, N. A. (2017). Process memory investigation of the Bitcoin Clients Electrum and Bitcoin Core. *IEEE Access*, 22385–22398. doi:10.1109/ACCESS.2017.275976

Hovhannisyan, A. (2021, September 28). *NFTs are a problem.* Blog. https://www.aleksandrhovhannisyan.com/blog/nfts-are-a-problem/

Howell, J. (2022, March 1). *MetaFi - Where DeFi Meets the Metaverse.* 101 Blockchains. Retrieved November 14, 2022, from https://101Blockchains.com/metafi/

Hsieh, Y. Y., Vergne, J. P., Anderson, P., Lakhani, K., & Reitzig, M. (2018). Bitcoin and the rise of decentralized autonomous organizations. *Journal of Organization Design, 7*(1), 1–16. doi:10.118641469-018-0038-1

Hu, E. (2022, January 30). *Clever NFT traders exploit crypto's unregulated landscape by wash trading on LooksRare.* Cointelegraph. https://cointelegraph.com/news/clever-nft-traders-exploit-crypto-s-unregulated-landscape-by-wash-trading-on-looksrare

Huang, R. (2019, January 7). *How Blockchain Can Help With The Refugee Crisis.* Forbes. https://www.forbes.com/sites/rogerhuang/2019/01/27/how-Blockchain-can-help-with-the-refugee-crisis/?sh=6c6721366562

Human Rights Watch. (2021, March 30). *IMF: Scant Transparency for Covid-19 Emergency Loans.* https://www.hrw.org/news/2021/03/30/imf-scant-transparency-covid-19-emergency-loans

Iansiti, M., & Lakhani, K. R. (2017, February). The Truth About Blockchain. Blockchain. *Harvard Business Review.* https://hbr.org/2017/01/the-truth-about-Blockchain

IBM. (2019). *We.Trade.* https://www.ibm.com/case-studies/we-trade-Blockchain

IBM. (2020). *Digital Health Pass.* https://www.ibm.com/products/digital-health-pass/businesses

Iluvium. (2022). *Home Page.* https://www.illuvium.io

In a first-of-its-kind initiative in the healthcare industry, Apollo Hospitals collaborates with 8chili Inc to enter the Metaverse . (n.d.). Apollo Hospitals. Retrieved June 8, 2023, from https://www.apollohospitals.com/apollo-in-the-news/in-a-first-of-its-kind-initiative-in-the-healthcare-industry-apollo-hospitals-collaborates-with-8chili-inc-to-enter-the-metaverse/

Insights, C. B. (2021). *How Blockchain Is Disrupting Insurance.* https://www.cbinsights.com/research/blockchain-insurance-disruption/

Insights, L. (2021). *NBA's Dinwiddie talks about tokenizing personalities on Blockchain.* https://www.ledgerinsights.com/nbas-dinwiddie-talks-about-tokenizing-personalities-on-blockchain/

Intelligence, I. (n.d.). *Empower yourself with the data, insights, and analysis you need to make strategic business decisions in a digital world.* Insider Intelligence. https://www.insiderintelligence.com/

International Monetary Fund. (2021, April 14). *Leveraging Digital Money to Facilitate Remittances.* https://www.imf.org/en/News/Articles/2021/04/14/sp041421-leveraging-digital-money-to-facilitate-remittances

International, F. (2022). *Fnality International.* Retrieved 7 August 2022, from https://www.fnality.org/home

Investing.com. (2022, July 26). zk-STARKs vs. zk-SNARKs explained. *Cryptocurrency.* https://www.investing.com/news/cryptocurrency-news/zkstarks-vs-zksnarks-explained-2854329

Investopedia. (2019). *What Is Money?* Investopedia. https://www.investopedia.com/insights/what-is-money/

Iredale, G. (2021). *How Tokenization Of Physical Assets Enables The Economy Of Everything?* Blockchain 101. https://101blockchains.com/tokenization/

Irrera, A. (2020). *S&P Dow Jones Indices to launch cryptocurrency indexes in 2021.* Retrieved 7 August 2022, from https://www.reuters.com/article/cryptocurrencies-sp/sp-dow-jones-indices-to-launch-cryptocurrency-indexes-in-2021-idUSL1N2IJ0TG

Israeli, D., Lee, C., & Sridharan, S. (2017). Is there a dark side to exchange traded funds? An information perspective. *Review of Accounting Studies*, *22*(3), 1048–1083. doi:10.100711142-017-9400-8

Jakub. (2021, August 2). Rollups – The Ultimate Ethereum Scaling Solution. Crypto. *Finematics.* https://finematics.com/rollups-explained/

James, M. (2022). *How blockchain technology is transforming climate action.* Investments. Bulgarian Financial Investment Agency (BFIA). https://www.bfia.org/2022/04/09/how-blockchain-technology-is-transforming-climate-action/

Jansen, S. (2021, December 6). *How to choose a secure DeFi wallet, explained.* Cointelegraph. https://cointelegraph.com/explained/how-to-choose-a-secure-defi-wallet-explained

Jenny. (2021). *What Is An Emerging Art Market?* Nomad Salon. https://www.thenomadsalon.com/post/what-is-an-emerging-art-market

Jentzsch, C. (2016b). *What an Accomplishment!* https://blog.slock.it/what-an-accomplishment-3e7ddea8b91d

Jha, P. (2022, April 20). Brain drain: India's crypto tax forces budding crypto projects to move. *Cointelegraph.* https://cointelegraph.com/news/the-state-of-crypto-in-northern-europe-hostile-scandinavia-and-vibrant-baltics

Jiang, X.-J., & Liu, X. F. (2021). CryptoKitties Transaction Network Analysis: The Rise and Fall of the First Blockchain Game Mania. *Frontiers in Physics, 9,* 631665. doi:10.3389/fphy.2021.631665

Johnson, B. (2022). *How Actively and Passively Managed Funds Performed: Year-End 2018.* Retrieved 3 August 2022, from https://www.morningstar.com/insights/2019/02/12/active-passive-funds

Kaal, W. (2020, July 18). DAOs — Governance & Legal Design Experimentation. *Medium.* https://wulfkaal.medium.com/daos-governance-legal-design-experimentation-25b2d0f58a29

Kahya, A., Avyukt, A., Ramachandran, G. S., & Krishnamachari, B. (2021, July). Blockchain-enabled Personalized Incentives for Sustainable Behavior in Smart Cities. In *2021 International Conference on Computer Communications and Networks (ICCCN)* (pp. 1-6). IEEE. 10.1109/ICCCN52240.2021.9522340

Kanellopoulos, I. F., Gutt, D., & Li, T. (2021). *Do Non-Fungible Tokens (NFTs) Affect Prices of Physical Products? Evidence from Trading Card Collectibles.* https://papers.ssrn.com/sol3/papers.cfm?abstract_id=3918256

Karjalainen, R. (2020). *Governance in decentralized networks.* Available at SSRN 3551099.

Kaushal, P. (2017). Evolution of bitcoin and security risk in bitcoin wallets. *Computer, Communications and Electronics (Comptelix), International Conference on,* 172–177. 10.1109/COMPTELIX.2017.8003959

Khaleej Times - Dubai News, UAE News, Gulf, News, Latest news, Arab news, Gulf News, Dubai Labour News. (n.d.). Khaleej Times. https://www.khaleejtimes.com

Khaleej Times [@khaleejtimes]. (2022, June). *"The idea of regulations is actually thinking of possibilities, not limitations," said @drmarwan, founder, CEO - #DubaiBlockchainCenter and Managing Partner at #AccellianceBuilder's tribe at the #MetaDecrypt Web 3.0 Summit.* Twitter.

Khan, F. (n.d.). *devteam. space.* https://www.devteam.space/blog/what-is-decentralized-cloud-computing

Khedkar, A. (2022). *Exchange Traded Funds (ETF) Global Investment.* https://ashokakhedkar.com/blog/exchange-traded-funds-etf-global-investment/

Kiel Institute for World Economy. (2019, August 26). *More than a quarter of development aid never leaves donor countries.* https://www.ifw-kiel.de/publications/media-information/2019/more-than-a-quarter-of-development-aid-never-leaves-donor-countries/

Knysh, N. (2021, November 22). Introducing Blockchain: Six Limitations For Enterprises To Remember. Innovation. *Forbes.* https://www.forbes.com/sites/forbestechcouncil/2021/11/22/introducing-Blockchain-six-limitations-for-enterprises-to-remember/?sh=4f239c79313f

Compilation of References

Koffman, T. (2020). *Google cloud joins forces with EOS*. https://www.forbes.com/sites/tatianakoffman/2020/10/06/google-cloud-joins-forces-with-eos/?sh=675440d7516f

Kong, D. R., & Lin, T. C. (2021). Alternative investments in the Fintech era: The risk and return of Non-Fungible Token (NFT). *Available at SSRN 3914085*.

Kong, D. R., & Lin, T. C. (2021). *Alternative investments in the Fintech era: The risk and return of Non-Fungible Token (NFT)*. Available at SSRN 3914085. https://papers.ssrn.com/sol3/papers.cfm?abstract_id=3914085

Korkmaz, E. (2018). *Blockchain for refugees: great hopes, deep concerns*. University of Oxford https://www.qeh.ox.ac.uk/blog/Blockchain-refugees-great-hopes-deep-concerns

Kozak, K. (2021, October 20). *Organizational Building Blocks for Blockchain Governance: A Survey of 241 Blockchain White Papers*. Frontiers. Retrieved May 30, 2023, from https://www.frontiersin.org/articles/10.3389/fbloc.2021.613115/full

Kruijff, J. D., & Weigand, H. (2017, June). Understanding the Blockchain using enterprise ontology. In *International Conference on Advanced Information Systems Engineering* (pp. 29–43). Springer. doi:10.1007/978-3-319-59536-8_3

Kurahashi-Sofue, J. (2022). What is a Blockchain validator? *Avalanche*. https://support.avax.network/en/articles/4064704-what-is-a-Blockchain-validator

Kuznetsov, N. (2021, January 28). *DeFi liquidity pools, explained*. Cointelegraph. https://cointelegraph.com/explained/defi-liquidity-pools-explained

Kwon, J., & Buchman, E. (n.d.). *A Network of Distributed Ledgers* [Whitepapers]. Cosmos. https://v1.cosmos.network/resources/whitepaper

Lantz, L., & Cawrey, D. (2020). *Mastering Blockchain*. O'Reilly Media.

Leader, S. S. L. (2022, July 10). RSA, ECC, ECDSA: which algorithm is better to choose when ordering a digital certificate in LeaderSSL. *SSL Help*. https://www.leaderssl.com/articles/484-rsa-ecc-ecdsa-which-algorithm-is-better-to-choose-when-ordering-a-digital-certificate-in-leaderssl

Learn, C. (2022). *How to set up a crypto wallet*. Retrieved 3 August 2022, from https://www.coinbase.com/learn/tips-and-tutorials/how-to-set-up-a-crypto-wallet

Ledger Academy. (2022). *Transactions Per Second (TPS)*. https://www.ledger.com/academy/glossary/transactions-per-second-tps

Lerner, S. D. (2021, February 25). Bitcoin Sidechains. Innovation Stories. *Medium*. https://medium.com/iovlabs-innovation-stories/bitcoin-sidechains-74a72ceba35d

Lettau, M., & Madhavan, A. (2018). Exchange-traded funds 101 for economists. *The Journal of Economic Perspectives*, *32*(1), 135–153. doi:10.1257/jep.32.1.135

Levesque, J. (2022, February 24). How to Utilize NFTs for Fundraising. *TechSoup*. https://blog.techsoup.org/posts/how-to-utilize-nfts-for-fundraising

Liebi, L. J. (2020). The effect of ETFs on financial markets: A literature review. *Financial Markets and Portfolio Management, 34*(2), 165–178. doi:10.100711408-020-00349-1

liechtenstein.li. (2021, December 20). *Liechtenstein has the clearest crypto tax regulations.* https://www.liechtenstein.li/en/liechtenstein_news/liechtenstein-hat-die-verstandlichsten-krypto-steuern

Lielacher, A. (2022). *Best Crypto Exchanges.* Retrieved 3 August 2022, from https://www.investopedia.com/best-crypto-exchanges-5071855

Li, J., Zhou, Z., Wu, J., Li, J., Mumtaz, S., Lin, X., Gacanin, H., & Alotaibi, S. (2019). Decentralized On-Demand Energy Supply for Blockchain in Internet of Things: A Microgrids Approach. *IEEE Transactions on Computational Social Systems, 6*(6), 1395–1406. doi:10.1109/TCSS.2019.2917335

Liu, Y. (2019, August 14). What are the challenges of the Cosmos and how to tackle them? The Startup. *Medium.* https://cryptoslate.com/cosmos-inter-Blockchain-communication-protocol-ibc-surpassed-11-million-transfers-in-february/ https://medium.com/swlh/what-are-the-flaws-of-the-cosmos-and-how-to-tackle-them-6c114f4f3bd7

Logan, K. (2021, December 3). *Cathie Wood says the Metaverse could be worth trillions and will affect the world in ways 'we cannot even imagine right now'.* Fortune. Retrieved November 14, 2022, from https://fortune.com/2021/12/03/cathie-wood-Metaverse-trillions-affect-every-sector/

Losing Paradise. (2012, October 29). *YouTube.* Retrieved November 19, 2022, from http://english.seoul.go.kr/seoul-to-provide-public-services-through-its-own-metaverse-platform/?keyword=metaverse&cat=46

Machine, W. (2022). *Wayback Machine.* Retrieved 14 July 2022, from https://web.archive.org/web/20171010210556/https://pdfs.semanticscholar.org/566c/1c6bd366b4c9e07fc37eb372771690d5ba31.pdf

Mackay, B. (2019). Evaluation of Security in Hardware and Software Cryptocurrency Wallets. School of Computing Edinburgh, Napier University.

Mackreides, J. (2022, April 9). How Blockchain technology is transforming climate action. *BFIA.* https://www.bfia.org/2022/04/09/how-Blockchain-technology-is-transforming-climate-action/

Macwan, A. (n.d.). *Coinbase Wallet Logo Redesign.* Dribbble. https://dribbble.com/shots/16062179-Coinbase-Wallet-Logo-Redesign

Mann, C., & Loebenberger, D. (2017). Two-factor authentication for the Bitcoin protocol. *International Journal of Information Security, 16*(2), 213–226. doi:10.100710207-016-0325-1

Manoylov, M. (2021, January 1). *Hackers stole $120 million via 15 DeFi hacks in 2020.* The Block. https://www.theblock.co/linked/89830/hackers-stole-120-million-via-15-defi-hacks-in-2020

Marcobello, M. (2022, June 29). What Are Layer 2s and Why Are They Important? Technology. *CoinDesk.* https://www.coindesk.com/learn/what-are-layer-2s-and-why-are-they-important/

Compilation of References

Mark Cuban shares his yield farming strategies | Yield farming 101. (2021, June 17). Novum Insights. https://novuminsights.com/post/mark-cuban-shares-his-yield-farming-strategies-or-yield-farming-101/

Marke, A., Nellore, S.K., Mihaylov, M., Khvatsky, J., Floyd, H.P., Symes, T., Schlumberger, J.A.F., Baumann, T., Yarger, M., Doebler, F., Mathley, N., Lin, N., Ruslanova, M., Miller, D., Thorne, S.R., Arslan, C., Kilic, S., Chávez, C., Angarita, R., ...Wainstein, M. (2022). *Blockchain for sustainable energy and climate in the Global South. Social Alpha Foundation and United Nations Environment program.* http://www.socialalphafoundation.org/wp-content/uploads/2022/01/saf-Blockchain-report-final-2022.pdf

Marketplace, E. (2021, September 15). *Voluntary Carbon Markets Rocket in 2021 On Track to Break $1B for First Time.* https://www.ecosystemmarketplace.com/articles/press-release-voluntary-carbon-markets-rocket-in-2021-on-track-to-break-1b-for-first-time/

MarketplaceE. (n.d.). *Carbon Hub.* https://www.ecosystemmarketplace.com/carbon-markets/

Markets in crypto-assets (MiCA) | Think Tank | European Parliament. (2022, November 9). Www.europarl.europa.eu. https://www.europarl.europa.eu/thinktank/en/document/EPRS_BRI(2022)739221

MarksMan Healthcare. (2022). *Tokenization in Real World Evidence Studies: What and Why?* Data Privacy. https://marksmanhealthcare.com/tokenization-in-real-world-evidence-studies-what-and-why/

Marston, J. (2022, February 18). Moss.Earth is using NFTs & crypto carbon credits to fight climate change in the Amazon. *AgFunderNews.* https://agfundernews.com/nfts-crypto-carbon-credits-moss-earth-is-using-to-fight-climate-change

Marta, T. J., & Joseph, B. (2010). *Forex Analysis and Trading: Effective Top-down Strategies Combining Fundamental, Position, and Technical Analyses.* John Wiley & Sons.

Mastropietro, B. (2021, December 19). What Is Proof-of-Burn (PoB)? *Coinspeaker.* https://www.coinspeaker.com/guides/what-is-proof-of-burn-pob/

Mathews, E., Mukherjee, S., Dang, S., & Samuel, M. (2021, October 18). *Facebook plans to hire 10000 in the EU to build a 'Metaverse.* Reuters. Retrieved November 14, 2022, from https://www.reuters.com/technology/facebook-plans-hire-10000-eu-build-Metaverse-2021-10-17/

Mayer, H. (2016). *zk-SNARK explained: Basic Principles.* https://blog. coinfabrik. com/wp-content/uploads/2017/03/zkSNARK-explained_basic_principles. pdf

Mayer-Schönberger, V., & Cukier, K. (2013). *Big data: A revolution that will transform how we live, work, and think.* Houghton Mifflin Harcourt.

McCall, I. (2021, April 1). How to Launder Money With NFTs. *Medium.* https://medium.com/yardcouch-com/how-to-launder-money-with-nfts-56f1789e5591

McDonnell, H. (2021, April 9). *The Unknown Legal Future of the Art Market's New Favorite Medium: Non-Fungible Tokens ("NFTs")*. Hughes Hubbard & Reed LLP. https://www.hhrartlaw.com/2021/04/the-unknown-legal-future-of-the-art-markets-new-favorite-medium-non-fungible-tokens-nfts/

McMorris, C. (2022, February 18). *Resources | Synapse*. Synapsefi.com. https://synapsefi.com/resources/stablecoins-guide

Medio Ambiente GIZ Federal Ministry for the Environment Nature Conservation and Nuclear Safety. (2019). *Blockchain for Mexican Climate Instruments: Emissions Trading and MRV Systems*. https://www.giz.de/en/downloads/giz2019-en-Blockchain-emissions.pdf

Meilich, A., Ordano, E., & Guide, S. (2022, August 3). *What is GameFi? 'Play-to-Earn' Gaming Explained*. Crypto.com. Retrieved November 14, 2022, from https://crypto.com/university/what-is-gamefi-play-to-earn-gaming-explained

Mengelkamp, E., Notheisen, B., Beer, C., Dauer, D., & Weinhardt, C. (2017). A Blockchain-based smart grid: Towards sustainable local energy markets. *Computer Science - Research for Development*, *33*(1-2), 207–214. doi:10.100700450-017-0360-9

Menon, S. (2018, February 24). Bitcoin Legacy vs SegWit wallet address. What is the difference? *Medium*. https://medium.com/@buddhasource/bitcoin-legacy-vs-segwit-wallet-address-what-is-the-difference-cb2e71ab8381

Merrill, Schillebeeckx, & Blakstad. (2019). *Sustainable Digital Finance in Asia: Creating Environmental Impact through Bank Transformation*. DBS and UN Environment. https://www.dbs.com/iwov-resources/images/sustainability/reports/Sustainable Digital Finance in Asia_FINAL_22.pdf

MetaFi. (n.d.). *Opportunity Encounter between Metaverse and DeFi*. Retrieved November 14, 2022, from https://inf.news/en/economy/6ae1d599ff088ab3539c3dd7f0748b60.html

MetaFi: Where DeFi Meets the Metaverse | MetaFi Token - Beginner's Guide. (n.d.). Token Development Company. Retrieved November 14, 2022, from https://www.securitytokenizer.io/metafi-defi-meets-Metaverse

Metaverse and Money - CitiGPS. (2022, March 30). Institutional Clients Group. Retrieved November 14, 2022, from https://icg.citi.com/icghome/what-we-think/citigps/insights/Metaverse-and-money_20220330

Metaverse maybe $800 billion market, next tech platform Insights. (2021, December 1). Bloomberg.com. Retrieved November 14, 2022, from https://www.bloomberg.com/professional/blog/Metaverse-may-be-800-billion-market-next-tech-platform/

Metaverse safety Week 2022 - 10-15 December. (n.d.). Metaverse Safety Week. Retrieved June 8, 2023, from https://metaversesafetyweek.org/

Metaverse. (2022, June 1). European Parliament. Retrieved November 15, 2022, from https://www.europarl.europa.eu/RegData/etudes/BRIE/2022/733557/EPRS_BRI(2022)733557_EN.pdf

Compilation of References

Metaverse: Opportunities, risks and policy implications | Think Tank. (2022, June 24). European Parliament. Retrieved November 15, 2022, from https://www.europarl.europa.eu/thinktank/en/document/EPRS_BRI(2022)733557

Metzger, J. (2019). The current landscape of blockchain-based, crowdsourced arbitration. *Macquarie L. J, 19*, 81–102.

Microgrid, B. (n.d.). *About*. https://www.brooklyn.energy/about

Miller, L., & Gregory, P. (2012). *The Role of Cryptography in Information Security. CISSP* (4th ed.). For Dummies., https://learning.oreilly.com/library/view/cissp-for-dummies/9781118417102/a2_13_9781118362396-ch08.html

Miltenberger, O., Jospe, C., & Pittman, J. (2021). The Good Is Never Perfect: Why the Current Flaws of Voluntary Carbon Markets Are Services Not Barriers to Successful Climate Change Action. *Front. Clim., 3*, 686516. doi:10.3389/fclim.2021.686516

Mitre shell | marine snail | Britannica. (n.d.). Www.britannica.com. https://www.britannica.com/animal/mitre-shell

Mmett, S. D. (2022, June). *DeFi Wallet Review: Crypto Wallet Choices – Cryptopolitan*. Www.cryptopolitan.com. https://www.cryptopolitan.com/defi-wallet-review/

MolochD. A. O. (n.d.). *Homepage*. https://molochdao.com

Montanez, A. (2014). *Investigation of cryptocurrency wallets on iOS and Android mobile devices for potential forensic artifacts. Dept. Forensic Sci., Marshall Univ.* Tech. Rep.

Morey, J. (2021, October 25). The Future Of Blockchain In Healthcare. *Forbes*. https://www.forbes.com/sites/forbestechcouncil/2021/10/25/the-future-of-Blockchain-in-healthcare/?sh=b2f9811541f5

Morgan, J. (2022). *Liink | Onyx by J.P. Morgan*. Retrieved 7 August 2022, from https://www.jpmorgan.com/onyx/liink

Morrison, R., Mazey, N. C. H. L., & Wingreen, S. C. (2020). The DAO Controversy: The Case for a New Species of Corporate Governance? *Front. Blockchain, 3*, 25. doi:10.3389/fbloc.2020.00025

Mostafavi, M. (2021). Explaining Solana and its Innovations without technical jargon. *Figment Learn*. https://learn.figment.io/tutorials/explaining-solanas-innovations-without-technical-jargon

Moura, S. (n.d.). *How to Buy Digital Real Estate*. Crypto Learning and Education. https://www.sarabmoura.com/how-to-buy-digital-real-estate/#page-content

Moyers, S. (2022, August 8). *Why Brands Are Entering the Metaverse! Future of Marketing*. SPINX Digital. Retrieved November 22, 2022, from https://www.spinxdigital.com/blog/why-brands-entering-metaverse/

Musungate, B. N., Candan, B., Çabuk, U. C., & Dalkılıç, G. (2019, October). Sidechains: Highlights and challenges. In *2019 Innovations in Intelligent Systems and Applications Conference (ASYU)* (pp. 1-5). IEEE.https://www.researchgate.net/publication/335368901_Sidechains_Highlights_and_Challenges

Naderi, N., & Tian, Y. (2022). Leveraging Blockchain Technology and Tokenizing Green Assets to Fill the Green Finance Gap. *Energy Research Letters*, *3*(3). Advance online publication. doi:10.46557/001c.33907

Nathaniel, P. (2016). *Digital Gold: Bitcoin and the Inside Story of the Misfits and Millionaires Trying to Reinvent Money*. Harper.

National Cryptologic Foundation. (2022, September 30). "On This Date in History" Calendar 1983: Three Inventors Receive Patent for Encryption Algorithm RSA. *Cryptologic Bytes.* https://cryptologicfoundation.org/what-we-do/educate/bytes/this_day_in_history_calendar.html/event/2022/09/20/1663650000/1983-three-inventors-receive-patent-for-encryption-algorithm-rsa/78258

Nazarov, S., Preukschat, A., Lage, O., & Fernández, M. (2022, April). *Managing Climate Change in the Energy Industry With Blockchains and Oracles.* Tecnalia and Chainlink Labs. https://pages.chain.link/hubfs/e/managing-climate-change-energy-industry.pdf?_ga=2.253807112.1649722747.1658841288-1828728476.1658841288

NeonVest. (2018). *The scalability trilemma in Blockchain.* https://aakash-111.medium.com/the-scalability-trilemma-in-Blockchain-75fb57f646df

netObjex. (n.d.). *NetObjex India - The platform for NFT MarketPlace and Web3 Wallet.* https://www.netobjex.com

New Delhi Municipal Council. (2022). *Information Technology: On Going Projects.* https://www.ndmc.gov.in/departments/information_technology.aspx

News Desk. (2019). *Liquefy security token platform aims to tokenize real-estate in MENA.* Unlock Media. https://www.unlock-bc.com/news/2019-07-22/liquefy-security-token-platform-aims-to-tokenize-real-estate-in-mena

NFT documentation and property deeds - Moss Amazon Forest NFT - White Paper and FAQ. (2022). https://moss-earth.gitbook.io/moss-amazon-forest-nft-faq/nft-documentation-and-property-deeds

Nibley, B. (2022, January 19). A Guide to Sharding in Crypto. *SoFi Learn.* https://www.sofi.com/learn/content/what-is-sharding/

Nicola, V. D., Longo, R., Mazzone, F., & Russo, G. (2020). Resilient Custody of Crypto-Assets, and Threshold Multi signatures. *Mathematics, 8*(10), 1–17. https://EconPapers.repec.org/RePEc:gam:jmathe:v:8:y:2020:i:10:p:1773-:d:427729

Njoroge, E. (2021, December 15). Understanding a 51% Attack on the Blockchain. *Section.* https://www.section.io/engineering-education/understanding-the-51-attack-on-Blockchain/

Compilation of References

Novum Insights. (2021, June 23). *Deep dive into decentralized governance - DAO*. https://novuminsights.com/post/deep-dive-into-decentralized-governance-dao/

Nyan Cat Owned by 73B28B. (2020). *OpenSea*. https://opensea.io/assets/ethereum/0x3b3ee19 31dc30c1957379fac9aba94d1c48a5405/219

Nystrom, M. (2019, December 5). *2019 Was The Year of Defi (and Why 2020 Will be Too)*. ConsenSys. https://consensys.net/blog/news/2019-was-the-year-of-defi-and-why-2020-will-be-too/

OAG (Open Access Government). (2019). *World Bank Blockchain pilot sows fresh narrative for Haiti's farmers*. https://www.openaccessgovernment.org/world-bank-Blockchain-haitis-farmers/61205/

Observatory of Public Sector Innovation. (2018). *Counterfeit Medicine Detection Using Blockchain and AI*. https://oecd-opsi.org/innovations/counterfeit-medicine-detection-using-Blockchain-and-ai/

OCHA reliefweb. (2022, February 22). *ECHO Factsheet – Kenya – (Last updated 03/02/2022)* [Press Release]. https://reliefweb.int/report/kenya/echo-factsheet-kenya-last-updated-03022022

Okaformbah, C. (2019, February 19). *Governance in a Decentralized Autonomous Organization*. Medium. https://justcharles.medium.com/governance-in-a-decentralized-autonomous-organization-425f56b3e8bb

Okonkwo, I.E. (2019). *Valuation of Intellectual Property: Prospects for African Countries*. Paper submitted in partial fulfilment of the mini-dissertation in LLM, University of Cape Town.

OpenEarth Foundation. (n.d.). Retrieved July 29 2022 from https://www.openearth.org

OpenMarkets. (2015). *Ripple Labs And The Internet of Value*. CME Group. https://openmarkets.cmegroup.com/10381/what-is-an-internet-of-value

OpenSea Fart #0420 Owned by 80168016. (2021). https://opensea.io/assets/ethereum/0x495f9 47276749ce646f68ac8c248420045cb7b5e/9545159878656362628604289601099116938787474 20455204951361402386249786689327105

Ossinger, J. (2022, February 25). *Polkadot Has Least Carbon Footprint Crypto Researcher Says*. Bloomberg Asia Edition. https://www.bloomberg.com/news/articles/2022-02-02/polkadot-has-smallest-carbon-footprint-crypto-researcher-says#xj4y7vzkg

Overgaauw, V. (2020). *What are NFT tokens?* Anycoin Direct. https://anycoindirect.eu/en/blog/what-are-nft-tokens

Owie, B. (2022). NFTs Enter A New Era As Solana Closes The Gap With Ethereum. *Bitcoinist*. https://bitcoinist.com/solana-closes-the-gap-with-ethereum/

Pagnotta, E., & Buraschi, A. (2021). *An Equilibrium Valuation of Bitcoin and Decentralized Network Assets*. Retrieved 21 July 2022, from https://papers.ssrn.com/sol3/papers.cfm?abstract_id=3142022

Panther Team. (2022, August 26). ZK-rollup projects: Inner workings, importance & analysis. Panther Academy. *Panther.* https://blog.pantherprotocol.io/zk-rollup-projects-inner-workings-importance-analysis/

Parisi, T. (2021, October 22). The Seven Rules of the Metaverse. A framework for the coming immersive.... *Medium.* Retrieved November 19, 2022, from https://medium.com/meta-verses/the-seven-rules-of-the-metaverse-7d4e06fa864c

Park, D. (2022, August 31). *South Korea's capital city launches first stage of "Metaverse Seoul".* Forkast News. Retrieved November 24, 2022, from https://forkast.news/headlines/south-koreas-capital-city-launches-first-stage-of-metaverse-seoul

PCMag. (2022). Consensus Mechanisms. *Encyclopedia.* https://www.pcmag.com/encyclopedia/term/consensus-mechanism

Pells, R. H., & Romer, C. D. (2019). Great Depression. In *Britannica.* https://www.britannica.com/event/Great-Depression

Perkins, K. (n.d.). *September 2022.* Cryptomeria Capital. Retrieved November 14, 2022, from https://research.cryptomeriacapital.com/Cryptomeria_Capital_Metaverse_Overview_September_2022.pdf

Peterson, B. (2017). *Thieves stole potentially millions of dollars in bitcoin in a hacking attack on a cryptocurrency company.* Retrieved 21 July 2022, from https://www.businessinsider.com/nicehash-bitcoin-wallet-hacked-contents-stolen-in-security-breach-2017-12

Pettinger, T. (2022). Brain Drain Problem. *Economicshelp.* https://www.economicshelp.org/blog/glossary/brain-drain-problem/

Phantasma. (2022). *The Phantasma Experience.* https://phantasma.io

Phemex. (2022, April 16). What Are the Blockchain Layers? Layer 3 vs. Layer 2 vs. Layer 1 Crypto. *Crypto Insights.* https://phemex.com/academy/bitcoin-layer-1-vs-2-vs-3

Platform, E. (n.d.). *Evercity.io.* Retrieved July 29 2022 from https://www.evercity.io

Popescu, A. D. (2021). Non-Fungible Tokens (NFT)–Innovation beyond the craze. *5th International Conference on Innovation in Business, Economics and Marketing Research.*

Powerledger. (n.d.). *The Power Behind New Energy.* https://www.powerledger.io

Preetha, M., & Nithya, M. (2013). A study and performance analysis of RSA algorithm. *International Journal of Computer Science and Mobile Computing, 2*(6), 126–139.

Prestmit. (2022). *What is Hash in Cryptocurrency?* https://prestmit.com/blog/what-is-hash-in-cryptocurrency/?amp=1

Project Management Institute. (2021). *Most Influential Projects 2021.* https://www.pmi.org/most-influential-projects-2021/50-most-influential-projects-2021/sand-dollar

Proof of Space. (2022a). In *Wikipedia.* https://en.m.wikipedia.org/wiki/Proof_of_space

Proof of Space. (2022b). In *Wikipedia.* https://en.bitcoinwiki.org/wiki/Proof-of-space

Prophecy Market Insights. (2022). *Global Real Estate Tokenization Market is estimated to grow with a significant CAGR during the forecast period - By PMI.* https://www.globenewswire.com/en/news-release/2022/03/10/2400892/0/en/Global-Real-Estate-Tokenization-Market-is-estimated-to-grow-with-a-significant-CAGR-during-the-forecast-period-By-PMI.html

Protocol, U. (2018). *Every Asset Class will be Digitized and Tokenized.* https://www.universalprotocol.io

Public consultation on FATF draft guidance on a risk-based approach to virtual assets and virtual asset service providers. (n.d.). https://www.fatf-gafi.org/en/publications/Fatfrecommendations/Public-consultation-guidance-vasp.html

Puhl, I. (2022). *Blockchain and carbon: How to scale climate action while protecting investors and ensuring environmental integrity.* South Pole. https://www.southpole.com/blog/Blockchain-and-carbon

PWC. (2022, September 28-29). *Metaverse Assembly Outcomes Report.* Retrieved December 31, 2022, from https://www.dubaifuture.ae/wp-content/uploads/2022/12/TheMetaverseAssembly-OutcomesReport-WP-English.pdf

Qayum, A., & Razzaq, A. (2020). A self-evolving design of blockchain-based open source community – IEEE conference publication. *2020 3rd International Conference on Computing, Mathematics and Engineering Technologies (iCoMET)*, 1–11.

QuantumQuest. (2018, December 23). Intro to Data Structures for Programming. *Physics Forums Insights.* https://www.physicsforums.com/insights/intro-to-data-structures-for-programming/

Quiniou, M. (2019). *Blockchain: The advent of disintermediation.* John Wiley & Sons. doi:10.1002/9781119629573

Radmilac, A. (2022, March 9). Cosmos' Inter-Blockchain Communication Protocol (IBC) surpassed 11 million transfers in February. *Cryptoslate.* https://cryptoslate.com/cake-defi-launches-100-million-venture-arm-to-fund-web3-gaming-and-fintech-startups/

Rangone, A., & Busolli, L. (2021). Managing charity 4.0 with Blockchain: A case study at the time of Covid-19. *International Review on Public and Nonprofit Marketing, 18*(4), 491–521. doi:10.100712208-021-00281-8

Ratan, R., & Lei, Y. (2021, August 12). *What is the Metaverse? 2 media and information experts explain.* The Conversation. Retrieved November 14, 2022, from https://theconversation.com/what-is-the-Metaverse-2-media-and-information-experts-explain-165731

Rauf, D. (2021). *TFR. UNICEF to launch NFT collection as new way of fundraising to celebrate 75th anniversary.* https://www.google.com/amp/s/tfr.news/news/2021/12/14/unicef-to-launch-nft-collection-as-new-way-of-fundraising-to-celebrate-75th-anniversarynbsp%3fformat=amp

Rawal, S. (2016). Advanced encryption standard (AES) and it's working. *International Research Journal of Engineering and Technology*, *3*(8), 1165–1169.

Rean. (2022, March 4). 10 Practical NFT Use Cases Beyond Digital Artworks. *Hongkiat*. https://www.hongkiat.com/blog/nft-use-cases/

Rebecca, M. (2018). *International Approaches to Digital Currencies*. Congressional Research Service. https://crsreports.congress.gov/

Rees, K. (2022, February 16). *These 8 Tech Giants Have Invested Big in The Metaverse*. MakeUseOf. Retrieved November 14, 2022, from https://www.makeuseof.com/companies-investing-in-Metaverse/

Rene, G. (2019). *An Introduction to The Spatial Web*. Retrieved 15 July 2022, from https://medium.com/swlh/an-introduction-to-the-spatial-web-bb8127f9ac45#:~:text=The%20Spatial%20Web%20integrates%20Convergence,and%20physical%20lives%20become%20one

ReportLinker. (2022, May 13). The global NFT market size is expected to grow from USD 3.0 billion in 2022 to USD 13.6 billion by 2027, at a Compound Annual Growth Rate (CAGR) of 35.0% from 2022 to 2027. *GlobeNews*. https://www.globenewswire.com/news-release/2022/05/13/2442960/0/en/The-global-NFT-market-size-is-expected-to-grow-from-USD-3-0-billion-in-2022-to-USD-13-6-billion-by-2027-at-a-Compound-Annual-Growth-Rate-CAGR-of-35-0-from-2022-to-2027.html

Research, E. (2022). *Web 3.0 Market Top Companies | Web 3.0 Industry Trends by 2028*. Retrieved 16 July 2022, from https://www.emergenresearch.com/blog/top-10-companies-in-the-world-revolutionizing-the-web-with-web-3-services

Riddle & Code. (2018). *We're Building the Tretyakov Gallery's Blockchain-Powered App to Bring Art Patronage to a New Level*. Medium. https://medium.com/riddle-code/were-building-the-tretyakov-gallery-s-blockchain-powered-app-to-bring-art-patronage-to-a-new-level-d3c2d6602b81

Risius, M., & Spohrer, K. (2017). A blockchain research framework. *Business & Information Systems Engineering*, *59*(6), 385–409. doi:10.100712599-017-0506-0

RiskHarbor. (n.d.). https://www.riskharbor.com

Rodda, K. (2022, August 18). The three challenges facing the Blockchain Trilemma. *IG Bank*. https://www.ig.com/en-ch/news-and-trade-ideas/the-three-challenges-facing-the-BlockchainBlockchain-trilemma-220818

Rodriguez, S. (2021, September 23). You can now get paid in bitcoin to use Twitter. *CNBC*. https://www.cnbc.com/2021/09/23/you-can-now-get-paid-in-bitcoin-to-use-twitter.html

Rodríguez, S. F., Woolcock, M., Castañeda, R. A., Cojocaru, A., Howton, E., Lakner, C., Nguyen, M. C., Schoch, M., Yang, J., & Yonzan, N. (2020). *Reversals of fortune*. World Bank Publications. https://openknowledge.worldbank.org/bitstream/handle/10986/34496/211602ov.pdf

Romain. (2022, June 29). SNARKs vs STARKs: A Deep Dive Behind Layer-2 Rollups. *Medium.* https://medium.com/coinmonks/snarks-vs-starks-a-deep-dive-behind-layer-2-rollups-d9b3ca6e1386

Rooney, K. (2018). *A Blockchain Start-Up Just Raised $4 Billion Without a Live Product.* https://www.cnbc.com/2018/05/31/a-blockchain-start-up-just-raised-4-billion-without-a-live-product.html

Rossolillo, N. (2022, September 22). What Is a 51% Attack? *The Motley Fool.* https://www.fool.com/investing/stock-market/market-sectors/financials/cryptocurrency-stocks/51-percent-attack/

Roth, S. (2022, May 7). An Introduction to Sidechains. *CoinDesk.* https://www.coindesk.com/learn/an-introduction-to-sidechains/

Rozas, D., Tenorio-Fornés, A., & Hassan, S. (2021). Analysis of the Potentials of Blockchain for the Governance of Global Digital Commons. *Front. Blockchain, 4*, 577680. doi:10.3389/fbloc.2021.577680

Saggs, H. (2019). Babylon | History, Religion, & Facts. In *Encyclopædia Britannica.* https://www.britannica.com/place/Babylon-ancient-city-Mesopotamia-Asia

Saive, G. (2021, January 20). What is dao. *UBC Digital Magazine.* https://ubc.digital/what-is-dao

Saltik, H., & Alemdar, S. (n.d.). *Secure Hash Algorithm–512 In Blockchain.* Academic Press.

Samia, R. (2022, January 17). *Ethical and Regulatory Challenges of Emerging Health Technologies.* IGI Global. Retrieved November 24, 2022, from https://www.igi-global.com/chapter/ethical-and-regulatory-challenges-of-emerging-health-technologies/291434

Samudoka. (2021, April 15). What is solana. *Remitano.* https://remitano.com/forum/ca/post/10633-what-is-solana

Sandbox. (2022). Buying, selling and renting LAND. *The Sandbox.* https://sandboxgame.gitbook.io/the-sandbox/land/buying-selling-and-renting-land

Sanddollar. (2022). *About Us.* https://www.sanddollar.bs/about

Sandor, D. (2022, January 28). *How Blockchain technology will reshape green finance in 2022.* Eco-Business. https://www.eco-business.com/opinion/how-Blockchain-technology-will-reshape-green-finance-in-2022/

Satoshi, N. (2018). *Bitcoin: A Peer-to-Peer Electronic Cash System.* https://bitcoin.org/bitcoin.pdf

Scale, G. (2022). *Grayscale.* Retrieved 7 August 2022, from https://grayscale.com/

Scheltz, M., Nassiry, D., & Lee, M. K. (2020). *Blockchain and Tokenized Securities: The Potential For Green Finance* [Working Paper Series]. ADBI Institute.

Schickler, J. (2022, November 2). *France, Switzerland, Singapore to Test DeFi in Forex Markets*. https://www.coindesk.com/policy/2022/11/02/france-switzerland-singapore-to-test-defi-in-forex-markets/?ref=gomry.co

Schletz, M., Nassiry, D., & Lee, M. K. (2020). *Blockchain and tokenized securities: The potential for green finance*. Academic Press.

Schneider, L. A., Channing, E., Garcia, J., Ho, J., Patchay, J., Pike, E., Saunders, W., & Thomason, D. J. (2021). *A Sensible Token Classification System*. Novum insights. https://novuminsights.com/post/sensible-token-classification-system/

Schweiger, P. (2021). *Improving Usability of Blockchain-Based Decentralized Applications* [Doctoral dissertation]. University of Applied Sciences Technikum.

Sealpath. (2020, June 23). Protecting the three states of data. *Data Protection*. https://www.sealpath.com/blog/protecting-the-three-states-of-data/

Sectigo. (2021, January 05). What Are the Differences Between RSA, DSA, and ECC Encryption Algorithms? *Blog Post*. https://sectigo.com/resource-library/rsa-vs-dsa-vs-ecc-encryption

Securities and Exchange Commission. (2017). *Company Halts ICO After SEC Raises Registration Concerns*. https://www.sec.gov/news/press-release/2017-227

Services Group. (n.d.). *Tokenization*. http://www.bullservices.co.za/#tokenization

Seth, S. (2022). *Technical Analysis Strategies for Beginners*. Retrieved 22 July 2022, from https://www.investopedia.com/articles/active-trading/102914/technical-analysis-strategies-beginners.asp

Shakirov, I. (2020, September 29). *Research on Decentralized Autonomous Organizations (DAO)*. Grom. Medium. https://medium.com/gromorg/dao-research-42709eda6675

Sharma, R. (2020, June 21). *What Are Cryptocurrency Custody Solutions?* Investopedia. https://www.investopedia.com/news/what-are-cryptocurrency-custody-solutions/

Sharma, T., Zhou, Z., Huang, Y., & Wang, Y. (2022). *"It's A Blessing and A Curse": Unpacking Creators' Practices with Non-Fungible Tokens (NFTs) and Their Communities*. arXiv preprint arXiv:2201.13233.

Shawn, T. (2018). The NYSE's Owner Wants to Bring Bitcoin to Your 401(k). Are Crypto Credit Cards Next? *Fortune*. https://fortune.com/longform/nyse-owner-bitcoin-exchangestartup

Sheriff, L. (2022, April 25). How a new generation of NFTs plans to cut its carbon footprint. *Fortune*. https://fortune.com/2022/04/25/how-a-new-generation-of-nfts-plans-to-cut-its-carbon-footprint/amp/

Shevchenko, A. (2020, August 29). *Uniswap and automated market makers, explained*. Cointelegraph. https://cointelegraph.com/explained/uniswap-and-automated-market-makers-explained

Should all digital assets be subject to financial regulation? - Introducing a "sensible" token classification system. (2021, June 10). Novum Insights. https://novuminsights.com/post/not-all-digital-assets-should-be-subject-to-financial-regulation-introducing-a-sensible-token-classification-system/

Shuaib, M., Alam, S., Alam, M. S., & Nasir, M. S. (2021). Self-sovereign identity for healthcare using Blockchain. *Materials Today: Proceedings*.

Shumba, C. (2021, July 25). *RealVision's Raoul Pal Says Social Tokens Are "Next Big Crypto Thing".* Markets Insider. Retrieved November 22, 2022, from https://markets.businessinsider.com/news/currencies/realvisions-raoul-pal-says-social-tokens-are-next-big-crypto-thing-2021-7

Shuttleworth, D. (2021, October 7). *What Is A DAO And How Do They Work?* ConsenSys. https://consensys.net/blog/blockchain-explained/what-is-a-dao-and-how-do-they-work/

Siegel, D. (2016). *Understanding The DAO Attack.* https://www.coindesk.com/understanding-dao-hack-journalists

Singh, A. K. (2021, July). *An Introductory Guide to IPFS (InterPlanetary File System).* https://www.linkedin.com/pulse/introductory-guide-ipfs-interplanetary-file-system-aman-kumar-singh/. LinkedIn

Singh, A., Click, K., Parizi, R. M., Zhang, Q., Dehghantanha, A., & Choo, K. K. R. (2019). Sidechain technologies in BlockchainBlockchain networks: An examination and state-of-the-art review. *Journal of Network and Computer Applications, 149.* https://sci-hub.se/https://doi.org/10.1016/j.jnca.2019.102471

Singh, J. (2020, September 26). *What is yield farming in DeFi?* Cointelegraph. https://cointelegraph.com/explained/defi-yield-farming-explained

SIX. (2021, June 1). *Communication - EQ71 Digital Twin.* Empa. Retrieved January 1, 2023, from https://www.empa.ch/web/s604/eq71-digital-twin

Solana (SOL) Price · Price Index, Charts. (2023, June 2). Cointelegraph. https://cointelegraph.com/solana-price-index

Solana. (n.d.). *Home Page.* https://rejolut.com/blockchain/solana-nft-marketplace-development/

Solstroem. (n.d.). *The CO_2 avoidance programme for off-grid solar.* https://www.solstroem.com

Solstrom. (n.d.). *The CO_2 avoidance programme for off-grid solar.* https://www.solstroem.com

SPACE Metaverse – The Virtual Commerce Platform. (n.d.). Retrieved June 8, 2023, from https://www.tryspace.com/

Spence, E. (2022, February 26). Retrieved November 15, 2022, from https://www.researchgate.net/publication/234824743_Meta_Ethics_for_the_Metaverse_The_Ethics_of_Virtual_Worlds

SSL247. (n.d.). What is RSA? *Knowledge Base.* https://myssl.ssl247.com/kb/ssl-certificates/generalinformation/what-is-rsa-dsa-ecc

SSL2BUY. (2022). Diffie-Hellman, RSA, DSA, ECC and ECDSA – Asymmetric Key Algorithms. *Information Technology Journal, SSL Information*. https://www.ssl2buy.com/wiki/diffie-hellman-rsa-dsa-ecc-and-ecdsa-asymmetric-key-algorithms

Staff, E. (2022). *ETF League Table As Of 24 February, 2021*. Retrieved 3 August 2022, from https://www.etf.com/sections/etf-league-tables/etf-league-table-2021-02-24

Statista. (2020). *Insurance*. https://www.statista.com/markets/414/topic/461/insurance/#statistic2

Steinberg, L. (2022). *Security Magazine*. Retrieved 14 July 2022, from https://www.securitymagazine.com/articles/96998-4-cybersecurity-risks-of-web-30

Stevens, R. (2022, September 7). What Are Rollups? ZK Rollups and Optimistic Rollups Explained. Ethereum. *CoinDesk*. https://www.coindesk.com/learn/what-are-rollups-zk-rollups-and-optimistic-rollups-explained/

STOScope. (2019). *Security Token Offering (STO) List*. https://stoscope.com/

Strack, B. (2022 April 19). *Blockchain Tech Is Key to Combating Climate Change Report Says*. Blockworks. https://blockworks.co/Blockchain-tech-is-key-to-combating-climate-change-report-says/

Stroponiati, K., Abugov, I., Varelas, Y., Stroponiatis, K., Jurgeleviciene, M., & Savannah, Y. (n.d.). Decentralized governance in DeFi: Examples and pitfalls. *Static*. Squarespace. https://static1.squarespace.com/static/5966eb2ff7e0ab3d29b6b55d/t/5f989987fc086a1d8482ae70/1603837124500/defi_governance_paper.pdf

SubDAO Protocol. (2021, October 9). Learn on SubDAO: DAO Governance Matters for DeFi. *Medium*. https://subdao.medium.com/learn-on-subdao-dao-governance-matters-for-defi-35ae40260f5b

Suberg, W. (2022, June 27). Google users think BTC is dead- 5 things to know in bitcoin this week. *Cointelegraph*. https://www.google.com/amp/s/cointelegraph.com/news/google-users-think-btc-is-dead-5-things-to-know-in-bitcoin-this-week/amp

Sun, C. (2022). *Financial Institutions Move Closer to Realizing a Blockchain Solution for Syndicated Loans*. Retrieved 7 August 2022, from https://www.credit-suisse.com/about-us-news/en/articles/media-releases/financial-institutions-move-closer-to-realizing-a-blockchain-solution-for-syndicated-loans-201703.html

Sur, A. (2021, June 2). *New Delhi Municipal Corporation To Introduce Blockchain For Birth-Death Certificate and Property Tax*. Medianama. https://www.medianama.com/2021/06/223-ndmc-Blockchain-birth-death-property/

Suresh, A. S. (2013). A study on fundamental and technical analysis. *International Journal of Marketing, Financial Services & Management Research*, 2(5), 44–59.

Synthetix. (n.d.). Synthetix.io. https://synthetix.io

tago-admin. (2022, June 16). *Decentralized finance (DeFi): A beginner's guide*. Tago | Tagoverse | Talk to Earn - TalkFi | Tago Soul | Mental Metaverse. https://tago.guru/decentralized-finance-defi-a-beginners-guide

Takahashi, D. (2022, August 5). *The DeanBeat: Why Web3 companies created the Open Metaverse Alliance*. VentureBeat. Retrieved November 14, 2022, from https://venturebeat.com/games/the-deanbeat-why-web3-companies-created-the-open-Metaverse-alliance/

Takyar, A. (2022). All About blockchain: Blockchain scalability solutions. *LeewayHertz*. https://www.leewayhertz.com/BlockchainBlockchain-scalability-solutions/

Tasca, P. (2020). Internet of Value: A Risky Necessity. *Frontiers in Blockchain*, *3*, 39.

Tasca, P., & Piselli, R. (2019). The Blockchain paradox. *Regulating Blockchain: Techno-Social and Legal Challenges*.

Team, C. (2022, October 13). *What Happened to Terra?* Corporate Finance Institute. https://corporatefinanceinstitute.com/resources/cryptocurrency/what-happened-to-terra/

Team, I. (2022). *Web 2.0 and Web 3.0 Definitions*. Retrieved 14 July 2022, from https://www.investopedia.com/web-20-web-30-5208698

Technology, R. (2022). *Renaissance*. Retrieved 7 August 2022, from https://www.rentec.com/Home.action?index=true

Tendermint. (n.d.). *Tendermint Core*. https://docs.tendermint.com/

Teshock, M. (2020, May 4). *How the FDA is piloting Blockchain for the pharmaceutical supply chain*. IBM. https://www.ibm.com/blogs/Blockchain/2020/05/how-the-fda-is-piloting-Blockchain-for-the-pharmaceutical-supply-chain/

Tezos (XTZ) Price · Price Index, Charts. (2023, April 22). Cointelegraph. https://cointelegraph.com/xtz-price-index

Thalhammer, F., Schöttle, P., Janetschek, M., & Ploder, C. (2022). Blockchain Use Cases Against Climate Destruction. *Cloud Computing and Data Science*, 22-38. https://www.wiserpub.com/uploads/1/20220225/cb1859265cfa6a25dfa0bc362237128c.pdf

The 2021 Geography of Cryptocurrency Report Analysis of Geographic Trends in Cryptocurrency Adoption and Usage. (2021). https://go.chainalysis.com/rs/503-FAP-074/images/Geography-of-Cryptocurrency-2021.pdf

The Future of Crowdfunding Creative Projects. (n.d.). *Kickstarter*. https://www.kickstarter.com/articles/the-future-of-crowdfunding-creative-projects

The Goalkeepers. (2021). *Global Progress and Projections for Maternal Mortality*. Gates Foundation. https://www.gatesfoundation.org/goalkeepers/the-goalkeepers/

The World Bank. (2018, April 25). *ID4D data: Global Identification Challenge by the numbers*. Data | Identification for Development. Retrieved July 21, 2022, from https://id4d.worldbank.org/global-dataset

The World Bank. (2018, October 1). UFA2020 Overview: Universal Financial. https://www.worldbank.org/en/topic/financialinclusion/brief/achieving-universal-financial-access-by-2020

The World Bank. (2022, May 24). *Countries on the Cusp of Carbon Markets*. https://www.worldbank.org/en/news/feature/2022/05/24/countries-on-the-cusp-of-carbon-markets

Theodorou, Y., Okong'o, K., & Yongo, E. (2019). Access to mobile services and proof of identity 2019: Assessing the impact on digital and financial inclusion. GSMA.

Thomas, F., Schaaf, B. d., & Sehlstedt, U. (2021, December). *Hyper-collaboration in the healthcare and life science industry – The new imperative*. Arthur Little. https://www.adlittle.com/en/insights/prism/hyper-collaboration-healthcare-and-life-science-industry---new-imperative

Thomason, C. A. B. (2022, April 4). *Regulating for a decentralised future*. CityAM. https://www.cityam.com/regulating-for-a-decentralised-future/

Thomason, D. J. (2022). *Web 3 and tokenization of everything*. Medium. https://medium.com/coinmonks/web-3-and-tokenisation-of-everything-19b53d4ca535

Thomason, J. (2017, May 4). Blockchain – Leapfrogging for the Poor? *LinkedIn*. https://www.linkedin.com/pulse/Blockchain-leapfrogging-poori-dr-jane-thomason/

Thomason, J. (2019, April 8). Money, Management, Medicines and Me - Blockchain and Emerging Health Systems. *LinkedIn*. https://www.linkedin.com/pulse/money-management-medicines-me-Blockchain-emerging-health-thomason/

Thomason, J. (2021, September 25). *DeFi: Who, what and how to regulate in a borderless, code-governed world?* Cointelegraph. https://cointelegraph.com/news/defi-who-what-and-how-to-regulate-in-a-borderless-code-governed-world

Thomason, J. (2022, April 23). Green Finance need voluntary carbon markets that work. *Cointelegraph*. https://cointelegraph.com/news/green-finance-needs-voluntary-carbon-markets-that-work

Thomason, J. (2022, April 9). How Blockchain technology is transforming climate action. *Cointelegraph*. https://cointelegraph.com/news/how-Blockchain-technology-is-transforming-climate-action

Thomason, J. (2022, April 9). How Blockchain technology is transforming climate action. *Crypto News*. https://cryptonews.net/news/analytics/4818663/

Thomason, J. (2022, February 16). *It's all oh so very Meta*. City A.M. Retrieved November 14, 2022, from https://www.cityam.com/its-all-oh-so-very-meta/

Thomason, J. (2022, January 26). Could a green DAO allow Blockchain to be used for climate action? *CITY.AM.* https://www.cityam.com/could-a-green-dao-allow-Blockchain-to-be-used-for-climate-action/

Thomason, J. (2022a). *MetaHealth - How will the Metaverse Change Health Care?* DergiPark. Retrieved November 24, 2022, from https://dergipark.org.tr/en/download/article-file/2167692

Thomason, J. (2022b). *The Metaverse could be just the tonic for social prescribing.* City A.M. Retrieved November 24, 2022, from https://www.cityam.com/the-metaverse-could-be-just-the-tonic-for-social-prescribing-2/

Thomason, J. (n.d.). *5 things we will do in the metaverse – Studyum Academy.* Studyum Academy. Retrieved November 22, 2022, from https://academy.studyum.org/5-things-we-will-do-in-the-metaverse/

Thomason, J. A. (2021, November 28). *New tribes of the Metaverse — Community-owned economies.* Cointelegraph. Retrieved November 15, 2022, from https://cointelegraph.com/news/new-tribes-of-the-Metaverse-community-owned-economies

Thomason, J. (2019). *Blockchain Technology for Global Social Change.* IGI Global. doi:10.4018/978-1-5225-9578-6

Thomason, J., Bernhardt, S., Kansara, T., & Cooper, N. (2020). *Blockchain technology for global social change.* Engineering Science Reference.

Thurman, A. (2021, February 18). *As faith in audits falter, the DeFi community ponders security alternatives.* Cointelegraph. https://cointelegraph.com/news/as-faith-in-audits-falter-the-defi-community-ponders-security-alternatives

Times, T. (2022). *Terrorists Turn to Bitcoin for Funding, and They're Learning Fast (Published 2019).* Retrieved 22 July 2022, from https://www.nytimes.com/2019/08/18/technology/terrorists-bitcoin.html

Towards Ontology and Blockchain Based Measurement Reporting and Verification for Climate Action – Hyperledger Foundation. (n.d.). Retrieved July 29 2022 from https://ja.hyperledger.org/learn/webinars/towards-ontology-and-Blockchain-based-measurement-reporting-and-verification-for-climate-action

Tradestrike. (n.d.). *We'll change the way you trade* [PowerPoint Slides]. StrikeX. https://strikex.com/wp-content/uploads/2022/07/TradeStrike-Pitch-Deck.pdf

TransActive Grid. (n.d.). *New Grid on the Block.* http://www.solutionsandco.org/project/transactive-grid/

Trautman, L. J. (2021). *Hofstra Law Review. Virtual art and non-fungible tokens.* https://www.google.com/url?sa=t&source=web&rct=j&url=https://www.hofstralawreview.org/wp-content/uploads/2022/04/aa.4.trautman.pdf&ved=2ahUKEwiI5_qSw6j7AhV0gP0HHTGhBtwQFnoECAkQAQ&usg=AOvVaw3w_0_yWSO-0FCUaz0LcNDD

TreeCoin. (2020, January 31). *2020: A big year for natural forests?* TreeCoin. https://medium.com/treecoin/2020-a-big-year-for-natural-forests-cb3437a2ef75

Triangle, B. (n.d.). Retrieved July 29 2022 from https://www.bctriangle.com

Truby, J., Brown, R. D., Dahdal, A., & Ibrahim, I. (2022). Blockchain climate damage and death: Policy interventions to reduce the carbon emissions mortality and net-zero implications of non-fungible tokens and Bitcoin. *Energy Research & Social Science*, 88, 102499. doi:10.1016/j.erss.2022.102499

Turner, D. M. (2017, August 7). Applying Cryptographic Security Services - A NIST summary. *Cryptomathic.* https://www.cryptomathic.com/news-events/blog/applying-cryptographic-security-services-a-nist-summary

Tutorials Point. (2022). Cryptography Digital signatures. *Cryptography Tutorial.* https://www.tutorialspoint.com/cryptography/cryptography_digital_signatures.htm

Tyson, M. (2022, July 28). Solana BlockchainBlockchain and the Proof of History. *Infor World.* https://www.infoworld.com/article/3666736/solana-BlockchainBlockchain-and-the-proof-of-history.html

U.S. Department of Treasury. (2022, May 13). *Treasury Announces 2022 National Illicit Finance Strategy* [Press Release]. https://home.treasury.gov/news/press-releases/jy0779

U.S. Treasury Sanctions Notorious Virtual Currency Mixer Tornado Cash. (2022, August 8). U.S. Department of the Treasury. https://home.treasury.gov/news/press-releases/jy0916

UMA - Universal Market Access. (n.d.). Uma.xyz. Retrieved June 3, 2023, from https://umaproject.org

Umer, S. M., & Kishan, V. (2021). *Application of non-fungible tokens (NFTs) and the intersection with fashion luxury industry.* https://www.google.com/url?sa=t&source=web&rct=j&url=https://www.politesi.polimi.it/bitstream/10589/182823/1/2021_12_Umer_Kishan.pdf&ved=2ahUKEwjjg-r1x6j7AhUM-aQKHdItCjwQFnoECBEQAQ&usg=AOvVaw276ippExoM8FoyMYnMIGvS

Uniswap. (n.d.). *Home Page.* https://uniswap.org

United Nations Department of Economic and Social Affairs. (2020, December). *Population Facts. No. 2020/2.* https://www.un.org/development/desa/pd/sites/www.un.org.development.desa.pd/files/undes_pd_2020_popfacts_urbanization_policies.pdf

United Nations Human Rights Counselling. (2022, May 23). *UNHCR: A record 100 million people forcibly displaced worldwide.* United Nations. https://news.un.org/en/story/2022/05/1118772

United Nations. (2021). *Climate Change - United Nations Sustainable Development.* Sustainable Development Goals. https://www.un.org/sustainabledevelopment/climate-change/

United Nations. (n.d.). *Take Action for the Sustainable Development Goals*. https://www.un.org/sustainabledevelopment/sustainable-development-goals/

United Nations. Climate Change. (2018, January 22). *UN Supports Blockchain Technology for Climate Action.* https://unfccc.int/news/un-supports-Blockchain-technology-for-climate-action

United Nations. Economic and Social Council. (2022). *Progress towards the Sustainable Development Goals Report of the Secretary-General.* United Nations. https://unstats.un.org/sdgs/files/report/2022/secretary-general-sdg-report-2022--EN.pdf

Universal Protocol Alliance. (n.d.). *Universal Protocol Alliance.* Retrieved July 29 2022 from https://www.universalprotocol.io

UNOPS. (2019). Building for a sustainable future. *The Economist.* https://content.unops.org/publications/UNOPS-Building-for-a-sustainable-future.pdf

UpLink. (n.d.). Retrieved July 29 2022 from https://uplink.weforum.org/uplink/s/uplink-contribution/a012o00001pTeuBAAS/carbonland-trust-esg-nfts

US Energy Media. (2022). Benefits of Tokenization in Energy Business. *Energies Magazine.* https://energiesmagazine.com/benefits-of-tokenization-in-energy-business/

Use Ethereum. (2022). Non-fungible tokens (NFT). *Ethereum Use Cases.* https://ethereum.org/en/nft/#how-nfts-work

Valeonti, F., Bikakis, A., Terras, M., Speed, C., Hudson-Smith, A., & Chalkias, K. (2021). Crypto collectibles, museum funding and OpenGLAM: Challenges, opportunities and the potential of Non-Fungible Tokens (NFTs). *Applied Sciences (Basel, Switzerland)*, *11*(21), 9931. doi:10.3390/app11219931

Vasile, I. (2022, July 29). Solana vs. Ethereum: An Ultimate Comparison. *BeInCrypto.* https://beincrypto.com/about/

Vaughan, E. J. (1996). *Risk Management*. https://www.amazon.co.uk/Risk-Management-Emmett-JVaughan/dp/047110759X

Verghese, R. (2022, July 31). Understanding The Blockchain For Beginners. *Eat My News.* https://www.eatmy.news/2022/07/understanding-Blockchain-for-beginners.html

Verma, A. (2022). A Beginner's Guide To Understanding The Layers Of Blockchain Technology. *Blockchain-council.* https://www.BlockchainBlockchain-council.org/BlockchainBlockchain/layers-of-BlockchainBlockchain-technology/

Vermaak, W. (2021). What Is a Hard Fork? *Alexandria.* https://coinmarketcap.com/alexandria/article/what-is-a-hard-fork

Vervoort, D., Guetter, C. R., & Peters, A. W. (2021). Blockchain, health disparities and global health. *BMJ Innovations*, *7*(2), 506–514. doi:10.1136/bmjinnov-2021-000667

Video Game Market Size & Share Growth Report, 2030. (n.d.). Grand View Research. Retrieved November 14, 2022, from https://www.grandviewresearch.com/industry-analysis/video-game-market

Vigna, P. (2016). Chiefless Company Rakes. In *More Than $100 Million - Group called DAO is running itself via computer code.* Wall Street J.

Vogelsteller, F., & Buterin, V. (2019, November 19). EIP-20: Token Standard. *Ethereum Improvement Proposals.* https://eips.ethereum.org/EIPS/eip-20

Volety, T. (2018). Cracking Bitcoin wallets: I want what you have in the wallets. *Future Generation Computer Systems.* Advance online publication. doi:10.1016/j.future.2018.08.029

Voshmgir, S. (2019). Tokenized Networks: What is a DAO? *Blockchainhub Berlin.* https://blockchainhub.net/dao-decentralized-autonomous-organization/

Walker, M. C. W., & Mosioma, W. (2021, April 13). *Regulated cryptocurrency exchanges: sign of a maturing market or oxymoron?* LSE Business Review. https://blogs.lse.ac.uk/businessreview/2021/04/13/regulated-cryptocurrency-exchanges-sign-of-a-maturing-market-or-oxymoron/

Wang, Q., Li, R., Wang, Q., & Chen, S. (2021). *Non-fungible token (NFT): Overview, evaluation, opportunities and challenges.* arXiv preprint arXiv:2105.07447. https://www.researchgate.net/publication/351656444_Non-Fungible_Token_NFT_Overview_Evaluation_Opportunities_and_Challenges

Wells, C. (2021, October 30). *What Is the Metaverse? Where Crypto, NFT, Capitalism Collide in Games Like Axie.* Bloomberg.com. Retrieved November 19, 2022, from https://www.bloomberg.com/news/features/2021-10-30/what-is-the-metaverse-where-crypto-nft-capitalism-collide-in-games-like-axie

Weng, I. (2022). *Linking RWE to Clinical Trials.* Komodo. https://www.komodohealth.com/insights/linking-rwe-to-clinical-trials

Werbach, K. (2016). *Trustless Trust.* SSRN Electronic Journal. doi:10.2139srn.2844409

West, T. (2022, July 29). Solana Blockchain & Proof of History. *CoderOasis.* https://coderoasis.com/solana-and-proof-of-history/

WFP & UNICEF. (2021). *Vulnerability assessment of Syrian refugees in Lebanon.* Author.

What are decentralized exchanges, and how do DEXs work ? (n.d.). Cointelegraph. https://cointelegraph.com/defi-101/what-are-decentralized-exchanges-and-how-do-dexs-work

What is a decentralized autonomous organization, and how does a DAO work ? (n.d.). Cointelegraph. https://cointelegraph.com/learn/what-is-a-dao#:~:text=as%20investment%20advice

Compilation of References

What is Polkadot (DOT): A beginner's guide to the decentralized Web 3.0 blockchain. (2022). Cointelegraph. https://cointelegraph.com/blockchain-for-beginners/what-is-polkadot-dot-a-beginners-guide-to-the-decentralized-web-3-0-blockchain

What, I. B. T. (2018 March 13). *GOBankingRates*. https://www.gobankingrates.com/investing/crypto/what-is-Blockchain-technology/?utm_campaign=1144566&utm_source=yahoo.com&utm_content=8&utm_medium=rss

What's the Plural for Metaverse ? (2021, July 14). Cognizant. Retrieved November 14, 2022, from https://www.cognizant.com/futureofwork/article/whats-the-plural-for-Metaverse

White, W. (2021, April 29). *Social Tokens: Get Ready for the Next Massive Crypto Trend.* Nasdaq. Retrieved November 22, 2022, from https://www.nasdaq.com/articles/social-tokens%3A-get-ready-for-the-next-massive-crypto-trend-2021-04-29

Whitten, M. (2021, October 16). The Amazing Things You'll Do in the 'Metaverse' and What It Will Take to Get There. *Wall Street Journal*. Retrieved November 22, 2022, from https://www.wsj.com/articles/the-amazing-things-youll-do-in-the-metaverse-and-what-it-will-take-to-get-there-11634396401

Wiener, G. (2022). NFTs for Nonprofits: Non-Fungible Fundraising. Digital Fundraising. *WholeWhale*. https://www.wholewhale.com/tips/non-fungible-fundraising-nfts-for-good/

Wikipedia. (2016). https://en.wikipedia.org/wiki/Steemit

Wintermeyer, L. (2021, March 19). Climate-Positive Crypto Art: The Next Big Thing Or NFT Overreach? *Forbes*. Retrieved July 29 2022 from https://www.forbes.com/sites/lawrencewintermeyer/2021/03/19/climate-positive-crypto-art-the-next-big-thing-or-nft-overreach/?sh=19d0c402b0e6

WithamJ. (2021). https://www.hopkinsmedicine.org/news/publications/neurologic_issues/neurologic-winter-2021

World Economic Forum (WEF). (2018). *Digital Transformation Initiative*. Collaboration with Accenture.

World Health Organization. (2022, January 28). *Child mortality (under 5 years)* [Press Release]. https://www.who.int/news-room/fact-sheets/detail/levels-and-trends-in-child-under-5-mortality-in-2020

World Metaverse Council. (2022). https://wmetac.com/

XRP. (2022). *XRP - Digital Asset for Global Economic Utility | Ripple*. Retrieved 7 August 2022, from https://ripple.com/xrp/

Yakovenko, A. (2019, April 19). Proof of History: A Clock for Blockchain. *Medium*. https://medium.com/solana-labs/proof-of-history-a-clock-for-Blockchain-cf47a61a9274

Zhang, X., Chen, Y., Hu, L., & Wang, Y. (2022). The Metaverse in education: Definition, framework, features, potential applications, challenges, and future research topics. *Frontiers in Psychology*, *13*, 1016300. Advance online publication. doi:10.3389/fpsyg.2022.1016300 PMID:36304866

Zhenzong | emperor of Song dynasty | Britannica. (n.d.). Www.britannica.com. https://www.britannica.com/biography/Zhenzong

Zhou, A. (2021, July 7). Blockchain can help us beat climate change. Here's How. *CITI I/O*. https://citi.io/2021/07/07/Blockchain-can-help-us-beat-climate-change-heres-how/

Zipmex. (2022, July 22). *Blockchain Layer 1 VS Layer 2 Scaling Solution: Key Differences*. https://zipmex.com/learn/layer-1-vs-layer-2/

Zizi, O. (2021, December 24). Ranking DAOs: We computed their "net community score" to see how they stack up. *Business of Business*. https://www.businessofbusiness.com/about/

Zwitter, A., & Hazenberg, J. (2020). Decentralized Network Governance: Blockchain Technology and the Future of Regulation. *Front. Blockchain*, *3*, 12. doi:10.3389/fbloc.2020.00012

About the Authors

Jane Thomason is the Inaugural Chair of the World Metaverse Council and a globally recognized thought leader on Metaverse. She holds distinguished roles on the editorial boards of "The Journal of Metaverse" and "Frontiers in Blockchain" and is an Industry Associate at University College London, Centre for Blockchain. She is the author of "Blockchain for Global Social Change," "Applied Ethics in a Digital World," and "Advancements in the New World of Web 3: A Look Toward the Decentralized Future" in press (2023). Dr. Jane is frequently invited to deconstruct the Metaverse and explain how this growing industry will impact the future. Dr. Jane was named as one of "8 Metaverse experts to follow," "top 100 women in Web 3 and Metaverse," and "Top 25 Women in Fintech and Blockchain, MENA" and was featured by CNN in their series on the Metaverse "Decoding the Secrets of the Metaverse." She was recently honored by AIBC Eurasia as "Web 3 Leader of the Year."

Elizabeth Ivwurie is a Lawyer and Blockchain Strategist with blockchain industry experience and certifications from the University of Oxford's Saïd Business School and ConsenSys. Elizabeth has a deep appreciation for the scale of investment in blockchain technology and the diversity and significance of the ecosystem. Elizabeth has worked with solutions architects and organisations in deploying blockchain in their business models and in publicised and non-publicised use cases.

Index

A

AR/VR 161, 262, 265

Artificial Intelligence 3, 162-163, 166, 179, 185, 187, 200, 209, 251, 261

Augmented Reality 176, 185, 200-203, 212, 253

Avatars 147, 150, 161, 166, 169, 171, 173, 176-177, 179, 181-182, 185, 189, 197-199, 202-203, 205, 266

B

Bitcoin 15-17, 21-23, 25, 30-32, 36-37, 39, 44-45, 50-57, 60-62, 71, 79, 99, 104-106, 109, 113, 116-122, 129, 134, 159, 214, 260

Blockchain 1-3, 11, 13-25, 27-32, 34-38, 40-47, 49-58, 60-64, 66-67, 73, 75, 77-79, 83, 86-89, 91-92, 97-105, 107-109, 113-115, 117-118, 121, 125-128, 130-131, 133-137, 140-152, 154-157, 159, 161, 163, 165, 167-169, 172, 177, 180, 182, 189-190, 194-195, 198-199, 201, 209-230, 232-239, 241-246, 248-263, 265, 267-270

C

Centralized Exchanges 63

Climate Change 134, 148, 209, 211, 214, 222, 232-233, 235, 237-238, 240, 247-250, 252-260, 268, 270

Composable 61-62, 164, 167

Confidentiality 10, 28, 31, 109, 144, 187, 223, 267

Consensus 11, 14-15, 17-20, 22-28, 31, 33, 38-42, 51, 85, 93, 161, 169, 196, 212, 248, 263, 265

Cryptography 8, 11, 14, 19, 28, 30, 33-34, 38, 47, 60, 116-117, 139, 195, 214-215

D

Decentralized Autonomous Organization 2, 83, 98-100, 172, 251

Decentralized Ecosystems 84, 91-92

DeFi 2, 5, 11, 52, 59-82, 84, 96, 98, 101-102, 130, 152-153, 161, 165, 168-169, 182, 191-192, 261-265, 269, 272

Digital Asset Space 64

Digital Assets 5, 8, 11, 66, 68, 71-74, 81, 102, 106, 108, 111-114, 123, 127, 129, 132-133, 136-137, 140, 149, 152, 162, 165, 171-172, 174, 180-181, 196, 212, 232, 249-250, 255, 264-265, 269

Distributed Ledger 15, 18, 28, 107, 127-128, 133, 244

E

Emerging Economies 209, 212, 224, 252, 269

ERC 20 125

Ethereum Improvement Proposals (EIP) 123, 134-135

Index

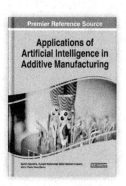

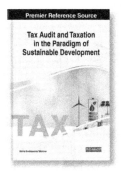